ACTING:
Onstage and Off

FIFTH EDITION

Robert Barton
University of Oregon

WADSWORTH
CENGAGE Learning

Australia • Brazil • Japan • Korea • Mexico • Singapore • Spain • United Kingdom • United States

WADSWORTH
CENGAGE Learning™

**Acting: Onstage and Off,
Fifth Edition**
Robert Barton

Publisher: Michael Rosenberg

Development Editor:
Megan Garvey

Technology Project Manager:
Jessica Badiner

Marketing Manager:
Erin Mitchell

Marketing Assistant: Mary
Anne Payumo

Marketing Communications
Manager: Shemika Britt

Associate Content Project
Manager: Georgia Young

Creative Director: Rob Hugel

Art Director: Maria Epes

Print Buyer: Susan Carroll

Permissions Editor:
Timothy Sisler

Production Service: Philominal
Bosco, Pre-PressPMG

Text Designer: Lisa Devenish

Cover Designer: Ross Carron

Compositor: Pre-PressPMG

For product information and technology assistance, contact us at **Cengage Learning Academic Resource Center, 1-800-423-0563**

For permission to use material from this text or product, submit all requests online at **cengage.com/permissions** Further permissions questions can be emailed to **permissionrequest@cengage.com**

Library of Congress Control Number: 2008923878

ISBN-13: 978-0-495-56604-5

ISBN-10: 0-495-56604-7

Wadsworth Cengage Learning
25 Thomson Place
Boston, MA 02210
USA

Cengage Learning is a leading provider of customized learning solutions with office locations around the globe, including Singapore, the United Kingdom, Australia, Mexico, Brazil, and Japan. Locate your local office at:
international.cengage.com/region

Cengage Learning products are represented in Canada by Nelson Education, Ltd.

For your course and learning solutions, visit
academic.cengage.com

Purchase any of our products at your local college store or at our preferred online store **www.ichapters.com**

Printed in the United States of America
1 2 3 4 5 6 7 12 11 10 09 08

To my son Andrew,
whose sense of wonder
renews my own

Contents

2   Relaxed Readiness / 39

Calm enough, yet energized enough to do your best

Warming Up / 39

Mental Warm-Ups / 40

Group Warm-Ups / 44

Physical Warm-Ups / 50

4   Stanislavski's System / 110

A complete process for characterization

Myth and Reality / 111

Ten System Steps / 120

Open Scenes / 134

5 Stanislavski Stretched / 146

The system twisted and expanded

8 Performance Process / 280

What to expect from first audition through closing night

Acting Etiquette / 281

Adaptations / 292

Process versus Product / 305

Offstage Performance Process / 307

Exercises

Illustrations

Appendixes

Index / 385

Acting to Understand

Acting is one of the best ways to learn about being alive. Because in our work we actors get to become other people, we get the chance to understand them and coexist with them. We stop making instant judgments of others when we get the chance to *be* them. Only shallow satirists can portray fellow humans, however strange or villainous, without gaining lasting empathy for their pain and comprehending their perspectives. A good acting class does more than impart knowledge; it humanizes. It helps each participant become less narrow and provincial, more a citizen of the world. Each actor can end up knowing more about herself, about others, and about ways the self and others connect. Each actor can learn the arts of compromise and collaboration. Along with these heady, high-sounding lessons, there can also be a lot of laughs.

This book is designed for the beginning acting student, for whom the life-enhancing aspects of actor training are a higher priority than technical skills. Its basic assumptions are (1) offstage performance can be effectively adapted for the theatre; (2) onstage training can be applied toward leading a full life outside the theatre; and (3) the two can feed each other in ways that both illuminate and amuse, a pretty good combination.

Acting: Onstage and Off is divided into nine chapters that address the areas of greatest concern to novice actors. The book begins by guiding each student through an exploration of his past and present offstage life, to help him find confidence and recognize experience that can be used in class. Once the actor no longer thinks of himself as inexperienced and inept, the text moves on in Chapter 2 into learning to warm up (body, voice, and mind; individually and collectively), then to understanding the actor's own equipment (Chapter 3). The assumption is that *self*-awareness is crucial before *other*-awareness can be accomplished, whether those others are living or fictional persons.

Warmed up and self-aware, the actor pursues basic means for putting together a character, in Chapter 4 as devised by Constantin Stanislavski and as adapted by others in Chapter 5. Once these fundamental principles of performing as someone else are established, Chapter 6 explores the need to balance honesty with precision and considers methods for blending the two. At this stage, the actor is ready to tackle the unique traditions and history of this art. Chapter 7 addresses the actor's relationship with the script and Chapter 8 addresses performance etiquette, the basic standards of behavior and support in the theatre. This chapter allows the new actor to quickly settle nagging procedural questions, so that he gets the help he needs, and avoids, as one of my students put it, "blowing it without knowing it." It is also geared toward teaching the student to quickly pick up the survival information needed for entering *any* new world. The book's final chapter helps the student decide among various options for more involvement, suggests directions actor training may take in the future, and teaches some ways of applying all that has been learned, even if this course is the student's last direct contact with the art form.

Each chapter leads to successively more complex levels of understanding. If in completing a chapter, the reader were likely to say, "Okay, this is fine, but what if . . . ," an attempt has been made to answer that question. Above all, this book aims to help each actor find some joy and wonder in herself as a performer. An actor needs many skills *eventually*, but joy and wonder should come first.

Using This Text

Acting classes vary from three hours a week for a single term to six hours (plus lab sessions) for a full year. It would be useless for an introductory text to try to serve everyone equally. There are, however, three ways to adapt this text to varying time strictures and changing class enrollments. It is possible to work through the book in sequence for a full year of activity. It is also possible to target a particular subject or skill (such as voice, which is dealt with in a number of sections throughout the book) or by sampling every chapter and doing only the earlier exercises of each. This last alternative is a suggestion for short-term classes, so that students get at least a taste of each area that concerns them.

An unusually focused or experienced group of actors may be able to move quickly over the background examination and warm-up activities of the first two chapters. Most students, however, will need the training in relaxation and channeling of energy provided in Chapter 2 before undertaking the relatively sophisticated demands of Chapter 3. The activities in Chapter 1 are largely passive and undemanding. By Chapter 3, each student is asked to accomplish acute, systematic analysis not only of himself but also of others in the class.

In our program at the University of Oregon, we read the entire book in the first quarter, then go back and review for greater depth during the subsequent terms of the school year. So we move swiftly and hit the high points in Acting 1, and then return for greater depth in subsequent courses. This allows the student who will be taking only Acting 1 to taste each of the basic elements and allows continuing students to more fully assimilate content in later terms.

An extensive list of scene suggestions is given in Chapter 7, and a sample scene, called *The Rehearsal,* appears in Appendix K. This scene may be used to apply all the concepts discussed here.

Ten elements in *Acting: Onstage and Off* distinguish it from most other acting texts:

1. The offstage connection, or learning to act one's own life better; a constant connection between life in the theatre and life removed from it.

2. A conversational, down-to-earth, accessible writing style.

3. No new lingo: Original terms, rather than invented vocabulary, for acting concepts.

4. Ample actor testimony from well-known performers, both proven veterans and successful newcomers near the ages of the students.

5. Clear interpretation of Stanislavski (the father of actor training as we know it) for modern readers.

6. No need to read specific plays because examples are drawn from lives rather than scripts. The book's basic approach focuses on life experience rather than on dramatic literature for instances and background material. Some instructors may wish to supplement this book with a scene anthology or play assignment of their own choosing.

7. Auditioning treated as a basic rather than an advanced skill. Auditioning is what you do to get into another class, to apply what you've just learned in a show, to get a job, to win a scholarship, to make any temporary and tentative condition permanent and definite. Far too often, beginning classes whet the appetite of novice actors without showing them how to get more chances to pursue this art. I believe it is this very postponing of auditioning that makes it so terrifying to the actor.

8. Systematic observation process for analyzing acting habits and personal tendencies. Checklists allow students to focus on the kind of detail that both leads to self-knowledge and provides ingredients for characterization.

9. Strategies for actors to become self-sufficient rather than overly dependent on guidance. An emphasis on the actor's responsibility for in-rehearsal active contribution and out-of-rehearsal exploration.

10. Abundance of choice: Enough exercises and approaches to allow flexible selection and adaptation. The book has far more activities and more questions than most readers will wish to attempt, so that teacher and reader may pick, choose, reject, and modify. These exercises may be cut back in scope easily, and written assignments adapted into thought-discussion questions and improvisations, in those instances where a minimum of academic work is deemed appropriate.

Adaptations

Acting 1 includes both shopping novices (many of whom move swiftly on to other shops) and serious students who already are (or quickly become) fully committed to actor training. Two features, added in the third edition and expanded in the fourth, are of particular interest to the latter. Chapter 5 deals with all the ways Stanislavski has been altered by others, and the section New Directions (in Chapter 9) covers innovative approaches that have begun to change the face of actor training. These give more depth and juice to students eager to move forward. For those programs, such as our own, that choose to return to the book over the course of several years, the new material will offer deeper dipping. For non majors classes, both these additions can be easily skipped over with no loss in either reading flow or discovery. For classes with both kinds of students, I suggest additional extra-credit reports or projects for the movers and shakers. A third alternative for some teachers is to assign only those post-Stanislavski contributors that appeal particularly to them or are appropriate to their circumstances. An instructor with some Meisner (Chapter 5) background, for example, may choose to cover him and skip the other American adapters. Someone teaching in a setting experiencing powerful social issues and wishing to give her students problem-solving strategies may choose to focus on Boal (Chapter 9) while omitting other contemporary innovators.

Though it should be of interest to all students, the Offstage Action (introduced in Chapter 1 and continued throughout the text) will be particularly useful to those who intend to use this training in venues outside the theatre. Often an acting class has a more profound and widespread impact on one's life than is at first evident. These ten Offstage Actions should provide a framework that enhances both the noticing of such impact and the planning of future choices. Offstage Action is also offered as a summary of the importance of our work for teachers dealing with college administrators and for students confronting parents who feel their study of performance may be inconsequential and frivolous. In its totality, this material now includes professional skills to supplement personal ones. The most significant additions to the fourth edition were sections on acting for the camera and acting scale. The first ("Onscreen versus Onstage") evolved as I observed more actors moving quickly to film early in (and in some instances before) their training and the shifting statistics that suggest a huge number of performers who never darken a theatre. The section titled "Scale" came out of my observation that actors seem increasingly insensitive to adapting to the space in which they are performing. They not only need to shift between camera and theatre, but between intimate and vast performance spaces. Although we consider many aspects of actor training outside the realm of a beginning class, I believe that adjusting to your context is actually a fundamental skill best instilled at the very start of one's acting education.

This New Edition

In addition to the usual infusion of new quotes and exercises, the fifth edition has five new features, offering advice on the following crucial parts of the acting process:

Coining—Methods of speaking a line as if for the first time, discovering and coining the words with a sense of freshness.

Memorizing—A new and greatly expanded guide to learning lines, with specific techniques for scenes and others for monologs.

Critiquing—A guide to offering nurturing but candid responses to one's class-mates with all students fully engaged.

Partnering—Ways of becoming what an acting partner should be, supportive, prepared and collaborative.

Burning—Advice on playing various levels of anger, from full out "red/orange" fireworks to more subtle, yet often more powerful "blue flame" fury.

The online Instructor's Resource Manual should provide both teacher guidelines and readily available forms for all observations and reports. It will be expanded during the life of this edition to provide continued and upgraded support.

Acknowledgments

Continued thanks to Wandalee Henshaw for permission to adapt open scene samples and Kathleen George for open scene concepts.

Reviewers for the first edition of *Acting: Onstage and Off* included Robert L. Amsden, Betheny College; Kate Beckman, St. John's University; Jon Beryl, Indiana University; Tod Fortner, Santa Barbara City College; Theodore Hersand, University of Oklahoma; Tom O. Mitchell, University of Illinois; Norman J. Myers, Bowling Green State University; Barbara O'Neill, University of North Dakota; James Panowski, Northern Michigan University; Pauline Peotter, Portland State University; and Marc Powers, Ohio State University.

Reviewers for the second edition included Wil Denson, University of Wisconsin, Eau Claire; Rozsa Horvath, Los Angeles Pierce College, Woodland Hills; and Porter S. Words, Colorado State University, Fort Collins.

Reviewers for the third edition included John Dennis, Louisiana State University; Stephen Guempel, Louisiana State University; Barbara Sellers Young, University of California, Davis; Scott Shattuck, Marymount College; Sara Thompson, Agnes Scott College; Ed Trujillo, Diablo Valley College; and Lou Anne Wright, University of Wyoming.

Reviewers for the fourth edition included John J. Conlon, University of Massachusetts, Boston; Robert D. Dunkerly, Community College of Southern Nevada; Scott Hayes, University of Findlay; Dana Smith, Truman State University; James Tompkins, University of Louisville; and Alan Tongret, Paradise Valley Community College.

Reviews for this edition include Matt Andrews, Marist College; Christine Frezza, Southern Utah University; Deborah W. McEniry, Palm Beach Atlantic University; Amy Sarno-Fradkin, Beloit College; and Scott Shattuck, Stephen F. Austin State University.

About the Author

Robert Barton is professor emeritus of acting and continues to teach at the University of Oregon. He has performed in most of the plays of Shakespeare and has directed half of them, including playing the title role in a PBS production of *Hamlet*. He is the author of several acting texts and co-author, with Rocco Dal Vera, of *Voice: Onstage and Off*. Robert's book *Style for Actors* was recipient of the Theatre Association's Best Book Award and he has been honored as Outstanding Acting Coach by the American College Theatre Festival. He has published numerous articles on acting, and his regular column, "Many Right Ways," appears in each edition of *The Voice and Speech Review*. His new introduction to theatre text, *Theatre in Your Life* (with Annie McGregor) and an anthology of plays titled *Life Themes* were published this year.

Acting Acknowledged

Already an experienced actor
and almost always acting

Acting is play, sometimes quite heavily disguised as work.
—Judi Dench

*I feel like I didn't have enough confidence in myself to do anything
but pretend. So I acted my life.*
—Jennifer Aniston

*As we act our lives, we have to make up our dialogue and create
ourselves as we go along.*
—Michael Caine

I was born to act. I was a showoff. That's all acting is—showing off.
—Morgan Freeman

Everyone acts almost all the time. You are a highly experienced actor even if you've never taken a class or been in a show. You may not be a skilled actor, but you *are* experienced. Acting is what we do with groups: to survive in an old group, to gain membership in a new group, or even to be left alone by a group we do not wish to join. We're learning to act throughout our lives. We're always trying to figure out how they (the current group members) want us to behave, what qualities to punch up or play down, which feelings to show or to hide, what behavior will be rewarded or punished. We try to give our audience what it wants and still stay as much ourselves as possible, to avoid feeling cheap and compromised. This is called "acting." This is what we do to survive.

All the World's a Stage

People are always trying to tell you how to act. Consider these familiar lines:

"That's no way to act."

"Stay in your room until you learn to act like a young lady."

"He's been acting so strange lately."

"You don't need to act as if you own the place."

"I can't go there. I'm afraid I just wouldn't know how to act."

"Stop acting as if the whole thing was my fault."

"Oh yeah, she acts innocent, but I know better."

"OK, so how would you have acted if you'd been there?"

"Do you think maybe this is all some kind of act?"

"He acts like he hasn't got a care in the world."

"When are you going to start acting like yourself again?"

"Don't worry about it. Just act natural."

And of course, this all-time favorite, which we may hear any time between birth and death:

"Act your age."

The world is full of actors. No one has said it better than William Shakespeare:

> All the world's a stage,
> And all the men and women merely players:
> They have their exits and their entrances;
> And one man in his time plays many parts,
> His acts being seven ages. At first the infant,
> Mewling and puking in his nurse's arms.
> And then the whining school-boy, with his satchel
> And shining morning face, creeping like snail
> Unwillingly to school. And then the lover,
> Sighing like furnace, with a woeful ballad
> Made to his mistress' eyebrow. Then a soldier,
> Full of strange oaths and bearded like the pard,
> Jealous in Honour, sudden and quick in quarrel,
> Seeking the bubble reputation
> Even in the Cannon's mouth. And then the justice,
> In fair round belly with good capon lined,
> With eyes severe and beard of formal cut,

Full of wise saws and modern instances;
And so he plays his part. The sixth age shifts
Into the lean and slipper'd pantaloon,
With spectacles on nose and pouch on side,
His youthful hose, well saved, a world too wide
For his shrunk shank; and his big manly voice,
Turning again toward childish treble, pipes
And whistles in his sound. Last scene of all,
That ends this strange eventful history,
Is second childishness and mere oblivion,
Sans teeth, sans eyes, sans taste, sans everything.

We recognize ourselves and others in each age. In contemporary, nonpoetic terms, this speech might read:

The whole world is just a stage and everyone is just an actor, entering and exiting. We all play roles during our lives. Seven major ones include:

1. Baby crying and throwing up while being held.

2. Whining child, dragging your backpack slowly to school, complaining about having to go.

3. Lover, groaning as loud as any furnace and writing sad songs to any part of your girlfriend's body.

4. Tough guy, swearing, growing a beard that makes you look like a leopard, wanting to win all the time, ready to fight over anything, trying to get famous. Not noticing that fame lasts no longer than a bubble, you're willing even to stick your head inside a cannon to get it.

5. Veteran politician, fat from eating so much fried chicken, looking serious, trimming the beard to look respectable, always dropping words of wisdom, even when nobody asked, acting all the time.

6. Skinny old-timer, glasses sliding down your nose, your old trousers in perfect condition but miles too big for you. What used to be a strong voice now cracks and breaks just like a child's.

7. Second childhood and senile emptiness, no more teeth, no more taste, no more anything.

The Seven Ages

1. Mewling Infant

Every baby learns to cry to get picked up, loved, changed, or fed, later learning to enhance the feeling of need and even to create the impression of need, whether need exists or not. My infant son sat blissfully with me while I wrote the first edition of this book. But if my wife passed through the room, he suddenly focused on her breasts and broke into a fairly convincing imitation of all the starving children of three, maybe four African countries. Since my wife and I both knew he had eaten within the hour, she would continue on her way. He would sigh and gurgle happily again, as if to say there was no harm trying. This age is never really left behind. Any of us may resort to mewling when we aren't getting enough (or the right kind of) attention.

2. Whining Child

We all give performances surrounding school. By this book's second edition, my son sometimes pretended to be sick (or sicker than he really was) to avoid going to school. And then later pretended to be well (or better than he really was) so he could go to some function he really wanted to attend. Haven't we all? We whine and pout through some responsibility that has been forced on us. We let everyone around know how much we're suffering, what a great sacrifice this is, how noble we are for plugging on, how much they owe us for being such a brick. Martyr routines are very popular performances.

School is also where one learns that even with group avoidance, some acting is required. If you are a bookish, artistic, wimp who does not want to join the jock bullies at recess, you still need to figure out how to act so they will not make your jocklessness the focus of their bullydom.

3. Sighing Lover

When smitten with somebody, many of our actions are guided by what we feel a lover should act like, by our observations of other, more experienced lovers from movies and books. Then there are the performances you give for the object of your affection. You're trying to act in such a way that the adored one is never disappointed, always pleasantly surprised. ("Maybe if I write her an eyebrow poem. I'll bet nobody else has done that . . ."), trying to be wittier, smoother, stronger, or wilder than you've ever been in your life—whatever your beloved seems to admire.

If the relationship is worth it, the forced acting eventually fades, with much mutual relief, into the sunset.

4. Reputation-Seeking Soldier

As I prepared the third edition, my son was a teenager who recently passed through a "soldier stage," where, in the presence of other young males, his main objective and primary performance was to appear unafraid, in control, tough, and possibly threatening. Sometimes we act the toughest when we really want to cry and run home for a hug. During adolescence, a time when we can be easily hurt, it seems important to pretend that nothing can hurt us.

Acting tough seems to be a crucial rite of passage into adulthood, but not everyone makes it through the pass. Some get caught up in this phase forever, lingering long in the land of swagger. Some are lucky enough to find an outlet.

Like many young actors, my son discovered, as I worked on the third edition of this book, that his more extreme performance impulses could be channeled onstage, making life easier for everyone offstage. As I was writing, he said to me one day, "Dad, I think I need to act in another play, before I start acting out." Like many of us, he did not necessarily go through his ages in Shakespeare's exact order. At this writing, he has only recently recovered from being totally smitten with a young woman. I will not embarrass him by recounting the more extreme ways he found to demonstrate his love for her, but let's just say that an eyebrow poem would be conservative compared with some of them.

5. Saw-Spouting Justice

These well-fed authority figures are always speaking as if what they say will be carved in granite somewhere. Everything out of their mouths has quotations around it. I find myself flirting dangerously with this phase, trying to skip it. Because I am in charge of an acting program, people are willing to listen to me and often even hover expectantly, pencil in hand. It's very easy to believe, for the moment, when someone gives you such authority, that Moses wasn't the only one to climb the mountain and chat with God. People who are used to being listened to, without fighting for an audience, can pontificate to the point of parody. A student returning home as a member of the winning debate team or the winner of a local beauty pageant may suddenly assume an exalted position as he or she passes on advice to mere mortals aspiring to the same glory.

At this fifth edition, my son is college student. While too young to move into full out, saw-spouting justice, his superior knowledge of technology can sometimes make him become, when called in as my technical consultant, patronizing and superior. He may sigh and pontificate when dealing with my profound ignorance, passing along the information with eye-rolling superiority. This is OK since he so often has to come to me for life advice and he deserves some satisfaction in return for being wise where I am not. It is turn around and payback time as I need to bow to his knowledge for a continued relationship with all the machines that run our home.

6. Lean and Slipper'd Pantaloon

Some seniors shrivel and are surprised at how small their impact suddenly is, after a lifetime of vigor. In this confused moment, some cling desperately to old casting and past power, exploding with rage when everything is no longer in place. Others begin to enjoy the freedom from responsibility, the lightness that comes with no longer being at the center of everything.

7.   Second Childishness and Mere Oblivion

Shakespeare's final image is sad and desolate. Some old people die long before their last breath. Others have a great final season. The universal image is "second childishness." Some seniors return to childlike wonder and discovery, to dealing with issues no more complicated than being caught being naughty by others, or possibly not discovering enough things to do today to have fun. Small children and old people sometimes discover themselves as kindred spirits, capable of complete sharing, as they reach casually past all the generations between them.

Shakespeare wrote of seven roles in the play of life. We don't all go through them in this order, but we never really leave an "age" behind. We store it in our repertoire. Mature statesmen may suddenly mewl and puke, tired old men may suddenly become brave soldiers again, and bona fide cynics can suddenly sigh like furnaces and write eyebrow poems, completely in love. As you review your own ages, have you already found yourself returning to some for a visit?

Exercise 1.1

Imitating Ages

If you feel fairly comfortable doing the voice and attitude of one of the ages (imitating a little kid, an old person, a politician, and so on), volunteer to read one of the following passages. Let each person spend about five minutes working on a character and then present them in the order of the seven ages.

1. Infant
   (Ad-lib baby noises.) "Goo-goo, gah, gah (giggle, gasp)." (Include gurgling, burping, mewling, and puking.)

2. Whining Child
   "I can't go. I just *caaaaan't!* My tummy is all achy and I forgot to do my math homework. . . . I mean I forgot to tell you that . . . that . . . that's not all! I feel hot and tired and slow and heavy and . . . icky!"

3. Lover
   "I think your eyebrows are completely awesome

   I'll never forget when I first saw some

   Of your eyebrows moving on your face

More awesome by far than precious lace.

Your eyebrows make me completely hot.

Will this poem give me at least a shot?"

4. **Soldier**
"Freeze, G, you think you bad, but you mess w'me, I take you out, you dig? Oh, you got a cannon there? W'big cannon balls? Listen Dawg, my balls is bigger than anything in your whole bigass cannon so shoot you stupid sonabitch!! Shoot!"

5. **Seasoned Politician**
"I've traveled far and wide across this beautiful country of ours and people always ask me, they say, 'What is the most important thing about being an American?' and I always answer, 'Freedom!' The freedom, for example, to let people who believe in you, contribute to your tax-sheltered annuities, your contingency funds, and your rolling market accounts. So, my friends, if someone suggests to you that I have done wrong, may I proudly reply that here in America, this so-called 'wrong' is one of our most important rights!"

6. **Lean and Slipper'd Pantaloon**
"So I got up and thought I'd take a little walk but, phew, those stairs just slowed me down. . . . So then I thought I'd just read the paper but I swear to God the print has gotten so tiny that no one could do that, so I tried to find the magnifying glass and I was sure I had put it down by the radio, but by golly it had totally disappeared. I suspect Mrs. Simpson down the hall. She's always said how much she liked that thing. . . . Oh, well."

7. **Sans Everything**
"I don't want it. . . . What pill? . . . No, I haven't. . . . I've never taken one of these. . . . I don't want anything. . . . I want to rest. . . . I want something to do. . . . I just don't . . . know."

Exercise 1.2

Ages Experienced, Ages Observed

You've probably already experienced the first five of Shakespeare's ages. What was your most vivid "performance" in each? Write a brief description of what you were like, and if possible, include a typical "line" you often delivered back then.

1. Infant

2. Schoolchild

3. Lover

4. Soldier

5. Justice

You may want to check your own memory against your parents', in the first three categories at least. Write a sentence describing the most vivid example you have observed in each of the other ages:

6. Pantaloon
7. Second childhood

How many of these performance ages, described by those who went on to become famous actors, remind you of some you went through?

HALLE BERRY: I was always dramatic. If I cut myself, I was bleeding to death, you know?

LEONARDO DI CAPRIO: My dad taught me not to be shy. I'd imitate people we'd just met for him. I liked to become someone else.

JULIA STILES: By the time I was ten, I could walk around the city by myself and no one would bother me because I had on my killer look.

JOHN LITHGOW: As much as my family moved, I was always the new kid on the block. I became accustomed to acting—by trying to fit in at each school. I found I could convince people that I really belonged.

WESLEY SNIPES: Early on I'd use my acting abilities to pick up girls. If I didn't get that phone number, I'd weep.

MARK WAHLBERG: My actor training wasn't at Julliard. It was in front of judges and cops, trying to get out of trouble.

ANTHONY HOPKINS: When I was drafted, I pretended to be deaf during my medical exam. It worked.

Seven Acts

In addition to passing through ages, we all perform "acts" or specialized performances in our lives outside the theatre. Most have their roots in simple childhood Let's Pretend. Here are seven varieties:

1. Pageants

> Toto in a grade school *Oz*? Third Wiseperson, carrying myrrh, in a church Nativity? Part of a Living Totem Pole in a Scout Jamboree? Ring Bearer at a wedding? Toastmaster at an anniversary party? Homecoming Queen's Court?

You're dressed up, it's a very big occasion, the place is packed—actually, many of the essential ingredients for theatre are present. You may be cast in a definite role, even though it might be an inanimate object, like a rock. Or, in public rituals, you may be cast as yourself, without convenient camouflage. But this is a *transformed* you, amazingly cleaned up, polished off, and sanitized. The stakes here are very high, the price of doing something wrong is beyond your means, and you usually feel very proud.

I made my stage debut as an altar boy or more aptly a falter boy. I used to trip over my cassock or light myself on fire.

—Mel Gibson

I was "The Amazing Adrien," an eleven year old with a magic act. That was my introduction to acting and to pulling the wool over adults' eyes.

—Adrien Brody

---

2. Disguises

A progression of ghosts and monsters for Halloween? A Disney or *Star Wars* character for a costume party? A sophisticated world traveler at some bistro where you hope not to get carded?

These performances are looser and more improvisational. Your intent is *not* to be recognized. You experiment endlessly with your costume pieces; you work on your walk, your gestures; you practice certain lines so you get the voice, the timing, the inflection just right. Then you enter the world. Sometimes you only make it downstairs before returning to your room for a few adjustments based on some early family reviews. But you get better and better as the evening progresses.

3. Alter Egos

The Super Jock You who enters the playing field? The Oxford Scholar You who stands up to debate First Affirmative? The Vogue Cover Girl You who glides onto the prom dance floor?

Alter egos are second selves, often with improvements: You with Cheek Bones and a Ph.D. Some of us click into the alter ego as a way of upping courage. Seeing yourself slightly enhanced often has a startling effect on observers, who may see you that way too. Some people go so far as to name their other selves, who tend to be more assertive and colorful than the main you. Many use these other selves as a means of *rising to the occasion*. Sometimes alter egos compete for your attention. Sometimes they even take on a life of their own.

> *My first successful characterization is what I devised for myself in high school. I played the blond homecoming queen for several years. I laid out my clothes for the week every Sunday so that I wouldn't repeat.*
> —Meryl Streep
>
> *So eventually the big brassy broad beat the crap out of the little torch singer and took over.*
> —Bette Midler (discussing two of her alter egos)
>
> *Acting is just a matter of farting about in disguises.*
> —Peter O'Toole

4. Role Models

You decide to lower your voice when angry, just like your father? To walk like a certain rock star? To emulate the unshakeable dignity of your favorite teacher?

Other human beings and literary figures serve as sources for the basic characterization you would like to present to the world. You may just want to shake your hair to the side like a certain actress, not necessarily to *be* her. You try on qualities like pieces of clothing, discarding one if it doesn't seem to fit. Borrowing may involve anything from a small mannerism to an entire outlook. Much borrowing may happen before you're satisfied with the whole package.

5. Understudying

Your folks aren't home and someone tries to deliver a gross of electric can openers— what do you do? Your boss is gone and a customer is getting unruly— what do you do? You're left entertaining your Great Aunt Helga who only speaks Swedish—what do you do?

Standing in for someone who usually handles a situation and attempting to effectively trouble-shoot involves more than just trying to figure out how the other person would handle the situation. It may also involve trying to get their actions down pat, their manner of authority, their way of ending a sentence firmly. It's harder than copying a role model, where you willingly pick whom you want to emulate. In understudying, you may not even like or understand the person for whom you're standing in, and you have no time to practice. Even if lines of dialogue come to you, you may find yourself struggling for the right word emphasis. You know the other (missing) person should be starring in this scene, and that you're merely an understudy. Like most understudies, you try to give a pretty good imitation of the star.

> *When I auditioned for my first TV job at nineteen, I had no idea what to do, so I pretended to be Barbara Walters. I'd sit like Barbara and I'd look down at the script and up at the camera because I thought that's how you act—all from what I had seen Barbara do. On the job, I started to forget to be Barbara sometimes and Oprah would start slipping through. But in the beginning, being Barbara was what saved me.*
>
> –Oprah Winfrey
>
> *I gradually created someone I wanted to be and finally I became that person.*
>
> –Cary Grant

6. Suppression

Mortified beyond human endurance, but determined not to appear upset? Flattered, but striving to appear as if compliments like this come to you hourly? Ecstatic over winning, but afraid the other competitors will not respond well to your leaping and shrieking?

Cooling down your first response to something more manageable, less foolish, or overbearing, is an acting challenge that may go on for hours before you can finally let it rip. If you win, you want to appear happy, even thrilled, just not obnoxious. If you lose, you want to appear transcendent, not devastated. Huge acting energy is invested in stifling emotional display and avoiding humiliation.

7. Deception

"It wasn't really you who emptied out the cookie jar, was it?" "And the reason your jeans are torn and muddy is that you were attacked by a band of Pygmies?" "You've never tried smoking that awful stuff, have you?"

We all act, to some degree, less guilty than we are. It can run from a few harmless fibs to profoundly immoral lies. Feigned innocence is a universally acknowledged form of offstage acting. If the deception helped bring off a surprise party or visit, we feel triumphant and skillful when the amazed recipient gets the joyous news.

Even the most honest of us may look back on a few occasions where we cringe at not 'fessing up,' but also feel some measure of pride in pulling it off.

> *When we got bored, Jules could be real creative. She could muster up tears in a second to get out of homeroom and I'd have to follow her out to help her.*
> —Julia Roberts' best friend (describing how she was in high school)
>
> *I have such a fear of embarrassing myself that I will do anything not to embarrass myself. That's it. That's the key to my success.*
> —Michelle Pfeiffer

While serving jury duty during the writing of this book, I was stunned one day to hear the judge instruct us that it would be our duty to figure out who was acting and who wasn't. He later said to me, "If there weren't so many actors in the world, I'd be out of a job." Some cases and some careers are based on lies. But most of our performances, particularly in the categories of suppression and deception, are humane, caring, even loving.

Imagine yourself getting up on any given day and following only your gut impulses, without any effort to accommodate others. The damage could be enormous. Daily acting involves sparing other people's feelings. You perform so you appear quite so bored, so offended, so amazed at their lack of sensitivity or tact, so appalled at the fact they missed the point or the appointment. If a friend is hurting, you and I try to figure out how to act so that our friend will feel supported and nurtured. We do not just figure out what to do, we figure out how to act. For many of us, even those of us who work in the theatre, the finest performances of our lives are given offstage.

Exercise 1.3

Striking/Successful Acting

Keeping your description again to no more than one sentence, pull out the most striking/ successful performances you can recall in each of the seven areas. It may have been striking but a total flop, or it may have been extremely successful but very low key. Or it may have been both.

1. Pageants

2. Disguises

3. Alter egos

4. Role models

5. Understudying

6. Suppression

7. Deception

Exercise 1.4

My Best Offstage Performance Ever

This exercise can be done in a single class period with everyone sharing or spread over the term with one or two people presenting each period.

> *People are incredible actors. We're masters at hiding what's really going on most of the time.*
> –Glenn Close

Pick what you consider the most impressive performance you have given in your offstage life. This may be a time when you felt something very strongly but managed to hide it, a time when you were guilty but managed to seem innocent, or may be impressive because you kept up an illusion for a very long time. Possibilities are limitless. (One student reported her best performance was one birthday when her boyfriend got her a china doll she did not care for at all, and that she was so good at convincing him that she loved it that he got her another one the following year!)

Working with a partner, describe the event and set it up so that you can narrate and move in and out of the scene with your partner playing one or more other participants.

Exercise 1.5

Dueling Performances

The toughest moments in life can be when you are cast in two roles that you cannot play with equal grace and believability. Your role as Loyal, Respectful Daughter comes straight up against your role as Feminist if your father makes recurring sexist remarks. It is especially difficult if both roles are essential to your concept of yourself, way up near the top of those acting parts you fully intend to run for many seasons.

1. Try to identify five times in your life when you wanted to play two roles that were at odds with each other.

2. Which ones won?

3. Were you ever able to successfully blend the two? Is there a way the two women's roles in the example could possibly be combined, without hurting either?

4. Work with a partner. Set up the conflict. Force yourself to choose. Make the choice you made. If the one you would make now is different, repeat the scene as you would play it now.

One of the main differences between acting in a play and in life is that in life you are the playwright as well, with both the chance and the responsibility to come up with your own dialogue. So offstage acting has no script, and onstage acting does. Right? Not entirely.

Exercise 1.6

Scripting and Improvising

People who require risk as a constant in their lives will work a lot of improvisation into each day. Others, craving constancy, will nearly script themselves, with only the slightest variation in day-to-day dialogue. Everyone scripts and rehearses certain crucial life encounters (a seduction scene, a telling-off-the-boss scene, a finally-persuading-the-folks scene) carefully, hoping the other persons will pick up the right cues.

Recall two each of your

1. most carefully scripted or planned encounters or

2. least planned, most challenging, freewheeling improvisations.

Write four single sentence descriptions, beginning with "The time I . . ." Keep these four memories in mind as you begin to explore other dimensions of your acting outside the theatre. (*See* Appendix A: My Acting History, at the end of the book, for an optional format for summarizing the acting you have experienced so far.)

Exercise 1.7

Shared Pasts

Sit in a circle and each share the following information with the others as a way of breaking the ice and getting to know each other.

1. **Your Acting History**
   As much onstage, as much *off* as you want to share. Only a summary, to give others a feel for what you've done. A paragraph tops. Don't dare say you don't have any.

2. **Your First Role, Your Favorite Role**
   Two highlights out of the general pattern in part 1. If you've not yet done a play, you must have done a pageant. No one totally escapes these things. We're talking about your debut here. The occasion you choose to think of as launching you as a potential ham. Your favorite may or may not be the same as your first. It may be one you've actually never played but dream of playing. It may be *on* or *off*. Try to identify, in no more than a sentence, why it's your favorite, what delights or thrills you when you think about it even now.

3. Why You're Here
The Truth. If this was the only open time slot in your schedule, fess up, so others will know you do not worship daily at the altar of Dionysus. If you have already decided to pursue a professional acting career, have the courage to say so in the open air. The real reason you happened to end up in this class, at this school, at this time. The more straightforward you are, the more you'll get from all this.

Observing Yourself Act

What happens at the exact moment that an actor acts? Ten ingredients are present in any life encounter. Take a look at your life. Any moment, involving you and someone else, will involve:

1. Some way of defining what you and this other person mean to each other (*relationship*)

2. Something you want (*objective*)

3. Something in the way (*obstacle*)

4. Your plan to get what you want (*strategy*)

5. Specific maneuvers within your overall plan (*tactics*)

6. Things said by you and the other person (*text*)

7. Things implied but not really said (*subtext*)

8. Times when you do not speak but are actively thinking, so a speech is going on in your head (*interior monolog*)

9. Moments when the other person says or does something that makes you pause, consider, and reject several different answers before choosing a reply (*evaluation*)

10. Small units in the scene that can be isolated as actable events unto themselves in which a single transaction is taking place (*beats*), and shifts within the scene (*beat changes*), signaling that this transaction has been completed and a new one is starting:

   A topic of conversation is changing

   Another attack is being tried

   A new person is changing the direction of the conversation

   A new objective is being pursued

The terms appearing in italics are actor language for scene ingredients. There is no simpler or more difficult lesson in acting than learning these ten items. They provide the basis of the Stanislavski System, which will be covered later in the book, but they are really the basis of all human interaction. Almost all actors who perform well identify these ten in every scene they play. Almost all actors who fail have forgotten this basic homework.

Imagine that you want to finish reading this chapter (only a few more pages), but your roommate's CD player is blaring. You decide to get rid of her. You try mentioning her promise to call her folks tonight. You inquire if she shares your hunger for a pizza. She's not interested. She wants to sing along with the music and to talk about how music has changed her life. Finally, you level with her that you can't concentrate and ask her for fifteen minutes of silence. She agrees. Curtain.

Active Ingredients

1. *Relationship:* Newly assigned roommate; don't know each other well, seem to have differing tastes and lifestyles
2. *Objective:* To finish homework (Chapter 1, *Acting Acknowledged*)
3. *Obstacle:* Roommate's blaring stereo
4. *Strategy:* Remove roommate
5. *Tactics:* Distractions (phone call, pizza), frankness (asking favor)
6. *Text,* and
7. *Subtext* (in following example, text is in regular type, subtext in *italics*)

> YOU: *(OK, here goes)* Say, didn't you . . . *(God, I hope this isn't too pushy)* promise your folks to call home tonight? *(Good, sounded pretty casual.)*
>
> HER: *(What do you care?)* Uh . . . Yeah. *(None of your business, bitch.)* So? *(Change the subject. Aha!)* I love this song. *(Let it go.)* Shake your body, your body, your BAHDEEEEE!!!! *(Can I shake it or what? I got the moves!)*
>
> YOU: *(I hope this doesn't sound too pushy)* Well, shouldn't you call them then? *(It was. I'm such a jerk.)*
>
> HER: *(One mother is enough, thanks.)* I already tried. *(Buzz off . . . Oh, I guess she means well.)* They aren't home. *(Christ!)* I left a message on their machine. *(Satisfied????!!!!!)* Ooh, I REALLY love this NEXT song! *(So back off.)*

8. *Interior Monolog* (takes place before the previous exchange):

> *That machine of hers is driving me crazy. Alright now, what is this? Observe myself act? What is this guy talking about? How many more pages? "I wanna bang, I wanna clang . . ." I can't get the stupid lyric out of my head. Please God, make the power go off . . . I have to write out all this private stuff?! I wonder who's gonna see this. "Clanga, banga, uh HUH!!!! Clanga, banga you- WOO!!!" You-woo? What does that mean? Damn it. I need quiet. I gotta get her outta here. What could I . . . Hey wait, what about that phone call she's supposed to make?*

Was some of this hard to follow? Re-read it. Almost everyone's interior monolog will confuse someone else.

9. *Evaluation:* Here's one possible continuation of the previous scene, in which you evaluate potential responses to her attitude. Text is in regular text, subtext in italic).

> HER: "Music makes me feel good."
>
> YOU consider saying:

1. "Shut that thing off or I'll kill you!" *(No, that's a little too confrontational. ...)*

2. "Well, I guess I'll go to the library and study now." *(Hey! Why should I give up my living space? What if this becomes a habit . . .)*

3. "Look, this room is half mine and I have some rights, some rights to peace and . . . and quiet. . . ." *(No, that's whiny. . . .)*

4. "This book is too hard to deal with over all that music." *(Well, that's the right idea. How about . . .)*

> YOU finally decide to say:

5. "Listen, I like that CD so much that it's distracting me, and I have got to get this reading done. Could you do me a favor and let me have fifteen minutes of quiet? I'll owe you." *(Much better. Now shut that thing off or I'll kill you.)*

> HER: "OK."

10. Titles of Beats

   1. Fuming Over Book Until Breaking Point

   2. Making Failed Pizza Pitch

   3. Making Failed Phone-Home Pitch

   4. Ode to Music Followed by Pause

   5. Request for Silence and Acceptance

The wonderful thing about this simple list is that if you concentrate on each item, you are so involved that you don't have room in your consciousness for nervousness, awkward self-consciousness, or distractions. People who fail to get what they want are often failing to play their *objectives* strongly enough or failing to switch *tactics* from one that is not going to work to another. Or they do not consider enough alternatives during an *evaluation* before choosing one.

Exercise 1.8

Playing Objectives

Improvise another version of the scene with a different objective and conflict provided by the roommate character. Identify the ten ingredients.

Go back and repeat the exercise, trying to persuade

1. Your parent to let you take one of the family cars back to school for a few weeks;

2. A police officer not to give you a speeding ticket;

3. A salesperson to take an out-of-town personal check;

4. A professor to accept a late paper; and

5. Someone working registration to let you into an overcrowded, closed acting class.

Exercise 1.9

Real Life

The scenes in Exercise 1.9 are just conjecture.

1. Find some real ones and jot down the ingredients before the encounter has passed from memory. Pick two scenes with different partners and quite different objectives.

2. Write down what happened in such a way that the outline or skeleton of the experience emerges. (See Appendix B: Acting Observation, at the end of this book, for an optional format for this observation and others to follow.)

3. Identify *relationship, setting, other character, basic situation, objective, obstacle, strategy, tactics, text* and *subtext* (at least four lines of dialogue), *interior monolog* (one or two paragraphs at a crucial moment), *evaluation* (including some random searching followed by at least four rejected alternatives plus the one chosen), and *beats.*

4. Repeat the process, for a different encounter, using the fewest possible words to describe the event. Don't let yourself get bogged down in description or detail. The result should scan easily. It should be clean and virtually free of verbiage.

5. Stop and notice during the next week when you shift beats, what range of tactics you employ, when you regret your choice during an evaluation and wish you'd gone with one rejected. You want to let the vocabulary become second nature and to heighten your own awareness of the theatre present in each life.

Exercise 1.10

Objectives on the Clock

Working in twos, either the teacher gives the actors a situation and then separately presents them with opposing objectives (on paper or by whispering to them) or the two actors leave the room and the class decides both.

The situations should involve two people wanting opposites. Here are some examples:

Two roommates. One has worked overtime for weeks, finally has a night off, and wants to be alone to relax in peace and quiet. The other's boyfriend or girlfriend is being sent off by the military, who knows when or if they will see each other again, and they want to spend the evening alone in the apartment tonight. Both roommates want the other to leave.

Two good friends have crushes on the same person and want to make a move. One is good friends with the crushee. She knows this and wants help making a move, not knowing how the friend feels.

1. Actors have three minutes to quietly plot a strategy for their scenes.

2. The scene is then improvised and timed at five minutes.

3. At least three different tactics must be used by each actor.

4. Characters may not win by talking over the other person. Each must listen to the other.

5. Try hard to win, but be true to the situation, and if your partner offers a powerful case, concede.

6. Have the actors share how the exercise felt and what they believe they each did that was most and least effective. Have the class give feedback as well.

Actor Guidelines

To keep choices active, clear, and strong, use the following reminders:

1. Objectives should be stated with the preposition *to* followed by an active verb. Never use the word *be* because it is too passive. Objectives like "to be happy" or "to be loved" are *both* so nonassertive that they cannot be actively acted. They give you nothing to pursue. "To find joy" and "to get a lover" are somewhat more actable. "To win the trip to Maui" and "to boff Lois" are even more actable. To goad, defy, needle, force, or tease are more actable than to tell, suggest, inform, wonder, or get angry because the former demand results.

2. Keep language simple. Keep words to a minimum. Use down-to-earth, unambiguous words that click quickly into consciousness. Your analysis of a scene should read like traffic signals, guiding you through the part.

3. Subtext may support the text, modify it, or qualify it. It may add dimensions that the text did not seem to imply by itself. It may actually contradict or work against the text as in the old vaudeville routine:

> STRAIGHT MAN: Nervous?
> > COMIC: NOOOPE!!!!! *(second line given with so much terror and anxiety that it wipes out the word itself)*

Subtext is an actor's food and air. Finding, changing, and shading subtext is what actors most love to do and what audiences most love to watch. Stanislavski says that *subtext* is what the audience comes to the theatre to see, that if all they wanted was the *text* they could have stayed home and read the script. A firm, hard remark is modified with a gentle, warm tone, and the most polite, civil re-sponse (words) can be filled with dangerous warning (delivery) not to tread fur-ther. Subtext is a phenomenal source of power. It may totally alter text.

> *I like the challenge of conveying an emotion or idea that*
> *isn't right there in the dialogue. I like to be able to say, "I*
> *think I'll have a drink," and let the audience know that what*
> *I mean is "I love you."*
>
> —Mel Gibson

Exercise 1.11

Text Versus Subtext

Two actors are given an activity, a circumstance, and a topic of conversation. They must stick solely to the topic of conversation. *Example:* A couple is packing suitcases. He is going off to war. They discuss only the weather. Try this with additional suggestions from the audience. What do you find out about the relationship between text and subtext?

4. Don't write out interior monologs like term papers, with formal word choices and perfect sentences. Interior monologs are jagged, incomplete, often interrupted thoughts with illogical twists and turns. The language (because it goes on in your head and doesn't need censoring) may be rough, crude, irrational, profane, even silly. Your interior monolog is like a tape that runs continuously day and night in your head, and when you are scat-tered or disorganized, it is doubly so. It is "stream of consciousness," but this stream has a lot of debris, driftwood, seaweed, and a few dead fish. No one's interior monolog is tidy. Notice how rude the interior remarks are in the roommate scene? And I had to cut back the original version for pub-lication. Because this stuff is unspoken, because it is behind the words, it is often quite socially unacceptable, which is why we usually don't say it. But it needs to be there to be real.

5. The relationship between *strategy* and *tactics* is like that in sports between a game plan and plays. There is always a general plan of attack, but then there are a wide range of maneuvers within the plan. The plan may not change, but the maneuvers may shift constantly.

Alternatives

Your *evaluation* period may have some random and desperate thoughts that do not lead anywhere because you are momentarily thrown off guard. These may include worrisome thoughts about what the other person will think of you before you even begin to consider an actual response. However, sooner or later your evaluation will include a subcategory called *alternatives*. These are answers you consider, but reject; they will vary from person to person and according to mood. If you're feeling ill and surly, your alternatives may include some insults and at least one obscene howl. Most however, include the following:

Response	Sample Lines
Complete rejection	"No way. Not in your lifetime, not in this century. Eat garbage and die."
Complete acceptance	"Whatever you say."
Stalling	"I don't get it. Could you run that by me again?"
Guarded, ambiguous response	"Thanks for your frankness. I hear what you're saying."
Logical, reasonable answer	"Let's go over each one of your points."
Emotional, passionate answer	"Oh God! I love it!!!" or "X#&@!!! You piece of *#^!!!"
Something menacing	"Go ahead. Make my day."
Something endearing	"You sure have a way with words."
Any combination of the above	

In the film *The Terminator*, alternatives are even considered (and shown electronically) by the nonhuman title character. In one scene, he is wounded and gives off an unpleasant odor. A guy comes to the apartment where he is hiding and shouts through the door: "Hey Buddy, you got a dead cat in there or what?" On Arnold's internal computer screen, six possible answers appear:

1. "Yes/No."
2. "Or what?"
3. "Go away."
4. "Please come back later."
5. "F _ _ _ you, asshole."
6. "F _ _ _ you."

He chooses 5, and the man goes away and leaves him alone.

Actors often leave out evaluations people would use in real life. Actors' words pop out too easily. The result is bad acting. It's easy to omit evaluating because the lines are already there and the actor doesn't have to search for words. This search, however, is compelling to watch. Great actors fill *evaluations* with original, powerful *alternatives*. Whenever they are handed a difficult cue, we watch, intrigued by what they consider but choose not to unveil, enthralled, as they prepare to respond.

Tactics can be characterized as *charm* ("I win, you win, we all win") or *threat* ("I win, you lose, so give up"). During an evaluation, we may hover and then move in one direction or the other. Here are some tactics most often chosen:

Charm Tactics

1. *Validate:* Make the other person feel important. Nod, smile, laugh appreciatively, flatter, pay tribute, bow, shrug, bend, appear powerless and impressed, give them an identity to live up to.

2. *Soothe:* Calm them down, lull, hum, hush, use a bedside manner, salve, quell, relax, caress, croon, offer reassuring sounds and comforting words.

3. *Open up:* Use candor. Claim to be open and frank because we honor their intelligence and character. Speak plain, shoot from the hip, be direct, be vulnerable, go for the bottom line. The idea is that some people might be hoodwinked, but not the listener.

4. *Play:* Amuse them, flirt, beguile, delight, find shared jokes, wink, whisper, captivate, convulse, get them to be silly with you and to drop their guard.

5. *Stir:* Inspire them, call them to wonder, challenge their ideals, turn them on to ideas or to you, get them hot, overwhelm them with fire of thought, deed, or action, whip them into a frenzy, whip up their patriotism, idealism, or gonads.

Threat Tactics

1. *Command:* Jump in and take charge, dominate, bulldoze, interrupt, seize the moment, grab leadership and authority. Take over.

2. *Intimidate:* Overwhelm with your height, size, physical strength, projection/volume, any ingredient bigger than theirs. Flex, clench, menace, bluff, appear dangerous. Overpower.

3. *Outspeak:* Speak with greater crispness, clarity, and assertiveness. Find more vivid word choices than theirs, dart with consonants, twist with endings of phrases, finish statements like curtain lines or by demanding a response. Use words as weapons.

4. *Scrutinize:* Stare at them as if you have the goods on them and know all their secrets. Study, undress with your eyes, glare, look through them. Answer questions with questions. Imagine you have a hidden weapon, dossier, evidence, photos (the shots with the donkey in Tijuana), a surprise witness, or secret arsenal.

5. *Yell:* Throw a tantrum, scream, appear irrational, nonnegotiable, at the edge of violence and past reason. (Use this one only selectively.)

Tactics raise ethical questions. For now, skip what is right or wrong and note what people do.

Exercise 1.12

Get the Dollar

Someone offers a dollar to the classmate who can come up with the best tactic. Let everyone who wants to try. Either the person with the dollar chooses the recipient or everyone votes on a winner. Discuss the range of tactics employed. Did any somehow combine both charm and threat maneuvers?

Exercise 1.13

Changing Tactics

Write out the tactic categories on slips of paper. Give two actors a basic situation to improvise with and periodically signal them to draw a different tactic to pursue until it is time to draw another. *Variation:* Side-coach the scene by calling out the name of the actor and the tactic to be tried next.

Exercise 1.14

Observing Alternatives

Take turns challenging others in the class with difficult questions (like pretending you hate the color of someone's sweater and how dare she wear it to class?) and listening carefully to the answers. Have class members identify alternatives they considered, but left unchosen, before the actual answer.

Exercise 1.15

Observing and Identifying

Sets of two volunteers get up and let the class give them a simple relationship (such as brother and sister) and conflict (like disagreeing over the best Mother's Day gift). Half the class "identifies" with one person and half with the other. The first person to observe three complete beats stops the scene. Everyone identifies the ten basics for the brief encounter that has just occurred.

Exercise 1.16

Observing Class

Designate someone at the beginning of the hour to stop class at a random moment during the first half-hour of the session. Then review the period so far for the ten basics. What were the shared objectives? What was the first noted obstacle? What was the most noteworthy evaluation? What general strategies and specific tactics have been employed? How has this class period divided into beats?

Exercise 1.17

Observing Offstage Acting

1. Observe and record an offstage encounter exactly as you did one in which you yourself starred in Exercise 1.15.

2. Do the same thing with another encounter, but pick one of the participants to support in your head, so that you have a much stronger sense of that person's subtext than the other's.

Exercise 1.18

Observing Onstage Acting

1. Attend a production and observe a single character with whom you feel some identification. Compare responses with your classmates.

2. Repeat number 2 from Exercise 1.17 with a character for whom you feel no identification or sympathy, and use the exercise to allow some understanding and compassion for the perspective of this character who is so different from you.

Why Study Acting?

If all the world is acting, why study it? Acting often does not necessarily mean acting well! Something this important to living fully is something we can all get better at.

A strong motive for acting is *l'Esprit de l'Escalier*, an evocative French phrase that literally translates as "the Spirit of the Stairs." Imagine yourself at a party where someone says something astonishingly rude to you. You are stunned and struck speechless. The evening goes on. You are leaving the party, descending the *stairs*, and suddenly the *spirit* comes to you. You think of the most devastating, witty comeback line in the world, a perfect retort, very civilized, but sure to end all such rudeness forever. Unfortunately, the party is over, you are outside, your rude assailant is nowhere to be seen, and too much time has gone by for an effective retort anyway. You would love to rewind the tape of your life. No such luck. But the line was perfect.

You arrive home and are sorely tempted to tell the story as if you did execute the key line at the key moment. Your ethics are strongly tested. If enough time goes by, you might start telling the story that way. You might even start believing it happened the way it should have, if there was real justice in the world. There is real justice in the theatre. Characters often do think of the perfect comeback. Life is more the way it ought to be.

Acting is where I get to yell at people the way I'd like to. And to be funny the way I'd like to be funny. And to be alive the way I'd like to be alive.
—Ethan Hawke

Theatre is life with the dull parts cut out.
—Alfred Hitchcock

And sometimes it rubs off. The more time you spend speaking the great lines of others, the better chance you have to think of them yourself. There is a poster/postcard/bumper sticker that reads, "If All the World's a Stage, I Need Better Lines." Proximity to better lines can help. You may develop into someone who gets the spirit long before descending the stairs.

A Richer Life

Acting is life-enhancing. Even if you never enter the door of a theatre after the last day of class, you can develop vivid personal awareness, higher communication skills, and a strong dose of compassion for others. Most disciplines study human behavior from a distance, looking at large groups with far more theory than experience. There may be no better, more involving way to learn about yourself and the phenomenon of being alive than by studying acting.

You learn how to relax and focus. You find out how your body, voice, and personality affect other people. You get tools for change if you do not like what you find out. You have a stronger sense of the kind of figure you cut in the world. You get to free dormant creative impulses, unchanneled emotional expression, and suppressed playfulness.

You also gain insight regarding others, as individuals and as groups. You observe more carefully and you interact with greater sensitivity. You may start out as an atheist, a pacifist, and a political liberal. Before your study of acting is over, you may get to play a fundamentalist preacher, a soldier, and a Birch Society member. You may even be in class with such people and bond with them. You will never be able to casually judge them or generalize about them again. You will never be able to think of them merely as members of their groups.

You understand connections between you and others: how to make connections, avoid them, solidify them, and break them. You sense hidden agendas, nuances, layers of interaction. There is a good chance of being able to "play" your own life better.

I come from a tight knit, conservative family. What kind of girl would go for that? They were looking for exotic, hotblooded Cuban boys with skintight pants and forbidden, dark-eyed lust. So I presented myself as that kind of guy. I was acting, even at that age.

—Andy Garcia

The study of acting allows you to return to Let's Pretend. You may replace playing Peter Pan with deciding to be French while you're in a restaurant, acting stinking rich as you peruse the sapphires in a jewelry store, or giving yourself a made-up background to share with the stranger you're seated next to on the plane. Most of us were much better at Let's Pretend, in days of yore, than we are now. Acting class can get you back in touch with the child in yourself. Acting can unlock the you that was there before the locks were put on your imagination, your capacity for delight, your sense of wonder. It can unlock your dormant ability to transform yourself and the world around you.

As much as actors like to pretend that we're these serious intellectuals, you only get into acting if you're a kid who likes to dress up and play pretend.

—Billy Bob Thornton

Actors are people who were good at playing "Let's Pretend" as kids and now we're getting money to play house.

—Michael J. Fox

Actors versus Others

Human beings all act, but what about the actor as a recognized artist, a professional, someone *known* as an actor? What makes some get up and perform, even show off, where others fear to tread? The story of Oog, the Caveperson, freely adapted here, is a possible explanation:

> Imagine a society of prehistoric types where strength and courage are admired above all. Imagine a small male Caveperson, named Oog, living in this group and not quite fitting in. Most males like to hunt and all take their turns killing dinosaurs [I told you this was freely adapted]. Oog likes to carve on walls, eat, talk, and mate. He is scared of hunting. But his day comes along like everyone else's.
>
> Oog spends the whole day observing dinosaurs and other powerful creatures, having neither the heart nor the courage to kill anything. He drags his club home at sundown, only to encounter all the powerful brutes standing around the cave entrance. "Hey, Oog, where's dinner?" one asks menacingly. Oog pauses nervously and considers trying to run away.
>
> Suddenly he is inspired. "Wait 'til I tell you about it," he says. "There I was on the plain, the sun beating mercilessly down on my neck, when suddenly this enormous green creature roars (he stops and roars) and rolls his head (he rolls) so fiercely that I got chills (his listeners get chills) and then . . ." (The details of his story can be omitted since, with some embellishment, he takes them through his day so vividly, that they almost feel as if they were there in his place.) Oog has his audience mesmerized. He imitates the dinosaur to perfection, he gets the sound of dinofeet on the sandy plain, all the details. Cheers follow the end of his story.
>
> All is forgiven. There is ample leftover dinosaur around anyway. The group quickly agrees that Oog should be excused from hunting from now on. Instead, he should follow the hunters and observe the hunt, recreating it for everyone at supper each evening, acting out all the parts. Well, most of the parts. Already others are volunteering to help out. He is happy to be excused and glad to have a function. As Oog and his mate head off to their corner of the cave, she says to him, "Oog, you've got it all over those dumb brutes. You're a real artist."
>
> As another couple moves to their corner, she says, "That Oog. Isn't he amazing? The way he got just how the dinosaur's head swings back and forth. It was perfect." Her mate replies, "Well, it was pretty good. Personally, I wouldn't have swung my head so far. It's more of circle than a swing, actually." And so the first actor is born. And minutes later, the first critic.

In every culture, someone finds she is better at showing society how it lives than at living at its center. Her gifts are for recreating human experience. She can literally give life back to an event from the past or give form to something in the mind. One of the questions you are probably exploring in taking an acting class is whether or not that sort of person is you.

> *When I got to do my first play, it was like somebody
> dropped me in the water for the first time. My God! To
> know who you are, to know how you're supposed to earn
> the breath you draw. It's such a release.*
> —Alfre Woodard
>
> *I think I first turned to acting out of a desire for love. Isn't that
> what we all want? And then I fell in love with acting itself.*
> —Matt Damon

Nearly everyone fantasizes about an acting career, and acting teachers are plagued by first-term students wanting to know if they have what it takes. This question is premature. No decent teacher will answer it until a student has studied the art for a few years. A teacher will tell you where your strong suits appear to lie, where you've made progress, what kinds of goals you should set, and what training you should pursue next. But no one should give you thumbs up or down but you. If you decide ultimately, down the road, to pursue the profession, it will be because you know you *must*. It will be because the art has chosen and possessed you and you have no choice. You may or may not be Oog.

> *When I found acting, I discovered a piece of me that had
> been missing all my life. It's almost like you miss a couple
> chapters in a book, but you keep reading confused. Then sud-
> denly there are the missing chapters and it all makes sense.*
> —Lucy Liu
>
> *Everything else in my life receded, once I discovered theatre.*
> —Bette Midler
>
> *I knew I wanted to be an actor as soon as I knew what one
> was. At age 3 I asked my parents to get me an agent and
> finally when I was 6, they did.*
> —Keira Knightley

Offstage Action

An actor also has access to many life skills that elude other people. Studying acting (both in class and in shows) can help you become skilled and resourceful in count-less offstage encounters. What follows is a *looong* list. At this point, just scan it for parts of your life you really want to improve. Let these be regular reference points throughout the term. Then return to the list as your awareness of how this class could affect you expands. Each subsequent chapter will ask you to reconnect with the list as a checkpoint in your growth.

1. Negating Newness

You want to make a good impression, but you don't know the other people or circumstances, so you're unsure how to "act":

- *First dates:* What does this person want and do I want to spend more time with this person? If you can get comfortable performing in front of groups of strangers, you can get loose and playful around one new person whom you think you like.

- *Handling interviews:* Even the toughest questions can be rehearsed; you can actually practice and prepare rather than just getting nervous.

- *Fitting in as a newcomer:* Theatre requires instant intimacy. People who have never laid eyes on each other suddenly must trust each other and work closely. This ability carries over into other contexts.

- *Visiting potential in-laws:* This is an audition and involves skills you will study. Also remember that you don't necessarily want the part for which you are trying out.

- *Making small talk with strangers:* Working with dialogue and improvisation gives you lots of lines and more ways to respond freshly when you might otherwise be coming up blank.

- *Hosting/chairing for the first time:* Actors need to learn new routines fast, swiftly figure out protocol, and get things moving. Plus you learn to act like a leader.

- *Giving impromptu speeches:* Again, these don't have to be altogether new. Acting allows you to learn stories, lines, and jokes and file them away for when they are suddenly needed.

2. Pleasant as Possible

You're in a situation that could get extremely unpleasant unless you develop an acting strategy to smooth out the encounter:

- *Creating, maintaining boundaries:* Acting classes establish guidelines for appropriate behavior. Actors get skilled at telling others what they will and will not accept.

- *Getting rid of pests:* If you pursue acting, you really will be too busy to give them much time, but you will also learn specific strategies for being left alone.

- *Taking rejection gracefully:* There are always so many more actors wanting roles, nominations, places in class, and so on than there are openings that getting comfortable with hearing "No" is simply an actor's way of life.

- *Handling criticism well:* Your work is constantly evaluated publicly with an emphasis on how it could change for the better. You learn to accept critical "gifts" without being devastated.

- *Airing grievances effectively:* Again, characters in plays do this better than most of us, and we can borrow from them. You develop the ability to complain succinctly, often with humor, in the way that works best.

- *Resolving conflicts swiftly:* Because there is always a looming deadline, actors learn to get right to the problem, solve it, and move on to be ready for opening night.

- *Settling disagreements peaceably:* Actors share a common goal—the show must go on—that powerfully unites and motivates them to get along. This skill transfers to other circumstances.

- *Ending relationships gracefully:* Theatre is a constant series of closeness suddenly ended when the show closes or the course ends, almost like having temporary families that then dissolve. You get very good at enjoying it while it lasts and then being able to say good-bye and walk away.

- *Negotiating skillfully:* Every rehearsal is a series of negotiations. Before you know it, you have mastered compromise and initiative.

- *Self-assertiveness in the face of opposition:* Unless you want to be a doormat, you learn to face up to all the strong personalities and make your voice heard. Actor training is in many ways about learning when and how to speak up.

3.   Keeping Cool

Major acting effort goes into not blowing up, breaking down, or freaking out. In fact, the most frequent form of offstage acting is dialing yourself down:

- *Not overreacting, subduing emotional excess:* Contrary to the stereotype of actors emoting excessively, one of the primary lessons we learn is how to subdue displays when excess is inappropriate.

- *Modulating degree or kind of emotion shown:* Actors become adept at masking or revealing feeling in increments, useful in countless life encounters.

- *Self-control, restraint:* Acting gives you power and choice. It teaches you to do just enough and no more.

- *Conquering destructive impulses:* Even the simple study of evaluations and alternatives *(see page 20)* helps you recognize when you need to ponder an action before fully taking it. The self-analysis of actor training helps you recognize early your own symptoms and tendencies to impulsiveness.

- *Handling stress, pressure gracefully:* There are so many sources of tension in performance that skills related to being ready and going easily with the flow are among the most important learned.

- *Anger management:* Because you study emotions across the board, you have much better chances to reign in those that do not serve you.

- *Quick recovery from tough encounters:* Switching gears from one scene to the next, getting ready for "show time" whether you are in the mood or not, getting over harsh criticism, and quickly bouncing back are all part of the acting process.

- *Maintaining perspective:* Actors examine plays from many points of view, must comprehend behavior they would never choose, and constantly need to look at the big picture.

- *Knowing when to substitute emotion:* Sometimes the situation is not going to change, and the only way to make it better is changing the way you feel about it. Actors have to do this.

- *Knowing when to exaggerate expression of feeling:* You punch up an emotion (in what behavioral scientists call "display rules") to avoid hurting someone's feelings, so you may act as if a mildly pleasant (or even disappointing) gift is the best thing that ever happened to you if the giver seems to need this kind of reassurance. You may also "enlarge" a negative response for something you wish never to happen again. Believably heightening response is a vital daily acting skill.

4. Sensing Signals

Actors study behavior closely and get much sharper than others are at recognizing what is really going on behind what is said:

- *Reading nonverbal behavior in others:* We study how to read the look in someone's eyes, body language, pauses, all the signals that many miss.

- *Sensing people's feelings accurately:* After learning the various masks used by those trying to cover a feeling, you become adept at seeing through those masks.

- *Responding appropriately:* Acting gives you more choices generally and the capacity to read signals to tell you how to proceed.

- *Grasping expectations:* Every acting teacher and director is different in what they expect us to do on our own, so we get adept at determining what that is, a skill essential for any new job.

- *Tuning in to subtle social signals:* Many people are so full of themselves that they fail to recognize a current running through a group. Actors learn to get their antennae out for shifts in the room.

- *Sensing and mastering behavioral modes:* In the world of any play, there is a dominant way of acting, which may be profane, aristocratic, whimsical, and so on, and the same is true of most groups we might join.

- *Recognizing, mastering protocol:* A code exists even in the most seemingly casual groups. There are things you always and never do to succeed. Acting gives you protocol radar.

- *Interactive synchronicity:* Actors develop powerful empathy and a connection with others and are more likely to get on someone else's wavelength with less effort.

5. Winning Ways

Whether you are selling an idea, project, plan, or yourself, for a season or a night, acting is a crucial part of persuasion:

- *Pitching an idea:* All performance skills are needed for an effective pitch, but most civilians lack these as back-ups to the ideas themselves.

- *Convincing parents/authority figures:* Actors begin to recognize the part of themselves that those in charge respond positively to and where their most effective arguments have been. Then they build on these for the next encounter.

- *Romance:* Wooing people is about figuring out what those people like, how they want you to act around them, and when to surprise them. Actors are naturals at this, and scripts offer some impressive models of successful lovers.

- *Seduction:* If you want others to drop their guard, whether the reasons are sexual or simply to persuade, the art of acting gives you a seductive edge.

- *Winning trust and confidence:* Class teaches you where your own behavior seems least truthful and helps you hone what others respond to as real.

- *Getting yourself hired, chosen, or awarded:* Again, the audition skills actors develop can give them a significant edge in competitive settings where being able to act confident is essential, even if it is not your first impulse.

- *Getting off light when you've gotten busted:* These skills should be used with high selectivity. Actors have countless stories of getting out of traffic tickets, detention—you name it—through skillful and subtle performances.

6. Improving Your Image

Many people don't like the way they come across to others, but feel trapped. Many don't even know how they come across. Acting students learn what they send out and how to make changes:

- *Breaking out of limiting behavior:* Acting training helps you recognize what you are doing that is not working and gives you other options.

- *Altering others' perceptions of you:* Constantly reading feedback and adjusting is part of the acting craft where there is no need to remain clueless.

- *Changing your personal image:* Because you learn to change yourself to play a character, you also pick up hints about refining what you project in the world.

- *Leaving an impression of both confidence and humility:* Civilians often think they need to come across as one or the other. Actors learn to blend.

- *Controlling impressions you leave:* Because you learn how to make a character seem more powerful, lighthearted, subtle, whatever, you have the wherewithal to do the same with your personal characterization.

- *Balancing being true to yourself with social skills:* Acting can teach you which battles are worth fighting. You learn how to lubricate some social occasions so you feel more free to speak your mind in others when it is needed.

7. Richer Relationships

Some of us get almost too good at number 3, "Keeping Cool." Opening up involves knowing not just how to feel like a friend, but how to act like one:

- *Demonstrating concern for those you care about:* Actors learn about actions, the sort of gestures or demonstrations that actually show people how you feel.

- *Nurturing important relationships:* Friendships don't just fall apart. They take some regular attention, a collection of the smallest gestures.

- *Finding ways to offer support:* As you study human behavior as a performer, you also study human needs and recognize what is needed and how to give it.

- *Providing consolation, or solace:* The fear of appearing sentimental or clumsy stops many from demonstrating real concern, but actors are less likely to be frozen by that degree of self-consciousness.

- *Encouraging, honoring others' accomplishments:* Non-actors are also often embarrassed that they will come off as cheesy or inauthentic, whereas actors learn how essential praise is to growth and give it.

- *Establishing trust:* We have no choice but to learn how to trust our scene partners and everyone who supports a production, which means we learn short cuts.

- *Effective self-disclosure:* Because we learn to conceal who we are, we also often feel more comfortable sharing what's inside when the time is right.

- *Demonstrating compassion:* Oddly enough, you may feel deeply for others, but not have learned how to show it. So you learn to act what you feel.

- *Making empathetic connections:* The mere fact that we are asked to go deep into the skins and hearts of others as we play them gives us an opening to do the same with our companions.

- *Developing support systems:* Acting requires us to learn quickly whom we can trust, learn from, and feel nurtured by. We have more clues to pick a better posse.

- *Full engagement with those close to you:* Simply allowing ourselves the freedom of identifying and experiencing fully with our friends is a tremendous relief and very hard unless you learn relatedness through acting.

8. Social Savvy

Acting is interacting, knowing how to connect with, listen to, and relate to others:

- *People skills:* There are myriad models both in plays and among performers of how to play people effectively rather than distancing yourself or putting yourself at their mercy.

- *Networking skillfully:* Most productions have fifty or more people working on them. Pay attention, and every one of them will be on your team by the time the show is over. Or not. Same for other groups later.

- *Interactive competence:* Models for getting directly to the point with vivid examples and getting results are offered to us constantly in scripts where most of the hemming and hawing of life has been cut out.

- *Mastering routine social exchanges:* If you aren't naturally good at life's improvisations, you can observe and rehearse these surprisingly predictable interactions. They don't have to be spontaneous; you just need to act them that way.

- *Being an interpersonal virtuoso:* The chameleon nature of versatile acting can mean quicksilver interactive adjustments as well, switching gears to get more on someone's wavelength, achieving instant rapport.

- *Easing tension, creating harmony:* Study the energy you bring into a room (especially a rehearsal hall or acting class) and model those who always seem to improve the mood and break the tension before it explodes. They have a specific kind of contagious harmonious sense.

- *Working with a wide range of colleagues:* There is probably no more varied a motley crew than those who people a theatre department or a production. We could hardly be less similar except for our love of this art, so we learn to get past all those differences and down to what binds us.

- *Actively collaborating:* Acting teaches you to ask questions, make requests, assert demands, compromise, and generally adjust to get the best results for everyone.

- *Keeping up morale:* A great ensemble actor learns to contribute to maintaining a sense of general well-being among company members, a great skill in any situation.

- *Being socially adroit:* Because we get to study characters making disastrous social errors and brilliant successes, we have a true and varied menu of choices available to us.

9. Prediction Potential

Acting forces you to face your fears, learn what works, and to look ahead:

- *Recognizing consequences:* Every choice in an acting program has reverberations (some of which can get one cut), so you get quite adept at looking ahead several steps, an invaluable kind of awareness.

- *Curbing impulsiveness:* Acting teaches you to learn to pause, breathe, and consider before taking action. Your work becomes more interesting and your decisions more mature.

- *Avoiding irrational reactions you later regret:* Similarly, you learn to red flag your own hasty choices from the past and particularly to extend evaluations in these kinds of encounters.

- *Setting achievable goals:* Actors must work in small units ("beats," *see pages 15–16*) each with objectives that can be attained and do not overwhelm. This is a tremendous life model for getting through tough times.

- *Not being inhibited or overwhelmed:* So many people are too frightened even to take an acting class that, just by being here, you are miles ahead of all of them in fear management! Every time you volunteer to get up and "make a fool of yourself," you are way ahead of the game because you recognize how much fun and how freeing that is.

- *Sensing ways to get yourself into "the flow" or "the zone":* These terms are used by social scientists and athletic counselors for the times you are so motivated and "into it" that everything comes easily and distractions fade away. Acting teaches us to carefully note how we get into our most creative space as well as the opposite. It teaches us to get where we want to be more swiftly.

10.   Career Capabilities

One of the secrets major employment agencies know is that those who have studied acting gain professional skills untouched by other fields. You may not get a job as a professional actor but your ability to get, keep, thrive, and advance in any job will increase through:

- *Meeting the public comfortably:* Turning audiences into your new 500 best friends is common theatre practice. You get used to it.

- *Maintaining a poised and pleasant manner:* Acting requires falling into an appropriate behavior pattern at every performance, whether you feel like it or not, in a smooth and confident way.

- *Making presentations:* Each public performance, class report, or activity prepares you for each time you need to stand up and present a plan.

- *General resourcefulness:* Actors learn multiple ways to approach a character and put together a performance, so the task of investigating and experimenting with a wide net becomes habit.

- *Taking initiative:* Self-motivating is the name of the acting game, in part because those who do not end up with weak performances or don't make the cut. It becomes pleasantly addictive to be a self-starter.

- *Finding innovative ideas:* The ultimate corporate cliché is the admonition to "think outside the box." We are always moving outside and *waaay* beyond the box, so innovation is like breathing.

- *Brainstorming:* Effective rehearsals prepare you to throw out ideas rapidly and grab the best, to just keep coming up with other possibilities.

- *Adapting within structure:* Theatre has very specific rules, but then allows freewheeling creativity within them, so you learn that you can both fit inside established processes and defy convention.

- *Changing strategies:* It is so clear in acting that if what you are doing now isn't working, try something (anything!) else. An amazing number of people just keep trying the same thing, but actors learn to make another choice or lose out.

- *Leading discussions:* Again, there are many models in theatre programs of how to lead and how to follow, plus when to open up and when to close down talk to get the group to move forward.

- *Balancing multiple tasks:* As you will see in Chapter 8, acting is a matter of juggling concurrent jobs in order to pull the performance together, a great advantage over those who think they can only do one thing at a time.

- *Managing time effectively:* From the time a scene or monolog is assigned or a show starts rehearsing until opening, there is a need to monitor and use time to the max every day. There is no cramming to catch up. As a result, actors learn how to get the most out of each limited time frame.

- *Meeting deadlines:* Theatre is the ultimate deadline art, with a due date that is set and is not about when you actually feel ready, invaluable in a world of procrastinators.

- *Working unsupervised:* Between each class and rehearsal, actors grow accustomed to major solo homework so they can bring great stuff to the next group meeting, not needing constant input.

- *Editing:* We always need to cut scenes and monologs to meet time constraints or to tighten our performances, which puts us in the editing mode and allows us a healthy openness to streamlining.

- *Retaining information:* The constant act of memorizing text and mastering acting concepts gets you primed to retention, to actually keeping salient information intact over long periods and hauling it out when needed.

OK, Wait a Minute . . . ?

Three questions come immediately to mind when you read a list like the one just presented:

1. If this is true, why are so many actors so messed up? Because many of them practice acting intuitively without really studying it. And some study it, but as an isolated art form without making life connections, even when the lessons are right in front of them. *Offstage* action mastery doesn't happen automatically. You have to observe and connect. Offstage skills are more available to you than to others, but you still have to grab and apply them.

2. If this is true, why isn't acting one of the most important classes taught at any school and one required of all students? Good question. It is one of the most important, but administrators and curriculum committees have been slow to recognize it. Taking an acting class is not going to solve your life problems, but I would challenge you to come up with any other course that offers you as much help for your future choices.

3. If this is true, isn't a good actor a manipulative user? Not of necessity. Acting is a powerful tool that can be used with or without integrity. The choice is yours. Much of acting is done to help others, spare their feelings, and offer them solace. Much of it is done to make everything run more smoothly, to keep more people content, to get the job done. You are going to act your life no matter what. You might as well do it well.

Exercise 1.19

Offstage Action Acknowledged

1. Review the list in the previous section and determine where you could use the most help in your offstage life. Keep your list to refer to throughout the term as you pick up tips on improvement in those areas.

2. Review the list for places you feel you already have mastery. Be alert for advice you might give others when they need it.

3. If there is time, compare notes in class about where people feel secure and where not. Consider coming up with a master list for the class of areas that are shared by enough people to be called class concerns.

4. When there is an opportunity to devise an improvisation, turn to this section for basic scenario ideas so that you can actually practice some life situations in advance.

Already an Actor

So you have an acting history. You have found situations you thrive in, fantasies and visions that inspire you, areas of vulnerability and strength in public, areas of child-like wonder that are still very much alive in you, and others that may need some resuscitation. You have places in your life where you script very carefully and those where you choose to wing it.

Many of your offstage experiences can give you confidence and texture onstage. Your acting experience can be brought into the theatre and used there. You have a giant résumé of performances. Some were Oscar-caliber triumphs. Others were such disasters you don't even like to think about them, unless enough time has passed to make them funny. All are a source of learning. Don't start acting class convinced that you are an acting virgin. Your life is a fascinating fund that can be drawn on to help you become both a better actor and a more complete human being.

You have an acting past and present. Learning more about this art form can give you a future that includes

A fascinating lifelong endeavor;

A chance to utter great words;

More insight and compassion;

Stronger self-awareness;

More successful human interactions;

Highly useful skills; and

A reawakening of the child in you.

Not bad for a single area of study. It's ironic that some regard acting as frivolous, not really an important, fundamental subject to study. What could be more fundamental than learning how to feel full of possibility?

The actor is Camus's ideal existential hero, because if life is absurd and the idea is to live a more vital life, the man who lives more lives is in a better position than the guy who lives just one.

—Jack Nicholson

2

Relaxed Readiness

Calm enough, yet energized enough to do your best

The most important acting advice is don't run before you can walk.
—Kate Winslet

If I can just stay focused, and then I can start to really breathe, my panic falls away, and I can act.
—Nicole Kidman

The best actors have a kind of stillness, with nothing distracting, just a compelling focus.
—Anthony Hopkins

Even in the beginning, when I was doing junk television, I still had one thing—focus.
—Michelle Pfeiffer

I like people with power. And in acting, power comes from focus.
—Danny Glover

Warming Up

Actors who are focused are fascinating. You are focused when you have a point of concentration, a center of attention, when your consciousness is controlled and directed where you want it to be. Your energies are so united that you cannot be distracted. Your powers are brought to bear upon one clear course. All irrelevancies and digressions fade away.

The best way to achieve focus is to learn how to warm up. Because acting challenges the body, the voice, and the spirit, all three deserve some attention. All three can be eased into a higher state of alert responsiveness and sharper focus. In the great offstage performances of your life so far, focus came suddenly, perhaps accidentally. But this state can be achieved deliberately.

> *The eye of a focused actor attracts the spectator . . . a blank eyed actor lets the attention of the spectator wander.*
> —Constantin Stanislavski
>
> *I'm not a talented man. . . . I'm a focused man.*
> —William Hurt

And you are not alone. In an acting class or a cast, everyone depends on everyone else. They have no choice. These groups need instant trust and mutual acceptance. Time cannot be wasted while each individual frets over when and how to open up to the others. Each person needs to warm up his own instrument, and he needs to warm up to those around him. This chapter will deal with preparing to act, as an individual and as a member of the group.

Balancing Opposing States

If you are too *relaxed*, you fall asleep. If you are too *ready*, you can explode. The actor seeks a balance between ease and eagerness, between indifference and anxiety. Someone heavily anesthetized is relaxed, but then so is a corpse. A guru of the 1970s used to admonish his Quaalude-besotted disciples that they were aiming to become "laid back, not laid out." Concentrate only on relaxation, and your performance is likely to come up short on energy, vitality, clarity, and power. At the other extreme is locker-room frenzy, which works for sprinting and high-decibel rock, but leads to acting that burns out quickly, to performance minus nuance, shading, and variety.

Images of cats permeate acting literature because no other creature seems quite so loose, yet alert. Acting warm-ups shoot for *relaxed readiness* because actors are not automatically blessed with the cat's perfect energy state. As you learn the following sequence (or any other used by your class), keep yourself open and responsive. Avoid pre-judging any exercise. Don't pick favorites, don't decide early which you don't like, don't decide at all yet. Just let go. It may seem for a while as if nothing is happening. When you finally get each exercise mastered and are free enough to allow it to work on you, then it will happen.

Mental Warm-Ups

The body and voice are worth little if the mind fails to respond. The mind can free your spirit, an elusive combination of imagination, energy, and openness to experience. We all recognize the spirit of, say, Christmas or brotherhood, without being able to trap and keep it. Your acting spirit is strongly connected to the child in you. You start by tapping your willingness and then turning with trust to those around you, letting them give you courage and conquering your own fear of unmasking.

You don't act alone. The old actor cliché goes, "I don't know what happened. It was great when I did it at home in front of the mirror." I often joke with casts, as we approach opening night, about the fact that the audience will soon come and interfere with everything we've done, audaciously interrupting us with their laughter and applause. But communion with other actors and the audience is the whole point. It just takes adjustment. The others often don't respond the way they did in your head (or your mirror) at home. You need to allow others to become your mirrors and your guides.

The first step is to exorcise yourself from the demons that follow all actors around. These are some of the things they whisper in your ear, so that it sounds like you speaking:

"These people are all much more talented than I am."

"They've all acted a lot already. I'm the only baby here."

"I'm the only one who looks bad in tights." (Substitute any clothing worn so far.)

"They're all so colorful. They'll think I'm too straight."

"They're all so normal looking. They'll think I'm too weird."

"Everybody remembers the warm-ups but me." (Substitute any topic covered so far.)

"They all know each other already. I'll bet they all signed up as a group."

"Maybe I should have taken Art History instead." (Or any other subject offered in the world.)

This list and this paranoia are boring. And a waste of time. All the things on the list are false and you know it. And most of the fears are shared fears. Yet nearly everyone gives in to some demons. Promise yourself not to.

Exercise 2.1

Dumping the Demons

1. Write out the preceding list of statements.

2. Cross out those items you haven't actually succumbed to yet.

3. Add your own additions. The possibilities ("The teacher already hates me;" "They'll never cast me here") are endless.

4. Scrawl something colorful over each item ("B.S." "Hogwash." Your own favorite retaliation.)

5. Have a private exorcism, where you dramatically shred the paper, toss it out to sea, burn it, or all of the above. If you do the exercise The Journey *(page 62)*, symbolically slay your own demons at the end.

6. Get on with your acting.

Class Commitment

If you decide today that you have an emotional investment in your acting class-mates, there will be dividends beyond any stockbroker's dreams. The dividends are intangible, inspirational, and impossible to exchange on any market. When you are invested in someone else, you want that person to excel and you project your hope onto her, you bend a little when she disappoints you, you always look ahead to what she might become with a little support. Instead of seeing this person as competition, you actually equate your own progress with hers. You want to be part of a group of actors who are, without exception, exceptional. You want your teacher to find the task of making qualitative distinctions impossible.

Acting classes are rarely graded on any kind of scale, so everyone in the class could get an A (or, of course, possibly an F). But with this fellowship comes mutual responsibility. If you are absent one day in your psychology lecture of 300 students, it matters to no one but you. In acting class, you may be partnered with different people to lead warm-ups, to perform someone's offstage memory, to (coming in subsequent chapters) imitate, to explore subtext, to perform a scene. If class time is devoted to these activities, you could leave a virtual platoon of partners in the lurch by not being there, on any given day. If you are late for some other classes, it doesn't really matter. If you are late for Acting 1, someone may be off in the corner by himself, because you were his partner for the activity that started the day.

Even if you have been a flake all your life, this is the time to feel responsible for others in the group, to move beyond your own habitual self-indulgence to a sense of community. You'll like how it feels.

The actors must understand each other, help each other, absolutely love each other. They absolutely must.

–Laurence Olivier

When I found acting, I finally found a place that accepted everybody and all their dreams.

–Kevin Spacey

Stage Fright Substitutes

The term "stage fright" has largely dropped out of use because we now know that dwelling on something this malevolent gives it power. If I tell you not to be afraid, you will dwell on your fear. If I say, "Do not think of fast-food burgers under any circumstances," an assembly line of them will parade in your mind. The key to most fears is substitution. On the simplest level, you replace the ogre with something less menacing, to fill your consciousness.

A great actor is like a great host. His concern is for the comfort and well-being of his partner and his audience. Great hosts ease you into a feeling that everything will be fine. They soothe you and make you feel effortlessly open to the next course. They never force you with overwhelming offers of "More dip???!!!" placing the green stuff millimeters from your mouth. For the hosts themselves, once they have concentrated fully on their guests, there is no room in their consciousness to be worried about whether the baseboards were dusted or if the stain on the rug will show. There's no room in the head for such monsters. Instead, project your concern to your listeners, really thinking more of their comfort than their verdicts.

The best advice I ever received from a veteran actor was, "Step out of the center of the universe." Once you do that, your perspective and your humanity are both back in place. And your "guests" will relax.

Accepting the Audience

An audience is an audience, whether it's one friend, a handful of classmates, or thousands of paying customers.

> *I don't think of the audience as someone separate from me. You have to seduce an audience. You can't beat 'em and you can't kiss their asses.*
>
> –Harrison Ford
>
> *All sorts of waifs and strays are admitted into the circle of actors. I think it was that side of acting and the love you get from people that work together, that first drew me in. I had never felt anything like it.*
>
> –Ian McKellan

Here are some other hints for allowing those out there to be *with* you, instead of assuming they're against you:

1. No matter who is really out in the audience, place a familiar, nurturing, warm somebody out there. Place the spirit of someone who supports you.

2. Make friends with a piece of furniture, a window, a radiator, a blackboard, any object that seems comfortable and familiar, perhaps reminiscent of some place you like. Connect back with it occasionally for assurance.

3. Remind yourself that at the same moment you are walking up front to tell your little joke in acting class, millions are being born and dying, a crucial piece of heart surgery is being performed, a couple is making hot love on some secluded Bahamas beach, someone toils in the lab trying to discover a cure for AIDS, a pilot has just landed a damaged plane with all on board grateful that only a few have been killed or injured. What you are doing is not the beginning or end of life. You are a grain of sand (albeit a great grain), and this moment is not even a semifinalist among the big triumphs and traumas going on in the world.

4. Tell yourself those people out there are potential best friends. In acting class, this is definitely true. In a performance hall, it is potentially true. You go out in front of a crowd. They are not merely a crowd. They are 1,200 of your best friends, or at least potential best friends. What you want with your audience (especially if you address them directly) is a sense of confiding in someone you trust. If you will project that trust out into the house, the audience will lovingly receive it.

5. No one sits in the audience hoping to be bored and disappointed. In fact, empirical studies have shown that when mistakes (line drops, fumbling pieces of business) have been deliberately inserted in performances to test audience response, that almost no one could recall these errors later because they had cheerfully edited them at the time. That's how much each of the people watching is on your side.

Group Warm-Ups

Trust can be projected onto strangers, but it helps a lot if you can simply stop being strangers. It's worth taking time, the first weeks of acting class, for people to get to know each other. I believe it's worth a lot of time. Here are some of the things others usually want to know. Sharing this information will help you skip steps and drop barriers.

Sharing Now

Some sharing of your past was suggested in Chapter 1. Now is a good time to share what you think and feel, not just what you've done. Think about what you would like to say or show in each category. Have an answer even if it is only a conjecture, your best guess at the moment.

Exercise 2.2

Shared Opinions

1. How You Would be Typecast

Whether you choose to accept your type, fight it, change it, or expand it is something to determine later. Now is the time to acknowledge it. You need to know how others perceive you, even if you elect to alter that perception. How would a casting director place you? What sorts of parts would she be likely to send you out for? How do most strangers perceive you? This question requires some self-awareness.

Remember, type has little to do with the way you are deep down. It is the impression you leave. It may also have little to do with your chronological age or the parts you've played so far. You may have done roles in your hometown because you were the only one around with the size or the voice to pull it off. In a larger casting pool, this may not be your perceived type at all. Offstage, you may have been cast as a leader, heading student governments, fund-raisers, you name it. But onstage, you may not look and sound like a leader at all.

Are you cringing at the whole idea of having to be any type when you want to be a great versatile, limitless actor? Of course you are. But you must know how you are viewed now before you do that. If you are uncertain, your friends will be glad to help you. Your best information will come from new friends, who do not have unfair information. Ask others:

What sorts of roles on TV they feel you could fit in (if the current actors disappeared)?

What celebrities you remind them of (if even just slightly)?

Which people in the dorm or in this class you are most like (and least like)?

This information can really be eye opening.

2. Your Favorite Actor

"Oh, I don't really have a favorite. There are so many great ones." Come on. Pick one. This isn't engraved in stone. You may change your mind next week. But right now, who is someone you really admire? And why?

Pick an actor, not just a star. Just a star, you say? There are actors who are stars, but there are stars who are not actors. If you're serious enough about the art to study it, you're ready to make that distinction. Pick people whose artistry, skill, or versatility you admire at least as much as their charisma, size, or sex appeal. When you think of an *actor*, you think of quality work, not just a great set of eyes or biceps. Pick someone whose art you admire at least as much as anything else about him.

3. Performance That Impressed You Most

Sometimes, watching an actor at work just fills you with awe. You are vividly aware that this is art of the highest order. You get chills, the works. What is the closest you have come to feeling that way?

Exercise 2.3

Shared Performances

4. Offstage Performance You'd Most Like to Share

You reviewed these as you went through the Chapter 1 exercises. Which, out of your vast repertoire, would you enjoy telling about? Or demonstrating? Which would be most likely to help these classmates feel they know you? To get a sense of you, acting in the world?

5. Offstage Performance of the Week

If a vivid one has not been thrust upon you by an unexpected visit, Rush Week, or new living arrangements, you may want to stage one, armed with all the information you now have. If you had to recreate this moment for the class, how would you cast it from among your classmates?

6. Favorite Story Joke

A story joke takes a minute or two to tell. You need to establish characters and circumstances that involve change, so that there is more than a setup and punch line. Again, imagine it two ways: one with you just telling it, the other with the story staged and featuring you and some of the other actors in class. If you don't have one you like, this is a great time to ask everyone you know to tell you theirs, until you find one you'd like to tell.

7. Character Identification Monolog

You've probably noticed that this list moves gradually from simple information sharing, to opinions and thought questions, to recreated events or small performances. This last item is the closest to traditional theatre—a written speech, which you memorize and present. Something one to two minutes in length is best. It does not have to be from a play. It could be from an interview, magazine article, essay, someone's advice column, your favorite novel, or even some restroom wall, as long as the character speaking is not you but rather someone with whom you identify. Your reason for identifying with the material could be that the humor clearly matches your own, the political or moral position is one you feel strongly about, the pain of the speaker deeply moves you, or this is the kind of situation you could see yourself getting caught in. Try to share, in a sentence, why you identify with this speech.

"But I don't read plays and have nothing in mind. I don't even know where to start." Not so. On this Earth, and probably on your bookshelf at home, there must be some speech that speaks to you and for you. You cannot possibly be that unformed. Give yourself credit. This is a chance to share something you love.

Too Much, Too Soon?

How will you ever share all this? You probably won't. Your teacher might elect to go through the whole sequence, but will more likely pick and choose and skip some items, as the sense of the group becomes evident. Whether it gets done in class or out, this gives you good stuff to talk about with your classmates as you get to know each other outside of class. These questions, incidentally, are fairly standard at an audition or actor interview, so many actors spend their lives refining and changing their answers as they change.

I suggest the following ground rules:

1. As others share, stop them and ask them for clarification of anything said. Question each other if curious. But try to stay with curiosity that is likely to be universal. If you wonder if someone had the same homeroom teacher you did, find out outside of class.

2. Everybody learn the line, "Just the high points." Chant it to the occasional motor mouth, who goes through everything he's ever done, a book of reasons for taking the class, or needs to pick ten favorite actors, with an ode to each. This can be done good-naturedly. Anyone can forget and rattle on.

3. If someone is genuinely drawing a blank, others might offer their impressions. If others in the group disagree with the actor's own perception of herself (this happens often with "type"), everyone should feel free to speak up. All here are in the process of defining the self and can use help.

4. This is nonjudgmental sharing. There are no right answers. There are no preferred responses. The whole idea is just to get to know others, so the work that follows will be grounded on awareness.

5. You shouldn't ask to have your answers, offstage performance, and monologs critiqued by a teacher or others. Critical response is not the point here. The whole experience should be completely free of evaluation. You want to share who you are, without others telling you, in any way, if that meets with their approval. Not every theatrical act needs reviews. The sharing is enough.

Exercise 2.4

Shared Viewing

As a group, decide on one or more audience experiences that everyone will experience this term. If a play is being performed by your theatre, everyone should try to read the script, attend the performance, agree on what acting elements will be observed, and use this show as the basis of discussions for the rest of the term. If everyone agrees to watch several episodes of the same TV series, another, different kind of basis for discussion and improvisation is possible. Acting concepts are much easier to understand if you've all experienced the same performances. Also, the act itself eases informal, offstage discussions among members of the group.

Names

Try to get everyone's name down the first week. Have pencil and paper nearby as these exercises progress. If you are terrible at names, draw cartoons of people or pick animals or old acquaintances they remind you of, words that rhyme with their names, particularly memorable things they have said about themselves—whatever it takes. Just as it is important to get past a stiff formality early in acting class, it's vital to know who your peers are. When people start to speak, say their names to yourself beforehand, then check to see if you are right. If there are lulls in class, look around the room and try to identify everyone in it. Remember, you are investing in these people, and the first step is knowing who they are.

Exercise 2.5

Name Trunk

1. Imagine an enormous trunk in the middle of the room, which will be packed with something belonging to each person in class. The first person pantomimes putting in an imaginary possession that starts with the first letter of his name (Terry's trapeze, Gloria's guitar, Sandy's skateboard).

2. Pick something that might actually express you, or at least your own sense of humor, not just because it's alliterative.

3. Each person repeats both the packing motion and the naming of items of everyone who went before. Once the trunk is packed, the names should also be firmly in place.

Exercise Adaptations

The following activities work well for establishing contact and rapport with others around you:

Exercise 2.6

Partner Greetings

1. Wander around the room until a leader signals when to stop. Find a way of making physical contact with the person closest to you, which will become your way of greeting each other.

2. Work your way through the whole group, finding a different way of contacting each. Look at each other for a moment and try to let an impulse hit you without speaking. No words should be exchanged.

3. When the teacher signals it's time to move on, pick something quickly and just go with it.

4. If you shake hands with someone, that's fine, but that's it, for that greeting. Soon you'll need to explore far less conventional ways of touching.

5. Stop halfway through the group, to write down your greetings in case you forget them.

6. Greet these people this way when you run into them on campus or in the hall.

7. At a later session, add a sound. Whenever the two of you are partnered, repeat the greeting.

Exercise 2.7

Group Greetings

1. At some point in the term, every pair should demonstrate their greetings for the class.

2. Some similarities of moves and sounds will be apparent, so that a group greeting may emerge out of all the partner ones. This can be silly and enjoyable to explore for quite some time. It's a good feeling to have a group greeting firmly established, at least by the end of the term, but the exploration is the main idea.

Exercise 2.8

Circle Jumps

1. Let the group pick a word or sound of the day. It might be something fun to say, like "Raspberries," or the Bronx cheer. It might be the name of someone in the group who has a birthday or who has had good news, or the name of some world political figure whom everyone would like to yell at.

2. Gather into a tight circle, arms locked, and begin dipping and breathing as a unit, saying the word lightly.

3. Let the word build in volume and the dips build into leaps so that there is a final group leap, quite high in the air, and the word explodes one last time.

Exercise 2.9

Group Breath and Sound

Sit in a tight circle, cross-legged with knees touching (and, optionally, arms entwined), or stand in the same configuration. Proceed to find a common group breathing pattern, an agreed-upon sound shared by everyone silently, a hum shared by everyone. Let the hum develop naturally into a group chord.

Exercise 2.10

Everybody's Esprit

Remember the concept of *l'Esprit de l'Escalier* or the Spirit of the Stairs in Chapter 1? *(page 24)*

1. Pick out a great lost opportunity from your own past and let the class help you act it out the way it should have been.
2. Cast your antagonist and any other characters needed from your classmates.
3. Get your cue, take a deep breath, and say the Killer Retort, which the Fates should have allowed before.
4. The class cheers you throughout, and goes berserk in admiration, once you finally get the line out. Everybody should get a chance at this little taste of psychodrama.

Physical Warm-Ups

Actors vary widely in their rituals of preparation, but the following sequence of activities is probably that most commonly used:

Meditation

Tensing/Releasing

Alignment

Shaking

Stretching

Breathing

Aerobics

The warm-up that follows employs one to two exercises from each category, plus an optional return to a meditation wrap-up.

The sequence is important even if you vary the activity because each phase prepares you for the next. Skipping steps in any designed exercise sequence could mean strain or even pain because you may not be loose enough, yet, for whatever you've jumped to. Read through, stopping to try something if you feel like it. You will need clothing that lets you roll around on the floor and either very soft-soled shoes or none at all.

Narrowing Your Circle

When it comes time to do the exercises in class, find a space for yourself and narrow your focus, so that you don't make eye contact with anyone. Listen to the instructions as side-coaching (you hear the words but don't look at the speaker), so you are alone, even though surrounded by others. Imagine that you have a circle surrounding your immediate territory, with no need to move outside it. Work in a state of public solitude, comfortably alone, even in the midst of a large group. This is a state the actor often needs to enter in performance.

Modify any exercise if it appears to give you strain today. Feel free to drop out of the activity if you don't feel well. No need to explain your decision. Instead, just fade subtly out until you feel you can rejoin. All these exercises are standard and tested, however, so experiencing consistent problems with any of them means you should see a physician.

Breathe fully throughout each exercise, alternating a complete inhalation in one position with a generous exhalation as you move to the next. Don't concentrate so hard on getting the moves right that you forget to breathe. Let breath move you along, and help you loosen up.

Meditation

Even a few minutes spent silent, still, eyes closed, focus narrow, can be calming. Meditation is usually done sitting or lying on the floor and involves repetition of a sound silently to yourself. Breathing tends to get more and more shallow as concentration turns inward. Example:

Exercise 2.11

Here and Now, Part I

1. Let go of responsibilities carried from the past and expected in the future. Past and future are like heavy, cumbersome layers of clothing you let drop aside so you can breathe. Give yourself permission to be in no time or place but right this moment, in this room, surrounded by these other actors. Feel the earlier part of the day, and the later part that's still ahead, drift away, so you feel completely here, in this moment.

2. Help yourself focus here and now by picking out small physical sensations: feelings of jewelry against your skin, places where clothes feel loose and draped, a radiator humming, your own shallow breathing, the places your body makes contact with the floor. Nothing is too tiny or trivial to notice if it is immediate.

3. Choose a word or sound that pleases you: a suggestive verb like *soothe, ease, release, complete, renew,* or something purely sensual and abstract like *velvet, music, embrace,* or *dawn,* the name of a favorite object, place, or a nonsense syllable that makes you feel good. Repeat the word silently to yourself, continuously, without any effort, letting the qualities of the word wash over you and allowing your mind to wander where it will.

The time devoted will vary depending on the need of the group. If everyone seems high strung today, this may be extended. If there is a sense of calm unity already in the room, even two minutes may be enough.

Tensing/Releasing

The principle of adding some tension to an area of the body just before letting that area unwind or fall free is widely accepted as a means of producing greater release. A moderately tensed muscle relaxes more when let go than it would from a neutral state, and the immediate contrast produces, for most people, a pleasurable, easy feeling. Example:

Exercise 2.12

The Prune

Lie on your back with arms and legs uncrossed and loose. As each area of the body is called, tense it up, keeping everything lower on your body loose and relaxed. The tension will accumulate, moving from head to toes, before you finally let everything go and float from the release. Each tensing is more effective if you imagine you are making that area of the body taut, as though protecting yourself from some shock.

1. First, tense all your facial muscles inward toward the center of the face, as if it were rapidly withering and drying up into a prune.

2. Tighten the surrounding skull as if it were suddenly locked in a vice.

3. Shoot the tension into the neck as if it were in a brace and frozen in place.

4. Shoot it across the shoulders, locking at the shoulder joints. (Remember everything below the shoulders is still loose.)

5. Tighten the upper arms, both sets of biceps and triceps.

6. Tense at the elbows, locking the elbow joints;

7. into the lower arms,

Figure 2-1   The Prune

8. locking the wrists as if they were tightly bound,

9. tightening the palms of the hands as if catching a ball,

10. drawing the fingers halfway into a fist that will not complete itself but remains suspended and part-closed.

11. Tighten upper chest and back,

12. stomach and lower back as if protecting against a blow.

13. Tense hip joints, which are then locked.

14. Tense the groin area and the buttocks,

15. stiffen upper legs,

16. lock the knee joints,

17. draw lower legs taut,

18. lock ankles,

19. stiffen feet, extending toes.

20. Point toes finally at the wall opposite you.

21. Final position: Pull upward toward the ceiling at the center of your body, so that your torso is lifted up off the ground and your body is supported only by the back of the head, the shoulder blades, and your heels, as if the whole body was drying up like a prune. Hold, then

22. release, letting it all go, feeling almost as if you're sinking into the floor or floating in the air, but in no way confined anymore by gravity. Relax and savor the sensation of easy, released floating.

23. Repeat more quickly, remembering to keep everything loose until it is called: Tighten face, head, neck, shoulders, upper arms, elbows, lower arms, wrists, hands, fingers halfway into fist, upper chest and back, stomach and lower back, hip joints, groin and buttocks, upper legs, knee joints, lowers legs, ankles, feet, toes pointed, body pulled up toward ceiling and release. And savor.

Alignment

The spinal column has become universally recognized as a primary center for the body—a center of energy and, unfortunately, tension. The vertebrae tend to literally close off in a way that shortens the spine and blocks your physical and emotional responsiveness. Fortunately, the column can be returned to a relatively open state by lying on the floor and allowing the space between each vertebra to return as the back stretches toward an aligned state and the rest of the body follows. Examples:

Exercise 2.13

The Accordion

1. Still on your back and, without pushing to achieve it, simply allow your spine to stretch out along the floor. Imagine your body is like thick syrup that has splashed on the floor, and slowly, easily spreads in every direction.

2. The back should be absolutely flat against the floor. For many, this feeling will be achieved more easily by raising the knees slowly or extending the elbows slightly to the side. Shift around until you find your own flattest, easiest position.

3. Imagine the spine as a hand accordion stretching to its full length but still undulating gently and feeling no pressure.

4. Imagine air whirling gently around each vertebra, as they all ease apart. Imagine that your head is several miles away from your tailbone, as these two ease gently in opposite directions.

5. Roll over on your side into a curled position and slowly move to a standing position by uncoiling, with the head the very last part to reach the top and the column returning to the same aligned, stretched sensation that it had when pressed against the floor.

6. Think of your head now as a balloon floating high above the rest of the body, which hangs comfortably from the balloon. Plant your feet firmly and imagine them many, many miles away from your head-balloon. You should feel as if your posture is terrific, but that it was achieved without effort and is maintained without strain.

7. Sense your accordion-spine moving imperceptibly, comfortably stretching.

Exercise 2.14

The Puppet

1. Drop the entire upper body forward like a puppet, breaking at the waist so that your hands almost brush the floor.

2. Let the knees bend slightly and use the lower body only for balance and support, ignoring it otherwise and letting the entire upper body hang loose and limp.

3. Test your own looseness by swinging arms and head, apelike, back and forth until you are really limp.

4. Imagine a string connected to your tailbone that begins to tug you up as if a puppeteer is pulling you into life. Imagine similar strings connected to each of the thirty-plus vertebrae all the way up into the back of your skull.

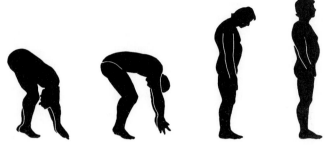

Figure 2-2 The Puppet

5. Allow yourself to rise very slowly, string by string, untensing slightly with each tug. Avoid any temptation to pull upper back, neck, and head up too early. They're the very last strings. You'll reach a completely erect position before your neck even begins to rise.

6. Collapse again and repeat.

Shaking

At any of the joints (wrists, elbows, shoulders, and so on), stiffness or the false sensation of cramp in a nearby muscle may be relieved by spinning the appendage in a circle or just shaking it out. The sudden rush of activity tends to awaken that area of the body, so it joins the rest of you and takes part again.

Exercise 2.15

Rag Doll

1. Imagine yourself as loose as a rag doll or scarecrow and simply shake out, standing in place, wherever you feel a little tight.

2. Spend some time on just the wrists, then elbows, then the whole arm from the shoulder joint, then alternating legs, finally all of these going at random.

Return to shaking at any point in the exercise sequence when you feel like it. Don't isolate it at this point, but return to shaking regularly, as a constant way of loosening and of filling time while you may be waiting for others to complete an exercise.

Stretching

In physical conditioning, stretching is an effective counterbalance to muscle-building activity. The muscles narrow and contract as they build, restricting flexibility, as in "muscle bound." Stretching gives pliability and helps add grace to strength. More than any single activity, stretching prevents injury, keeps muscles supple, and keeps the body flexible. It can be profoundly healing. Oddly enough, while animals seem to know instinctively how to stretch, humans have largely forgotten. The upper back and neck area tends to gather tension and benefits particularly from stretching.

The following exercise may be the one most widely used by actors:

Exercise 2.16

Head Rolls

1. Standing tall, with feet firmly planted, let your head drop forward into your chest, chin landing gently on your clavicle.

2. Begin slowly rolling your head in either direction in a moderate circle that grows in size with each repetition, without ever having your head move more than ever so slightly to the back while allowing it to go more fully to each side and to the front. It is as if your circle, no matter what its size, favors forward movement.

3. Change directions after you work your way to a wide circle.

4. Keep the rest of the body upright and isolate the action to the head and neck so the shoulders and chest are in no way active. Make no effort to keep your mouth closed or eyes shut, but let them drop if you feel the impulse. Make no effort for any sort of regularity of rhythm; if you feel like lingering briefly as the head is over the right shoulder to relish the stretch there, go ahead. Let yourself sense where you need to linger. If you feel like it, increase the speed of the circles, but only if that feels good today.

5. It may help to think of the neck as a ball bearing at the connection between torso and head, a ball bearing firmly placed but capable of a large range of safe motion. (The only potentially unsafe action is in dropping the head backward.)

A stretched body is capable of reaching farther without strain. Physical stretching can make you feel more capable of emotional, creative stretching as well. The following exercise may be difficult for those with lower back problems. With this and all warm-ups, trust your body to tell you when you need to step out. Don't feel the need to prove anything.

Exercise 2.17

The Sun

This is one of many variations of a Yoga-based exercise that stretches the whole body and can be infused with optional spiritual connotations as you worship the sun, salute it, or (if the day is overcast) try to will it into appearing.

1. Hands

2. Salute

3. Ankles

4. Side Stretch

5. V

6. Cobra

7. V

8. Side Stretch

9. Fetus

10. Salute

11. Hands

Figure 2-3 The Sun

There are eleven positions or asanas. Positions 1 and 11 are the same. So are 2 and 10, 5 and 7. This will be more complicated than anything we've done so far, but the stretch is worth it. And don't forget to breathe!

1. Stand tall, hands clasped, palms together, as in prayer or traditional Asian greeting.

2. While inhaling, explode into a giant X figure, arms and legs wide and open, leaning back slightly to face the sun.

3. Pull your legs together, and keeping them straight, bend your upper body over (as in toe touches), with your hands grasping your ankles, getting full stretch along the back of the legs, while exhaling.

4. Spread your hands out on the floor, supporting your body (as at the beginning of a push-up), but with only one leg extended behind, while the other is bent beneath the upper body, stretching the extended side of the body, while inhaling. The overall position is similar to a sprinter about to take off. (In each of these full body stretches, the head is tilted slightly back so that the line from head to foot is a very moderate C-curve).

5. Extend the leg that was bent to join the other and, exhaling, move your body into an upside-down V with your buttocks being the point of the V and high in the air.

6. Lower your upper body as if to do a push-up, but as your face nears the floor, curve your torso back into a cobra position, providing a gentle stretch along with lower back and upper legs, inhaling.

7. Repeat the upside-down V, while exhaling.

8. Inhaling, repeat the stretch in position 4, reversing extended and bent legs so that the stretch is on the other side of the body.

9. Bring your feet together and, supporting your weight, curl your body into the smallest possible position (approximately fetal), head against knees and arms wrapped around lower legs. Squeeze yourself inward in preparation to explode out. Inhale, exhale, and inhale again in this position.

10. Exhaling, repeat the X full-salute of position 2.

11. Repeat the hands-clasped stillness of position 1.

Eventually, when all moves are second nature, aim to perform the Sun as one continuous, flowing action. Pulse slightly in each location, but imagine a floating, unbroken, easy dance, with all moves having the fluid, spineless quality of the cobra for which position 6 is named.

Alternative: If time and space make it difficult to do the Sun, just take a few minutes to stretch anywhere you feel tight, working your way gradually through the body as a simple substitute.

Breathing

The term "breath support" means more than having enough air to speak. The manner and depth of breathing you choose can produce differing energy states. Research shows that changing breathing patterns can change the way you feel. The act "supports" you in varying ways: from the calm stillness of shallow meditation breathing to the highly energized, almost juiced sensation of full diaphragmatic breathing and the stamina of lower back breathing. The actor needs at different moments to call on a whole range of support. The following exercise touches on the deepest breathing, because most of us need to be reminded of the reserves of breath storage. Also, in this warm-up sequence, it's time for something energizing.

Exercise 2.18

Lung Vacuum

This exercise literally cleans out stale air and replaces it forcibly. Some dizziness is natural, particularly for smokers, at the very beginning.

1. Collapse exactly as in the Puppet, simultaneously blowing air out vigorously (and audibly) through the mouth.

2. In the collapsed position, continue to blow out air in short, powerful spurts until you feel completely emptied of air. Imagine that you need to get rid of harmful fumes and replace them with clean air, but that it will only work if you are totally empty. (At this point, all should proceed at their own rate, with no need for group coordination.)

3. Rise slowly, keeping air out, making sure your footing is secure and solid. Keep air out as long as you can manage it. Note: *Do not* try to do this in sync with others in the group. This is not a competition, and lung capacity varies between people who are identically fit.

4. When you feel you must breathe, allow air to sweep in, feeling it pour almost to the end of your fingertips and toes. You should feel much like Woody Allen looked in his balloon suit in *Sleeper.*
   Notice the rush of air to the small of the back. You should feel an intense rush as the new air sucks in with a vacuum force.

5. Repeat sequence at your own rate.

Good actors always work to inhale faster (so they don't waste valuable time) and to exhale more slowly (so they can speak longer and more confidently). This exercise is an intensification of that sensation, with exhalation extended for quite a while, and inhalation happening in an instant.

NOTE: The following two sequences should be considered optional, depending on the needs of the group. If the vocal warm-up is being included, it should be inserted at this point.

Aerobics

The value of a regularly raised, sustained heartbeat has been established for cardio-vascular fitness and health fringe benefits. Some kind of aerobic activity is standard for anyone pursuing fitness, and the payoff is especially strong for actors who need endurance and controlled breathing.

Long-term benefits are not the reason for aerobic exercise in this warm-up, however. A minimum of fifteen minutes three times a week is needed for that. The following activity is designed to get the heart pumping and the blood flowing after the calmer earlier exercises:

Exercise 2.19

The Blender

This sequence is performed as fast as the group can manage it, and, unlike earlier activities, usually done watching someone lead the movement. The leader calls moves with a definite, clear beat. Everyone bounces lightly on the balls of the feet throughout.

1. *Two jumping jacks:* Familiar exercise with leader setting time.

1. Jumping jacks

2. Elbows to knees

Figure 2-4   The Blender

3. Touch feet in back

4. Side jacks

5. Kicks

6. Starbursts

Figure 2-4 The Blender (continued)

2. *Two elbows to knees:* Elbow touches opposite knee, as the other arm swings high in the air, then other elbow touches other knee.

3. *Two touch feet in backs:* Hand-slap shoe in same opposition as step 2 (left hand to right foot, right hand to left foot) as foot is raised in back. Again, unused arm swings high in air.

4. *Two side jacks:* Same as jumping jacks, except body is turned sideways each time with one arm to the front and the other back, one leg bent to one side and the other leg straight and extended to other side.

5. *Two kicks:* One leg up and forward, with both arms extended out to the sides.

6. *Two starbursts:* Similar to positions 2 and 10 in the Sun. Dip with hands just above knees, then leap off the ground into a big, open X in the air.

Alternative Exercise 2.20

The Journey

Imagine that you're on a wild journey through various terrains, being pursued by some monster or demon. Go through the following maneuvers, continuing to dip or jump up and down in a stationary position. Explore as a group how best to represent the activity while remaining in one spot:

1. Swimming
2. Climbing a ladder
3. Skating
4. Climbing a rope
5. Riding a horse
6. Slalom skiing
7. Rowing a canoe
8. Trying to fly

Finally, decide to stand up and assault the demon (as David did Goliath):

9. Wind up your sling and fire your victorious stone at the Demon, jumping for joy as the monster crashes to the ground.

Alternative Exercise 2.21

Anything Aerobic

Find a theme to keep everyone active and engaged for at least a full minute and a half. Act out as many sports as possible with quick changes. Become as many different animals as you can in the time. Run outside and around the building and back into the classroom—anything that gets the pulse up and charged.

Exercise 2.22

Here and Now, Part II

Return to a sitting or lying position, close your eyes, and renew your sense of here and now, with the added stimuli of the preceding exercises. Drop away any lingering past or future distractions, touch on some immediate physical sensations, repeat a word or sound that makes you feel good.

Allow yourself to feel a part of the group around you with whom you've shared the activity. Let yourself be the same as those around you, still you, but even and comfortable with others.

Changing Images

Countless exercises could be substituted for any of the ones described. Don't give in to the temptation, however, to want new exercises every day. If you're bored with a warm-up, it's because you're not yet giving yourself up to it. Acting warmups don't work until you can do them mindlessly, without struggling to remember what's next. The variety and enhancement can come with the *images* you change in your head.

Here are some possibilities:

- *Prune:* You age radically with each tensing. You're a hideous crone (like *The Picture of Dorian Gray*) by the last "pruning." Youth and vigor all return as you release. You are rejuvenated and renewed.

- *Accordion:* As your spine lengthens, so do you. You are Gulliver being tugged at gently by the Lilliputians or Paul Bunyan napping luxuriously over acres of timberland. When you stand, you can see across continents.

- *Head Rolls:* You are Samson or Rapunzel. You have an amazing mane of hair that whirls in slow motion around you like a cloud. Each roll of the head increases your own power, beauty, pride in your mane.

- *Puppet:* You're an ape when you collapse. At each tug along the spine, you move through an evolutionary cycle from primitive to a fully formed human of the future (passing through Oog about one-third of the way up), bright, complete, and ready to conquer new worlds.

- *Sun:* You are a much-revered priestess-dancer or medicine man. Your people have pinned all their hopes for survival on you. Each move is a supplication to nature for spring to arrive and save your people from the cold. You literally will the sun to come out and warm those under your care.

- *Lung Vacuum:* You are saving the world. At great peril to yourself, you have breathed in toxic fumes, which you now blow out of your body and off the planet. You are successful, and when you inhale, you are cleansed and safe.

- *Blender:* It is an Olympics far into the future, and you have been chosen healthiest and most beautiful human in the world. You are dancing for a throng of people who wish to emulate you. Each move has them gasping with wonder. Each move fills you with power, which those who watch share because your energy is contagious.

It helps warm up the mind if the physical maneuvers are accompanied by a rigorous workout of the imagination. You might pick a theme for a given session (the examples given are all about *power* and *heroism*), depending on your interests or needs that day. If you are warming up for a character, you might direct images to the character's background/perspective, so you are entering her world through each exercise.

Vocal Warm-Ups

This sequence should take about five minutes, once mastered, and is more effective if it follows a complete physical warm-up. (*See* the suggested point of insertion in the preceding sequence.) When the body has been relaxed, aligned, and stretched, when breath has been tapped, then the voice can be freed. A vocal warm-up that isn't preceded by a physical one is like a building without a foundation. A standard progression involves the following stages:

Releasing
Breathing
Rooting Sound
Shaping Sound
Precision

Releasing

The muscles of the face and throat need to be allowed to relax so breath and sound aren't constricted. It's as if a free, open passage needs to be created before the voice can pass untroubled. Some moderate tensing will be introduced again so the relaxation is fuller when it follows:

Exercise 2.23

Letting Go

1. *The Lion:* Stretch your face open and out in all directions, bug-eyed, like a Kabuki Lion or like the Munch painting *The Scream*. It's as if you are executing a silent scream. Your

mouth is wide open, tongue extended downward. Imagine a silent scream with full desperation but no sound.

2. *Skin Slide:* Let the scream disappear. Allow all the facial muscles to collapse slowly, including the jaw, which drops open. Imagine the skin almost sliding off the skeletal structure of the face, because it is that relaxed. Your eyelids may drop half-shut. Let them.

3. *Jaw Drop:* Open and close your mouth several times, effortlessly allowing the opening to increase slightly each time. Test to see if you can easily get two fingers into the opening, without strain. From now on, let the jaw drop open or closed, with no effort to control it, unless an exercise calls for it.

4. *Full Body Yawn:* Let your whole self participate, the body doing a big stretch, forming a loose X, with a full audible, lengthy sighing sound released as your arms drop to your sides again.

5. *Shoulder Drops:* Raise your shoulders very high, then let them drop. Repeat twice more, raising the shoulders slightly less each time.

6. *Inclines:* Incline your head to right and left, back and forth, in a gently rocking motion, feeling a light soothing sensation in the throat with each move.

7. *Nods:* Do the same movement to the front and back as if you are agreeing with someone. Allow head to fall back as far as it falls forward. Remember, let the jaw hang loose.

Breathing

Now that the path is clear, breath is needed to help reach for sound and carry it forth. This sequence also works breath storage to the small of the back, more gradually than in the Lung Vacuum. Consciously record air passing through each of the following areas:

Exercise 2.24

Respirating

1. *Nose and throat:* Deeply inhaling.

2. *Upper chest:* Letting air pass through without any expansion in this area.

3. *Floating ribs:* Three sets of lower ribs are unattached at the front, so when they part, air flows fully. Feel them open like a double door of welcome for the air.

4. *Diaphragm:* Normally in an arched and raised position (*see* Figure 2-5), it both lowers and flattens (Figure 2-5) as deep breathing occurs. Feel the area in the lower torso expand to its fullest as the diaphragm descends.

5. *Lower back:* Finally the air reaches deeply into this most efficient, often unused, storage room.

Now sigh out in exhalation, recording the reversal of the process, as the air moves out and past:

6. Lower back

7. Diaphragm

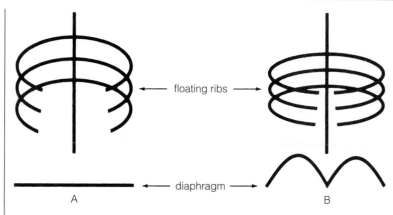

floating ribs

diaphragm

A   B

Figure 2-5 Active Breathing

8. Floating ribs
9. Upper chest
10. Mouth

Repeat the process a few times, then follow with another Full Body Yawn.

Rooting Sound

With air to ride, sound can be strongly summoned from deep in the torso, where your fullest, most resonant music lives. The specific physiological location is less important than what it feels like. Sound that feels rooted, like a firm, proud tree, will fill a space and vary itself with little deliberate effort.

Exercise 2.25

Sounding

1. *Planting:* Plant feet firmly and imagine your voice planted way down in your tailbone, with roots passing down through you, through your legs and into the ground beneath you.

2. *Humming:* Reach down for sound on inhalation and hum on exhalation. Explore the tones and colors available. Let sounds resonate in the facial mask.

3. *Roller Coaster:* Work the hum up and down your register from lower to higher pitches and back, like a roller coaster, rooting deeper each time sound descends. Note the sensation of vibrating sound along the front of your torso as you resonate. Note all the places the sound can vibrate if it needs to.

4. *String:* Imagine a string pulling sound louder as it tugs away, then softer as it returns to your mouth. Hum, then evolve into an *aaahhhh* sound. Let the volume increase and

decrease, without pitch going up, tension in the throat, or stridency in the sound, but by confidently rooting. As it gets louder, feel the string confidently extending to some great distance. As it gets softer, the sound is no more comfortable, but capable of greater subtlety.

Shaping Sound

Parts of the body may be exercised separately, for particular attention. Organs for shaping sound into words can benefit from individual exercises. Just as some parts of your body tend to add fat or lose flexibility more easily than others if not worked, your organs of articulation may need degrees of attention to keep them in shape. The consonants and vowels used in the drill sections are those that give most people difficulty. These exercises can all be performed quite rapidly (not tensely, but quickly, for dexterity) once they are mastered. Most of these consonants (except *F, V, S,* and *TH*) can be struck more cleanly, quickly, and simply than is often done. They need to be tapped, not bludgeoned.

Even though the animal images are evocative, the consonant and vowel drills are helped by making up specific occasions, messages, languages, or attitudes as you speak them (*"Pay, pay, pay,"* cries the Cossack to the Czar; *"Kay, kay, kay,"* orders the Galactic ship captain to his staff), filling the exercises with both imagination and purpose.

Exercise 2.26

Isolations

The Lips

1. *Fish:* Isolate and expand your lips as if moving through water, stretching them like you are a guppy, as if you have fish lips.

2. *Horse:* Make an unvoiced *P* sound that explodes like a horse when it shakes its head. Work for maximum vibration of the lips.

3. *Motor Boat:* A *vvvvv* sound, slowly starting the motor, taking off, changing gears, choking the engine, dying out.

4. *Lip Drill:*

   paypaypay paypaypay paypaypay pah

   baybaybay baybaybay baybaybay bah

   maymaymay maymaymay maymaymay mah

The Hard Palate

5. *The Fly: zzzzzzzz* sound, varying pitch and volume

6. *Snake: sssss* sound threatening prey, varying intensity

7. *Palate Drill:*

   zayzayzay zayzayzay zayzayzay zah

   saysaysay saysaysay saysaysay sah

The Tongue Tip

8. *Cat Lap:* Lap at imaginary milk from all different directions and distances as rapidly as possible.

9. *Tongue Tip Drill:*

   laylaylay laylaylay laylaylay lah

   taytaytay taytaytay taytaytay tah

   daydayday daydayday daydayday dah

   naynaynay naynaynay naynaynay nah

The Back Tongue

10. *Jungle Heart Beat: Repeat* the *ng* sound several times through an extended sigh.

11. *Tongue Back Drill:*

    kaykaykay kaykaykay kaykaykay kah

    gaygaygay gaygaygay gaygaygay gah

    (final sound in each line an extended sigh as in *kaaaah* and *gaaaaah*)

Precision

Articulation drills can increase the crispness and clarity of sound, but should be preceded by full warming and releasing so that they don't add unneeded tension. Because of the challenge, some actors, even warmed up, lose the benefits they have just acquired. They get tight in anticipation. It is important to keep a sense of looseness and enjoyment, which is why this last exercise is designed to play off of a partner.

Exercise 2.27

Lip Reading

1. Pick a partner and lock eyes with him.

2. Repeat together very slowly and precisely the following simple list of articulatory organs:
   The tip of the tongue

The roof of the mouth

The lips and the teeth

3. Gradually speed up your delivery and mutual lip syncing of these lines to the point where delivery is rapid-fire, highly crisp, but with no increase in tension, tightness in the throat, volume, or rise in pitch.

4. When your eyes tell each other you have gone as fast as possible, slow down gradually again, step by step, to a very measured, leisurely pace, and then stop.

5. Mirror each other on one last Total Body Yawn.

NOTE: This exercise doesn't have to be done with a partner. It's just more fun that way.

Alternative Exercise 2.28

Twisters

Substitute or add the following tongue twisters to the corresponding consonant drills above.

P: "Pulchritudinous Paula provided poor, parched Paul a passionate passage through puberty."

B: "Bitter bitch Bette bested Blake by buying back Boston for big bucks."

M: "My mogul mother might make many more major monster movies, Marilyn."

Z: "Zany, zealot Zelda's zenith was Xeroxing zinc zodiac zippers."

S: "Sarcastic Sheila slowly sashayed South, Sunday, speaking several sharp, sick satires."

L: "Loathsome leech Louie lazed listlessly around Loretta's, lapping liquor like a lounge lizard."

T: "Due to too much testosterone, Todd tended to tirelessly tackle two-ton tyrants."

D: "Divinely decadent Dorothy delightedly destroyed downtown Dallas, daily."

N: "No new naked nervous nerd knows near enough novelties, Norm."

K: "Carpingly critical Carrol called Carl's Caliban a crude caricature."

G: "Go grab Grant's grandma's grotesque green garters, Gloria."

Vocal Progression

Because there are so many short exercises in a vocal warm-up, take time now to review all those just covered. If you can't recall any single one, go back until you can float through the sequence quickly:

Letting Go	Respirating	
Lion	*Inhaling:*	*Exhaling:*
Skin Slide	Nose and Throat	Lower Back
Jaw Release Drop	Upper Chest	Diaphragm
Full Body Yawn	Floating Ribs	Floating Ribs
Shoulder Drop	Diaphragm	Upper Chest
Inclines	Lower Back	Nose and Throat
Nods		Full Body Yawn

Hard Palate

Sounding	The Lips	Drill	TongueTip	Back Tongue
Planting	Fish	Fly	Cat Lap	Jungle Heart Beat
Humming	Horse	Snake	Tongue Tip	Tongue Back Drill
Roller Coaster	Motor Boat	Palate Drill	Drill	
String	Lip Drill	Twisting		
	Lip Reading			

When and Where to Warm Up

Should you do this standard sequence in every single performance situation? No. That won't be possible. But all these exercises have been tested repeatedly. There is nothing kinky here. These are classics used in many acting programs, so you'll start with a sound, basic pattern and sense of progression. If you will persevere, warming up can free your own instrument to respond fully.

Members of the class should take turns leading the warm-ups here, possibly working in pairs. You don't really know it until you can speak it and guide others through it. The ability to lead this activity is also a skill that every performer wants. Any director should be able to turn to you and say, "Could you lead us in a warm-up?" without you dissolving into Jell-O. Work briefly from this book, then from note cards with exercise names, then from memory. The time when you will most want to get a group warmed will probably not be when you have your books or notes with you.

> *I know that when I feel strong and my back is the source of strength, I feel the earth beneath my feet, I feel something going right up through me, very strong, clean and washed all the way through. It is of the utmost importance for one's body to be so obedient to the impulses that come, that they obey you.*
>
> –Vanessa Redgrave

Edit, vary, or expand an exercise according to the occasion and your own needs. If you're in a crowded room, a quick Prune *(page 52)* isn't possible, physically or emotionally. If you've only got two minutes, a complete Here and Now *(pages 51–52, 63)* can't be done. But you can tense and release along the spine and both sides of the torso, even sitting in a chair if you work with modifications. And you can think of soothing images, focus on something in this strange room that isn't strange, but comforting. You can repeat a sound that settles you, even for just a few moments. The secret of warm-ups is in adapting them, but not neglecting them.

Offstage Adaptations

Every situation you encounter in the theatre has some parallel outside. Every activity in this chapter has potential offstage use. The Prune is a great muscle relaxer, if you are having trouble sleeping (and if we didn't move immediately on in class, many actors would doze off). Rooting Sound may be just what you need before a difficult conversation with your parents, especially if your objective is to be viewed as an adult. If you still suffer from "baby voice," it's hard for anyone to seriously listen to you as a grown-up, no matter what the other facts of your life may say about you. A Here and Now may help you enjoy the family reunion at hand, and stop dwelling on the fight you had with your girlfriend before vacation, and the paper that will be due (but you know you won't write until) the week after next. It may help you be with your family, so you don't miss the moment. Actors are hardly the only people tempted to get so caught up in their pasts and futures that they seem to overlook their presents altogether.

Exercise 2.29

Offstage Action: Readiness

What new information do you have from this chapter that could influence your progress in each of the OA areas? If needed, review the subcategories on pages 29–37.

1. Negating Newness	3. Keeping Cool
2. Being Pleasant as Possible	4. Sensing Signals
5. Winning Ways	8. Developing Social Savvy
6. Improving Your Image	9. Improving Prediction Potential
7. Building Richer Relationships	10. Jump-Starting Career Capabilities

Specifically: How might finding ways of warming up help you prepare for certain life encounters that tend to unsettle you?

Exercise 2.30

Warm-ups in Real Life

1. Try to remember at least three major encounters within the last year in which it would have helped you perform more effectively if you had been able to warm up beforehand.

2. Identify three or more regular situations, ones that are constant, predictable parts of your life, in which you could warm up to function better.

3. Project into the future for occasions similar to those in step 1. Where could you plan now to give yourself more of a feeling of control by planning a warm-up as part of your preparation?

Exercise 2.31

Nadi Shodhana

This is one of numerous Yoga-based exercises that are especially useful in helping actors overcome stage fright and achieve a calm state of focus in performance. This may serve you in preparing for any potentially fearful or stressful situation. It is sometimes called The Sweet Breath. Nadi means channel or pathway. Shodhana means cleansing. So this exercise cleanses energy pathways.

1. Hold your right hand up and curl index and middle fingers toward your palm. Place your thumb next to your right nostril and your ring finger and pinky by your left. Close the left nostril by pressing gently against it with your ring finger and pinky. Inhale through the right nostril in a slow steady full inhalation.

2. Close the right nostril by pressing gently against it with your thumb, and open your left nostril by relaxing your ring finger and pinky. Exhale in a slow, steady, full exhalation.

3. Inhale through the left nostril, close it and exhale through the right nostril.

4. Repeat 10 rounds (a round being an inhalation and exhalation through each nostril).

Some find Nadi Shodhana effective in combating allergies as well. Almost everyone experiences a sense of calm, focused well-being.

The body, the voice, the mind, and the spirit can all be helped toward being ready to respond with warmth to all the potential goodwill waiting for you when you perform, as an actor or as yourself.

> *All of us are playing roles in real life dramas that we are not only starring in but have been scripting too. We are each the author and leading player in the entertainment called "my life."*
> **–Shirley Maclaine**

3

Individual Inventory

Know enough about yourself to use everything you have

I need to know myself well enough to lend my flesh to a role.
I'm not just going to lend the bones.
—Terrence Howard

Having a rich personal life and taking time to know who you are
makes your acting much better. You can't just work, work, work and not
figure s—t out. You need to find out about yourself.
—Kirsten Dunst

Knowing enough about yourself to use everything you have. You have to
know yourself in order to pull from inside and connect to other people.
—Angelina Jolie

When you look in the mirror, know who is looking back at you.
When you know your strengths and weaknesses, then you can create art.
—Debbie Allen

If you don't lead a real life and use it, you lose truth in your work.
—Mel Gibson

Taking Stock

Actors need to take *inventory*, like stores. They need to know their own merchandise. No matter how similar an actor may be to others in small ways, the sum total is *individual*. No other creature has been put together just like you. So your Hamlet, your Blanche DuBois, your Tinker Bell won't be quite like any other actor's. As comforting as that is, it helps if you have some idea how yours will be different. This chapter is about checking and counting *you*.

You won't like all information you uncover. You may be carrying a self-image that needs to adjust, maybe even collapse. But you'll get to know yourself better and then feel more as if you live inside your own body. If you have an inflexible vision of what you should be, you'll miss a lot. If you've picked some god or goddess as the only image you can accept, you'll be devastated. But if you want to act well, you can only kid yourself for so long anyway. There's no point in doing inventory if you don't want to know what's really on the shelves.

Knowing Your Instrument

> *The actor's instrument is only himself and the more*
> *interesting your instrument is, not only are you going*
> *to be remembered, but the more use you can be put to.*
> —Richard Dreyfus

Your own inventory is a challenge because, unlike the merchant, you can't stand back and look objectively at the merchandise. The concert violinist can reverently place his Stradivarius in the case and look at it. The master mechanic can clean up and then go back out to look over his engine. The writer can flip through the pages and read his product, then put it down and walk away from it. *You* are the product.

I once worked as an assistant to a brilliant, eccentric, somewhat out-of-touch professor, who worked herself into a frenzy trying to get students to experiment with new vocal and physical techniques. She'd shout during a lecture, "You each need to go out and play with yourself!" The whole group would fall apart laughing, and she would mutter, confused, "I mean play with your . . . (interminable pause here) . . . instrument!" And the class would again collapse. This communication breakdown was a perfect example of the actor's dilemma. The very stuff you need to work with is tied to matters private. So the most innocent suggestion can seem suggestive. And the most professional advice can sound personal.

Your body, your voice, your mind are your materials for acting effectively offstage and on. Your inventory will be helped if you allow yourself the same measured objectivity any craftsman would give to examining tools of his craft—even when you're examining your own thighs.

Body Awareness

Public interest in the body and health is at an all-time high. Never have so many studied so much about diet and exercise. This awareness is good for an actor, but he needs to move beyond body as machine to body as interpretive instrument. We'll focus on the constant interpretive choices you make by just standing, sitting, walking, or gesturing, as well as on your own particular mannerisms.

There's nothing inherently wrong with a mannerism. The acting profession is packed with successful and mannered artists. People like Katharine Hepburn and James Stewart are almost too easy to imitate, their quirks are so pronounced. But you want to be aware that you have them and that sometimes they may be distracting to the observer. You don't want to lose a role (a client, a scholarship, an interview, a job, a date) because of a nervous gesture or because of the way you shift your weight. These are tiny things, but they may be getting in the way of an audience's capacity to believe you. And they can be modified.

Check your own body in three overlapping categories: habits, adaptations, and cultural binding.

Habits

When you are in no particular mood, simply passing through the world, what choices are you most likely to make? No matter how these personal tendencies first came about, now they are habitual, happening without thought or effort, automatically. *Habits* can be subdivided into Still (you caught in repose, in a photograph) and Active (you caught in motion, on film).

Consider both the whole package and isolated body parts, any of which may acquire a life of its own. From foot tapping to knuckle cracking to teeth grinding to shoulder shrugging, an isolated movement may be a response to stress or it may just be an unconscious, acquired taste. Some heads may lean in all of a sudden on every key word spoken ("chicken neck," as many actors call it), others tilt to one side when listening, toss hair back suddenly, nod repeatedly, or sink down so far in the torso that the neck almost disappears. And this is just the start of a head list.

Adaptations

When you add stress or stimuli to an otherwise average day, how does your body respond? Alone or in a group, as you're touching someone or being touched, as your mood changes, how do your responses change? Note yourself adjusting to Space Invasions. You have an amount of space that you like to keep between you and others, as if you carry an invisible bubble around you. It may be larger or smaller (or more or less flexible) than someone else's bubble. It is your desired distance for most interactions. If you're on a mountaintop or a crowded elevator, your bubble adjusts in size because you know what to expect. But your bubble bursts and you're unhinged when someone unexpectedly invades what you regard as personal space.

Some people respond with genuine horror to the most accidental "space invasions" of their bubble, forgetting that it's invisible. Others are mindless invaders, forgetting that just because they like bear hugs and pats on the fanny doesn't mean everyone they meet craves that kind of contact.

You can invade another's space by moving very close without touching (as in certain South American cultures, where people like only three or four inches between them for conversation), by enveloping or trapping, by grabbing hold, by gentle touching in an area the recipient considers off limits, or by simply staring so that your eyes invade. Omitting overtly violent or sexual moves (in our culture someone three or four inches away may indeed have one or both of these in mind), there are still a wide range of invasions. It is easy not to share the same covert limits as someone else.

Cultural Binding

Any group whose members share the same behavior is called a *culture*. Behavioral scientists call it *binding* when you're tied so strongly to the group that you have trouble breaking away from group limitations, even when you need to. You can be bound to a culture like a prisoner bound to a stake. Group membership not only helps define who you are, but can be a source of pride, especially in your heritage. You may be bound emotionally, even spiritually, but you may also be unaware of binding by geography, conditioning, age, sex, family, and personal interests. Binding becomes a problem when you want to be believably cast as a member of another group.

Go through the list of questions on the following pages. When the question makes no sense or you draw a blank, get up and move around. Take a look in a full-length mirror. Skip over questions that are still puzzling, but jot down responses when you think you know how you fit into the category. Study yourself. Ask people who've been around you for a while. If you haven't got a clue now, give yourself permission to start noticing. It's time to do some research, and what could be a more interesting research topic than you? You don't even have to go to the library. You *are* the library. Start watching other people in repose and in action to see ways in which others use their bodies like or unlike you.

Expect to be overwhelmed by more questions than you can answer and more categories than you can immediately comprehend, but also expect everything to get easier and clearer, the more accustomed you get to studying you.

Exercise 3.1

Habits

Answer as many as possible of the following questions about you still and you active.

Still

Standing

1. Where is your weight placed in your typical silhouette? Which part of your body really carries the load?

2. Where are you centered? Does energy or drive radiate from one spot?

3. How close to symmetrical are you? Do you lean or cross yourself or favor one side?

4. What is your posture like? Do you slouch? Does it vary?

5. Does any part of your body seem to dominate or draw focus?

Sitting

1. How collapsed or erect are you when sitting or reclining? How much do you sink or release into the chair or floor?

2. Do you lean? In what direction?

3. Is your body crossed in one or more places? How tightly? Do you appear to be covering yourself anywhere? Are you sitting on any part of yourself? Your own leg? A hand?

4. How much space are you taking? Do you thrust out or exhibit any part of yourself? How open and expansive is the spread of your arms and legs?

5. What curves are present? In the spine? The appendages? The tilt of the head? In more than one direction?

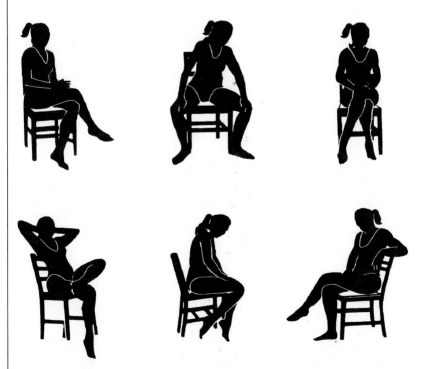

Figure 3-1 Habits (Sitting)

Expression

1. What is the typical look you tend to have on your face? What are the three runners-up? What range of facial change do you habitually go through?

2. Is your eye contact with others usually direct or not? How intense? How long before look-ing away? Do you squint, narrow your eyes, droop your lids, or open your eyes wider?

3. Any changes in other parts of the face? Do your eyebrows move? Do you wiggle your nose? Purse your lips? Suck in your cheeks?

4. Do expressions generally linger or disappear abruptly? How are they timed? Does your smile come suddenly or slowly expand?

5. Are you easy to read or are you somewhat "poker faced?" Are your expressions pro-nounced or subtle and muted? How lively and open is your face?

Active

Tempo/Rhythm

1. Are your movements fast, slow, medium? What is your basic rate?

2. How constant is your tempo? Are you fairly predictable or do you change radically?

3. Do you land with full weight or glide, making only minimal contact with the ground? Are your steps heavy or light?

4. Do you punctuate or stress each move with any part of the body as you walk? Could someone tap your movement patterns like playing a drum?

5. What is the relationship between your speed and your rhythms? To what extent do they affect each other? Are you fast and erratic? Slow and steady? What combination?

Motion

1. When walking, sitting, or leaning, where do you make contact with the surface below? Is the contact flat and solid or gradual and curved?

2. Do you prepare to move (shifting weight, adjusting clothing, swaying slightly) or do you just take off? When you stop, is there a recovery period of similar adjustments? Do you settle (even squirm) into stillness, or just land and stop?

3. What kind of support do you give yourself? Do you reach out with your hands to furniture before you sit, lean on walls or corners as you round them, grab railings on stairways?

4. Is your pattern of movement fluid, smooth, effortless, or is it jerky and labored? How obvious is the changing of gears as you accelerate or change direction?

5. Are the moves straight and assertive? Do you face your target directly and shoot for it or approach it indirectly? Do you ease into furniture sideways, sidle up to people, curve across a room, insinuate yourself into a space?

Gestures

1. Are your arm and hand movements expansive and wide? Or do you work tight to the torso and economically?

2. How frequently do you gesture? Can you sit on your hands without going crazy with the need to use them? Or are your gestures occasional and selective?

3. Do you have moves that are predictable and repetitive? How standard are they? Are they shared by many, or unique to you? Do you have props you always seem to be playing with?

4. Do you literally demonstrate your feelings/experience physically? Could someone who doesn't speak English figure out what you are saying because of the pictures you are drawing? Or are your hands more likely to move in abstract, less literal ways?

5. Do the shoulders get engaged, do you lean in to make points, does the head join in? How connected are your gestures to the torso? How free or independent are they from the rest?

Exercise 3.2

Adaptations

Identify how you react when external elements change, as in:

Public versus Private Behavior   Do you react differently in groups? When the focus of a large number of people turns to you? Do you find yourself shifting posture, relating to furniture in a different way, walking more or less lightly, changing your timing? Are you consistently yourself in intimate groups, or are you one of those people who only really come alive when there is an audience?

Space Invasions (Initiating and Receiving)   What if actual physical contact with others is involved? Are you more likely to be an invader or a receiver? Do you initiate physical contact? What is your own desired distance? How unsettled are you when others close in? Do you adapt well? Are you more likely to touch a particular place on another person?

Mood Shifts (Up and Down)   To what extent does your physical life express your emotional one? Is the receipt of good or bad news likely to show in your body language, while you adjust to what you've heard? Does the kind of day you're having affect your posture, eye contact, the freedom of your gestures? Does intense feeling explode into movement of some kind? Or are you unlikely to change at all? Do you mask shifts in feelings?

Exercise 3.3

Cultural Binding

Try to identify these influences on your physical life.

Geography   Does everyone guess where you were born? Even if they don't hear you speak? Do people know you are from the city or the country without having to ask?

Family   Is your ancestry obvious? Do you share a set of moves with other people whose parents were the same nationality, religion, or any other dominant affiliation?

Conditioning   Do you send information that you have been told for years not to assert yourself in groups, lest you be thought overbearing? Or to push, shove, shout, get seen, grab attention, whatever it takes to get what you deserve? How evident is the rewarded behavior and the punished behavior that was part of your home, school, or church? Ironically, the habit may linger long after you have actually altogether changed your feelings about that area of your anatomy.

Interests Can others tell your special skills and favorite activities? That you are a dancer, athlete, pianist, body builder, scholar? Have you picked up all the trademarks, along with the love of the activity?

Age Do people get your age right or wrong, and can this be because of how you carry yourself?

Sex On a scale of extreme sexual stereotypes, where are you? Do you fall into a traditional masculine/feminine image? An androgynous mix? Neutral or ambiguous? How flexible and changeable are you?

I Am What I Am

You may look at the Body Awareness Checklist that follows, say, "I am what I am!" and reject the idea of changing. But remember that adjusting and changing are not the same thing. The truth is that cultural binding limits your casting. If you're "a nice Jewish girl from the Bronx," you are three wonderful things to be. But imagine yourself cast as Antigone, one of the great tragic heroines. She is "a nice Greek girl from Thebes." The actor cast in the role must achieve a classic, universal quality. Too much Bronx in stance, gestures, eye contact, and there's no way the audience will successfully place her in the ancient world. You cannot get in the way of the audience's imagination. You want to unleash its imagination.

So how can you win? Learn to recognize your own binding, modify it when appropriate, but do not lose it! First, you never want to lose your own heritage. Few things are worse than going home and finding you have forgotten how to be at home there. Second, the minute you virtually wipe out all the Bronx from your body and voice, guess what the next part to come along will require? Guess what kind of accent and physical life? And guess who will have conditioned herself out of consideration? What you want is control and flexibility. Being other people does not need to mean losing who you are.

Body Awareness Checklist

Habits (Still)

Standing	Sitting	Expression
1. Carriage _____	1. Release _____	1. Typical _____
2. Center _____	2. Leaning _____	2. Contact _____
3. Symmetry _____	3. Crossing _____	3. Parts _____
4. Posture _____	4. Space _____	4. Timing _____
5. Focus _____	5. Curves _____	5. Clarity _____

Habits (Active)

Tempo/Rhythm

1. Rate _____

_____

2. Changes _____

_____

3. Weight _____

_____

4. Punctuation _____

_____

5. Relationship _____

_____

Motion

1. Contact _____

_____

2. Preparation/Recovery ___

_____

3. Support _____

_____

4. Pattern _____

_____

5. Assertiveness _____

_____

Gestures

1. Expansiveness _____

_____

2. Frequency _____

_____

3. Predictability _____

_____

4. Demonstration _____

_____

5. Connection _____

_____

Adaptations

Groups

Public Behavior _____

_____

Private Behavior _____

_____

Contact

Receiving Invasion _____

_____

Initiating Invasion _____

_____

Mood

Up _____

_____

Down _____

_____

Cultural Binding

Geography _____

_____

Interests _____

_____

Family _____

_____

Age _____

_____

Conditioning _____

_____

Sex _____

_____

Exercise 3.4

Using the Body List

Make a copy of the Body Awareness Checklist *(pages 80–81)* and jot notes to help you remember information gathered about your physical life. If terms are unclear, go back over that section in this chapter. There are far more categories than you can probably handle. Fill in what you can. See if a clear physical profile emerges. If there are a lot of empty spaces, promise yourself to start observing yourself closer in those areas.

So far you've looked at your offstage life and your potential casting. Take another look at the list, imagining that you've already been cast and are beginning to put together a characterization.

Pick any role you've ever wanted to play. Ask yourself about the character's center, gestural range, personal bubble, adaptations, and the rest. Find concrete ways of building a full performance, considering the range of options open to you, finding ways of building on pure intuition with tangible technical choices.

I usually collect a lot of details or characteristics, and then I find a creature swimming about in the middle of them.

—Laurence Olivier

I always try to figure out, Where in his body does he live? In his head? His heart? His cock? His stomach? His feet? I try to play the bodily ego of the person and then bring it from there. That helps me get started.

—David Duchovny

Imitation for Double Awareness

Actors are observers. They ride the bus or wait in line and watch. They note a walk, a nervous gesture, a set of eyebrows knitting close together. They use people they see as a limitless encyclopedia. They store away, translate, imitate, and interpret what they've observed. And often they learn more about themselves in the process. Actors develop that highest form of flattery, imitation, to an art form.

If an actor can find the personal rhythm of a character, he's home free. And one of the best ways to do that is to follow a person down the street, unbeknownst to him. Pick up his walk, imitate it and continue it, even after he's out of sight. As you're doing it, observe what's happening to you. By zeroing in on a guy's personal rhythm, you'll find that you've become a different person.

—Dustin Hoffman

Physical Life Project

Everyone will be a spy in this next assignment. Do this research without consulting anyone. You'll be observing, on the sly, two other actors in class, for about two weeks, while actual class time is devoted to other activities. You are capturing the physical life of two other people. Your mission is to observe these two performers in as many different contexts as you can: officially "acting," just "being," in groups, alone, one to one, calm, excited, going through their behavioral repertoire.

Step 1: You draw a slip of paper, which will have on it two names (these same two names will have been drawn by another classmate, but for a while you're on your own) that you will show only to the teacher. Your espionage career is launched.

Step 2: Everyone comes to class prepared to complete the following "self-imitation" exercise designed to help the people who are observing you.

Exercise 3.5

Self-Imitation

Only two chairs will be placed at the front of the room, with some space between them. Both chairs face the audience. Everything else you fill in, from your past or imagination. Carry your usual life props.

1. Enter imaginary classroom.
2. Look for a place to sit.
3. Move past imaginary others to sit down.
4. Once seated, change your mind and move to the other chair.
5. Interact with an imagined classmate.
6. Take notes on a lecture or demonstration going on.
7. Attempt to get the teacher's attention but fail.
8. DO SOMETHING INTERESTING.
9. Let something in your circumstances make you angry.
10. Leave imaginary classroom.

You'll wish to run through this sequence a few times before doing it in class, so that it comes easily and believably. Use a situation drawn mostly from your own life. If the class isn't made up primarily of undergraduates, any shared activity (grocery store trip, sale at the mall, some kind of registration hassle) can be substituted.

Remember, you are completely yourself in a typical but intensified situation. Make no effort to entertain or charm the audience. In fact, let yourself be boring. If your concentration is complete, even in this simple set of tasks, you will probably be fascinating. Questions to consider:

1. **Enter the classroom:**

   How large?

   How light or dark?

   Cold or warm?

   How many people in here?

   Where are the authority figures located?

   How closely are the authority figures observing?

   What time of day is it?

   Are you late or on time?

   Where have you been just before this?

   What is your attitude toward this class?

   What do you expect to happen here today?

   What are your plans once the period is over?

2. **Look for place to sit:**

   How crowded is it already?

   Is your favorite place taken?

   Do you hope to sit next to someone in particular?

   How close to starting or started is the lecture?

   Was there a crowd jammed up at the door?

   How easygoing or rude were they?

   How relieved or indifferent are you to just arrive?

3. **Move past others to sit down:**

   How difficult is this task?

   How narrow are the aisles?

   How cooperative are those you need to pass?

Do you have to ask anyone to clear your path?

How self-conscious are you?

How likely is it that you're being observed?

4. **Once seated, change your mind, move someplace else:**

   What is your motive for moving: Something puts you off where you are?

   Something attracts you over there?

   Something beyond your control?

   How much of an endeavor is this going to be?

5. **Interact with another classmate:**

   Do you need this person's help?

   Does he or she need/want yours?

   Is it related to class or personal?

   How much do you enjoy this interaction?

   How well do you know this person?

(Remember, this is silent. Say real words and hear real words, but silently, so that to the audience it looks like the sound has been turned off, but everything else is realistic. Make us have to read your lips if we want to know exactly what's being said.)

6. **Take notes on lecture/demonstration:**

   How do you go about getting out a notebook and something to write with?

   Do you need any other supplies?

   What is your attitude toward the material presented?

   Is it clear, fascinating, obscure, boring?

   How much do you need to understand this stuff?

   How crucial is this class to your survival?

7. **Attempt to get teacher's attention and fail:**

   Why do you make the effort?

   What exactly do you do?

   What's going on, up there, that makes the prof ignore you?

   How aggressively do you pursue this objective before giving up?

   How devastating or inconsequential is being ignored to you?

   How often does this happen to you?

8. Do Something Interesting:

Number 8 is up to you. You can have some fun with it, or you can agonize over it. Try to find something interesting from the scene you have created, so that it moves organically out of the situation. It may be an extreme reaction to being ignored, a mischievous impulse from you, or motivated by someone else in the imaginary room. Infinite possibilities.

Actors are always being given impossible tasks like "Do something interesting," especially at auditions. The best solution is always to go back into the situation, instead of worrying about imposing something clever from the outside. These are chances to explore your own creativity and capacity to discover everything a situation has to offer.

9. Let something make you angry:

The teacher?

The person next to you?

The chair?

Your broken pencil?

Your frustration at what just happened?

An entirely new atrocity?

10. Leave classroom:

(Let's assume bell has not rung, so class is not over. You decide to leave.)

How has your life changed since you came in here?

What do you know now that you didn't before?

What do you care more or less about?

How much of what you hoped for has happened?

How much do you care who notices you leave?

How much do you want to make a disturbance?

What is the next objective you are shooting for?

Interlude: Now, while the class officially turns its attention to other matters, you embark on your spy mission. Start by making comparisons between your two subjects and yourself. Use the checklist to help you organize your observations.

Step 3: After you've been working alone for awhile, your teacher will reveal the name of the other student who is spying on the same twosome you are. Meet your partner and compare notes. Begin working together, checking in with each other daily, alerting each other to new developments in the case

("Did you notice how *X* stands when he's coming on to somebody?" "Look at how *Z*'s expressions change when she talks to the teacher." "I think he's going to be at *Y*'s party tonight. See if you notice anything different when he's just hanging out, having a few beers.") The research should be enjoyable, even addicting.

Interlude: As the time approaches to present your findings in class, you may have reservations about "doing" another actor. Will it seem cruel or condescending? No. When the time comes, everyone enjoys this activity. The observees get so much new information (Remember all the blank spots on your self-observation sheet?) that they're actually grateful. Why not just videotape actors and have them watch themselves? Because they don't see what you see. Early in their training, actors watch videos of themselves, focus on their noses, moan at the size of their hips, and discover resemblances to Aunt Harriet they never noticed before. Their vision is scattered and personal. (Video can be a great tool later on, once some self-awareness sinks in.) The real, valuable lessons for your subjects will come from seeing their physical tendencies through you. It helps objectify the experience and systematize the information. The habits themselves are what come to the foreground.

Remember to identify what you see, without passing judgments. You will not go into class and say, "You have this weird walk and this bizarre gesture you do" but, rather, something like, "You land heavily with the full foot, especially when you're preoccupied. And your right fist sometimes opens and closes when you grasp for ideas or words." No mannerisms are inherently positive or negative. They just are.

It helps if some form of written report is turned in and eventually read by the observees. (*See* Appendix C: Physical Life Observation, an optional, more streamlined version of the checklist, with more room to write.) When words fail you, you may draw (stick figures sitting, a facial expression sketched, a diagram of a series of gestures) to help clarify points you want to make.

At some point in the work with your partner, you will decide which of you is going to be the Primary Presenter of which observee, probably because you have more of a knack for one subject than the other.

You and your partner (*A* and *B*) have drawn names of two other actors (*C* and *D*), but even though you're both working on the other two, each of you will gradually take more of the responsibility for one of them. The Primary Presenter will be the first one up to demonstrate what he has discovered.

Step 4: Results are due and this is what happens:

Exercise 3.6

Imitation Sequence

(Let's say *A* is specializing on *C* and *B* is specializing on *D*.)

1. *A* gets up and walks through a silent imitation while the class calls out their guesses. *A* ignores the guesses until someone gets it right (and shouts, "*C!!!!*"). *A* nods to show that the guess was correct but continues until the planned imitation is completed.

2. *A* then restarts the imitation, this time adding narration ("When you walk into a room you always look around and then down at the floor. You tug your book bag back up onto one shoulder and walk in, putting your weight on the balls of your feet and bouncing slightly, keeping your eyes on the floor . . ."). The execution of the imitation is exactly the same, but this time *A* is telling *C* the details while doing them.

3. *B* now joins *A* up front and adds any pertinent details *A* may have left out ("I also notice that you often swallow just before starting to move into a room and you place both hands around the handle of the book bag when you tug at it . . ."). *B* may also share an area of disagreement or a different observation ("I really think you put your weight more on the outside of both feet, not toward the front.")

4. *A* and *B* now talk their way through the list on the observation sheet, making sure each relevant category is covered, if possible, through both demonstration and description.

5. Once the work on *C* is completed, *A* and *B* reverse roles and cover *D*. *B* first does the imitation once, then with narration, *A* adds details for *D*, then the partners once again work their way through the list. It is the same exact procedure, with *B* leading the way this time.

6. The class may wish to add the occasional two cents, and *C* and *D* may have a few questions based on the information they have gotten.

After a few imitations have been completed for the class and the procedure is clear, it is possible that only steps 1 through 3 may be done in front of the whole class. Breaking into smaller groups to go through the checklist can save a lot of time and still give both observers and observees the benefit of the experience.*

*Note to Teachers: After watching a few complete demonstrations all together, the class can benefit from working in smaller groups, although for this to work, it will take some figuring on your part pairing up partners. Actors rarely shortchange each other on this assignment. They feel a strong responsibility for a complete and systematic observation. Your only real monitoring will be in checking the extremely subjective or naive observations and to suggesting other alternatives.

Exercise 3.7

Alternative Imitations

If time doesn't allow the full spy exercise, any number of reduced versions are possible, in which both the act and the observation are abbreviated. Classmates might be imitated:

1. Walking to the front of the room and writing names on the board.

2. Raising a hand and participating in class discussion in a typical manner.

3. Performing in any other assignment presented in class so far.

4. Sharing brief examples of the biggest differences between their onstage and offstage personas.

5. Doing just a few assigned categories from the checklist, instead of the whole thing.

Smaller imitations can also be used to warm up for the big one. While some of the suspense is lost, it can help actors check in with the class at various stages in their observations. If the class stays together for a year or more, additional imitations can be blended in, adding layers of sophistication.

Exercise 3.8

Celebrity Imitation

This is an interesting variation on imitating classmates. Let the class throw out names of celebrities and, if there are no objections to a name, keep adding them until there are as many celebs as class members. No need to limit the list to actors. Politicians, talk show hosts, athletes, and musicians—any public personalities will work.

1. Draw a name and observe your target in the same categories as listed on pages 80–81.

2. Locate a videotape of the celeb so that you can stop and re-play it as you try to identify specific behaviors.

3. Imagine that your celeb is either presenting or accepting an award.

4. On presentation day, make a full entrance from the wings. As soon as someone guesses who you are, she can shout out the name. If no one guesses, keep ad-libbing until someone does guess. (*Note:* Do not have your athlete play a sport or your singer sing unless the audience has failed to guess and you are desperate for more evidence.)

5. Discuss any details that might be added for each imitation to make it more complete.

6. After the individual presentations, imagine you are at a reception where your celebrities mingle. Explore improvising inside this persona in a social situation.

Imitation Payoffs

What has all this accomplished?

1. You've looked at yourself in quite a few physical categories, to begin to get a sense of the kind of figure you cut in space and how you use the space around you.

2. You've presented yourself in an everyday situation to the class, demonstrating basic acting principles firsthand. You've performed realistically with a heightened reality.

3. You've observed other actors (and others have observed you) going through the Self-Imitation to get precise information and personal insight.

4. You've spied on your subjects in every possible situation to sharpen your sense of detail, for nuance of movement, and your sophistication regarding the body.

5. You've partnered with someone, making all the negotiations and compromises that always need to happen between sets of actors.

6. Two people closely watching you have helped you recognize, for better or worse, many of your own tendencies.

7. You've given a gift to other actors, by mirroring them, so they experience a friendly but revealing reflection.

8. You've experienced the sensation of performing with both involvement and objectivity, of becoming someone else, but then removing yourself and describing the event. You've maintained that balance, essential for an actor, between being onstage and in the audience at the same time.

9. An exchange of mutual benefit has happened between a group of actors starting to trust and support one another.

10. You now have many resources to put together a physical characterization for a character in a script. You do not have to play only parts that are already perfect for you. You can begin to characterize.

11. You've been able not only to watch, but to organize what you see, so that a system of physical characterization is available to you.

> *It was challenging playing a gracious and contained woman [in* Crouching Tiger, Hidden Dragon*], because the character was so far from who I am and what I know. So I just started working with one detail after another.*
> —Michelle Yeoh

Applying Body Awareness

What do you do with this information now? It depends on how close or distant your "mirror" was to what you'd expected. How pleased or distressed you are by what has just been reflected to you. A beginning acting class aims to enlighten, not necessarily change. Ask yourself if any of your mannerisms interfere with the effectiveness of your communication. Don't do anything without reflecting. What you communicate may be just fine, and you now have self-awareness to add to self-acceptance. Or you may choose, gradually, to proceed with some changes. If you want to change, you can apply some of the skills you developed in imitating others.

Vocal Awareness

Body work comes before voice work because it's easier. You know your body better. You can see it and feel it. You can look at most of it, even while you read this page. The rest you can see in the mirror. The family album is full of you in various sizes and shapes. Imagine the family voice album. The body is out there to be counted. You have known yours for years; you may not like it, but you know it. The voice can't be seen or touched. It's hiding. Your own voice may, in fact, still be a stranger to you.

The result? A whole society of people who have no idea how they sound. The world is full of women who spend many daily hours working to look breathtaking, but they sound like Bambi. Of men who pump enough iron to look like warrior chiefs, but talk like Thumper. They don't seem to notice. It's almost as if they think like a silent film.

Yet, countless crucial moments depend on the voice. Onstage, the action of the play stops, an actor sits on the edge of the stage, and beautifully speaks a soliloquy that may be the heart of the whole evening. Offstage, speaking on the phone, reading aloud to a group, talking with a lover in the dark of the night, encouraging hope in a friend whose eyes are closed in anguish, over and over again, the full expressiveness of the voice is essential to acting your own life.

Body work also tends to precede voice, because the body houses the voice. If the body is free and aware, the chances are better for the voice to follow. The good news is that much body awareness is transferable. The bad news is that you probably have a lot of catching up to do. You may be starting with twenty years of voice habits and no voice thought. But you can work on your voice in the grocery store, the car, the shower, wherever you have the inclination. First, some basic terms.

You see women who are absolutely stunning, in $10,000 worth of clothes and jewelry. And there they are at Spago [an exclusive Los Angeles restaurant] and they say, "Well, I'd like a prosciutta pizza" [said in a Minnie Mouse voice] and you think, Oh shit, what did they waste their money on this for [pointing at some imaginary Balenciaga gown]? It's ugly. I mind it very much.

—Kathleen Turner

Quality

Your voice has a tone and texture unlike any other. *Quality* is the feeling of sound you produce. It's determined largely by a combination of surfaces inside you (facial bones, nose, sinus cavities, mouth, pharynx, chest) where sound resonates. Voices are traditionally described as harsh, mellow, thin, full, light, dark, husky, nasal, strident, resonant, large, small, breathy, hoarse, or in more metaphoric terms like silken or velvet.

Tempo/Rhythm

You have a rate of speaking and a stress pattern within that rate. The relationship between speed and emphasis has been explored in the body section of this chapter. The tempo/rhythm of the voice uses the same principle, frequently with surprisingly little connection to the timing of physical movement.

Articulation

How crisp or precisely do you form sounds? Articulation is determined by how your consonants are completed, where the articulation organs are put (placement), how long the contact is sustained (extent), how much force is behind it (pressure), and whether or not your vocal folds are engaged (vibration). When someone says he can't hear you, most of the time he actually can't understand you, because of poor articulation.

Pronunciation

How close to standard is the way you speak? To the speech heard most often in performance, which does not seem to come from a particular, recognizable region or group? Some confuse this category with the articulation. Pronunciation has nothing to do with how precisely you say something, but with how close you say it to the way most other people say it. The standard pronunciation of a word can actually be quite slurred.

Pitch

Your speech could be written out on sheet music identifying the various notes employed from the top to the bottom of your own register. Your tendency to repeat certain pitch patterns is like having your own theme song. Research shows that people respond more positively to the lower pitches, but most speakers actually restrict themselves to the upper half of their range.

Volume

Most of us are aware of tendencies toward loud or soft (Are you someone who is always being asked to speak up? Are you someone who is always being shushed?), but it takes a sophisticated understanding of projection to adjust to varying listeners and spaces.

Word Choice

Do you tend to choose primarily complex, four-syllable words? Explicit four-letter words? Or both, depending on the occasion? Since the same event can be described with infinite variety, the choices you make strongly define you.

Nonverbals

No one utters just words. There are countless noises or spurts of sound, beyond recognizable language. These express emotion beyond words. Nonverbals add color and interest to vocal life. Oddly enough, beginning actors frequently fail to use them in scene work, in part because the playwright usually leaves it up to you to add them. A scene will often seem too clean to be real, but once sprinkled with nonverbals will breathe with a whole new believability. Nonverbals are used heavily offstage, especially when we're surprised and thrown off by the cue we've just received. They help fill our evaluation period while we recover. ("Hmmmm . . . I . . . uhhh . . . (sigh) . . . think we . . . ummmm . . . (tiny laugh) . . . need to talk about this.")

Influences

You can look at your vocal life from the same perspectives we used for your physical life.

Habits: What are the characteristics of your voice in standard, low-key, daily circumstances?

Adaptations: How does it change in public, when your bubble alters or your mood swings?

Cultural Binding: Which of the influences of geography, family, conditioning, interest, age, and sex figure strongest in what other people hear from you?

The Voice Awareness Checklist that follows the next set of exercises will help you remember all these terms and categories.

Exercise 3.9

Basic Parts of a Vocal Life

Unlike the body, the simplest vocabulary regarding voice may be unfamiliar or unsteady to you. You may need to track down some of the following terms in the dictionary. In each of the following categories, jot down one- or two-word responses as they come to mind.

Quality

1. What is the basic tone or texture of your voice?
2. What adjectives or abstract words best describe the feeling of your voice?
3. Where do you primarily resonate?

Tempo

1. What is your standard rate? Fast, slow, medium, or somewhere between?
2. How does your vocal tempo connect with your physical movement?
3. Are you constant or do you use different tempos? When do you change?

Rhythm

1. Do you stress certain words or give all relatively equal value?
2. What kinds of phrasing patterns do you use to separate parts of your statements? Where do you take pauses or breaks?
3. Is the overall impression smooth or jerky and erratic? How fluid is your speech? What does it sound like if you try to capture your own timing by tapping out what you consider typical?

For *Tempo* and *Rhythm* together: What does it sound like if you try to tap out your own timing like beating a drum?

Articulation

1. How precisely do you shape each sound? Is it crisp? Do you mumble? Or have lazy speech?
2. Are there particular words and sounds that always give you trouble? Which challenge you most?
3. Do you drop consonants or syllables? Swallow endings? Which sounds do you tend to omit?

Pronunciation

1. Is your way of saying words standard? If not, how far off? How? Regional? Ethnic? Idiosyncratic?

2. How easy is it for you to slide in and out of various accents, dialects, mimicry? How sharp is your ear?

3. Are you aware of substituting one sound for another? Which ones?

Pitch

1. Is your voice higher or lower than most peoples' for the notes used in everyday speech? Where is your basic placement?

2. Do you have a regular melody pattern, so that graphing your pitch would show repetitions?

3. How close to the top and bottom do you venture? What restrictions do you place on pitch? Lock in one half? Do you explore without strain? What is your range?

Volume

1. Are you basically loud, soft, where on the continuum? Do you project or fill a room effortlessly?

2. Does your voice seem to have power, or are your aware of needing to push in large space?

3. Under what circumstances does your volume knob get adjusted? Are you sensitive to being too loud or soft for others' comfort? How adjustable are you?

Word Choice

1. Is your working vocabulary relatively large? Is your language formal, casual, full of slang, big words, fad words, meaningless phrases?

2. How do you arrange your words in sentences or thought clusters? Verbs first? Non-sentences? Your typical syntax?

3. Are there certain words and phrases that are definitely yours? Specific vocabulary choices (like computer language or theatre terms) used no matter what the circumstances? A fondness for certain kinds of images? Personal favorites? Your own lingo?

Nonverbals

1. How many stalling sounds do you make when you are pondering a question? What kinds?

2. How likely are you to sigh, groan, growl, moan, chuckle, pop your lips, or yawn audibly? To hum, whistle little snatches of tunes, or make percussive sounds? Which sounds dominate your communication?

3. What is your laughter like? Squeals of delight? Guffaws? Escalating bubbles that gurgle up like a pot boiling over? Sudden, brief explosions? Little titters?

Voice Awareness Checklist

Habits

Quality	Tempo	Rhythm
1. Tone _____	1. Rate _____	1. Stress _____
_____	_____	_____
2. Description _____	2. Connections _____	2. Pausing _____
_____	_____	_____
3. Resonance _____	3. Change _____	3. Fluidity _____
_____	_____	_____

Articulation	Pronunciation	Pitch
1. Precision _____	1. Standard _____	1. Placement _____
_____	_____	_____
2. Challenges _____	2. Ear _____	2. Melody Pattern _____
_____	_____	_____
3. Omissions _____	3. Substitutions _____	3. Range _____

Volume	Word Choice	Nonverbals
1. Projection _____	1. Vocabulary _____	1. Stalling _____
_____	_____	_____
2. Power _____	2. Syntax _____	2. Dominance _____
_____	_____	_____
3. Sensitivity _____	3. Favorites _____	3. Laugh _____

Adaptations

Groups _____	Contact _____	Mood _____
_____	_____	_____

Cultural binding

Geography _____	Family _____	Conditioning _____
_____	_____	_____
Interests _____	Age _____	Sex _____
_____	_____	_____

Exercise 3.10

Using the Vocal Awareness Checklist

Use this checklist *(page 96)* exactly as you did the Body Awareness Checklist. Analyze yourself, then listen to others, using what you hear and imagine when putting together a character so that you hear the character speak. Sharpen your skills with imitation each time you recognize a new vocal twist. Most of us begin to notice voices much later than we notice bodies. Try these small awareness exercises:

Exercise 3.11

Resonators

The sound of the voice is strongly influenced by the place where someone resonates. Here are dominant locations and the resulting almost stereotypical sounds:

Head: "Heidi's head voice gives me heartburn and a headache."

Mask: "Max's mask makes for major magnification."

Nose: "Norm's nasality and neckties are noticeably nerdish."

Sinuses: "Selma's sound search settles sharply in her sinuses."

Throat: "Thelma's throat thrashes, throttles, and throbs."

Pharynx: "Phil's FM fullness comes from his pharynx."

Chest: "Charles' chest sound challenges, charms, and takes charge."

Exercise 3.12

Classic Voices

Use the same approach to this list of standard voice descriptions. Start close to the stereotype the line suggests, then move away to subtler variations. There will be some inevitable overlap with the resonator list.

Harsh: "Hey, Harry, howscomes Helga hates your hide, huh?"

Mellow: "May tomorrow mean more music and magical memories."

Thin: "Think thankful thoughts throughout your thrashing, Theodore."

Full: "Ferdinand's final fanfare filled and overflowed the farthest foothills."

Light: "Lovely Lily looks luminous in lace and lurid in lamé."

Dark: "Don't dare double-cross Delores or you die."

Husky: "Hey, hot stuff, how's about holding hands?"

Nasal: "Nadine is nowhere near normal."

Strident: "So far season sales simply suck, Sam."

Resonant: "Raoul reveled in Rio with the ravishing Ramona."

Large: "Laurence loves to laugh and longs to live."

Small: "Silly, shy Suzy sat stiffly at Sorority Sing-Along."

Breathy: "Baby wants a big blue Buick, boys."

Hoarse: "Watching Harry's horrible Hamlet hurt. It gave me a hernia."

Exercise 3.13

Around Town

Find examples of extremes on each list on each of the items on the chart, on trips to the bank, the grocery store, a restaurant, or a bar. Become certain about when you are hearing a really low voice or a distinct regional pattern.

Exercise 3.14

Mosts and Leasts

Who in class has the highest and lowest voices? Who is loudest and softest? Work your way through the list. If there are disagreements, discuss differences in the way you hear people. Have an election with winners in the following categories:

Quality: Most mellow, huskiest, most nasal, breathiest, most strident

Tempo: Fastest, slowest, most varied, most consistent

Rhythm: Most predictable, heaviest contrasts, most fluid, least expected pauses

Articulation: Most crisp, most slurred, least consistent

Pronunciation: Most standard, most unusual, best ear, most regional

Pitch: Highest, lowest, most use of range, least use of range, clearest melody pattern

Volume: Loudest, softest, most varied

Word Choice: Most formal, most casual, most idioms

Nonverbals: Most distinct laugh, most stall sounds, most unusual nonverbals, least use of nonverbals

Announce the winners with much applause and fanfare for all recipients.

Exercise 3.15

Do the Teacher

You observe the teacher (and any teaching assistants) long and hard day after day. Try to capture their vocal lives. Work as a class trying to top or outdo each other, referring back to the list so you don't just mimic, but identify what you've done. Try to do other members of the faculty as well.

Exercise 3.16

Famous Voices

Who in the class does a voice of someone extremely well known? This may be an actual person, a cartoon figure, a famous puppet, any voice that tends to be instantly recognizable. Everyone try your best one, and let the natural mimics do several. Then go through the chart and state what happened when the new voice was created. Identify the physiological changes that create the new voice.

Exercise 3.17

Voiceovers

The following are standard voices, used by people who work in commercials and narration. The list represents our own cultural stereotypes. Since radio spots are brief, each voice must be recognizable after only a few words of dialogue. The more of these and other voices you have, the more usable you are to a recording studio or agency. Try each. Consider taping them.

You probably have more voices in you than you think. Try to identify vocabulary, what you do to achieve any of these sounds:

Tough guy (detective, sergeant)	Little kid	Romantic
Starlet	Adolescent	Vivacious
Sick person (cold, sore throat, headache)	Grandparents	*Impersonations:*
Cowboy	Ancient agers	Movie stars
Snob	Animals	Comics
Wimp	Santa Claus	Politicians
Executive	Disney characters	*Dialects:*
Secretary	Fairytale characters	Regional American
Homemaker	Witches	British Isles
Farmer	Dracula	MiddlEastern
AM frantic announcer	Deity	European
FM mellow announcer	Cultured	Slavic
Greaser	Sexy	Asian
Airhead	Country (C&W)	

Vocal Life Project

This time you're not a spy, you are an investigative reporter. (*See* Appendix D: Vocal Life Observation, for an optional form to use to record your observations.) Your subjects know you're after them. You might draw new names or keep the old ones, depending on time factors. In either case, build the vocal work on sound physical observations. If time allows, everyone in class might read the same paragraph aloud and describe the same event, so you have a ready comparison of the group's different vocal lives. Like any good reporter, you'll uncover and even invent ways of studying these voices, but here are some standards:

1. Call them on the phone. Experience the voice in isolation.

2. Interview them on tape and study it, replaying each phrase until it's yours.

3. Tape them when they perform in class, so you can hear the differences between regular conversation and acting.

4. Determine other voices that are similar, among classmates and teachers, and among well-known actors and celebrities.

5. If possible, listen to someone from these actors' families, hometowns, any groups you suspect may have a binding influence.

Here are two possible ways to approach this assignment, one solo and one with a partner.

Exercise 3.18

Solo Vocal Imitation

Come up with five sentences that this person speaks or probably would speak. Try to capture the person in a variety of circumstances and moods.

Presentation: Make an entrance as the person and let your "character" be present physically before you speak. Introduce your "self," say the five sentences, and make an exit.

Exercise 3.19

Partner Vocal Imitation

Use the same basic rehearsal process as in the Physical Life assignment, only this time you're putting together a scene in which *both* your observees appear. Where might these two meet? What would they be likely to talk about? What kinds of conflicts might be present? What strategies and tactics would each employ with the other? Cast yourselves according to your aptitude for imitating one of the subjects. Do whichever one you are better at doing. Be sure to switch roles some time in your rehearsal to experience what your partner does and so you don't get too locked into your own assumptions.

Pick a scene that is physically varied, so you have a chance to base your vocal work firmly in their physical lives. The less you choose to do with your bodies in the scene, the less chance you have for capturing the home where their voices live. Your bodies will reveal vocal choices once you are carrying yourself the way your subject does. It's also more fun to explore the space between these two people. Each person wants a clear objective in the scene. Don't just feature them sitting around, shooting the breeze. Idle chitchat can be part of the scene, but for dynamic acting, each person is there for a reason and with a strategy.

Since everyone knows the subjects this time, the game is not one of who is it, but what is it. There is still a strong sense of recognition, this time of vocal tendencies heard all term, but never really recognized, until they come from another actor. Perform the entire scene first. Then go back over the checklist. Walking through a narrative is not really possible, but do get up, move around, and actively demonstrate every chance you get.

Applying Vocal Awareness

It's important to leave this class understanding the vocal instrument you have and what you do with it. It's far beyond the capacity of this class to bring about sweeping vocal changes. Be patient with yourself. You are already far more vocally sophisticated than you were a few weeks ago. All the material following the body section can be applied here as well. For now, be content to listen more carefully and to master even small changes. And begin to recognize elements of the voice as ingredients for character recipes. ("If I lower my pitch and use a slightly more nasal quality, then slow down and smooth out my delivery, then the character can express . . .")

> *You can do so much if you learn to be with your voice. To me, there's a melody behind every character's speech pattern.*
> —Thandie Newton

Personal Awareness

Your body and voice are primary tangible equipment, what you use to communicate offstage and on. But you're obviously no robot or mere machine. You bring to each performance a whole complex personality, a fascinating history of textured experience and perception, dreams, memories, ideas, and imagination. The finest actors and most fascinating people manage to bring all of these into their work. When you are fully present in a performance, you bring more than the cognitive processes of your mind. You bring what many call your spirit. However, if the voice is less tangible than the body, then the mind and spirit are even more elusive than the voice.

Examine the following incomplete statements. Some you could fill in now. Other statements you'll just want to think about for a while. These are all questions you'll be asking later, about a character in a play, when you prepare a standard character analysis. Some you've already considered. The best answer to each question is usually the first one that comes to mind.

Exercise 3.20

Your Past

Complete these basic statements, making no effort for answers to make sense to anyone but you.

1. I come from . . .
2. My childhood was . . . Family conditions were . . .
3. Major influences on me include . . . Experiences making the most lasting impression on me were . . .
4. Five people whose opinions are most important to me are . . . My outlook on life was primarily determined by . . .
5. The ten most important facts about me are . . .

Areas to consider in answering each of these:

Early years: (Happy? Forgettable? Terrifying? Ideal?)

Hometown: (Influence? Roots? Memories? Sense of connection?)

Parents: (Living? Married? Rich? Poor? Happy? Successful?)

Siblings, caregivers, companions: (Bonds? Influence? Significance?)

Family offerings: (Affection? Rejection? Overprotection? Drive? Discipline?)

Home conditions: (Divorce? Alcoholism? Religion? Illness? Financial comfort?)

External influences: (War? Travel? Political climate? Exposure to other worlds and perspectives?)

Lingering forces: (Image of God? Role models? Idols? Best friend? Worst enemy? Important fantasy/ literary figures? Chief nurturers/authority figures?)

Exercise 3.21

Your Present

At the exact moment you are reading this and jotting down responses, what's going on in your life right now?

1. I am basically . . . Other people tend to describe me as . . .
2. My physical appearance is . . . My usual style of clothing and type of accessories are . . .
3. My temperament could be described as . . . For example . . .
4. My lifestyle involves . . .
5. I am most and least interested in . . . Above all else, I believe . . .

Suggestions for identifying your present:

Self-descriptions: (Healthy? Ill? Bright? Extravagant? Independent? Thoughtful? Cute? Confident? Troubled? Powerful?)

Appearance: (Style choices? Way of wearing/handling clothing? Hair? Amount of artifice? Neatness? Colors? Degree of awareness?)

Choices: (Foods? Music? Pastimes? People? Places to go?)

Exercise 3.22

Your Future

A large amount of anyone's time is spent planning things to come or daydreaming things you hope will come. With the world waiting before you, what do you see ahead?

1. What I want most to achieve in life is . . . If I have a life plan, it would be . . . Other important objectives would include . . . Obstacles I face are . . .
2. My strategy could be described as . . . Specific tactics I am most likely to use in my life are . . .
3. In five years, I see myself . . . In ten years . . . In twenty . . . If I work hard, I believe I can have a future where . . .
4. If I am remembered, it will be for . . .
5. In my darkest fears, I'm terrified that I end up . . . In my wildest fantasies, I . . . If all my dreams come true, I will . . .

Bringing Yourself Onstage

Consider the preceding lists for things you may be ready to share with new friends and with the audience if the role warrants it. Which of your own answers surprised you? Note, but file away, experiences too raw, new, or uncertain to use. Later, this checklist will help you compare yourself with a character you play. It gives you a clearer idea of where you stop and the character begins.

One of the biggest problems any actor faces is acting more onstage the way she does off. We have an unfortunate tendency to edit some of our best stuff. Actors are always being critiqued by those who know them with lines like these:

"I've heard you do very forceful things with your voice. Why are you whining so much in this scene?"

"You personally have a wonderful stillness, but you're too busy in this part."

"Why isn't any of your joy and vivacity in the scene? No one is more fun than you, but this character is stiff right now."

"You're so bright. Please don't deny the character's intelligence."

"Get some of that urgency you've just shown me discussing politics, into the character, discussing her marriage."

Undeniably, some of your own qualities will work for a given role and some could use alterations to suit the character. Edit those parts of yourself that would be imposing you on the role. But find as much of yourself in the role as you can. Offer as much of yourself to any important life encounter as you can. Don't edit at random. The performance is yours, not someone else's.

Whoever I play, whoever I become, I must have a starting off point. I must be sure of who I am, so sure it doesn't worry me, before I become someone else.
—Bob Hoskins

You have to bring who you are offstage, onstage.
—Rita Rudner

I think people perceive of me as funny, down-to-earth, accessible. And basically not different onstage and offstage.
—Lily Tomlin

Acting has a lot to do with living in the real world.
—Russell Crowe

Acting Journal

One of the most effective ways of recording and keeping your Individual Inventory is an acting journal. Sometimes this is a class requirement, sometimes an option. It's always useful in later years to look back on, and it feels good to have a place to store your acting experiences. Some actors are not comfortable keeping journals, but almost all agree that if you can take the experience and put it into words on paper, you are more likely to keep it and own it.

A journal helps you capture what you live and act. Theatre is the most ephemeral of arts. You invest months of your life in a show, then one day it's over and this big piece of you is just a newspaper clipping, a telegram, some opening night good luck notes, maybe a pressed dead flower, all in a drawer. The journal makes memories tangible. It revives them. Actors have a tendency to repeat the same old bad habits. Some always get paranoid the second week of rehearsal, some always get morose once the show opens, some always fall in love with their scene partners and then fall quickly out. If you have a record to read over, you can catch yourself falling into old patterns and stop before you sabotage yourself one more time. The journal helps you trap moments. It gives you a better chance of not repeating the bad moments. It gives you a shot at repeating the good ones.

Trust that honorable acting teachers universally uphold the principal of absolute confidentiality, so that what you write will not go beyond the reader. On the other hand, remember that this is an acting journal, not a diary or something you might submit to your therapist. This is a very fine line. Because of the personal sharing that goes on in acting classes, some students feel compelled to kick it up an inappropriate notch. Some share extraordinarily intimate, deeply private details and raise life issues that intersect only tangentially, if at all, to their progress as actors. Some recount virtually everything going on in their lives with no attempt at analysis or synthesis. This is a difficult distinction since your most profound and private experiences often feed in powerfully into who you are as an actor. Just ask yourself if you are simply pouring out your experiences, or if you are making an honest attempt to apply the pouring to your growth as a performer in the theatre and your life.

Exercise 3.23

Keeping a Journal

Your teacher may design a specific series of journal entries or ask you to simply respond as ideas about acting occur throughout the term. The following is a format that may work for you.

Each class period:

Notes on lecture, discussion, and exercises

These should not be just preparation for a test or quiz. Catch any vital experience you might forget later. If the class does a great exercise that is not in the book and you think you may want to use it again, be sure to get the various steps recorded so that you can. If the teacher says something that has a profound impact, get down the exact words so you can return to them for inspiration.

Notes on critiques

Carefully record what is said to you because sometimes the adrenalin rush after performance clouds your brain. Remember, this is your guideline for rehearsing the next and usually last time the work will be presented. Don't miss a word. Expand beyond your own presentations to things said about other actors that you feel have relevance to you.

This class and you

What happened for you in this class and how would you rate the event and your participation in it?

Once a week:
Progress update

Where are you as an actor this week compared with last? How have you moved forward? Have you taken any steps back? What new skills and knowledge are in your repertoire that were not there before? Any new fears? How are your critical responses changing as you see more? Be sure to re-read your response from last week to see if you have changed since then.

Offstage connections

What happened this week where you were able to apply lessons from class? What happened where you could have but forgot to? What will you do otherwise next time?

Performance Observation

Pay close attention to another actor's performance at least every week. It may be live theatre, film, or tube. It may be at auditions. It may be another actor in class. Select performances that for some reason either work spectacularly or fail to reach their potential. Try to put into words what the actor did or did not do that made that happen.

Every two weeks:
Class is . . . ?

How are you feeling about it? How is class going for you? How are you enlightened? How confused? Any suggestions? Are you getting enough (or the right kind) of attention? What is helping you most? What least? What would you like to share with your teacher that is easier to write about than talk about?

Offstage Observations

What do you notice about people in the world that might help your acting? What are you discovering about yourself in both your behavior and your own imagination? Which of your life experiences would you "play" differently given the chance to repeat? What have you learned from them to prepare you for the future?

Ongoing:

Rehearsal journal

Record your experience on each assignment from initial brainstorming to postmortem. What happened at your rehearsals for class work this term? Note especially any times you experienced a breakthrough.

Audition/Performance journal

How did you feel about each session? Which of your offstage performances might apply directly to your work onstage? When did you audition and what occurred? What did you find out that you can take to the next audition? Were you cast in any shows this term? Use the same guidelines to capture the experience.

Special entries:

These may be assigned or you may submit them for extra credit:

Trust

How willing are you to trust strangers? Friends? Co-workers? Family? What types of actions or behaviors enable you to trust others more? What kinds cause you to mistrust others? Describe a situation in which you caused someone to lose trust in you. What actions could you take to make yourself more trustworthy?

Groups

Where are you most and least effective in groups? What makes it so? What responsibilities do you tend to accept or shirk within groups? How much of a team player are you? Where do you score and where do you come up short? What groups do you tend to view and judge in the most sweeping way? How do people tend to misjudge you on first impression? Do others tend to assume you are a member of certain groups? What about you makes this happen?

Warm-ups

What warm-up elements have you taken into your offstage life? Which kinds of challenges that you regularly encounter would probably go more smoothly if you warmed up physically, vocally, or emotionally? How might you remind yourself to take the time to do so next time? Which of the warm-ups you have learned seem to serve you best and least? Which seem most powerfully adaptable to your offstage life?

Surprises

As you have watched your classmates this term, which ones, for better or worse, have surprised you? How did your initial impression change? Was this because of your own snap judgments or because they sent out false signals? Was it because they actually blossomed or bottomed out during the term? Where have you most surprised yourself in your willingness or reticence to take risks? How would you like to surprise your classmates and instructor by the end of the term?

Feedback

How skilled are you at gracefully giving and receiving feedback? Do you offer constructive criticism in a way such that other actors feel comfortable hearing it? Are you able to find what is useful in a comment you get, even if the tone or word choice seems harsh? Do you avoid any unpleasant confrontations and so avoid giving critical feedback unless it is demanded? How similar is your tendency when class gathers in a circle to your offstage interaction? Where on a scale from outspoken and critical to meek and noncommittal do you fall? How does this compare to where you would like to be?

Futures

As you review past encounters without actor training, how would these have gone differently if you had been trained as an actor? If you have some theatre experience, how would you now approach auditioning, rehearsing, interacting with castmates and the director, and responding to performance pressure? As a human being, how might your approach to any context in which you have not acted as you would have wished alter? What vows are you making to yourself about how you will "perform" the next time this particular challenge faces you?

Offstage Action Analyzed

Take any of the alliterative categories: Negating Newness, Pleasant as Possible, Keeping Cool, Sensing Signals, Winning Ways, Improving Image, Richer Relationships, Social Savvy, Prediction Potential, and Career Capabilities. Examine how your offstage life has been or might be altered because of shifts in perspective and some new strategies that acting class has provided. Identify some lost opportunities you regret, some brilliant moments where you intuitively made the exactly right acting decision, and some promises to yourself for the future about how to have less of the former and more of the latter.

Within the structured journal format, try to personalize the whole document, so it becomes a tool for your growth and a reflection of you. Some actors need to make it a kind of scrapbook, with photos, drawings, cartoons, signs, and fold-out entries. Do what works. If your journal is turned in for class, but there are entries that you wish not read, indicate that. Trust that your privacy will not be violated. If you want the reader to listen to a particular CD while reading, attach it. Limit the inclusion of recorded sharing as a substitution for writing. Some auditory actors like to record their thoughts, but submitting tape is not a good idea unless you have gone back and edited so that your teacher does not need to wade through hours of rambling. If there is something that you absolutely cannot write but must say, so be it. But be selective.

If you make this a strong reflection of your experience this term, you will love picking it up and pouring over it many times in the years to come. And do consider continuing your journal after this class.

Exercise 3.24

Offstage Action: Inventory

What new information do you have from this chapter that could influence your progress in each of the OA areas? If needed, review the subcategories on pages 29–37.

1. Negating Newness
2. Being Pleasant as Possible
3. Keeping Cool
4. Sensing Signals
5. Winning Ways

6. Improving Your Image
7. Building Richer Relationships
8. Developing Social Savvy
9. Improving Prediction Potential
10. Jump-Starting Career Capabilities

Specifically: What about your physical and vocal changes might be influencing the kind of impression you make that is not what you want? What adjustments might change that?

Choosing for Yourself

By now you have a clearer idea of how others see you, whether that is the person inside you or not. You're foolish to fight your type, and you're foolish to accept it. Work toward a never-ending expansion of your range and power. But work in a way that lets you grow step by step.

The best scenes and monologs for Acting 1 are those that allow you to focus on the truth of the moment, to concentrate fully, to commit with all your energy to what the character wants. If you have to keep remembering to be anorexic and sixty-two, you are unlikely to accomplish the more important objectives mentioned. That's why your first choices in acting class should be close to type, and why you should not let type upset you or in any way stop your desire to change and grow.

Getting yourself onstage, just the right amount, so the performance has a sense of sharing and intimacy, without self-indulgence, is an accomplishment. Once you have been completely who you are onstage, who you are can be limitless. The best means of being yourself in front of an audience has been designed by Constantin Stanislavski. Ironically, it involves finding yourself by forgetting yourself.

I'm interested in getting out of my own way and letting the character happen.
—Shirley MacLaine

I most enjoy the loss and discovery of self that can only be achieved through detailed understanding of another life.
—Daniel Day-Lewis

I was always a character actor. I just used to look like Little Red Riding Hood.
—Paul Newman

4

Stanislavski's System

A complete process for characterization

Acting is a way of practicing compassion—because you learn that everybody is in some way lovable.
—Maggie Gyllenhaal

Even when I played a rodent in Charlotte's Web *in 5th grade I asked myself, "What would a rat do? How can I be more rat-like? I read up on rats and got into their psychology."*
—Don Cheadle

I think a lot more attention could be paid to Stanislavski as there is still a great deal of very messy acting.
—Vanessa Redgrave

To all Method actors: speak clearly, don't bump into people, and if you must have motivation, think of your paycheck on Friday.
—Noel Coward

"I really don't believe in all that Stanislavski stuff."

One hears this statement often. The person who says it does not know the Stanislavski stuff. The speaker has picked up some distorted version, indirectly, from someone who didn't know what he was talking about in the first place. The speaker has neither read all of Stanislavski's major works, nor studied his actual precepts. No one has contributed more to our progress as actors, and no one has been more misunderstood for it, than Stanislavski.

Constantin Stanislavski created the only known complete system for putting together a character, and it is used to some degree by every reputable acting program. Programs expand and vary "The System," may even move in a different direction, but always acknowledge the principles Stanislavski gave us. So why all the bad-mouthing?

Myth and Reality

Information about the System came to Americans in scattered doses. Just as you can quote one piece of scripture and distort the Bible, people have been quoting this particular genius out of context for decades.

He suffered from unclear translations of his works, reaching these shores out of his intended sequence, decades apart. His complete vision took quite a while to get here. (In fact, we still do not have many of the 12,000 documents found at his death, and there are major differences between Soviet- and English-language editions of works. Stanislavski's ideas suffered at the hands of American studios, which took bits and pieces of his work, adapted them freely, and sometimes twisted them almost beyond recognition. The biggest twist?

The Method

> *I'm a Methodist, but not in acting.*
> —James Garner

The Method is not Stanislavski. People who call themselves Method actors probably did not study the real deal. The Method is a tiny fraction of Stanislavski, as little as one-twentieth. The System itself has at least twenty major ingredients. The Method has one. (Some Method actors push it up to three or four.) Imagine having a large home and using one room, a whole paintbox and using one color, a playground and never moving beyond one ride. You get the picture.

Stanislavski never regarded this one ingredient (*emotion memory* or *affective memory**) as anything more than one of a number of tools in the actor's toolbox. And he found it a less useful tool every year he worked, even discarding it from his own toolbox toward the end of his career. Ironically, in the same period that he began to find it less and less important, it grew prominent in our country and became the centerpiece of much training. "The Method" (a term he never used and a concept bearing only marginal resemblance to his Method of Physical Actions) is nothing more than shorthand to the System.

Even *Reader's Digest* versions of Stanislavski, however, work well for certain scripts, particularly for film, where sustaining, repeating, and projecting performances are not always necessary, because "one great take" will do it. Even Stanislavski in

---

*Richard Boleslavski distinguished affective memory as a very specific beckoning of an event that happened to you and is now powerful as different from emotion memory, which includes the whole range of such similar experiences, but almost everyone uses these terms interchangeably.

shorthand can have merit. But after a while, people began to realize that the Method could lead to the worst kind of self-indulgence, self-absorption, muddy, mumbled communication, and a general confusion of the actor's feelings for those of the character. Guess who got the blame?

Because it is so incomplete, Method acting also tends to be almost as unreliable as any other quick fix.

> *My approach to acting? Take a shot of vodka and hope for the best.*
> —Nathan Lane

Who Was Stanislavski?

Constantin Stanislavski (1863–1938) was a brilliant actor, director, and teacher who co-founded the Moscow Art Theatre in 1898 and changed the way actors worked forever. He did as much for performance as Darwin, Marx, and Freud (his contemporary) did for biological science, political science, and psychology. Actually, there are similarities in the way these four helped open new ways of understanding human behavior. Stanislavski wrote four famous books *(An Actor Prepares, Building a Character, Creating a Role,* and *My Life in Art),* which eventually make their way into the personal library of almost any serious student of acting. In the first three of these books, he uses a brilliant device: a master teacher, called Tortsov, takes a group of acting students, including the book's eager narrator, Kostya, through several years of classes. Both Tortsov and Kostya are really Stanislavski at different points in his life. (Kostya is, in fact, the common nickname for Konstantin.) So the elderly Stanislavski meets the young actor he once was and the books distill his own learning process. There is no relaxation, concentration, imagination exercise, no warm-up, no improv, no script experiment currently practiced for which the basic principle and at least the germ of the exercise itself does not appear in these works.

Fortunately for us, when Stanislavski started acting, he was not a "natural." He was awkward, ungainly, and ill at ease, so he was motivated to study what all the great performers did to calm and focus themselves, and to report the results in a systematic way. He later found himself working with new plays (by writers like Anton Chekhov and Maxim Gorky) that cried out for truth in acting, instead of the more extravagant and bombastic attacks many actors had been using. He found a system to achieve this calm and truth, now taught all over the world. Organized classes and degrees in acting were unknown when Stanislavski started working, so it might be argued that without his contribution, your class might not even exist today. Many of the spiritual gifts you receive, as you train as an actor, come, indirectly, from him.

Basic Ingredients

You already experienced the basic Stanislavski System, back in Chapter 1, when you identified these crucial ingredients:

1. Relationship
2. Objective
3. Obstacle
4. Strategy
5. Tactics
6. Text
7. Subtext
8. Interior Monolog
9. Evaluations
10. Beats

Go back and review anything that fails to come immediately to mind. This is the actor's fundamental vocabulary. You want it secure and working for you. (For simplicity and clarity, the terms on this list are those most widely used by actors now, whether they were part of Stanislavski's original working vocabulary or not.)

Stanislavski determined that in any life situation (or theatrical encounter), the person (or character) always determines her choices based on her feelings about others around her. She has something she wants, something in the way, and a constantly changing plan to get what she wants. She experiences words spoken, but also other meanings implied, actually a constant series of words going on in her head. She and her partner each consider saying a number of things that they actually end up rejecting along the way. Stanislavski recognized that any encounter between humans could be broken down into sections, when changes (a shift in topic, method of persuasion, someone arriving or leaving, an uncovering of new information) occurred. Therefore, instead of being one long, confusing blur, the encounter could be seen in easily understood parts. (The acting terms have been deliberately avoided in this paragraph. Can you substitute acting words for the ones used?)

The Legacy

> *Stanislavski's System lays the groundwork for inspiration. Doing this work is like erecting lightning rods to attract lightning. The more rods you build, the more likely the bolt will strike. The System is a magnet for the subconscious, our major source of inspiration.*
>
> –Richard Brestoff

What is so magical about all this? Well, like most brilliant discoveries, it seems like common sense once you think about it. If an actor really does each of these things, his attention will be fully engaged, his instrument will respond honestly, and he will be compelling to watch.

Certain actor blocks, like tension, stiffness, and self-consciousness, tend to fall away, because the mind can only hold so much. (Researchers say seven separate categories are the maximum, at any moment, for most people.) If "I don't know what to do with my hands," or "I hope the critique isn't devastating" enter your head, you aren't concentrating in the mode described, so you aren't using the System.

The elements mentioned identify only a single interlude in the whole major event that is a play or a life. They help you enter an isolated encounter, while the total Stanislavski System helps you put yourself in a character's complete world. The list addresses only those facts of which each person is consciously aware. The System involves the subconscious as well. It embraces a larger picture and multiple levels. Stanislavski has summarized his vision into three overall ideas he calls "propositions," paraphrased here:

Proposition 1

The actor needs to achieve a state that is like a normal person in life. To do this, he must be:

1. *Physically free and controlled:* His instrument should be available to him and under his control.

2. *Alert and attentive:* Combined with freedom, this amounts to the state of relaxed readiness.

3. *Listening and observing:* He must be in genuine contact with actors who play opposite him.

4. *Believing:* He must accept and be able to live convincingly inside the reality of the character.

Proposition 2

If the actor puts himself in the place of the character, he will then be able to achieve honest action onstage by combining:

1. *Psychological action:* Strong motives drive the character forward toward his objectives. An involved, feeling actor automatically executes organic physical actions.

2. *Physical action:* Feelings are powerfully sustained and expressed through movement. Physical action supports and beckons psychological states.

The beauty of the Method of Physical Actions is the way the ingredients sustain each other. You see a symbiotic relationship between them. On a very simple level, let's say you achieve a state of anger and forcefully grab the back of a chair. The movement is just right, and you may never have discovered it without immersing yourself in the character's perspective. In performance, even if you are not always fully angry, the power of the move, as the body remembers it and anticipates it, is likely to help you generate anger and consistently communicate it to an audience.

Stanislavski understood very clearly that the body was more directly reliable and available than the emotions, which "run through your fingers like water," and that the body should therefore be used as a pathway to elusive feelings. Of course, your likelihood of discovering both the physical and psychological actions is stronger if you are truly sharing in the character's own perspective.

Proposition 3

The organic action that results from this combination will give rise to sincere, believable feelings by the actor, but only if he has thoroughly researched and analyzed the role. The actor's meticulous preparation ensures he is in the play, rather than some fantasy of his own, and his homework frees him to experience "metamorphosis."

Most Misunderstood

In all fairness, Stanislavski's writing style is dense and florid by today's standards, his sentences are intricate and complex, he does not always name each concept, and sometimes he appears to call the same idea by different names. He also changed his mind continuously as his system evolved, and much information has been passed on by various disciples, who happened to be working with him at one point in his life, went their own ways, and didn't grow as he did. As one of his most celebrated spiritual descendents, Jerzy Grotowski, has said, "Stanislavski's method evolved, but not his disciples. Each disciple is limited to his particular period." Yet there are five widely accepted myths for which there is no sustained support in his work:

1. Truth is what it's all about, so you don't need to bother with technical work.
2. You should be yourself, instead of bothering to develop a characterization.
3. You should use all your own memories and feelings onstage and think about your own past.
4. You should forget the audience altogether.
5. You should wait until you really feel it before you do it or say it.

You can probably see why lazy, narcissistic actors would grab at these half-truths, and why conscientious artists would be appalled. The fallacious five constitute a license to follow your whims, without work. You can also see why even these System distortions might succeed in isolated contexts. In filming, all you need is one good take. There is an old Hollywood story about a ruthless director, who supposedly would walk up to his little child star just before a shot, and say something mind-boggling like, "Someone just killed your little dog," then to the crew, "Okay, roll 'em!!!!" Let's hope it's just a sick, funny story, but what is true is that, regardless of how he got the tears he wanted, he did get them—once. The audience, seeing the film, would never know the child was crying about something unrelated to the movie. And there would be no need to repeat the scene on Thursday, as there is in the theatre. All five myths are false.

1. No Need for Technique?

Stanislavski was so convinced of the need for painful, meticulous technical work that he didn't always write about it. You know how you assume certain truths to be self-evident? He was working in a culture and for a company where discipline and daily, lengthy classes were so standard that he probably never dreamed that some jerk would presume to walk in front of an audience raw and untrained. The actors described in his books are, in addition to their sessions on the System, taking classes in dancing, gymnastics, fencing, other swordplay, tumbling, voice place-ment, diction, movement, "plasticity," boxing, and mask work! There are constant references to daily "drill sessions." He maintained consistently that the actor needed to be tuned, to induce the desired automatic responses. Otherwise, it just wouldn't work. The vessel would be too weak to carry the water.

2. Yourself Instead of Characterization?

Where does the actor stop and the character start? Stanislavski's concept of "The Magic If" suggests that the actor imagine herself in the character's place. NOTE: There is a crucial difference. The charge is not to imagine yourself there instead of the character. The character's place is her whole life. It is all her training, all her fears and prejudices, all her habits. You do not ask, "What would I do if I were there?" but "What would I do if I had experienced this person's entire life up to this moment?" If anything, this technique ensures that you will not impose who you are on the character's life. This concept is often not just misunderstood, but entirely reversed.

3. All Your Own Memories?

Perhaps the most controversial technique in the whole System is called "emotional memory," where actors summon up feelings from their own pasts to achieve emotion onstage. It is, however, recommended as a rehearsal rather than a performance de-vice, and then only with experiences that are not so raw that they threaten your sanity and control. Actors should use everything they have, but only when they are masters of the emotions instead of vice versa. Everything onstage is under control. Or as

Stanislavski puts it, "It is only permissible for an actor to weep his heart out at home or in rehearsals." What the actor uses in performance is simply triggering impulses and images discovered in rehearsal, not detailed summonings of his own past.

Dwelling on the past? The System asks the actor to dig deeply into the character's past to determine reasons for his behavior and help clarify motives. But Stanislavski never suggests that any of this is what the actor thinks about onstage. It is part of the process. The System demands enough present and future thinking to occupy the actor. But without the past research, the future thinking might be empty. You've been asked, in this book, to dig back into your own history. But that is to give you self-awareness and a sense of all you have to work with. You don't think about those things at the moment of performance, but they help clarify the thinking you do.

4. Forget the Audience?

Stanislavski helps the actor keep the audience from invading the actor's work. He never suggested the audience be excluded. He suggested that you keep yourself busy and focused enough that the audience couldn't inhibit you. His operative word is *concerned*. ("As soon as the actor stops being concerned with his audience, the latter begins to watch the actor.") The actor performs as if he were alone and in a state of public solitude.

His tool called "circles of concentration" identifies a way of working the audience in and out of your consciousness as necessary. You focus on a specific task right in front of you whenever you feel your concentration or involvement wavering. The smaller and more physical the task, the better (sort of a tiny Here and Now). You spiral out your circle to include your acting partner, when the two of you need to interact. You spiral out further, to include the entire stage at the appropriate moment, and further to take in the audience when there is a specific audience response to deal with, or when you know there is a difficult moment of projection. Basically, these circles keep widening and narrowing according to the needs of the moment. Stanislavski has described them as "elastic," letting the actor's awareness stretch, expand, and contract with minimal effort as is necessary. Clearly, the actor does not wish to be preoccupied or obsessed with the audience. But he wishes to have at his disposal the means of widening and narrowing his perception because "the audience constitutes the spiritual acoustics for us. They give back what they receive from us as living, human emotions."

5. Wait Until You Feel it?

Not on your life. Stanislavski suggests taking action aggressively onstage because it is likely (although not certain) that feeling will follow. His writings are filled with concern for maintaining the right Tempo-Rhythm, and he would probably have wanted to assassinate contemporary actors who indulge themselves by taking huge amounts of time to summon up feelings from some dark hiding place, while everyone else waits. The investment of time, for the System, is in actor homework and careful rehearsal, all geared toward making it unnecessary for the actor to stumble around in front of an audience searching for his lost emotions.

Leaving behind the five fallacies, let's consider the fundamental truths of the System.

Empathy

Acting is a crash course in empathy. You are forced, day after day, to be in somebody else's shoes.
—Susan Sarandon

You can't be a bigot and be a great actor.
—Joseph Gordon-Levitt

If one had to summarize the whole Stanislavski approach in one word, I think the best choice would be *empathy.* You empathize with someone when you so completely comprehend what that person is going through that you share his feelings, thoughts, and motives. Empathy is a far more powerful connection than sympathy or pity. It generates an involuntary physical response, beyond an intellectual/emotional one. You may watch a fight and actually feel a blow being struck with your whole being. Depending on which fighter you identify with, you may feel the blow received or the one given. This is empathy on the simplest level. You may also empathize to the degree that you can comprehend actions that most observers would find inhuman and beyond justification.

Exercise 4.1

Comprehending

What would it take to get you to empathize with the following people?

1. A woman who would steal another's child
2. A terrorist who would try to assassinate the Pope
3. A dictator who would order an entire race of people terminated
4. A mother who would murder her own two children
5. A spy who would betray his country and family for money

When, in your own life, have you found an act or a person beyond comprehension, but then something happened to you that made you empathic with the person you used to despise? On a personal level, developing empathy is a profound, troubling, deeply humanizing experience. It feels wonderful to be able to stop judging others, but disturbing to find your crisp, black-and-white world turning muddy and full of maybes. On an acting level, empathic response is essential. You may be cast as any of the five people in the list in Exercise 4.1. Those parts are all written and waiting.

Stanislavski showed us that actors are nonjudgmental, very compassionate artists. You play any role, saint or demon, with an equal amount of involvement. You play Hitler or Ghandi with empathy. It prevents you from presenting a generalized performance, full of vague attitudes. You play everyone as the everyday hero of his own life. You play everyone as just some guy doing the best he can with what he's got, since that's the way most guys see themselves. Ghandi didn't view himself in a celestial glow. He was just getting on with life, doing what he had to.

If there is any part of the System that might be said to possess magic, it is that point where you immerse yourself so thoroughly in the character that appropriate, involuntary actions occur. This is empathy, and if it is a miracle, it is also, as Stanislavski was the first to point out, simply a law of nature and an everyday experience.

You've got to find out how to love her, because you can't play a character that you don't love.

–Richard Dreyfuss

Even with the most outlandish character, it works to approach it as if what I'm doing here is the real thing. That character in the funny outfit isn't trying to be funny.

He's trying to look good.

–Will Ferrell

Drug dealers, gangsters, wife beaters, yes I have played them all and have tried to do them each with a sense of dignity.

–Laurence Fishburne

Hitler didn't think he was a monster. Stalin didn't think he was a monster. Lestat [in Interview with the Vampire] doesn't think he is a monster.

–Tom Cruise

Humane, loving people experience empathy all the time. As do sensitive, responsive actors.

Once you understand, not just intellectually but deep within, you're not just on your way to a decent performance, you're also freed from your own prejudices. And, in the vivid words of Stanislavski, "Prejudices block up the soul like a cork in the neck of a bottle."

> *The great gift of human beings is that we have empathy. We can all cry for each other and sense a mysterious connection to each other. If there's hope for the future of us all, it lies in that. And it happens that actors can evoke that event between hearts. They can make us feel enhanced. In the audience, I can be drawn out of myself into someone else's life and yet suddenly I myself feel more alive! I'm pulled out of what I do every day into something larger and more lasting, into humanity. That's what an actor can do.*
>
> —Meryl Streep

How do empathic responses get started, when you have a role where you feel you hardly know the character, much less function deep within his being?

Ten System Steps

To add to the ten ingredients you experienced early in this book are ten more that embrace the entire system. If you wish to inhabit someone else, you:

1. Learn all the relevant facts that influence this person's behavior *(given circumstances)*.

2. Use these facts to place yourself inside his life perspective *(Magic If)*.

3. From his point of view, determine what he wants most in life *(super objective)* and his range of lesser but still important goals, both conscious and unconscious *(objective hierarchy)*.

4. Experience his particular way of dealing with a variety of obstacles and setbacks. Find the connection between all the moments when a psychological motive prompts a physical impulse, through rehearsal experimentation, until a pattern emerges *(through-line of actions)*.

5. Write down the results in manuscript form and mark the script into workable units *(score)*.

6. Project onto people and objects, real and imagined, qualities from your imagination and experience that bring them to life *(endowment)*.

7. Use your five senses to awaken memories of both physical sensations and emotions that can be filtered into the character's feelings *(recall)*.

8. Add to your constantly playing interior monolog a film of the mind, then speak, not to the ears of your partner but to her eyes, trying to get her to see what you see *(images)*.

9. Alter your own tendencies (physical and vocal) to suit those of the character, particularly your sense of time and intensity of experience *(tempo-rhythm)* so none of your inappropriate mannerisms are imposed on the role *(external adjustments)*.

10. Allow yourself to use all the previous research to free your entry into the heightened reality that allows you to both discover and control simultaneously *(creative mood)*.

The ten steps come in this order, but one step does not stop while another takes over; each is layered in, as the others continue to be actively engaged. Take a look at each of them as they operate in your own life:

Step 1: Given Circumstances

Those details you considered in the last chapter regarding your own past and present are your own *given circumstances*. They are life factors that influence how you now behave. Relationships, training, conditioning, social life, financial status, age, and period of history all shape behavior. Your life has provided you with these circumstances, for better or worse. The playwright gives some of them to a character to help you inhabit that character's world. You fill in the others. You ask all the basic journalist's questions that begin with *who, what, when, where, why,* and *how.* Then determine which of a multitude of circumstances are most important. Almost always there are a few given circumstances that are breakthroughs in your understanding.

Exercise 4.2

Other's Givens

1. What are the seven most important given circumstances of one of the actors you imitated for class?

2. Of your best friend?

3. Of the person you most admire?

4. Of someone you dislike intensely?

5. Of the historical figure you find most fascinating?

Step 2: The Magic If

Next, you take the given circumstances and ask yourself how you would respond if you were in his shoes. The legendary Native American adage to hotheaded young warriors—"Do not judge another brave, my son, until you have walked in his moccasins"—is probably repeated in some fashion in all cultures by the wise, experienced, and forgiving to those too ready to fight. It is the capsule *Magic If.* You step into the other brave's moccasins and try to walk around for a time. The *if* is the means of entering the character's *givens.*

You particularly employ the *Magic If* in those areas where you have the least in common with your character. If you are an agnostic cast as a Bible-thumping revival tent preacher, you engage that character's early literal visions of God the Father, the prayer meetings that were the source of great thrills and visions, the time he was literally spoken to by Jehovah and told to spread the word, the triumphant cleansing he feels every time he leads another sheep back to the flock.

You leave behind your own experiences of disillusionment and scientific perspective. You do this, as much as is necessary, to stop feeling superior or judgmental, and to play the character from a full heart, in his own vision of reality. You end up feeling that in his place (his total place) you would be bound to act as he did.

I think all good actors use the Magic If.
—Jane Alexander

Exercise 4.3

Planting

1. Pick anyone from the last exercise and "plant" his given circumstances on yourself, replacing your own when they're incompatible.

2. Spend half an hour giving yourself over to the Magic If.

3. Perform any simple physical task (sweeping? setting the table?) entirely from the character's perspective.

4. Observe an event (a TV show? a ball game?) and see it from his eyes.

Exercise 4.4

Class Ifs

1. Imagine three separate classmates, each cast as you. Where would each of these actors need to use the *Magic If* to play you fully?

2. Reverse the process for three other classmates, imagining yourself being cast as them and as playing them well.

3. Pick the one of the three most removed from you. Use the *If* to act out any event that would be more comfortable for the person you're playing than it would be for you.

Step 3: Super Objective

We have already examined the objective involved in a single encounter, but everyone has something she wants out of life (or in the course of the play) more than anything else. For most of us this is the driving force, the cause we would go to the mat or even to war for. By moving through the character's given circumstances and immersing yourself in the *Magic If*, the super objective may become clear. It is usually actor-detective work because playwrights rarely come out and state it. It should always be emotional rather than intellectual and strong enough to involve "our whole physical and spiritual being." It should be stated in the simplest, most active terms. The super objective unifies all the tiny objectives that occupy moment-to-moment living into a major motive for living.

> *The more you can be specific about what it is the character wants, the more you can build inner need. If you're doing it right, it becomes liberating.*
> —Annette Bening

Objective Hierarchy

From the super down to the smallest, our lives are full of objectives pursued. Some objectives you consider for super, but do not choose. These go right near the top of the list as finalists, because they are still very important. Some are not conscious, but are very strong motivating forces. Strong subconscious objectives should be considered as well as conscious ones. A character often has a dominant objective for each act, and always for each scene, in the play.

Exercise 4.5

Hierarchies

1. Try to put into simple phrases what you
   a. Want most out of life
   b. Want very strongly but not quite most
   c. Wanted most during each of the past four weeks
   d. Wanted most during each of the past four hours
   e. Wanted most (if your objectives changed) during the last four minutes.

2. Try to review and uncover several moments in your life when you thought you were pursuing one objective (conscious), but then suddenly realized you were unconsciously pursuing another.

3. Recreate one of these scenes. Have classmates act other participants, based on your description of the rough scenario. Hierarchize the objective you had and let them all work to motivate you.

Exercise 4.6

Class Objectives

Discuss as a group, with someone writing choices on the board, the shared class super objective for the term, other contenders, and the class hierarchy for the term. Do the same for each week so far and for today's class meeting up to this moment. Conjecture about hidden or subconscious objectives that may also be shared by more than one person in the class.

Step 4: Through-Line of Actions

Each isolated action you perform in life has an inward dimension (the need to do) and an outward (what is done) dimension. Whether you get a glass of juice because you need to quench your thirst, or you get a Fulbright because you need to validate yourself as student, large or small actions all combine the psychological impulse with the physical attack. The actor needs to discover both elements for a character.

The physical action discovered through rehearsal experimentation is "the bait for the emotion," aiming to "rouse your subconscious." Emotions cannot be directly summoned (and trying to do so is usually disastrous), but the body can plant conditions and open doors in the hope that "the spirit cannot but respond to the actions of the body." This physical action may be overt, violent, extravagant, or it may involve no discernible movement at all. "Action, motion, is the basis of the art followed by the actor," writes Stanislavski, but "external immobility does not necessarily imply passiveness. You may sit without a motion and at the same time be in full action." In such a case, the tension in the body, the light in the eyes, the commitment to stillness is likely to communicate at least as strongly as a large sweeping movement will.

Over an entire play or life, patterns occur as the character keeps running into various obstacles, which Stanislavski calls "counteractions." People tend to repeat choices. When confronted with obstacles, some people give in all the time and even change their objectives rather than fight. Some employ largely threat tactics, yelling, physically intimidating, presenting themselves as irrational, confrontational, and disrespectful. Others always smile, nod, laugh appreciatively, charm, seduce, or gently lure to get what they want. Some always work indirectly and never say what they really have in mind. Some stick relentlessly to the same strategy, whereas others change easily, making *adaptations* as they go along. Look for patterns of behavior through the role that tie the whole together just as your life patterns begin to define your own through-line of behavior. The through-line ends up like the spinal column, with each action finally connecting to its neighbor in one continuous, fluctuating organ, which is why the *through-line* is often called the *spine* of the role. No action is too small to contribute.

The very smallest actions are often called *bits.** Not to be confused with "doing a bit" or piece of stage business of some kind, the bit is like the smallest piece of information *(byte)* that can be contained in a computer. I return home from a walk, and the first bit might be hoping I have remembered my keys, which I hear jingling, so that objective is achieved. I reach into the right pocket of my jacket, hoping the keys are there, but they aren't, so that bit did not end with an achieved objective. I reach into the left. They're there. The objective is achieved. I hope the house key is easily accessible on the ring. It's not. It's not even close to the top. Not achieved. I get the key after sorting through several, and, because I'm entering a door I don't usually use, I hope I have it inserted at the right angle, and I do! The door opens and life goes on! These silly, tiny little triumphs (sometimes called moment-to-moment victories) are the way we get through life.

Actors often fail to break the role down into enough bits, and the result is a performance that is too general. Stanislavski says that "in general" is the worst enemy of the actor. Most people playing the admittedly less than riveting scene I starred in above would do a very general looking-for-the-keys thing (one muddy bit, tops) without getting it *bit by bit* (there are six separate ones described), the way we actually do in life.

If you are cast as Hamlet, you can be overwhelmed by the size, the grandeur of the role, by all the great "others" who have played it. Or you can break it down from his *super objective* to the smallest victory. In your first scene, all you have to do for a

---

*There is some controversy over Stanislavski's use of *beat* and *bit*, partially because of translation confusion and because they are pronounced the same by Europeans teaching Americans. For our purposes, bits are always smaller, and it takes a number of them to constitute a beat, or a complete transaction.

while is successfully avoid your Uncle Claudius. Then your mother approaches you, and you just have to hide from her how distraught you are. She speaks to you, and all you have to do is think of the briefest possible answer to get the conversation over . . . And before you know it, you're dead and someone else is saying, "Good night, Sweet Prince." You work your way bit by bit, objective by objective, and the role is not frightening, because each unit in it is manageable and then you move on to the next. "Proceed," says Stanislavski, "bit by bit, helping yourself along by small truths."

Exercise 4.7

Tiny Triumphs

Break down the following experiences into the smallest bits possible:

1. The next time you arrive home
2. The next time you arrive for acting class, the period from entering the building to taking a seat
3. The first two minutes after you wake up in the morning
4. The last two minutes before you go to bed
5. Any short excerpt from a rehearsal with a partner in which the text is not involved.

Exercise 4.8

Triumphant Entries

Volunteers enter the room in one of the situations in Exercise 4.7. Class members call out iden-tifications of each attempted small triumph, then "Yes" or "No" if it was successful or not. Cheer the actor each time one is achieved.
Variation: Act is performed silently, with each observer jotting down victories. See if all agree on total tried, lost, and won.

Remember that all objectives from super to bit are positive. Even characters who appear bent on self-destruction are usually acting to still some demons inside them-selves. A pathetic, diseased wino lying in the gutter, reaching out to the bottle on the curb for one last swig of "rot-gut" vino isn't trying to make herself sick; she's trying to achieve peace, to sleep, to settle nagging self-doubts, at least for tonight.

As his work progressed through the years, Stanislavski preferred attempting to define the role in larger units and breaking the performance into bits only when a section was not working. The through-line of actions represents the total effort at achieving objectives, the various sections of the character's struggle.

Step 5: Scoring the Role

Stanislavski recommends that you score your script and accompanying notebook much like a musician sits down and notates a musical score, with important things like "super objective" at the front, probably in big letters. Then each scene has its own means of being highlighted. You take each of the ingredients listed in this chapter and find a way of notating them, perhaps drawing a line where each beat begins and ends for you, so that what emerges is like "a long catalogue of minor and major objectives, units, scenes, acts" designed to "draw the actor as a human being closer to the real life of his character or role." Many actors end up doing a great deal of scoring in their heads, but I recommend that you do it on paper at least a few times, to lock it in place for yourself. It also takes a while to work out your own codes, to determine how best to lay out information for yourself.

The score relates to the acting journal and may be combined with it. While no one else should tell you how to prepare a document this personal, and a great deal of what you write may be virtually incomprehensible to others, there is enormous value in the process of writing (sketching, drawing, coding) it down. Actors who score go back over and over for help and inspiration from the document. And, of course, it is one more way of making a very elusive art form recorded and concrete.

The first thing I do with a script is divide it up into beats and measures—a measure being a sequence of beats—to get at the fundamental rhythm of the part before playing it in rehearsals.

—Jack Nicholson

I secretly structured myself to play Ripley like [Shakespeare's] Henry V and like the women warriors of classic Chinese literature. From her director: "Her copy of the script was marked with 17 different colors of ink. In her margin notes, she got the dramatic significance of almost every line of dialogue and how each one might tie in with a later scene."

—Sigourney Weaver (on her role in *Alien*)

What I remember most is how knowledgeable he is. He does incredible, almost intimidating amounts of research. When he gets there, he's there.

—Morgan Freeman (describing Denzel Washington)

You don't complete the score before rehearsals begin and then keep it perfect like scripture. You revise and alter it throughout the whole rehearsal process and even during the run of the show. It's usually messy looking, with lots of erasing and crossing out. It is a dynamic, ever-changing work, always in progress.

Step 6: Endowment

You had no problem, as a child, making a stick into a magic wand or into Excalibur, with taking an old sheet and endowing it with great beauty, weight, and even ermine trim as it became your cape. Onstage you endow plastic swords and capes trimmed in rabbit fur or cotton batten. Props and set pieces tend to be lightweight, cheaply made, and unreal. You endow a glass of tea, which is supposed to be bourbon, with aroma, a burning sensation as you sip, a rush of lightheadedness as a possible aftermath. You endow some stiff plastic flowers with invigorating scent, softness, freshness, and the cheap plastic vase you are putting them in with the weight, coldness, and smoothness of porcelain or crystal. You endow a partner with great beauty to find him irresistible.

Endowing something or someone requires a clear memory of the original. If it's not in your experience, you do research. Actors need to keep all the senses awake with each new experience, for the possibility of having to recreate the sensation. They also need to go beyond the obvious, into creative conjecture. The bourbon may be a rare vintage given to you for your twenty-first birthday and sipped on the rarest of occasions. The flowers may be a hybrid developed by a gardener who worshiped you and was sent away by your snobbish parents. The vase might be something your mother brought back from a trip to China, quite expensive, but a color you abhor and she knows it. The cape may have been sewn by angels before history.

The script will suggest some endowment, but the vast majority is up to you and is full of creative possibility. The audience will never know the details as you are sipping or arranging flowers, but there will be a sense of depth, texture; you will look as if you really live in that space and the performance can take on the qualities of a tapestry.

Stanislavski divided endowment into *external*, where feelings are used to give imaginary life to tangible existing objects, and *internal*, where your own memory is used to create altogether imaginary objects, such as those that might appear on the fourth wall or in the character's offstage life.

Exercise 4.9

Adding Consequence

1. Try wandering around the house and endowing objects that are of no consequence to you. Stop and note those that have giant sentimental value, and study what happens to you as you contemplate, savor their history, flash on the relationships they symbolize. Go back and endow one to which you have been largely indifferent.

2. Pick some objects that are available in large enough numbers so that everyone in the group can endow them (empty paper cups, coins, notebooks, or other common items). Work on adding physical properties and then layering in emotional ones.

3. Each person brings an object to class. Work with a partner, first taking the other person's object and endowing it from your own imagination. Compare your own addition of consequence to that of the person who brought in the object.

Step 7: Recall

Repeated feelings, according to Stanislavski "are the only means by which you can, to any degree, influence inspiration." He also warns "the moment you lose yourself on the stage marks the departure from truly living your part." The primary tool for untapping controlled, repeatable emotion is memory of the senses. Although sight is probably the most powerful, all five (visual, aural, smell, taste, touch) can release with great strength. You need to stay alert for any untapping of your own life that might intrude on the character's experience rather than help you connect to it.

On a simpler level, each of the actual five senses is used onstage to assist in endowment where the theatrical object lacks the fullness of the real thing or where the real thing (an actual blow fully struck, a genuinely repulsive smell) would be dangerous to the actor or beyond the tolerance of the audience.

Exercise 4.10

Bringing it Back

Let each of the suggestive phrases below hit you in the appropriate sense, with the first memory to come along. Let the image expand to include the given circumstances and allow the feelings to return.

A landscape where you felt small and lost

A song that used to get to you

The voice of a lost loved one, soothing you

Something baking at your grandmother's home

The perfume/cologne of someone with whom you were infatuated

Your father's handshake or hug, your mother's embrace

Your first taste of an "adult" beverage

The taste of your favorite birthday cake

Release Pictures

When calling on emotional memory, often a single lingering image, like a photograph in the mind, summons back all the feelings in a rush and opens that emotional vein. Finding these images (once the experience is repeatable) can be far more effective than trying to recall the entire lengthy experience, which can get muddied by sheer overload of material. You may recall an entire romantic summer affair by the image of one sunset, watched seated quietly behind your lover. The tanned back of your lover and the colors in the sky, reflected on the loved one's skin, can be so vividly etched that the rest unlocks. You may recall your attachment to a favored grandparent by the image of a rocker with an afghan thrown over it. The icons of our times (a flag, a cross, a swastika) serve as *release images* for many, every time they are viewed.

Sometimes, when you look through a photo album, you stumble across a release shot, unexpectedly, after pages and pages of photos that were enjoyable, but did not unlock emotional memory. And suddenly you are flooded with feelings.

Exercise 4.11

Release Album

Identify a release photo for an emotional memory for each of the following. Experiment with variations of long shots, close-ups, slow motion, and other visual alterations to make the image even more evocative for you.

Childhood delight	Triumphant accomplishment
Awakening sexuality	Humiliation
Inspiration	Feeling utterly insignificant
Romantic love	Complete freedom
Heartbreak	Selfless compassion

Exercise 4.12

Total Recall

Select a moment where you know you had a strong, genuine emotional response. Instead of trying to summon the feeling, go through all your senses for the occasion.

What you were wearing, everything down to your underwear

What you were touching and what it felt like

What you were smelling

What tastes were in your mouth

What sights in the space, on the other people, images that jump out

What sound, including background or white noise

Any muscle tension or physical sensation

The way you were breathing

Step 8: Images

If you have a definite picture in your own head as you speak a phrase, and if you try to get your listener to see the same picture, your words are likely to be more vividly expressive and your connection with your partner more intense. It is as if you are plugging your energy into your listener and causing him to catch your vision. Thinking in images instead of just words is exciting and evocative. You have a film of the imagination for which your interior monolog is the soundtrack. Here are some examples of the way Stanislavski uses images:

Excessive gestures	Trash, dirt, spots on a performance
Involuntary, nervous movements	Convulsive cramps causing blotches on a part
Sloppy pronunciation of a word's beginning	A face with a bashed-in nose
Swallowing a word's ending	A man minus a limb
Dropped letters or syllables	A missing eye or tooth
Actor who speaks well	A phonetics gourmet, savoring the aroma of each syllable and sound
A comma	The warning lift of a hand, making others wait for you
An unfilled pause	A blank hole in the fabric of artistic creation
Accenting a word	A pointing finger singling out
Use of an adjective	To color a noun and set off this particular "individual" from others

You see how much more exciting these standard suggestions for stage movement and speech become when a picture is painted? The mental picture increases the chances for intense partner connection.

Exercise 4.13

Imaging

1. Working with a partner, speak the following lines with Stanislavski's images in mind:

   "You need to get rid of all those extra gestures."

   "I don't think you mean to make all those nervous little movements, but they are really distracting."

   "I can't understand the beginning of your first three words."

   "What happened to the last part of what you were saying?"

   "You're just not saying everything, so I can't get what you mean."

   "You really speak well. I love to listen to you."

   "You made it clear to me where the punctuation, especially the comma, was."

   "You took pauses, but I couldn't figure out why or what for."

   "You need to show which words and phrases are important, which need to stand out for attention."

   "Those adjectives are there to help you. Try to alert the dark, shadowy, reticent recesses of my sluggish, tired imagination by the way you use descriptive words."

2. Describe any brief experience you've had in the past few days, once with just the words, then with the movie of the experience (and occasional striking still photographs) in mind, trying to get your partner to see the same movie and notice the same still shots. Discuss the comparative "look" of your film and his.

Step 9: External Adjustments

No matter how much of yourself you find in the character, some altering of your own habits is going to be needed so you can portray this other human being. Some adjustments will have occurred automatically in setting up each of the previous conditions, but others can be layered in from the outside. These *externals* may involve any of the physical or vocal tendencies explored in earlier chapters. Were your body and voice just not right for this character? Now is the time to adjust them. Stanislavski believes, above all else, in experimenting with various *tempo-rhythms*.

The character "in time" is crucial to untapping who he really is. Character detail is liberating. "A characterization," says you-know-who, "is the mask which hides the actor-individual. Protected by it he can lay bare his soul down to the last intimate detail."

Exercise 4.14

Time Games

1. Take the lines in Exercise 4.13 and try to get your listener to change mood just by your changes in tempo-rhythm. Try to get her to:

Fall asleep	Get angry
Giggle	Get inspired
Beg you to stop	Get sad
Leave the room	Feel sexy

2. Perform a simple pantomime of any basic household task, first in a neutral state or in your own habitual tempo-rhythm. Then repeat with the following adjustments:

Rapid, low intensity	Medium external, slow internal
Rapid, high intensity	Erratic, internally and externally
Slow external, rapid internal	Extremely slow external, high intensity

Discuss both the way the change made you feel and the impression left on observers. Take other suggestions for adjustments from the class.

3. Keep the same task but add narrative, first where you are describing what you are doing, then where your conversation is unrelated to your activity. Experiment with vocal tempo-rhythms that match your physical choices as well as those that contradict.

Step 10: The Creative Mood

When an actor is able to pull together all these elements, she has an excellent chance to enter a state in which she's open to inspiration. Stanislavski compares the *creative state* to "the feelings of a prisoner when the chains that had interfered with all his movements for years have at last been removed." In this state of metamorphosis, she is able to think as the actor and as the character, without either interfering with the other. The performer functions simultaneously on two planes, with actor perspective running parallel to role perspective "as a foot path may stretch along beside a highway."

Far from naive or mystical about the state, Stanislavski is quick to point out that you only have a shot at achieving it if

> You have understood the play correctly, analyzed the character accurately, have a good appearance, clear and energetic diction, plastic movement, a sense of rhythm, temperament, taste, and the infectious quality we often call charm.

Nor does he claim that the Mood will come whenever called but, rather, will emerge between stretches of struggle. Much of the time an actor onstage isn't functioning in "a second state of reality," but wavers back and forth between actor and character awareness. The creative state is always worth pursuing. The careful preparation involved will ensure that decisions made will be honest ones. "Plan your role consciously at first, then play it truthfully." Because if the internal and external work are both "based on truth, they will inevitably merge and create a living image."

Open Scenes

One of the best ways of applying the basics of the System is the *open scene*. It is called "open" because the lines of dialogue are essentially nothing, waiting to be filled. Here is a sample.

Exercise 4.15

Open Dialogue

This dialogue is so open that the characters are just called 1 and 2:

    1: Ah.
    2: So?
    1: All set?
    2: No.
    1: Well.
    2: Yes.

Try it in class or simply imagine it with the following contexts:

1. Leaving home for a very long time (parent and child)
2. A drug bust (dealer and narc)
3. Revealing notice of academic probation (parent and child)
4. Picking out a new outfit (two friends)
5. Answering an ad in the classified section (advertiser and customer)

Repeat with the class suggesting more specific given circumstances to alter the scene.

Open scenes provide a comfortable introduction to the System because you are allowed to make up things. You get to be a little bit of a playwright as you master the basic terms. Then, later, when you approach a work scripted in greater detail, you're able to respond more sensitively to the playwright's vision as you investigate the same elements you created for your open scene.

Closing Scenes

You can tell already that no scene is completely open. Even in one this simple, one character is obviously more aggressive, the other more defensive or indecisive, one inquiring, the other responding. This and every scene is to some degree *closed* by information implied. Some open scenes are put together by a random computer search of short lines of dialogue. No matter how objectified the process, an implied relationship always emerges in the resulting text. There is also no such thing as a closed scene, where everything is defined. No matter how simple-minded or explicit the material, there's still a dimension left to the performers. All scenes are only relatively open or closed. Look at any script, asking yourself right away how open the material is. How much information has the playwright provided or closed for you, how much needs to be inferred, then invented by you?

The following open scene script is a favorite because it is so potentially complex in its twists and turns. It is a classic used in many theatre classes, for both directing and acting projects:

1: Oh.
2: Yes.

1: Why are you doing this?
2: It's the best thing.

1: You can't mean it.
2: No, I'm serious.

1: Please.
2: What?

1: What does this mean?
2: Nothing.

1: Listen.
2: No.

1: So different.
2: Not really.

1: Oh.
2: You're good.

1: Forget it.
2: What?

1: Go on.
2: I will.

What can we close at a glance? Character 2 seems determined to do something. Character 1 tries, with various tactics, to discourage 2. By the end, however, 1 is encouraging 2 to do something, which may or may not be what 2 originally set out to do. Are there any other implied closures on this scene? Let's look at two of many possible interpretations of these lines:*

Open Interpretations

Setting: A bedroom

Characters: A young married couple

Script: As provided

These three elements are the only things shared by the two scenes.

Example 1: The couple lost their only child before the baby reached age three. The tragic death occurred about six months ago. Lately the wife has often been found sobbing hysterically over the child's basket of toys. The day has come when the husband is determined to get rid of the toys, because of the way they continue to haunt his wife and himself.

Example 2: This couple does not get along well because their sex life is unsatisfying to both of them. The wife usually takes a book to bed, and tonight it happens to be a *Love Without Fear*-type manual. The husband often wakes the wife, to have a go at it, when he can't sleep. She hates these sessions, and does her best to discourage him.

Set and props: Both scenes require something to represent a bed and, if the cover is plain, both can share the same book. *Also needed for Example 1:* Basket containing variety of toys, including a doll and a music box. *Also needed for Example 2:* Sheets and pillows, water glass, aspirin bottle, cold cream jar, any invented props for first beat.

Example 1: Time to Let Go

Activity	**Intention**
1. She enters bedroom	*To find something to distract her*
2. She finds and opens book	*To grab first available diversion*
3. She sits on bed	*To calm herself*
4. She pages through book	*To occupy her mind*
5. She hears noise, starts, recovers	*To suppress her fears*
6. She crosses to door	*To somehow stop what she expects*
7. He enters with basket	*To make her understand his plan*
8. She says, "Oh"	*To get him to stop*

*The two scenes are adapted and extended from directing projects first presented under the supervision of Wandalie Henshaw, now Artistic Director for the Clarence Brown Theatre Company and Professor at the University of Tennessee, and originally published in an article entitled, "The 'Open Scene' as a Directing Exercise," in *Educational Theatre Journal*. Professor Henshaw wishes to acknowledge Kathleen George, Professor at Pitt University and author of *Rhythm in Drama*, for basic concepts and dialogue.

9.	He says, "Yes"	*To make her understand that it is time to do this*
10.	She touches the toys	*To somehow touch her child as well*
11.	She asks, "Why are you doing this?"	*To cause him to change his mind*
12.	He says, "It's the best thing"	*To get her to admit they need to do it*
13.	She takes the basket	*To stay close to the toys*
14.	She says, "You can't mean it"	*To intimidate him*
15.	She kneels, puts toys on the floor	*To keep them near her*
16.	He moves to put a hand on her shoulder	*To comfort her*
17.	He says, "No, I'm serious"	*To get her to comprehend how determined he is*
18.	She picks up doll from basket	*To cling to it*
19.	She says, "Please"	*To get him to give her some time*
20.	He says, "What?"	*To force her to at least speak of it*
21.	She holds the doll like a baby	*To bring back the feeling of comforting*
22.	She says, "What does this mean?"	*To arouse his grief*
23.	He turns away	*To escape the devastating sight*
24.	He says, "Nothing"	*To regain some control of his emotions*
25.	She picks out music box	*To find a more powerful weapon*
26.	She plays it	*To pull him into her perspective*
27.	She says, "Listen"	*To remind him of better times*
28.	He says, "No"	*To fight the music's effect*
29.	He crosses to other side of room	*To regain firmness and purpose*
30.	She rises and faces him	*To confront him combatively*
31.	She says, "So different"	*To accuse him of insensitivity*
32.	He turns to face her	*To stop the charge*
33.	He says, "Not really"	*To get her to feel his hurt, not just hers*
34.	She says, "Oh"	*To acknowledge his feelings*
35.	She goes to him	*To make peace*
36.	She embraces him	*To apologize and comfort*
37.	They hold each other	*To gain strength*
38.	He looks at her	*To check if she is ready*
39.	He holds on to her, says, "You're good"	*To assure her she has the strength to give the toys up*

40.	She slowly returns to the toys	*To say good-bye*
41.	She stands up, looks away	*To end her attachment*
42.	She says to herself, "Forget it"	*To discipline herself*
43.	She picks up basket	*To test herself*
44.	She hands it to him	*To free herself from any temptation to change her mind*
45.	He says, "What?"	*To get a verbal commitment from her*
46.	She quietly says, "Go on"	*To encourage him to do it quickly before she weakens*
47.	He says, "I will"	*To accept the offer firmly and close the discussion*
48.	He exits with toys	*To accomplish his task*
49.	She listens to music box fading as it gets farther away	*To linger an instant longer in the past*
50.	She sits on the bed	*To support herself*
51.	She lies down and curls up on the bed	*To comfort herself and to help her resolve*

Example 2: Try It, You'll Like It

Activity   **Intention**

1.	They enter from opposite sides	*To go to bed*
2.	They stop to glare at each other	*To keep the other at a distance*
3.	They go through separate preparations (he rubs feet, stretches; she applies cold cream, takes aspirin, for example)	*To avoid physical contact*
4.	They get into bed	*To go to sleep*
5.	They fight over the sheet	*To spite each other*
6.	She falls immediately to sleep	*To forget she married him*
7.	He tosses and turns	*To find some position to get to sleep*
8.	He sits up	*To admit he can't sleep*
9.	He looks at her	*To decide whether to try or not*
10.	He looks away	*To find courage*
11.	He shrugs	*To get up the gumption to go for it*
12.	He nudges her awake	*To warn her*
13.	She groans	*To get him to back off*
14.	He clears his throat	*To signal her*

15.	She says, "Oh"	*To wither his resolve with her sarcasm*
16.	He says, "Yes"	*To double his determination*
17.	He attempts passionate kiss	*To turn her on*
18.	She stops him	*To prevent him from smothering her*
19.	She asks, "Why are you doing this?"	*To distract and discourage him*
20.	He answers, "It's the best thing"	*To get her to go for it*
21.	She says, "You can't mean it"	*To remind him of past times*
22.	He kisses her	*To encourage her participation*
23.	He says, "No, I'm serious"	*To get her to experience the new hot him*
24.	She picks up the book	*To avoid dealing with him*
25.	She reads while he caresses	*To entertain herself*
26.	She pushes him away	*To free herself to concentrate*
27.	She says, "Please"	*To keep him off while she studies passage that interests her*
28.	She slams book shut, stunned	*To grasp fully what she has found*
29.	He says, "What?"	*To find out what is so interesting*
30.	She shows him page in book	*To share her discovery*
31.	She asks, "What does this mean?"	*To get help comprehending*
32.	He takes book, reads	*To mollify her*
33.	He slams book shut	*To suppress shocking information*
34.	He says, "Nothing"	*To cover his amazement*
35.	She says, "Listen"	*To suggest book's suggestion may be worth trying*
36.	He says, "No!"	*To free himself from experimenting*
37.	She reads passage again	*To memorize procedure*
38.	He lies down	*To protect himself*
39.	She looks at him	*To plan her attack*
40.	She grabs him and they disappear	*To act out passage in book beneath the covers*

BLACKOUT (May be accomplished by couple just flailing beneath sheet, out of audience view, for a while)

41.	They emerge from covers	*To come up for air*
42.	They sit up smiling	*To glory in their success*
43.	She says, "So different"	*To get him to feel good about what they did*

44.	He says, "Not really"	*To persuade her he is fully capable of this and more*
45.	She pokes or tickles him	*To make loving contact* .
46.	She says, "Oh"	*To tease him* .
47.	He says, "You're good"	*To get her to acknowledge her own prowess*
48.	She says, "Forget it"	*To give some back*
49.	She taps him on the shoulder	*To get his attention*
50.	He says, "What?"	*To play coy, to encourage her aggression*
51.	She points to bed beneath them	*To show him the way*
52.	She says, "Go on"	*To get him to take initiative*
53.	He says, "I will"	*To accept the challenge*
54.	They disappear again beneath covers	*To pursue their mutual pleasure*

Exercise 4.16

Motivation Units

1. Go back over each scene and mark where you think changes in beats occur. Then discuss to see if your choices matched others'.

2. If time allows, two couples should volunteer to present the scene regarding the dead child, and two others couples the sex problem scene, trying to follow closely the motivational units on the list. Discuss the differences between each couple doing the same scene. Which elements of subtext will vary, simply because of what any single actor will bring to a role?

Exercise 4.17

Open Scene Project

1. Stick with the sample script and format, but devise two entirely new scenarios. Working with a partner, begin brainstorming various situations that contrast as strongly as the examples.* For each scene, turn in a tentative title, conflict, description of the action, and a simple statement about how each character is different at the end. (*See* Appendix E: Open Scene Scenarios for suggested form.)

*Four to Avoid: Since no scene is truly open, four ideas should be mentioned because they lend themselves so obviously to the lines and offer little challenge: (1) Suicide, (2) Substance abuse, (3) Leaving home, and (4) Visiting a new hairdresser who is trying kinky techniques. Try to stretch your imagination beyond these first obvious choices. You are more creative than this.

2. Look for opportunities to explore the power of subtext. While a comic scene and a serious one have immediate contrast, consider all the other ways contrast is possible.

3. This is one of the few times in your life when you get to cast yourself any way you want. It may be your only chance to play Abraham Lincoln, Pooh, a talking horse, Mother Teresa, Mother Nature, a hustler, God. Consider the possibilities.

4. Plan to present both of your scenes in class and to turn in a written breakdown of the scenes into beats and bits just before performance. (*See* Appendix F: Open Scene Score.)

Start by looking at situations and characters instead of moods. At least one of the scenes could be played in an entirely different mood. A couple having an unsatisfying sex life is not inherently amusing, certainly not to those involved. Though in questionable taste, "dead baby" jokes have been around for years, treating that subject satirically. Sometimes an idea that starts funny develops sad. The scene switches emotional gears so that the final product has tragicomic balance, beginning in one mood and moving into another. Start with interesting people in intriguing predicaments, and then let them respond honestly. No character or encounter is too outrageous if the responses are truthful to the people and the event. Stanislavski says that acting is behaving truthfully in imaginary circumstances. This is a chance to let your imagination fly, free as a kite. The string is truth.

As you work on writing up motivational units, concentrate especially on what happens between each actual line of dialogue. Notice there are only twenty lines, but more than fifty bits in each scene. In both scenes, there are more nonspeaking motivational units than there are speaking ones. Novice actors tend to rush open scene work, particularly the first beat, and to neglect the tiny stages (Remember the door example?) that make up real lives. Don't ever be tempted to neglect subtext, particularly when your text is as negligible as this one. Each line in the motivation column should begin with the preposition "to" followed by an active (or actable) verb.

Since you will probably be revising your score right up to the last minute, work with pencil and various rough drafts. If you prepare a document that looks too finished too early, you will be tempted to make yourself stick to it. Wait to finalize what you turn in until after your last rehearsal. Determine the ten basics for each character, plus the ten more advanced ingredients: Given Circumstances, the Magic If, Super Objective and Objective Hierarchy, Through-Line, Score, Endowment, Sense and Emotional Recall, Images, External Adjustments, and an open, responsive attitude toward the Creative State.

As with the imitation assignments, this is a collaboration, but you may find it easier for each partner to take the primary responsibility for one scene, from conception through writing up the score. There should still be maximum input from both actors, but the process itself can be simplified if each partner focuses on the mechanics of one scene.

Rules

1. This is an exercise in subtext, so the text, such as it is, should remain absolutely intact.

2. Actors may switch who is 1 and who is 2 between scenes, but no other switches are possible. No single person ever gives two lines in a row, and no reversals in the middle of the scene are fair.

3. Actors have complete freedom of line delivery, but are not free to change wording. By all means, put in unexpected pauses, change a declarative statement to a question, change the intent of a line right in the middle, add numerous nonverbals—those are all actor tools. But do not turn "You're good" into "You are good" or "Yes" into "Yeah," or make other small changes.

Dealing with a difficult line by changing it is always a last resort. In this exercise, it's cheating.

> *I can't understand actors who learn their lines approximately.*
> *If it's a good script, the writer has sweated over every part*
> *of it and a single word can throw everything. If it's a bad*
> *script, you shouldn't be doing it.*
> —Katharine Hepburn

Open Scene Presentations

If time allows, scenes should be presented twice in class, with actors able to go back and work between showings. When it's your turn to present, give the audience no more than a title or a headline ("Tycoon Weds Martian") by way of introduction. If any more background is necessary, you haven't really done your homework. Every other piece of information needs to be on the stage. You're seeking strong, clear physical actions that reveal strong, committed psychological states. If two characters share a long friendship and you can't get it into the title, explore ways in which that friendship may manifest itself in their behavior.

It's a good idea to use props and costume pieces in an assignment of this kind. Your attention needs to be on the truth of the moment, not on the precision of miming. Keep all these things minimal, however, just what actually is used. Not set decor. In your last few rehearsals before the day you present in class, start rehearsing setting up the stage, introducing your material, getting quickly from one scene to the other, shifting props and costume pieces, and clearing the stage. I have seen actors, otherwise well prepared, simply collapse because they forgot to work on how to get up there, how to switch from scene to scene, how to get off, on the bookends of their presentation. You work on these things not to achieve some slick level of polish, but to put your own mind at rest, to keep yourself from being unnecessarily distracted or scattered, and to avoid wasting the time of your classmates who must sit and wait while you fuss over your scarf. If you can avoid it, why do this to yourself?

Exercise 4.18

Upping Objectives

Often objectives aren't played strongly enough because they haven't been stated strongly enough. You want powerful verbs that imply action, that almost get you moving as you speak them. Here is an alphabetical list of contenders:

A   annihilate, amaze
B   beguile, bully
C   convince, crucify
D   destroy, delight
E   ensnare, excite
F   frighten, frustrate
G   goad, give
H   hurt, hook
I   incite, intimidate
J   jab, join
K   kibosh, knock
L   lead, lash
M   mislead, mash
N   nurture, nail
O   overwhelm, open
P   provoke, pacify
Q   quit, quench
R   rip, rush
S   seduce, smother
T   tease, topple
U   usurp, unveil
V   vilify, vanquish

W   win; whip

Y   yank, yield

Note: X and Z are rarely used for verbs of any kind much less action words. Extra credit points for you if you can find some.

The powerful verb is the first ingredient. A receiver (usually him or her) is the second. A third is a desired response that probably involves "get" or "want."

Example:

1. I want to convince.

2. I want to convince him.

3. I want to convince him to love me.

Start with your first idea of a basic objective for your character in either open scene, scripted scene, or monolog. Then:

1. Spend some time with a dictionary or thesaurus trying to find an action verb that kicks the intensity of what you want up a notch.

2. Identify the receiver.

3. Turn the statement into an actively desired response.

Remember that the System is all preparation. Don't get bogged down with your homework when it comes time to perform, but give yourself permission for freedom, earned through your homework. As the inventor himself said, "You cannot act 'The System'; you can work on it at home, but when you step out on to the stage, cast it aside, there only nature is your guide."

Stanislavski created an acting system that is as flexible and misunderstood as any political system, including our own. It is based on behaving truthfully in imaginary circumstances. His contribution has been effectively summed up by the most renowned actress in the history of the Moscow Art Theatre (who was also the wife of Anton Chekhov):

> *[Stanislavski deserves credit for posterity for] summoning us all to be scrupulous and honest in our approach and understanding of art. His name is our conscience.*
> —Olga Knipper

The System includes a close, careful look at the world of the character, and then gradually enters the character's perspective. It is composed of objective means for taking on the subjective views of the character. It allows the actor to portray any person, however despicable at first glance, without judgment. It is based on the most humanizing trait, empathy. Any actor who chooses not to accept and employ the gifts of the System has a minimum obligation to do so informed, rather than ignorant. Stanislavski's System is likely to provide you with the basics on which you develop your own. His contagious spirit may give you the courage to change.

5

Stanislavski Stretched

The system twisted and expanded

*Create your own method. Don't depend slavishly on mine. Make up
something that will work for you. But keep breaking traditions, I beg you.*
—Constantin Stanislavski

How did I prepare to play a stoner [in True Romance*]?
Method, baby! A lot of research!*
—Brad Pitt

*There's a fine line between the Method actor
and the schizophrenic.*
—Nicolas Cage

Beyond Stanislavski

He got more than he bargained for. Huge gaps of time separated English-language
translations of his three major works. *An Actor Prepares* was published in 1936,
Building a Character in 1949, *Creating a Role* in 1961. So thirteen years went by
before the second major part of the System was revealed in this country, and another
twelve before anything like a complete overview was available. No wonder there
was and still is so much misunderstanding! Stanislavski's admonition to go beyond
his concepts presumes that one will at least *know* those concepts first.

Stanislavski has been stretched in many ways. His ideas have been distorted, dis-
tended, and pulled out of shape by some. They have been expanded, augmented, and
amplified by others. Developments in behavioral sciences have helped his flexible
system thrive into the twenty-first century. His ideas have proved to have plenty of
elasticity.

As a brilliant teacher, he had a powerful influence on other teachers, who in
turn influenced many others. Six of them are particularly worth your attention

because they took his ideas and developed them into their own. Stanislavski always encouraged this kind of innovation, welcoming experimentation and exploration. However, these teachers are so closely associated with him that many people mistake their ideas for his.

Stanislavski in Russia: Three Artistic "Sons"

Stanislavski mentored three great artists who were each part of the Moscow Art Theatre (MAT). They each had a distinct vision of what the work of the actor should be. Stan gave them what they needed to start them on their way. In many ways, they were his artistic "sons."

Evgeni (Eugene) Vakhtangov (1883–1922)

Although twenty years younger than Stanislavski, the brilliant Vakhtangov was the co-founder of MAT First Studio after only one year's membership in the company. Vakhtangov eventually headed the Third Studio on his own. His short brilliant career ended when he died of cancer in 1922 at age thirty-nine. His wife and other supporters continued his work for many years at what was then named the Vakhtangov Theatre.

Significance

He combined Stan's inner technique with a vivid and exciting theatricalism and was dedicated to exploring the "grotesque." Though he was fond of exaggerated and distorted characters, all were based on inner truths. You could say he pushed the envelope on how large or eccentric a character could be and still have actors thrive using a deep inner technique.

Key Ideas

- *Adjustment:* Using motivations completely unrelated to the content of the play, secrets unconnected to the dramatic events, impulses that no one in the audience would recognize but would produce powerful emotion. For example: An actor playing a character avenging his mother's death might find asbestos or some other dangerous material in the dressing rooms and consider suing the theatre management, "avenging" all the actors who might be potential victims of management's carelessness. This is not quite what most actors consider "substitution" because the performer is not really attempting to find a similar or parallel situation from his own life (an experience with his own mother or an actual murder) but, rather, an entirely different source of emotion.
- *Justification:* Finding reasons to come to the theatre (such as that you are the one hope your character has to ever come alive again and be heard) that

"justify" your participation in the play. In this case, putting yourself in the service of something higher may motivate you to a higher level of commitment. Again, this moves the actor outside of self-preoccupation but also outside the immediate needs of the character.

Exercise 5.1

Outer Before Inner*

1. Move around the room and, at a given signal, strike whatever pose your body chooses. Just make sure that your whole body is engaged and that the poses are not small or pallid.

2. Examine the pose, and encourage feelings or a strong attitude to emerge from what your body has done to find a justification for it. Take the physical attitude that has come first, then allow it an inner life to be released through the "pose."

3. Let a line of dialogue or simply a sound emerge from your inner life.

4. Continue to explore, freeze, pose, then justify until you are comfortable letting the body discover and then inhabit each physical attitude.

5. Continue this approach in the rehearsal of a scene, allowing random and extreme physical responses to invade your conventional blocking. Experiment with the emotional extremes in the scene, seeing how far you can push the emotional content without violating essential truths in the script.

Contribution

Vakhtangov managed to employ the Stanislavski System beyond the confines of realism, bringing it into other periods and genres, including classical theatre and highly "stylized" performance. He showed the System worked with numerous styles beyond realism, including what he called "fantastic realism." He was profoundly influential on the practice of giving honest inner lives to characters in large, exaggerated circumstances. Vakhtangov influenced Richard Boleslavsky, who taught MAT techniques in New York, and who in turn influenced Lee Strasberg.

Who Should Study Him?

Anyone who believes the System cannot be applied to nonrealistic contemporary works and anyone seeking inspiration for doing so.

---

*Exercises 5.1–5.10 are inspired by the artists in question, but I have designed or adapted them for a basic class. They are "in the style" of the innovator, but not necessarily exercises that would occur in that person's class or rehearsal.

To Read More

Simonov, Ruben. *Stanislavski's Protégé Eugene Vakhtangov.* Translated and adapted by Miriam Goldina. New York: DBS, Inc., 1969.

Vsevolod Meyerhold (1874–1940)

A founding MAT member, Meyerhold acted with the company for four years, leaving in 1902 to start his own theatre ("Comrades of the New Drama") after a falling-out with the management. He always maintained good relations with Stanislavski, however, who set him up several years later with a studio of his own. Stanislavski always hoped that Meyerhold would take charge of the experimental branch of the MAT, but Meyerhold's ideas were too extreme for many of its members (the master sometimes referred to him as his "prodigal son") and for various governments under which he worked. He craved a dynamic theatre that would be transformed by the same factors that were transforming basic life in his country. He sought a revolution in the theatre and supported the Russian Revolution of 1917, but was later defeated and extinguished by the Socialist Realism movement and repeatedly incurred the displeasure of authorities. He was arrested, exiled, and died (and may have been executed) in 1940.

Significance

Meyerhold sensed a fatal flaw in many of Stanislavski's actors; a lack of physical expressivity. He turned to commedia, pantomime, circus, Kabuki, Noh drama, boxing, and gymnastics to help train the actor's body to respond fully. From the Eastern theatre, he took the idea of centers of gravity; from clowning, ideas for the expressive mask, exaggeration, foolishness; from pantomime, an actor's need to develop strength and flexibility; from commedia, the idea of mastering *lazzi* or bits; and from all of these, committing to theatrical excitement. He felt that art is not an imitation of life, with audience members looking through a keyhole but, rather, always something more. He always asked what was theatrical about theatre and pursued it. He rejected naturalism as irrelevant. He sought an Expected Unexpectedness, in which actors bring a sense of mystery and anticipated excitement to their work.

Key Ideas

- *Constructivism:* The set as playground, with its bare bones uncovered, even flaunted, with many different performance levels and possible routes, with actors "playing" in highly gymnastic fashion on the space.
- *Biomechanics:* A way of training actors to use the least amount of energy to best convey emotion, desire, movement, and gesture, through rhythm, dynamics,

economy, and focused attention. Actors seek centers of balance, employing their bodies as expressions in space. A series of exercises that produce an actor/athlete/machine/clown (though not with the improvisational freedom we often associate with clowning, but more a mastery of clown techniques). Mind and body are disciplined to acrobatic precision, conventional and stylized gesture. Biomechanics trains:

1. Balance and general physical control
2. Rhythmic awareness, both in space and time
3. Overall responsiveness to one's partner, the audience, stimuli
4. Ability to attend closely and to react

- *Sixteen Etudes:* A series of precise exercises containing all the basic expressive situations in which an actor might be asked to respond.
- *The Acting Cycle:* Intention, Realization, and Reaction, Refusal, or Point of Repetition.

Exercise 5.2

The Stick

This exercise focuses on developing balance, coordination, and a strong awareness of a center of gravity. Use a dowel or section of a broom handle 36–40 inches in length. Throughout, allow the stick to be light, always handling it gently, not grabbing. Stand with legs apart, knees slightly bent, holding the stick about three-quarters of the way down in one hand. At all times, keep the focus at the top of the stick, aware of your environment but focused on the top of the dowel.

1. Bend knees to get momentum and rise, tossing the stick up so it arcs, then catch the other end in your hand easily. Repeat this action several times.

2. Now throw it so it twirls completely, catching the same end you threw with the other hand. As your confidence grows, toss the stick so it arcs as many times as possible before you catch it. Keep relaxed and loose throughout.

3. Hold the stick in the middle vertical to the ground. Toss from one hand to the other. Hold it horizontally with the back of your hand upward. Bend knees and then straighten them, lifting hand and opening fingers so the stick flies out. Bring your hand down, catch the stick with the back of your hand still upward. Repeat, letting go with one hand and catching with the other. Expand this action as well, passing the stick under your leg, behind your back, and so on around your body.

4. Place the stick in your palm, toss it, and catch it without closing your hand around it. Now when it is in the air, turn your hand over and bat it back up with the back of your hand or wrist.

5. Balance the stick on your middle finger and toss it up with that finger, catching it between your fourth finger and pinky. Continue tossing and twirling with various finger combinations.

6. Balance the stick on your palm, the back of your hand, one finger, your wrist, your elbow, your shoulder, foot, knee, back of neck, forehead, anywhere you can get it to remain perfectly still.

Exercise 5.3

Throwing the Ball

1. Start by sitting on the floor with your knees tucked under you.

2. Stretch toward an imaginary ball some distance away. Let it be a significant reach.

3. Give the ball a definite shape and weight, and let these influence your actions.

4. Move slowly into a standing position and prepare to throw the ball the farthest distance possible with a definite place at which you want it to land or be caught by someone.

5. Throw the ball and continue the motion into a follow-through position and a rebalancing or recovery before returning to the ground.

6. Repeat the action with balls of various kinds, sizes, weights, and surfaces and with other imaginary thrown objects such as rocks and sandbags.

7. With each act, note your shifting centers of gravity. Let each "throw" go through a cycle of acting: Intention (wanting to throw), Realization (surge of energy as ball leaves you), and Refusal of the Action (the way the body recoils in opposition after such an act).

8. Work with actual objects at various times, then return to imagined throwing to test the memory and accuracy of your work.

Contribution

Meyerhold developed a purely external path to emotion: surface to core, arousal of feeling from the outside. And his concern (unlike that of Vakhtangov) was not for the inner life of the character/actor but for the response of the observer. His work was a constant reminder that creation of feeling in the audience is far more important than that within the actor. He continued a long tradition that emotions are not necessarily felt but shown in performance, a direct link back through Delsarte (1811–1871) to Quintilian (first century A.D.).

His insistence on bare-bones theatre helped clear out the clutter and unessential elements that tended to burden older theatres. He also drew in various physical disciplines that often constitute the body training part of acting programs today and influenced Bertolt Brecht's and Jerzy Grotowski's ideas of performance and training.

Meyerhold's concept of actor/athlete is widely supported, an actor with the ability to command specific gestures because he has trained his body to receive these commands. His emphasis on the lower body was soon adapted by Michael Chekhov, then picked up many years later by Tadashi Suzuki.

Who Should Study Him?

Those interested in the theatre's effect on the spectator, on bare-bones theatre presentation, and on an intensely physical approach to actor training.

To Read More

Bruan, Edward. *Meyerhold on Theater.* New York: Hill and Wang, 1969.

Leach, Robert. "Meyerhold and Biomechanics," *Twentieth Century Actor Training.* Edited by Alison Hodge. New York: Routledge, 2000.

Michael Chekhov (1891–1955)

The nephew of the legendary playwright Anton Chekhov was himself admitted to MAT in 1910. As an actor, he was widely admired for being able to become wildly eccentric in performance without ever losing believability. He often wrote affectionately about Don Quixote, whom he admired and used as a model for employing brilliant and even feverish imagination to transform the commonplace into the magical. He left Russia in 1927, taught in numerous countries, and his professional career as an actor even brought him to Hollywood, where he was nominated for an Oscar for his role in Hitchcock's *Spellbound.*

Significance

Chekhov strove to place more emphasis on our imagination than Stanislavski had. He encouraged actors to move past emotional memories from their own lives to imaginary events and images, to get emotional stimulation from things that have never happened to anyone. He taught performers to seek stimulus from totally fanciful experiences, quite impossible in a literal world, but highly suggestive. For example, actors might be led to achieve a sense of giddiness and joy by imagining that they were walking on clouds or a rainbow with almost none of the gravitational limitations they would feel on Earth.

Key Ideas

- *Atmospheres:* A source of moods and waves of emotion from one's surroundings, a relationship, or an artwork, equivalent to musical keys.
- *The Higher Ego:* Creative individuality that makes each actor's performance of a role different from that of any other actor, including the actor's sense of

ethics, sensitivity, control, compassion, and humor, which all free her from the restrictions of its alternative—the narrow, selfish ego.

- *The Psychological Gesture (PG):* A physical action that reveals the inner feelings and personality of the character. For example, a character with great ambition but constant self-doubt might rise from a chair and then immediately sit down again. Although the actor might do this several times throughout the performance as a kind of defining physical manifestation of a troubling psychological state, it will far more likely remain a rehearsal device. This PG might also become a single move, with half the actor's body reaching up and out while the other half clings to the chair and safety. At various moments, the audience might sense an impulse of this kind without the actor actually standing up and sitting down, so that the PG provides a subterranean support for basic character urges.

Exercise 5.4

The PG

1. Working with a character you are performing in a monolog, scripted, or open scene, try to come up with a statement that summarizes the character's desires and feelings, such as, "I want more than life is giving me."

2. Experiment with nonrealistic but strong full body gestures to capture the essence of this character's emotional state. Work with moves that are archetypal, strong, simple, and well formed while you make the statement. Then leave the statement behind and work with some of the actual dialogue.

3. Once you feel you have the PG, use it as a way of accessing the scene as you warm up, then let the energy of it support your actual work.

4. Be sure to experiment with both inner and outer tempos (you may be moving slowly and carefully but be a nervous wreck, or you may be moving swiftly but are quite indifferent) as you refine the PG to one that is consistently evocative for you.

Exercise 5.5

The Castle

1. Imagine the interior of the castle or mansion of your dreams, how it would be furnished and decorated. Imagine that you own such a palace and that it is late at night on your first day after having moved in.

2. Walk around savoring how much you love this place and how perfect it is.

3. Begin the activity again with the knowledge that you are bankrupt, will have to sell the place, and that this is one of a few nights you will be able to spend here.

4. Repeat the action, replacing step 3 with each of the following:

   You have killed several people to make this place yours.

   All your favorite childhood characters and imaginary friends have come to live with you here and play with you again.

   You sense ghosts in each of the shadows and corners.

   It is so dark that you can barely see across each room or corridor.

   There is a lovely scent of flowers permeating each room but you cannot find them.

5. Select other physical and psychological actions to layer in.

Contribution

His Psychological Gesture, used throughout the world, is perhaps Chekhov's shining achievement, though he also influenced our use of abstract, fanciful, even illogical imagery to achieve effects. What we now call *conditioning forces* (*see pages 171–2*) originated with Chekhov, though he never named it. All our behavior is based on two kinds of immediate influences: physical (such as a sweltering hot day or a brisk one) and psychological (a feeling of foreboding or a sense of playfulness). Both change how we might do the simplest act, like combing our hair or buttoning a shirt, an idea developed and refined by Chekhov.

He influenced acting teachers by the unleashing of imaginative and fantastical elements in the Stanislavski System and in actor training generally. He strongly promoted the idea of each performance during the run of a show as being different and to some degree improvisational, within set limits. His use of visualization has become nearly universal.

Who Should Study Him?

Any actor or teacher interested in finding more abstract, fanciful, and purely imaginative ways to approach performance.

To Read More

Chekhov, Michael. *To the Actor.* New York: Routledge, 2002.

Chekhov, Michael. *The Path of the Actor.* New York: Routledge, 2005.

Chekhov, Michael. *On the Technique of Acting.* New York: HarperCollins, 1991.

Stanislavski in the USA: Three American Adapters

How did the influence of Stanislavski and his "sons" manage to travel so far from their homeland? In the early 1920s, the Moscow Art Theatre toured the

United States for a year and a half. Everyone was knocked out by them and wanted more. Americans had never seen such depth, ensemble, and incredible detail on-stage. The demand was so great for training of the kind offered to this company that two members, Richard Boleslavsky and Maria Ouspenskaya, opened the American Laboratory Theatre offering a two-year program in the basics of the System. (Un-fortunately their leaving the company at this point meant that they were therefore not exposed to Stanislavski's continued growth and development of the System.)

The MAT tour led to the formation of other companies trying to emulate them. The first and most influential was the Group Theatre, founded in 1931. The Group strove mightily to become an "American Style MAT" and had astonishing success with many of its early productions. These shows, for the first time on our home-grown stages, had deeply focused, genuine ensemble work. Three members of the Group Theatre eventually became teachers of great consequence. Their names are still an important part of actor training, and schools they have founded still thrive.

Oddly, each of them picked up some part of the System and left out many others. And they each chose different parts. Nevertheless, their collective influence on actor training in America has been huge.

Lee Strasberg (1901–1982)

> *Our whole theatre would have been less vital and ambitious without the influence of this one man, Lee Strasberg.*
> —Elia Kazan
>
> *Lee Strasberg tried to take credit for teaching me how to act. He never taught me anything. . . . To me he was a taste-less and untalented person. . . . He never taught me acting.*
> —Marlon Brando
>
> *I think Stanislavski got strangled, mostly by Lee Strasberg.*
> —Anne Bogart

Probably no one is more responsible for misinformation about Stanislavski than Lee Strasberg. Much of what he presented, however, he never claimed to come straight from the master, and he was sometimes even openly critical of Stanislavski. He tended to describe his work as a "reformulation" of Stanislavski. So the deception is largely accidental. Strasberg is probably the most famous American acting teacher of the recent past century and is widely revered as a great guide. Still, there are many falsehoods out there. First, he never taught Marlon Brando, the performer most associated with his Method Acting. Strasberg was not a founding member of the Actor's Studio, the place where the Method has flourished, and he had no real influence there until a number of years after it was formed. And while he did study with MAT teachers Boleslavsky and Oupenskaya, he dropped out of their program before the second year. Their program, like Stanislavski's two main books, dealt with technical matters in the second year, all of which Strasberg missed.

Lee Strasberg developed the Method based on a small part of the System, placing huge emphasis on emotion memory (in practice now largely used synonymously with *affective memory*) and neglecting almost altogether actions, given circumstances, objectives, characterization, and other elements. He mentored numerous famous actors (Al Pacino, Dustin Hoffman, Paul Newman, Robert De Niro, and Marilyn Monroe, just to name a few) during his lifetime, and countless film actors in particular revere him.

Significance

Strasberg ironically defended and widened the use of emotion memory even as Stanislavski moved away from it. Without Strasberg's evangelical emphasis, it is quite possible that this concept would have faded from use rather than becoming the very center of many actor training programs. He is sometimes unfairly accused of encouraging actors to indulge in immediate real emotion, even though he was always quite adamant that it is important to use remembered emotion from circumstances distant enough (at least seven years) to have control. He differed vividly from Stanislavski, however, in changing the "Magic If" to include one's own response without the necessity of sharing the character's cumulative background, allowing what he called a "substitute reality."

Although the production of genuine emotion in performance is a widespread goal, Strasbergian actors have sometimes been accused of displaying emotionalism and he of violating a core of privacy within performers.

Key Ideas

- *The Method:* While the concept of an inner technique for expressing deep feeling came from Stanislavski, the idea of its great importance and the value of using one's own personal history as such a strong resource is definitely Strasberg's. The name is his. And placing it at the center of one's work rather than as simply one of a number of items in one's toolbox is definitely Strasberg.

- *Private Moment:* A far more extreme version of Stanislavski's public solitude, involving doing something others never see you do and that you would normally alter considerably if you thought they were, as a means of losing self-consciousness in the presence of an audience.

Exercise 5.6

Personal Object

1. Find an object at home for which you have special feelings, but not new ones— something that has been around for years that is associated with powerful experience.

2. Hold it and experience the sensory details (color, size, weight, scent, feel, surface texture, temperature) of the object rather than focusing on the feelings it evokes.

3. In class or later alone, recreate the object in memory without it being physically present. First just look at it, then pick it up. As you move through the physical characteristics, if the emotion associated wishes to come, let it.

4. Locate other objects with strong personal histories and repeat the process of recreating them when they are not specifically present and exploring associative emotions.

Contribution

Strasberg developed very specific processes to help actors achieve relaxation that we now widely use as warm-ups. He also came up with finite ways to help concentration. Actors tend to be sabotaged by tension and distraction, so these are important aides in process.

His emotion memory and private moment techniques remain controversial, but they clearly have proved useful to many actors. Many believe the techniques work better on film than in the theatre. Onstage actors may appear to drop out of the scene to get their "moments" as they search within themselves and in fact to be preoccupied with themselves. The nature of film is that an actor can take time to achieve such moments just before the camera rolls, or his dropouts can be edited later. And it only takes one good take to preserve a moment forever.

To Read More

Strasberg, Lee. *A Dream of Passion*. Boston: Little, Brown, 1987.

Hethman, Robert, ed. *Strasberg at the Actor's Studio*. New York: Theatre Communications Group, 1965.

Stella Adler (1901–1992)

> *Stella stresses imagination and Lee stresses reality. You use Stella's imagination to get to Lee's reality.*
> —Ellen Burstyn

> *What an extraordinary combination was Stella Adler—*
> *a goddess full of magic and mystery, a child full of innocence*
> *and vulnerability.*
>
> —Elaine Stritch
>
> *Don't use your conscious past, use your creative imagination*
> *to create a past that belongs to your character. I don't want*
> *you to be stuck with your own life. It's too little! It's too*
> *bitty-caca.*
>
> —Stella Adler
>
> *Stella was kinda like [infamously tough basketball coach]*
> *Bobby Knight. Hey, I'm a lazy f_ _ _. Everybody can be. We*
> *need somebody to push us so we can learn to push ourselves.*
> *Stella was like that. Stella made Bobby Knight look like*
> *mashed potatoes.*
>
> —Benicio Del Toro

An original member of the Group Theatre, Stella Adler came from a family of prominent actors and was probably the most successful actor in the organization. Frustrated with some of Strasberg's classes, she went to Paris to visit Stanislavski in 1934 and worked with him for much of that summer. He told her that he had abandoned emotion memory because it had led to hysteria in some actors. He provided her with less direct ways of summoning emotion.

She returned and taught classes for the Group, then eventually opened her own studio in 1949. Two schools bearing her name continue, one in New York and one in Los Angeles.

While Lee Strasberg spent a great deal of time opening up the actor's own emotional life, Stella Adler focused on the actor's creation of character through evidence in the script.

Significance

Adler felt that delving into her personal life, as emotion memory required, was unnecessarily invasive, so she aggressively pursued and developed other paths. Her teaching helped bring forth the greatest emphasis on imagination, circumstances, and actions, just as Stanislavski intended. She taught that emotion should come from the actor's commitment to the circumstances and that a clear and deep understanding is critical for an actor's expressive truthfulness. She trained actors to do research into the world of the text and the world surrounding it, not unlike an actor/anthropologist.

Key Ideas

- *Defictionalizing the Fiction:* A process by which the actor fills in the details within the character, events, and place as if they are real, to live within those circumstances. Where, when, what, who: An actor investigating character and circumstances with the same active tenacity as a journalist might pursue a hot news story.

- *Paraphrasing:* Trying to do lines that are similar to but not the actual ones in the text by way of creating the sense of coining and newness when actually speaking the text. These paraphrases might ultimately be lines that your character rejects just before selecting the actual scripted ones, just as, in real life, we all consider and reject some things to say before we make an actual choice.

Exercise 5.7

Living with Pain

1. Select a minor injury of some kind: a sprained wrist or ankle, a sore shoulder, a cut finger, something that does not prevent you from venturing out and about, but which limits your full range of motion and causes you to adjust to avoid pain.

2. Go about a simple task such as getting dressed. Note where your weight is placed and the compensations you make. Keep all activity as economical as possible.

3. Pull forward sense memory to help you recall past experiences with this tiny disability, focus on clear muscle control, employ imagination, and continue to act logically within the circumstances you have established.

4. Work through other physical conditions that add small distractions to your daily activity.

Pick one each week to master by recalling it detail by detail.

Exercise 5.8

Your Own Words

1. As you read a newspaper, a magazine, or a play, begin to develop the habit of stopping after key passages and paraphrasing them in words of your own.

2. After the initial paraphrase, repeat your words very quietly, then project at least across the room.

3. When you work on a role, do the same for crucial important speeches of the character. Simply take the words into ones that could have been devised by you. This will make the ideas seem more as if they belong to you and help you feel as if you are in partnership with the author.

4. When you deliver the actual text, let your paraphrase personalize the delivery and consider the paraphrase as what you consider saying (*see* Alternatives, *pages 21–22*) before you actually choose the playwright's words.

Contribution

Adler served as a strong reminder that not focusing on emotion itself but, rather, the physical embodiment of it—gestures, voice, animation—can be the most effective pathway to feeling. Even more important, she established the value of the actor putting himself in the place of the character rather than vice versa. She also took the concept of actions and broke them down into actable units. More than anything else, Stella Adler brought into public awareness all the close careful attention to text and analysis Stanislavski endorsed.

To Read More

Adler, Stella. *The Art of Acting.* Edited by Howard Kissel. New York: Applause Books, 2000.

Adler, Stella. *The Technique of Acting.* Edited by Howard Kissel. New York: Bantam Books, 1988.

Sanford Meisner (1905–1997)

If there is a key to good acting, this is it, above all others.
—Gregory Peck

Out of his passion and his brilliance, Sandy developed a profoundly organic and healthy approach to training actors.
—Larry Silverman

If Strasberg is the most famous U.S. acting teacher of this century, Meisner is probably the most revered, one of the few whom actors have consistently honored in their acceptance speeches for various awards. An original member of the Group Theatre and a successful actor himself, Meisner, like Adler, was troubled by Strasberg's heavy emphasis on emotion memory. Meisner was greatly influenced by the work of Michael Chekhov and interested in finding techniques that worked beyond the confines of realism.

More than anything else, Meisner, who founded the Neighborhood Playhouse, wanted acting to come from the heart, not the head, and was bothered by a loss of connection between actors, particularly Strasberg actors who would go into their own reveries, often losing touch with other performers.

Significance

Meisner focused his work on one of the most neglected aspects of Stan's system and one that the master had held in the highest esteem—communion, a sense of profound connection between actors. He knew that crackling energy and tension in a scene comes from interaction between characters, and virtually all of his work is between partners—while most Strasberg and Adler exercises are done alone. A primary area of disagreement between Meisner and Adler was in the use of paraphrasing, which he never employed.

Meisner required actors to learn lines by rote away from partners (unlike collective line runs), so that textual encounters would be sure to surprise. His favorite metaphor was that the emotional life of character is a river with the text riding on top of it like a canoe. His work is primarily aimed at creating a truthful exchange between actors.

Meisner did not dwell on actions, objectives, beats, obstacles, and strategies, which he considered overly intellectual and dry "head" work. Nor did he deal with emotion memory, which though arguably "heart" work, tended to be so private as to potentially block communion.

Key Ideas

- *Preparation:* Creation of offstage emotion, coming onstage with something going on, with a full inner life.

- *Particularization:* A series of very specific inquiries to move forward the results of the Magic If.

- *Impulses not Cues:* Working not with the end of your partner's line but the place within speeches or silences where the will to respond comes.

Exercise 5.9

Repetition

1. Work in groups of three, with two partners and an observer. Partners sit facing each other, not quite touching knees.

2. Partner *A* makes a simple observation about the person that is without judgment, such as a comment on a color or garment they are wearing, for example, a "dark blue backpack." Make it the very first thing you notice. Don't take time to consider and reject choices.

3. Repeat the line at least seven times, finding a slight difference in connection each time.

4. Your partner listens closely and now repeats the line as "dark blue backpack." You then repeat your line and she hers as long as there seems to be something between you.

5. You continue this exchange for some time, letting whatever new information and connection flows between you permeate your work. Surprising ranges of connection may be involved.

6. The observer monitors the exchange and helps remind participants when needed of the following guidelines:

   Don't imitate or mimic your partner.

   Don't try to top her.

   Don't interrupt or anticipate before they have spoken, even though you have heard what they are saying before.

   Keep talking through laughter or any other response that comes up.

   Take out any pausing between what *A* says and what *B* says in response so you just respond without evaluating in any way.

7. At a point of mutual consent, change the person who is making the observation. Your partner now comments on something factual about you or your possessions. Do this for at least 15 minutes.

8. Move into actual sentences such as, "You have a dark blue backpack," and "I have a dark blue backpack."

9. When you have reached a genuine point of trust, change the observation into something about how the other person reacts ("You smile a lot"), something you have noticed about their feelings ("You are a little nervous today"). Repeat the previous process with lines that are less purely objective and more intuitive.

Exercise 5.10

One-Two-Three

Same conditions as in Exercise 5.9.

1. (One) *A* thinks of a highly intriguing, provocative question and asks *B*. (For example: "Are you lonely?" "What do you hate about acting?" "Has someone ever worshiped you?")

2. (Two) *B* repeats the question right away, allowing an immediate response.

3. (Three) *A* tries to describe *B*'s behavior when repeating the question suggested. ("You turned beet red." "You gasped for air." "You found that funny and intriguing.")

4. Alternate who asks the question and who responds. Each partner initiates at least five questions.

   Remember, you are never going to answer the question. This is simply about response, and noticing.

Contribution

Meisner gave us one of our most respected definitions of acting: "behaving truthfully under imaginary circumstances." His attention to communion brought forward one of Stan's major concepts, all but neglected by other disciples and descendents. Although Meisner himself did primarily partner work, his ideas have contributed to ensemble and group dynamics by those who would have otherwise overlooked these in class or rehearsal. His belief that others in the show or class are your lifeline, that your work will depend on theirs, that just as mountain climbers are roped together because their safety depends on it, so too will scenes live or die depending on the invisible rope connecting actors together, has had a profound influence on the elimination of petty competition and on the building of trust between actors.

His intensive partner work helps people get fully present in each moment because you are never certain how your partner is going to respond. You need to listen with everything you've got. Developing this habit in class and rehearsal has also influenced actors in being attentive and respectful to what is new and different at each performance.

To Read More

Meisner, Sanford, and Dennis Longwell. *Sanford Meisner on Acting.* New York: Random House, 1987.

Silverman, Larry. *The Sanford Meisner Approach.* 4 workbooks: *1. An Actor's Workbook, 2. Emotional Freedom, 3. Tackling the Text, 4. Playing the Part.* Lyme, NH: Smith and Kraus, 1995, 1998, 2000, 2001.

Summary

Each of these six teachers stretched Stanislavski forward in time. Each gave us a whole new direction. From Vakhtangov, we received expansion of the System into stylized and exaggerated works beyond realism. From Meyerhold, a greater emphasis was placed on audience response and the concept of the actor/athlete, the need to rigorously train one's physical instrument to respond fully. From Chekhov, we evolved the use of abstract and purely imaginative sources of inspiration, the actor's creative mind as source for characterization.

The Americans stretched Stan's ideas differently. Strasberg developed an intensive central focus on emotion memory; Adler developed a careful process of analysis and characterization; and Meisner renewed and further developed a sense of communion between actors. Because each of them stressed some but not all aspects of the System, each may be to some degree responsible for the incomplete knowledge so many actors have of its totality. Strasberg placed huge emphasis on the individual actor's resources, Adler on the text, and Meisner on connections with one's partner and the audience. All three developed text-related improvisation, for Strasberg the use of gibberish in place of script, for Adler paraphrasing, and for Meisner repetition. None of the three ever worked much outside the limitations of contemporary realism, nor did they work with college freshmen. Actors tended to work with them after they already had some training, experience, and maturity.

Strasberg's home, The Actor's Studio—a kind of glorious acting gymnasium—remains a revered haven for performers at all levels of experience. The Stella Adler School and the Neighborhood Playhouse, where the other two taught, continue as among the most prominent professional academies in this country.

Postmodern Stanislavski
Playing with Dials

Postmodern performance is characterized by irony. It juxtaposes the old and new, affection and contempt, the wonderful and the terrible. It often mocks itself, tending to be highly self-aware and to generate preemptive, reflexive laughter and emotional disengagement. *Seinfeld* was a postmodern sitcom, *The Simpsons* a cartoon, and *Letterman* a talk show. The smash hit musical *The Producers*, though in many ways downright old-fashioned, is postmodern in that it is a musical about making a musical that laughs at itself for being a musical. A postmodern performer has an ability to step outside the material and even wink at it on demand.

It is common for those lacking "Stanislavski smarts" to claim that his system is ineffective for the newest plays and productions. In the postmodern age of semiotics, didactics, deconstruction, dialectics, and problematizing (do not worry if these terms have no meaning for you now), a careful, internalized process can certainly seem inadequate, even inappropriate. You may be required to present a bold, self-referential performance with constant audience interaction. You may be asked to make sharp, sudden changes, following no psychologically clear behavior pattern. You may have to be outrageously in-your-face with your audience and to constantly change what you want and even who you are.

How can this careful, truth-based system support such a performance? This question is as naive as asking how democracy can embrace changing views of women, local government, privacy, family, drug abuse, poverty, or public access. The answer is in its flexibility. This acting system, like our political one, is designed to adapt. That is why it remains preeminent. Although other thrilling, even invaluable exercises, experiments, training methods, and approaches have emerged, so far none have included an all-encompassing process. Nothing else offers assistance that starts with basic training ideas followed by a progression of suggestions for how an actor's training might develop over a period of years. Nothing else starts with the very first time you pick up a script, takes you through every phase of rehearsals and all the way through the final performance. This is why it deserves to be called a System—because advice is offered for each step in class, rehearsal, and performance. All other approaches address only part of the process, so everything else is still bits and pieces, no matter how exciting those bits and pieces may be.

Why don't we offer much postmodern training to beginners? Because most acting teachers believe you need to learn to fully inhabit a character before you learn to step outside and comment on one, that you need to find an immediate tangible truth before shooting for a more abstract one. In fact, many inept novice actors are constantly stepping outside of character by mistake. It is a skill to be developed consciously, with the actor in control.

It is also far too common for new approaches to claim incompatibility with others and to declare the irrelevancy of past approaches. Most actors learn, sometimes by painful digression, that the most useful approaches are infinitely compatible. "Stan's Plan" will remain where most actors start. He never even considered that this would be where they would finish. It is fascinating that almost any "new" position on where actor training needs to move is simply a variation on one taken many years ago by Vakhtangov, Meyerhold, or Chekhov. So the same concerns and possible solutions have been around for a very long time.

There are two major pitfalls in using the System. One, characterized in the last section, is to take only one or two of its parts, elevate these to a status Stanislavski never intended, and neglect the other crucial elements entirely so you never really have anything more than a systemette. The other is to slavishly grant all ingredients equal status in every situation. This is like cooking with an equal quantity of every ingredient in a recipe instead of considering each time you cook how much of any ingredient to use. Stanislavski had provided the ingredients in the hope that you will develop your own recipe.

> *When I act, I imagine I'm a mixing board at a sound studio.*
> *The pattern in the board is me. When I play a character,*
> *I go "I'll turn these knobs down and these ones up."*
> —Heath Ledger

Imagine that you have a control panel in front of you with twenty dials. The first ten are labeled:

1. Relationship	6. Text
2. Objective	7. Subtext
3. Obstacle	8. Interior monolog
4. Strategy	9. Evaluation
5. Tactics	10. Beats

These first ten dials deal with any moment onstage.

Now, one level below them on your panel, you have the following:

11. Given circumstances
12. Magic If
13. Super objective
14. Through-line of actions
15. Scoring the role

16. Endowment
17. Recall
18. Images
19. External adjustments
20. The creative state

These next ten deal with the whole performance.

As an actor, you train to master all twenty, not with the idea that each will have equal importance in every performance, but to be able to dial them up or down to suit any script, any production concept, any occasion. For a performance asking for outrageous, self-referential behavior and quicksilver shifts in moods, even identities, while affronting audiences, you might dial 1, 4, 5, 7, and 10 way down and 6, 8, and 9 way up, so that the moment-to-moment struggle of the character becomes subservient to quick changes and connections with those in attendance. The System provides you with an overview, a thorough set of questions to launch your performance.

You may look at 1 (relationship) and decide there is none. This is always a possibility. You may also find that your primary relationship is not with other characters, but with your audience, your schizoid other self, an obsessive memory, an inanimate object, or even an abstract idea. But asking what relationship, if any, exists each time you go onstage is always worth asking. If you are playing an archetype, your given circumstances are dialed down to relative insignificance because you do not wish to particularize this character. But given circumstances are always worth examining. All twenty dials deserve dialing, even if the direction is down.

And as exciting as the work of some of the artists noted in Chapter 9 is, the idea that these replaces the basic system is absurd. Actors with professional aspirations need to be trained for where the work is, and the work is largely realistic, almost exclusively so for film and TV. Student actors with no interest in professional aspirations need to be trained so that their lives are greatly enhanced and the System connects most viably to their day-to-day concept of performing their lives.

Why so strong a defense of Stanislavski in a book designed to embrace all possible sources of actor wisdom? Because he has taken so much false flack and because there is really nothing to object to if you get what he has to say. There is no way his ideas can ever hurt your performance if you fully analyze the work. And there are countless ways in which it might help you. So it's a no-lose alternative.

No matter how much innovative, nonfacsimile performance grows in popularity, there will always be a huge appetite and market for convincing, realistic portrayal. Many of us are tired of a steady diet of realism, and, yes, we want to see plays deconstructed, turned, twisted, invented, and reinvented, but we don't want to see them all the time! We may tire of traditional, established plays and crave created works, but that doesn't mean we actually want to reject, cast away, and dismiss everything old. Sometimes we want to watch stories where everyone behaves as most of us do. Sometimes we just want to sit and watch people like us acting like people like us.

Stanislavski Bozos

If you are new to Stanislavski, you don't need this section yet. It may just satisfy your curiosity over the kinds of debates in which theatre people engage. If you move on in acting, it will prove useful. Whenever I can't make something work, I always like to blame whoever told me how to do it. Don't you? So if I think I've followed the Stanislavski System, but I'm not getting cast, how comforting to believe it's the System and not me that needs work. If I think I'm teaching Stan, but not getting results from my students, it must be Stan, not me, who sucks. The same is true if I am directing a play and it is not coming together. Alas, Stan's Plan has been so wildly diverted that bogus ideas are commonly presented as gospel. Most of these people aren't following the System at all. Most criticisms of the System are, in fact, criticisms of Strasberg and, to a lesser extent, the other adapters of Stan's work.

Then there is the fact that Stanislavski has been around so long. Isn't it time for something newer, hotter, more cutting edge and beyond? Well, sure. I think no matter what we have, we tend to be looking around for something better to show up. Well, probably. But in all the arts, contemporary concepts *add* to our choices beyond the classics. They don't replace them.

The world is full of those willing to offer opinions (often harshly negative) about Stanislavski without ever having done their homework. Some are heads of important theatre departments, major playwrights, stars, even officers of international theatre organizations. Some are so revered and have been so meticulous in their other homework that it seems shockingly unbelievable that they could be misinformed and misinform others. But they do! A highly respected colleague of mine announced to me that a highly respected colleague of his had totally disproved Stanislavski; he showed me the article in a highly respected European (this was supposed to have particular weight) journal "proving" it. What the article dissed was pure Strasberg, not the System. How embarrassing. How (unfortunately) common.

I suggest three solutions. One, shrug it off. This one doesn't work for me, because spreading ignorance gets on my nerves. Two, conduct a simple interrogation to reveal the ignorance of an uninformed (though perhaps prestigious) spouter. Three, if such a person continues spreading ignorance, simply think of him as a Stanislavski Bozo, a term I find strangely comforting. You can have respect for certain people in all other areas, but they can still be an S.B.

If you have S.B. suspicions, ask any one or more of these ten questions:

1. Could you describe the System for me in a nutshell? (If they start on emotion memory, they're dead.)

2. What are the twenty or so basic ingredients?

3. Where did your Stanislavski knowledge come from?

4. What have you read that he himself wrote? How long ago?

5. Have you read *Building a Character* and *Creating a Role*?

6. How did these two books change your ideas from those you gathered from *An Actor Prepares*? (This assumes the S.B. has at least read the basic book, but many have not.)

7. How did Stan encourage actors to approach a role externally rather than just internally?

8. Can you tell me how S's ideas changed (especially about emotion memory) throughout his life?

9. What other acting system covers all the bases?

10. Where does Stan actually say (or even imply) that the ideas of (insert whatever Guru in vogue is being revered) are wrong? How does the System not welcome such ideas?

S.B.s often spread B.S. If someone else quotes an S.B.B.S. to you, simply say, "He's a brilliant historian (or whatever) but doesn't know his Stanislavski." NOTE: Save the term for those for whom this is a lapse in an otherwise admirable life. Some people are Total Bozos (or T.B.s). For example:

> *The very first thing a casting director ever said to me was, "We often have a problem with Broadway actors because they tend to be too broad." I'm thinking, ohmygod, she thinks that's why it's called Broadway!*
>
> —Peter Gallagher

> *When I got to Hollywood, this fat man with a cigar asked what I'd done, and I said I'd got some good reviews in "Of Mice and Men." And he took the cigar out of his mouth and said, "You played a mouse?"*
>
> —Liam Neeson

Stanislavski Extended

Many fields of knowledge have opened up since Stanislavski worked and wrote. Acting has benefited not only from the work of those mentioned in the previous section, but also from sources as diverse as behavioral and computer sciences. Stan was in favor of anything that worked. In fact, one of his admonitions was that each actor should move beyond Stanislavski to his own discoveries.

If anything would upset the great man as much as the degree to which some of his concepts have been misunderstood, it probably would be the degree to which they have been slavishly imitated. There are disciples who refuse to tolerate an exercise or a phrase not dropped from the master's lips. But his System is open-ended. It grows, suffers, adapts, gets battered, and survives.

The following techniques did not come from Stanislavski himself but, rather, through those using his methods. They are in the Stanislavski "way of thinking," springing naturally from what he started and are well worth your attention.

Private Audience

Your own private audience is that group of people whose opinions are important to you, those to whom you have always felt the need to prove yourself. They influence you so strongly that you can't get them out of your head, at least not easily. Imagine that you are walking along, dragging your feet, slumped over at the shoulders, and you hear your mother (who lives 500 miles away) telling you to "Stand up and walk right." Now, you may automatically straighten up, or you may mutter "Buzz off" and keep slumping, but she is very much present in your audience in either case.

This group includes supporters and nurturers as well as major detractors, competitors, and those who have abused their authority over us. So some members are not friendly at all. When you have a triumph, and you think of someone and mutter to yourself, "I wish the S.O.B. could see me now," you have acknowledged a member of your private audience. Ex-husbands and wives are always private audience members. I keep waiting for the day when someone wins the Oscar or Tony and instead of thanking the world, says something like, "I won't bore you with thank-yous, but I do have a list of people who tried to stop me. I'd like to name them. First there was my terrible second grade teacher, Miss Markowitz, who didn't cast me as Cinderella. Then there was . . ." and so on. The winner would be acknowledging those truly unsung members of the private audience.

Your own vision of God has membership, whether it is abstract, such as the Force, literal—an elderly man with a beard and a scroll on a throne—or, like Jerry in *The Zoo Story*, who maintains that "God is a colored queen in a kimono." A variation involves those whom you idolize but have never actually met, such as a worshiped favorite author or actor.

Exercise 5.11

Naming Members

1. Jot down at least two names in each of these categories for yourself:

   a. Family

   b. Nurturers

    c. Detractors

    d. God

    e. Idols

2. Replace your members with those of your open scene characters. Run each scene, leaving your character open for any of the members to make an appearance in her mind and influence her decisions.

The identification of the character's private audience helps you with the Magic If. It also clarifies where you stop and the character begins, which influences you share, and which you, the actor, need to take on, to perceive the world as the character would.

Grouping

Grouping involves looking at others in general terms instead of as individuals. It is a way of endowing in large numbers. Bigots are the worst Groupers, branding all members of a race or creed with the same qualities, seeing cultural binding where it doesn't really exist. But everyone groups to some degree. Theatre majors tend to view business majors as aliens. Liberals tend to view conservatives as selfish. No one is entirely guiltless of the sweeping label.

    Grouping others (as powerful if you are cast as a timid soul, ignoramuses if you are playing an intellectual snob, thieves if you are a miser) helps you actively use all the other people onstage and in the character's world in a collective Magic If. It also helps you avoid playing an "attitude." You can't play "timid," "snob," or "miser" as isolated clichés. The more eccentric or unbalanced a character is, the more essential this technique becomes, so you aren't tempted to play her zaniness or craziness, but instead let yourself see people as she does. If you place these qualities on others, quite a bit of your behavior is likely to be automatically appropriate and free of stereotyped choices.

Exercise 5.12

Group Bias

What groups do you view in the most sweeping way? Write the name of the group and the one or two words you would use for them. Consider people who differ from your convictions in each of these areas.

1. Politics

2. Religion

3. Pastimes or recreation

4. Attractiveness

5. Discipline

Imagine someone whose views are the polar opposite of your own. What terms would she use to cluster you and those who feel as you do into a single group?

Substitution

While actually inserting your own experience in the place of the character's may seem thoughtless and shallow, there are certain instances when you may have no choice. Something in the character's life may be outside your experience. Now, nothing should be outside the spiritual or imaginative experience of an actor. You certainly shouldn't have had to rule a kingdom to play a king. But you may not have a ready frame of reference. Uta Hagen uses two of the best examples when she writes about shooting someone and being shot. Killing and being killed are experiences that are, I hope, foreign to you. She suggests that stepping into the shower, expecting warmth but being hit with and stunned by ice-cold water, is a reasonable sensation for a bullet hitting you. And, while you may have never hounded another human with a pistol, you have probably pursued, swatter in hand, a fly or wasp that has been driving you crazy, stalking with genuine menace and malevolence. Her suggestions act as "triggers" for the imagination. I think some actors would categorically deny that a character's actions are in them to perform. Substitution is a superior solution to denial.

For many actors, substitution also happens naturally. I have played several roles in which the people in my life who treated me similarly to the way the character was treated, and the feelings I had at that time, would simply superimpose themselves in my mind as I spoke the lines—unbidden but welcome, giving the moment a powerful boost. As long as this did not change the moment so suddenly that it was about me and not the character, it did not hurt and often helped the performance.

Conditioning Forces

Isolate within the given circumstances *(see pages 121–2)* factors influencing the character's behavior of the moment, which may change from beat to beat. Conditioning forces are immediate, physical, and sensual. Although many given circumstances influence your behavior in general ways, if it's raining outside and you enter the stage wet, this force conditions the very first moments of the scene, influencing each decision you make. Think of a hierarchy of given circumstances, starting with your whole life (how you were raised, family traditions and values, major events) to the last year (recent events that influence you: perhaps a death in the family, the end of a love affair, or a change in your financial status) to right now, this minute (like it's too dark to see to put your key in the front door). Conditioning forces are about right now. Standard ones include:

1. *Temperature/weather:* How hot/cold, wet/dry, constant/changing? May include variable conditions, as in a cold palace room with one fireplace, so that proximity changes feelings.

2. *Light:* How bright or dark, and what kinds of difficulties do you have as a result? Are there pools of light and shadow so that your vision and sense of security vary from space to space?

3. *Comfort:* Any irritating little aches or pains? Any discomfort that comes and goes, depending on how you move? Any stiffness? How do your clothes fit? Do you need to go to the bathroom? Is your foot asleep? Are you hungry or thirsty?

4. *Time:* Actual hour? Are you running late? How late? How long have you been up? How fatigued or energized? How anxious are you to get this over with? How willing to play around and sustain the encounter? What is the relationship between your outer and inner tempos? Do you need to accomplish something quickly but are feeling sluggish inside? Or do you need to move slowly so that you do not mess up a job, but your heart is racing with excitement and tension inside?

5. *Space familiarity:* Who owns it? How much right do you have to be here? How well do you know it? How curious are you about it? Who do you know here? Has it changed since your last visit?

6. *Distractions:* Are there loud noises from the street outside? From the next room? Is there an unpleasant, intriguing, or tantalizing odor in the space? Are your senses diverting you from your objective? Are you terribly curious about something? Terribly aroused by someone? Is any force or activity making it hard to focus your attention?

7. *Mood:* Do you feel unexpectedly buoyant and optimistic? Do you have a strange foreboding? Are you influenced in this encounter by your last one with this person and your anticipation of what this will mean?

Actors often mistakenly play in a space that seems utterly neutral, without any discernible physical influences. They also tend to play only two physical states: vibrantly healthy or dying. Consider the effect on the scene if your character had one glass of wine too many last night, and while not truly hung over, has this tiny little irritation at the side of the temple and is just a bit sluggish. Then there's that silly cut on your little finger where the Band-Aid won't stay on. And the neon light above is a bit glaring, but you don't have the energy to turn it off and a lamp on.

But there is a nice breeze coming in the window, relieving the heavy humidity in this room. Our state of well-being is relative, not perfect or terminal. Like endowment, a conditioning force may or may not read to an audience, but the sense of a complete human being in crisis probably will. Conditioning forces are especially important as you enter the scene because it is here that they often change (moving from dark movie theatre into glaring sunlight, heat wave into air conditioning, space uncertainty to relieved familiarity) and their effect on you may then modify as you grow accustomed to the new environment.

Exercise 5.13

Adding Conditions

1. Run the first several beats of one of your open scenes, adding a strong influence from one of the six forces listed, then with another force until you've tried all six. Now go back and layer in all six, one by one, so that all are finally working at once.

2. Have volunteers improvise situations where the audience identifies a basic relationship for the actors to start with. Do the scene once in a neutral state, then select two crucial conditioning forces to add.

Exercise 5.14

Crazy Car Conditions

Set up four chairs in two rows like the front and back seats of the car. Three actors get in and assume identities, driving along. A fourth is a hitchhiker, who, upon entering the car, brings in a distinct conditioning force, which everyone catches. Another actor hitchhikes, and when picked up, one of the first actors leaves. The new actor brings in a conditioning force that everyone also catches. After the group gets the idea of taking on the force, be sure that a conditioning force does not leave the car until the person who brought it on leaves the car.

Rehearsed Futures

The same way actors rehearse for the opening of the play, most of us are rehearsing our futures in our heads, thinking about some moment ahead when our lives will come together, or possibly fall apart. There are three kinds of rehearsed futures: *best possible*, *worst possible*, and *wildest dreams come true*. Most of us feel that our present circumstances will somehow change. Rehearsing your future is a way of holding onto your sanity and surviving present misfortunes. The future can be freely fantasized in both practical/possible visions and in wild/unlikely terms that require windfalls or even miracles.

For many actors, a best possible future would include getting a Master of Fine Arts degree from a respected program, working for some regional repertory companies, and perhaps doing some successful runs on Broadway. A worst possible might include flunking out of your present undergraduate program, never getting the courage to leave town, and spending the rest of your days bussing tables. A wildest-dream-come-true future might include being discovered tomorrow, becoming a household word overnight, winning Oscar, Tony, Emmy, and Grammy all several times over, having all the great writers of the world beg to create vehicles for you, and all the great lovers of the world beg to sleep with you, as you somehow manage to create peace and harmony among the peoples of the world with your art and have a newly discovered planet named after you, in honor of your accomplishments.

Taking the time to develop your character's rehearsed futures adds to the liveliness and energy of your performance, beyond the obvious additional dimension to the Magic If. Knowing your character well enough to fantasize from his perspective gives great confidence. Thinking about and yearning toward his future tends to make your performance alive with anticipation.

Exercise 5.15

Open Futures

1. Identify all three rehearsed futures for both of your open scene characters. The suggested assignment is to prepare two separate contrasting scenes as in the examples in Chapter 4. (*See* Exercise 4.17.)

2. Run the scenes, keeping yourself open to moments when the character might fantasize about the future.

3. Discuss any immediate impact on the scene.

Suppression

Much of our energy during time spent with others is devoted to trying *not* to reveal how we feel or how strongly. This *suppression of emotional display* helps us avoid making complete fools of ourselves, but can also stifle our freedom and spontaneity. Review the section on offstage suppression in Chapter 1 *(see page 11)*. Research has shown that instead of trying to cry, if you can identify, as Stanislavski has suggested, the conditions of the body that lead to crying (maybe you start to pause at odd places, your voice moves back into the throat, your fingers begin small spasmodic moves of their own) and then play directly against revealing those symptoms, the result will either be tears or a truthful struggle. So most actors who attempt to cry are approaching the phenomenon exactly backward. Having planted the character's given circumstances, next plant physical symptoms he wishes to avoid revealing. Remember that what is hidden just under the surface, what is not fully shown, is often what is most interesting.

> As an actor, you tend to want to show everything—but that's not true to life. What's compelling is the sense that something isn't being revealed—you just see little flashes that give you a hint as to why somebody is acting the way he is. That's what draws people to characters—that mystery or possibility. Will we know? Will we be shown?
>
> —Glenn Close

Exercise 5.16

Playing Against

1. Observe yourself for the next week, whenever you are trying not to show your feelings but are not entirely successful. Note your physical symptoms. Begin to put these in your mental acting file to employ when needed.

2. Go back to your open scenes and identify each point where your character wishes to suppress displaying emotion. Plant the symptoms to be avoided. Rehearse the scene with the focus on playing against what the character fears to reveal.

Exercise 5.17

Observing the System Plus

Attend a performance and identify each of these techniques for an individual performer (*see* Appendix G: Stanislavski Observation *at the end of the book*):

1. List ten of the character's most significant given circumstances.

2. Specify conditioning forces at work at the character's very first entrance and describe how and when these changed throughout the evening.

3. How would you, if cast in this role, employ the Magic If to help you absorb yourself convincingly in the character's perspective?

4. How would you employ grouping if cast in this role?

5. Write three paragraphs on three different versions of the character's rehearsed futures: (a) Best possible, (b) Worst possible, (c) Wildest dreams come true. Write as the character in his own words.

6. Find three instances where the actor was required to use endowment to make use of props or set pieces effectively. Do the same for the character view of three others in the play. Extend at least one of these endowments into detailed conjecture.

Working with a Partner

Stanislavski suggests that one must learn to infect a partner with your very soul. Never one to understate, he establishes throughout his works the need for complete respect, trust, and connection between acting partners. You share so much responsibility with and for your partner that the working relationship should be one of self disclosure, nonpossessive caring, trust, risk taking, mutual acceptance, and open feedback. Stanislavski calls this working relationship a state of "communion," which is a step higher than simple communication toward complete sharing.

Partnering

When you work on a scene, it may be the first of many times you need to learn to partner. If you have tended to be self-absorbed, this is the time to shift gears. The two of you are in this together. You have no right to sabotage the work of someone else, even if it is through ignorance, and you need to step up. This collaboration can prepare you to partner well in projects far beyond theatre.

Good partners:

1. Always call

   If you are going to be late for class or rehearsal, if you are going to miss either of these, you call your partner to warn her. Call her about today's class if she was not there or even if she was late and may have missed some important announcements.

2. Will try anything

   Whatever your partner suggests, you never say, "That makes no sense," "That's lame," or "My character would never do that." You try it. If it falls flat, okay, but you always give it a chance. Never pre-judge and never sabotage the idea with your total lack of commitment to it as if your intention all along was to show how bad that idea was. Instead, regard it as a great new way of potentially opening up the work and just give it all you've got.

3. Do their homework

   If you are in a scene it is a universal given that if the whole play is available you will read it. If you are conscientious you will also read about it. There should be no moment in rehearsal in which a question about the scene comes down to your not understanding how this particular moment fits into the whole play or how tied to the time period the attitudes of the characters are.

4. Bring stuff to the table

    A good partner has ideas, experiments, stuff to try when you meet. Don't show up without contributions. You may have an easygoing self-concept, thinking of yourself as willing to just go with the flow but that is not enough in collaboration. You need to be flexible and stimulating. Think of both of you as lightning rods who are full of ideas and may make sparks at this rehearsal.

5. Have your back

    If do need to miss class, a good partner will always take good notes to pass onto you, collect an extra copy of any hand-outs distributed, and contact you to make sure you are up to speed on where the class is now and what is going to be required next time. If you drop a line or mess up some moment in class presentations, a good partner will never blame you, but accept that in fact more rehearsal may have served you both.

6. Compensate for you

    If you are not feeling well and cannot give your all in a class presentation or rehearsal, your partner should respond to that with increased energy and commitment to keep the scene alive. This is similar to 5, but is more about being in the moment and sensing what is necessary right now to make it all work. This is like a dance. It is very much about being in the moment, staying connected, and being willing to step up to make the scene work.

7. Ask for help, never direct

    You may want your partner to change something because you critically do not think he is making the right choices. But you always need to remind yourself that you are not experiencing what audiences are so it is possible that his performance is reading differently than you are experiencing it. Ask for help if your partner is slow in picking up cues or not giving you enough anger or not seeming to be sufficiently devastated by your big pronouncement, but always do so in terms of your own needs as an actor instead of a critical assessment of this person's work. So instead of saying, "You need to pick up all these cues," you say, "It would really help me if you could almost cut me off at the end of my lines. I'm having trouble keeping the energy going."

8. Give you full candor, no B.S.

    Partners sometimes get caught in the need to falsely praise and encourage each other, like some pathetic parents at soccer matches who will praise any effort as beyond brilliant. The two of you should establish a contract of candor, right at the beginning of rehearsal, vowing to always tell each other the truth. The hard feedback should not be given insensitively, unless it is, but when it comes, it needs to be direct and honest.

9. Gently raise the bar

The ideal partner will stimulate you to be better. To make bolder choices, to work harder, to try stuff you never even considered before. Try to be that person. All theatre departments have actors everyone is anxious to work with, not necessarily just because of their talent, but because through their work ethic and quality of performance, they always set a standard.

10. Give you permission.

You need to feel able to get silly, wacko, experimental, edgy, to just *try* things in rehearsal. You never deny your partner's suggestions and your partner in return will also never get in your way and always encourage you to just go for it today, trusting your judgment about what to keep and what to pull back from these adventurous explorations. Rehearsals should often be about stretching the limits and comfort zones of the scene to determine what about this stretch is good to keep. A good partner will accept and applaud any damn thing you want to try because you are willing to try.

Your relationship is like a small, short-term marriage, with all the give-and-take and need for mutual support that implies. The two of you need to know each other better than can usually be accomplished accidentally. The following exercise imposes some structure and speeds up the process. It does not force an artificial instant intimacy, however, because you always have the freedom to reveal only as much information as is comfortable.

Stanislavski and his company had the extraordinary luxury of working and living together for many years, so that members of the Art Theatre were like family. This is the best exercise I know for gaining some semblance of self-disclosure between people who have no choice but to trust each other.

Acting is an intimate thing. You entrust your partner with something very private, a tremendous bond develops and that intimacy is like love.

–Kevin Kline

You work with some people who may be hot, but when you look them in the eye, they don't really look back. You can see they just don't have it. Connection. And they know it, and they know you know it.

–Ving Rhames

Exercise 5.18

Partner Sharing

Decide who will speak first, and take turns answering each question. Whenever possible, the listener should repeat in her own words what she has just heard. It is sometimes helpful to say, "What I hear you saying is . . ." and then complete the statement. If the speaker agrees that this was what he intended, then it is time to go on. Don't look ahead, and do not plan or "rehearse" any answers, but respond in the moment.

In a statement, such as number 2, you have the freedom to reveal as many or as few nicknames or titles as you want. This way you are not forced to share more than you want. When a question (as in 6 and 15) is repeated, answer it for the specific moment at which the statement is made. The exercise takes most people about an hour. If you are given some class time, but do not finish, why not begin your next rehearsal by completing it together?

1. My name is . . .
2. My other names are . . .
3. My romantic status is . . .
4. I come from . . .
5. The reason I'm studying acting is . . .
6. Right now, I'm feeling . . .
7. When I am in a new group, I . . .
8. When I enter a roomful of people, I usually feel . . .
9. When I'm feeling anxious in a new situation, I usually . . .
10. In groups, I am most comfortable when the leader . . .
11. Social rules make me feel . . .
12. If a situation is ambiguous and unstructured I . . .
13. I am happiest when . . .
14. The thing that excites me the most is . . .
15. Right now I feel . . .
16. The thing that concerns me most about the theatre is . . .
17. When I am rejected, I usually . . .
18. To me, belonging means . . .
19. The thing that is most difficult for me to do in public is . . .
20. Breaking rules makes me feel . . .
21. I most like to be alone when . . .
22. The thing that turns me off the most is . . .
23. I feel affectionate when . . .

24. Toward you, my partner, I feel . . .
25. I cry most easily when . . .
26. I laugh most easily when . . .
27. When I have a day all by myself, I am most likely to . . .
28. As a performer, I feel most insecure about . . .
29. I am most likely to get really angry if . . .
30. If I believe anything strongly, it is . . .
31. The thing I am most curious to know about you is . . .

After completing the list, take a few minutes to discuss the experience generally, and anything that may have come up during the rehearsal period so far that you would like to explore.

Exercise 5.19

Offstage Action: Stretching

What new information do you have from this chapter that could influence your progress in each of the OA areas? If needed, review the subcategories on pages 29–37.

1. Negating newness	6. Improving your image
2. Pleasant as possible	7. Richer relationships
3. Keeping cool	8. Social savvy
4. Sensing signals	9. Prediction potential
5. Winning ways	10. Career capabilities

Specifically: How might you apply strategies designed for working with a scene partner in other contexts where you need to collaborate with someone?

The amount of terminology associated with the System may seem vast, but there are really only thirty-six core terms worth committing to memory. These constitute your working vocabulary.

Exercise 5.20

Pulling it All Together

Review the next three paragraphs, which summarize the basic vocabulary of the Stanislavski System as originally designed by the man himself with additions brought about by time. Go back and review any idea from this chapter still not entirely clear to you. Don't reject any of these actor's tools until you know you have tried them.

Begin by determining the *given circumstances* of your character and using the *Magic If* to place yourself inside those circumstances, including *endowment* of real and imagined objects and people with physical and emotional qualities. You explore the character's *relationships* with everyone she encounters, developing her *private audience* and her *grouping* of others. You use your five senses to *recall* impressions, with *sense memory* adding detail and texture. You sometimes tap *emotional memory* to connect with the character's feelings. *Release pictures* can be especially powerful in this process. You explore not just the character's past and present but his *rehearsed futures*, including his fantasies. Each time the character appears you identify *conditioning forces* that may influence his behavior in an immediate, sensual way.

As you explore the *text*, you seek *images* to bring each line to life so you can connect fully with your partner. You work closely and in sufficient trust with your partner for mutual *communion* to occur. You discover the text's underlying *subtext*, including the character's *interior monolog* and *evaluations* where *alternatives* are explored. In each scene, you find her *objective*, the *obstacle* in the way, and general *strategy* and specific *tactics* employed to make it happen. You find many small *actions* or *bits* where any inner impulse has an outer execution, and you experiment with the *method of physical actions*, balancing the psychological and physical ingredients of each action. Instead of trying to feel the emotions for each moment, you concentrate on *planting* the physical symptoms of emotions, sometimes including *suppression* of emotional display. You section the role into *beats*, changing as individual transactions are completed.

You attempt to identify the character's *super objective* and to find the *through-line of actions*, connecting all the strategies, tactics, and individual maneuvers executed by the character along the way. All this work is placed in the *score* to guide the process. Although a number of changes in your own habits have occurred automatically, some *external adjustments* are likely to occur as your own body and voice change to suit the character. Attention to *tempo-rhythm* is especially important in entering the character's experience. If all these ingredients have been carefully pursued, you have a good chance of entering the *creative state* and are almost certain to achieve a performance based on *truth*.

6

Truth/Technique

Balancing spontaneity with consistency

It seemed to me that one without the other meant bad acting. But the two together, meant you had a shot at doing well.

—Philip Seymour Hoffman

We're just trying to tell stories and connect with the soul of the character we're taking on, so that we can help other souls in the world out there connect with each other. But what is the best way to do that?

—Naomi Watts

I'm getting better at doing the work, then leaving it behind at the end of the day. It's important not to lose yourself altogether in the role.

—Angela Bassett

Being bone real is not the big problem in acting in the theatre. The problem is to express what you are expressing at close distance, fifty yards away—that is the problem.

—Laurence Olivier

At first it just comes. Then you get much more self-conscious as you get older and that's your worst enemy as an actor.

—Natalie Portman

Which Way?

"Is it better for an actor to work from inside out or outside in?"

"For a performance to have emotion or precision?"

"Should the actor show the audience his face or mask?"

"Should the feelings be real or calculated?"

"Which is needed most? External form or internal conviction?"

"Is it more important to be honest or interesting?"

This is everyone's favorite debate topic regarding acting. It is no less interesting for being unresolvable. Like most debate topics, you can learn from it without settling the issue.

Why don't we just ask the great actors and get it over with? Because they can't agree. From Eleonora Duse (truth) and Sarah Bernhardt (technique) in the nineteenth century through countless others in the twentieth, there have been celebrated advocates for both sides. Great actors, like all geniuses, skip steps, so their work process and their statements can be deceiving. And many of them simply will not speak of what they do, lest they lose the magic.

Not only do actors work differently from each other, but the same actor will work differently depending on the medium, the space, and the script. Is there a microphone? Is my partner a camera or a person? Are there 50 people out there or 5,000? Is it intimate or do I need to fill a barn? Am I playing someone like me, or am I Mephistopheles, Hercules, the Mad Hatter, a potato chip? The same actor will even work differently from scene to scene. I was once in a musical in which I had a scene that always came straight from the heart, but minutes later was involved in a dance routine in which my interior monolog never got beyond "Step-ball-change. Step-ball-change. Don't forget to smile." The same actor may even work differently moment to moment. Ultimately the first steps will probably depend on the role.

> *My character in Beetlejuice is clearly an outside-in, with a walk and voice coming before an attitude. In Getting Straight, it was an inside-out. Who is this guy and where is he in me?*
>
> —Michael Keaton

As True as Possible

I believe that most actors, if pressed, would say they prefer to work internally, if possible. It is more fun to dig inside and tap real emotion, to cry tears that are genuine, to summon laughter that isn't forced. It's more of a genuine rush to share the character's feelings. However, it simply isn't always possible. How can you enter the character's soul if you can barely remember his dance steps? You could risk bumping into the other dancers, but there would be consequences. Nearly every actor, early in his training, experiences something like the following:

Example 1

You're in performance and it all seems to be happening for you. In your big scene, the tears come out in floods, everything is real, you're inspired, you're absolutely in the moment. You know you are at last an actor in the fullest sense. Then the director comes backstage and says something like, "You know, in scene 7, when you started blubbering, not only could I not understand a word you said, but you personally added five minutes to the running time of that act. What's wrong?" Others come backstage and do not praise. They give you sympathetic, curious looks, or they look away. A few may inquire about your health.

You have learned firsthand one of the classic truths of acting:

> An actor's first obligation is to be seen and heard.

By *heard* here, of course, we mean "understood." Emotion, when it finally overtakes you completely, prohibits clarity of communication, especially if you are trying to speak.

Example 2

You give a performance that seems calculated and hollow to you. You feel you were too aware of each effect and were probably stiff as a result. People come backstage. They are weeping. Your performance is eulogized. The director and other company members say you have never been better, that tonight you finally flew.

You have learned firsthand another classic:

> The audience doesn't care whether or not you are having a personal moment.

They care whether or not *they* are having a personal moment. The theatre is an art based on illusion, and ultimately, what matters to the people out front is what plays out front.

Actors prefer to be as truthful as they can, while still technically sound. If you can play from deep inside and still hit your marks, project to the back row, and give your partner support, then you have begun to marry these partners in art.

A Marriage of Necessity

Lee Strasberg, often associated with emotional acting, still criticized actors who were all feeling with lines like, "Blood, without flesh and bones, only spills," and "Without will, sensitivity is of no value." A purely technical performance risks looking like a lifeless, empty skeleton. A purely emotional performance risks looking like blood with no framework to flow through. Stanislavski demanded a completely trained instrument, with the technical repertoire to know how to respond fully to the impulses from within.

The actor's task is to become knowledgeable enough in technique to have at her disposal the means of transmitting emotion. A basic technical framework involves:

1. Mastering a working vocabulary of rehearsal and performance communication
2. Being able to execute a variety of physical maneuvers
3. Being capable of vocal experimentation, change, and clarity
4. Adjusting your behavior to suit the needs of the character and nature of the playing space
5. Developing the capacity to make decisions quickly and to commit to them with high concentration.

At a later, more sophisticated level, the actor's task can include such diverse techniques as speaking dialects, handling rapier and dagger, scanning verse, mastering styles, and a multitude of additional specialty skills, advanced techniques called on when you're ready to tackle characters from other worlds and times.

Body Maneuvers

We've dealt with the body in a number of contexts. Now it's time to identify what it needs to do onstage. If you're new to the stage, think of this as a crash course in the jargon used there. If this is review for you, skim the lists quickly to brush up and see if there are any new terms. Try to tour the theatre itself, associating each item with something concrete.

The Acting Space

The following items represent theatre geography. They are the landmarks on the map, helping you explore this world. Knowing where each is helps communication in rehearsal. If a director asks you to move to the third stage right and face the teaser, you don't want to be looking at real people's legs and looking God-knows-where to find the teaser.

above Area away from the audience, upstage

apron Part of the stage that projects into the auditorium, close to the audience, downstage of the proscenium arch

arch Short for *proscenium arch*, the frame that defines the stage, the opening through which the audience sees the stage

arena Form of staging where the audience surrounds the stage on all sides, sometimes called **theatre-in-the-round**

backing Flats or drops used to mask the backstage area by limiting the audience view through doors, windows, or archways on the set

batten Long pipe or strip of wood on which scenery or drops are hung

below Toward the audience, downstage

border Short curtain hung above the stage, used to mask the flies

box set Standard set for contemporary, realistic theatre, showing a back wall and two side walls, with the fourth wall understood to be the transparent one, through which the audience views the play

callboard Bulletin board backstage, where notes for a show are posted

cyclorama Curtain or canvas hung at the back of the stage, usually to represent the sky, also called the **cyc**

downstage Part of the stage nearest the audience

drop Curtain or flat hung above the stage and dropped or lowered when needed

flat Single piece of scenery, usually made of muslin, canvas, or linen, stretched over a wooden form, used with other similar units to create a set

flies The area above the stage where curtains, flats, and other scenic elements may be stored until it is time to "fly" them down into view

forestage Part of the stage nearest the audience; *see* **apron**

fourth wall Imaginary partition through which the audience watches the action

Green Room Actor's lounge backstage

grid Framework of wood or steel above the stage, also **gridiron**

ground plan Scaled floor plan that shows the ceiling view of the set, including entrances, windows, doors, and furniture

house All areas of the theatre not onstage or backstage: auditorium, lobby, box office, lounges

legs Flat or curtains at extreme right and left of stage used to mask wings; *see* **tormenters**

mask To conceal from view of the audience

props Any articles handled or carried by the actor

proscenium Opening through which audience views the stage; *see* **arch**

rake To place the floor of any area of the set on a slant; like a ramp

scrim Net curtain, stretched taut, which can become transparent or opaque depending on how it is lit, so that the audience may or may not be able to see through it

sight lines Areas of the stage visible to the audience

spill Light leaks around the edges of a lighting area

stage left Left side of the stage from the actor's point of view, facing the house

stage right Right side of the stage from the actor's point of view, facing the house

teaser Border curtain just upstage and in back of the front curtain

thrust Form of staging with the audience on three sides of the stage, which is thrust from the fourth side into the house

tormenters Flats or curtains at the extreme right and left of stage; *see* **legs**

wings Left and right offstage areas

Acting Areas

The terrain of the stage is mapped out with the following major areas. Some directors elect to break up the acting area into more or less separate areas, but these are where you move on major crosses during the process of staging a play (see Figure 6-1).

Which of these areas are stronger and which weaker? The centerstage areas are relative, but the most commonly accepted hierarchy for the others, from most powerful to least, is shown in Figure 6-2.

Can you see why? Areas 1 and 2 are center and are framed by the arch. As a culture, we are trained to look left first, because we read that way. Any of these factors may be changed by adding a platform (which will put a character on a much higher, more compelling level) or any number of other manipulations of the space. The relative power of areas also alters with nonproscenium staging (see Figure 6-3).

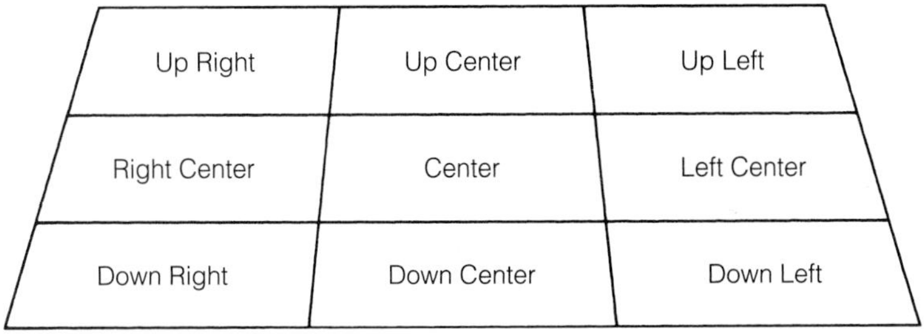

Up Right	Up Center	Up Left
Right Center	Center	Left Center
Down Right	Down Center	Down Left

Figure 6-1   Acting Areas

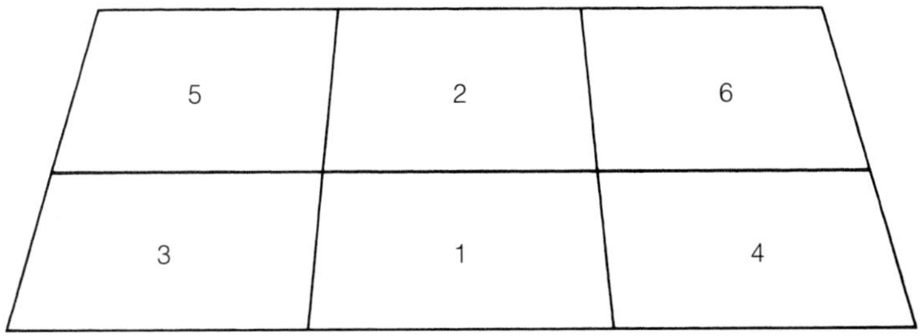

5	2	6
3	1	4

Figure 6-2   Area Power

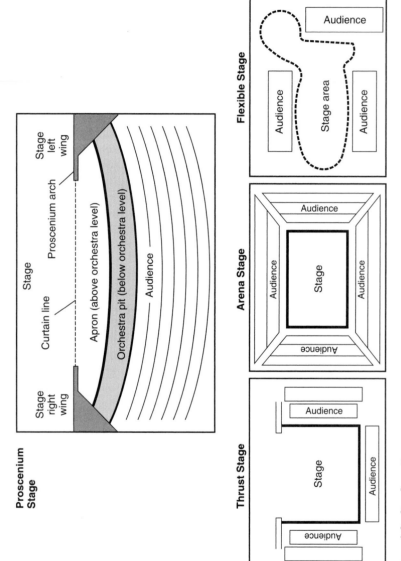

Figure 6-3 Stage Perspectives

Exercise 6.1

Using the Map

Execute the following basic moves:

1. Walk from the *cyc* to the *apron*, then to the *downleft leg*.
2. Stand downstage of the downleft tormenter and look at the grid.
3. Start at the *border* and move in a triangle, with the other points being a *tormenter* on either side of the stage.
4. Move from the *right arch* to the *cyc*, then to beneath the *batten*.
5. Make up additional problems for individual class members to practice.

Have each person write down a three-part problem and then draw slips of paper. Do the map maneuver written there.

Stage Movement

As anyone who has ever been lost will tell you, reading a map and using it aren't the same thing. Once you have locations down, there is a new vocabulary for using the space:

bit A particularly striking or theatrical piece of business, not to be confused with a single motivational unit

blocking Those movements of the actor that are set by the director at some point in the rehearsal process

breaking* Dropping character suddenly, often by laughing or in some way "breaking up"

bridge Transition from one unit to another

business Pantomimed action with or without props, the smaller movements not involving full crosses

cheat To turn toward the audience while appearing to focus on another player onstage to be seen better

closed turn Turn executed so that the actor turns his back to the audience

composition Stage pictures created by placing actors and properties in various arrangements

counter Small move in the opposite direction from a move made by another actor to balance stage composition

cue Final word, move, or technical change that signals you to proceed to your next line or movement

cue to cue Skipping lengthy passages and running only those moments where change in responsibility occurs, moving from one cue directly to the next

focus To direct attention toward a focal point so that the audience's attention will follow

front curtain Curtain hanging in the proscenium arch, concealing the stage from audience view

freeze To suddenly stand completely still to form a tableau

give stage To assume a less-dominant position in relation to another actor

hold Any deliberate pause in the play's action

indicating[*] Showing the audience, rather than letting them see; playing actions without intentions

mugging[*] Exaggerating facial expressions and reactions to the point of caricature

open turn Turning so that you are always facing the audience during the movement

places Instruction to take positions for the beginning of the play or scene

presentational Acknowledging the audience, the theatricality of the event, and playing generally toward the house

read To register with the audience, often used to describe the difference between the way an action feels onstage and the way it actually looks from the house, also **play**

representational Creating the impression that the audience is not present, that a real-life situation is being represented onstage so that the audience seems to be eavesdropping

run-through An uninterrupted rehearsal of the play, an act, or scene

schtick Silly or cheap piece of business, usually designed for laughter

share stage To assume a position of equal importance in relation to another actor

stretch To take longer to execute something than would normally occur, often done to allow time for a difficult costume or set change

strike To remove an object from the stage

take A reaction of surprise, usually involving looking again at the source or the audience; takes may be single, double, or triple depending on how many times the look is repeated

take stage To draw audience attention, to assume a stronger stage position

---

*These three terms represent degrees of failure in physical reaction. The actor moves himself farther and farther from the character's perspective and truth as he "progresses" from indicating to mugging to finally breaking, where complete control is lost.

Exercise 6.2

Maneuvering

Execute the following maneuvers. Two actors together onstage.

1. *A* cross downright, *B* counter, both cheat.
2. *A* and *B* face each other. *A* do a closed turn to face the wings. *B* start an open turn a beat later, and *A* stretch your turn so you both finish at the same time.
3. *A* and *B* stand downcenter. *A* take stage from *B* through movement. *B* regain focus by a piece of schtick.
4. *A* and *B* move freely, conversing about the theatre in a presentational manner, finding as many opportunities for takes as possible.

Add other problems from the class for pairs of classmates onstage, either with the audience calling out directions or drawing tasks.

Movement as Technique

> *The place where you stand, the way you use your space,*
> *how to stand in relation to other people in scenes, how you*
> *dance with them, that's what acting's all about.*
>
> —Sean Connery

Once you understand stage vocabulary and maneuvers, you are ready to use the space to achieve effects. The more you know about how stage pictures are continually created and dissolved, the more comfortable you'll be in the space. It will feel more and more like home, and you will look, to the audience, as if you really live there.

Exercise 6.3

Living Pictures

If you and your partner are onstage, before you ever physically move to another spot, there is the feeling of an active relationship between the two of you and between each of you and the audience. Try each of the following pictures. Ask yourself, what is the impression if:

1. The two of you stand quite close, facing each other, in profile to the audience?
2. Same as situation 1, but with considerable distance between the two of you?

3. Same as situation 2, but with pieces of furniture actually separating you?

4. You are standing close, but your partner's back is turned to you?

5. You are standing close, but your back is turned to your partner?

6. You are close, but both of you are facing opposite directions?

7. If the distance of situation 2 and the separations of situation 3 are added to the relationships of 4, 5, and 6?

8. You are standing close, but both of you are facing full front?

9. Both of you are full back?

10. Both of you are one-quarter left or right? Three-quarters left or right?

11. One of you is one-quarter left, the other one-quarter right? You switch?

12. The same combinations of three-quarter left and right?

13. One of you full front and the other full back?

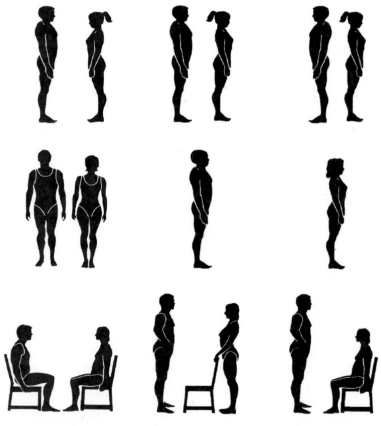

Figure 6-4 Implied Relationships

14. Any other combination, including profile?

15. Take any of the close-to-each-other combinations and put it up center?

16. Move it down center?

17. Move it to any of the other four major acting areas?

18. Take situation 4, but you are in the upright area and your partner is down center? The two of you reverse?

19. Any other situation with the two of you in different acting areas?

20. Same as 19, but with varying proximities to pieces of furniture?

21. Back to situation 1, but you are both sitting?

22. You are both kneeling?

23. Both of you are on a staircase or ramp? Both up on a platform?

24. Any situation listed, with both of you reclining? Both lying down?

25. Any situation listed so far, with each of you in one of the following positions, but always different from each other:

On a platform	Kneeling
On a staircase or ramp	Reclining
Standing	Lying down
Sitting	

See Figure 6.4.

Before even adding business or overt movement, strong messages would have been sent about how open the two characters were to each other and to the audience, about how equal they were, about who was dominant and who subservient, about degrees of dominance, about barriers to contact, and about the relative involvement or indifference of each participant.

Exercise 6.4

Offstage Pictures

1. If you are not already aware of this from the imitation exercises in Chapter 3, try to note whether you have a tendency to face people at one-quarter instead of straight on, whether you tend to stand when others are sitting, which of the physical tendencies mentioned are most and least characteristic for you in life.

2. When you see two people from a distance, note the immediate judgment you make regarding exactly what might be going on between them.

Exercise 6.5

Adding Motion

If the two of you are standing in profile, as in the very first situation in Exercise 6.3, what is the impression if:

1. You are both gesturing with full large bubble, extending arms all the way out and even involving legs in the conversation?

2. You gesture in a normal, everyday range?

3. You gesture in a tight, close-to-the-torso manner?

4. There is any contrast between the two of you in gestural patterns?

5. You both use hand props to emphasize everything you wish to say?

6. One of you uses hand props, but the other does not?

7. You both make long crosses every time you speak?

8. You both make short crosses of just a few feet?

9. One of you moves a great distance and the other a short distance?

10. One of you moves and the other is always still?

11. One of you moves a lot but does not really gesture, while the other stands in place but gestures fully?

12. The movements are relatively constant throughout the scene?

13. Large moves come after at least a minute of no movement at all?

14. One of you moves in an erratic, varying pattern while the other is quite predictable?

15. You both tend to move directly and then stop, or instead both move to an intermediate location, then change directions before you finally stop? If there is a contrast of directness between you?

16. Recalling your basic body positions when static, your movements tend to be largely pointed straight upstage or downstage?

17. There is constant countering, with moves seeming to go back and forth between the proscenium arch?

18. There is a greater use of the diagonal by both or one of you?

19. There is a tendency to circle each other and to move in curves, S-shapes, or figure 8s? If one person uses these circular moves while the other is always heading straight for a target?

20. The movements themselves are rapid and darting?

21. All movements are slow, steady, almost lugubrious?

22. There is a contrast in tempo-rhythms between characters or at various moments in the scene?

23. A movement comes just before a line?

24. The line comes first, then the cross?

25. The line is broken, with a movement occurring somewhere in the middle? If one character falls into a movement pattern while the other is quite varied?

These tools, combined with the list in Exercise 6.3, give the actor an almost unlimited combination of ways to communicate a relationship. The more you practice and observe these maneuvers as pure technique, the more responsive the body becomes to discovering appropriate moves in a more spontaneous way. Once you've been exposed consciously to all the modulations, it is amazing how many simply come to you when you are exploring within a scene.

Exercise 6.6

Exchanges

Use the following brief exchanges of dialogue to explore the staging relationships covered so far. Which changes in basic stage picture, business, stage movement, and timing alter the impact of the lines most significantly?

1: Your place or mine?
2: Neither.

1: I'm so excited. I'm just going to hold my breath 'til we get the news!
2: You do that.

1: How cold, crude, and rude.
2: Yes, those are my lawyers. You'll be hearing from us.

1: How do you like my outfit?
2: You know, a lot of people couldn't get away with a look like that.

When you get larger groups of actors in the space, many variables are added. The most important principle is *contrast*. Whenever an actor does something differently from all the others, it will take focus. So you may be sitting in a weak area of the stage with your back to the audience, but if it is full of actors in stronger areas, all standing and facing forward, you will be what we watch. Also, no matter what kinds of pictures exist, the minute someone moves, all eyes will go in the direction of the moving target.

Exercise 6.7

Contrast

Go back over the lists in the preceding exercises, and find situations in which an actor might position himself in such a way that it would normally be considered a weak choice, but could be quite powerful, simply because of contrast.

Onstage/Offstage Comparisons

Simple good manners offstage need to be modified for purposes of audience attention onstage, just so the right person can be seen and heard. These are not rules, but they are principles almost universally followed:

1. You usually cross in front of another character, unless that character is seated and you can be seen the whole time.

2. Generally, look at people who are entering or exiting to help direct attention.

3. Entering characters move well onto the stage and do not linger at the entrance. They also leave completely. Half-moves distract out front.

4. Actors do not often move at the same time unless momentary chaos is intentional. The audience gets confused about where to look.

5. Move on your own lines and usually remain absolutely still on those of other actors.

6. Remain as open to the audience as possible when speaking, with particular awareness of keeping your face, especially your eyes, visible much of the time.

7. All other factors being equal, if you are standing and the other person is sitting, you will dominate. Even though possessing the chair may seem the more powerful position, as it would be offstage, the audience, looking through the picture frame, sees one person looming powerfully over another. The possession does not read nearly as strong as the height. All such assessments of dominance need to be considered as seen through a picture frame.

8. Minimize eye contact. Inexperienced actors look at each other either not at all or too much. Michael Shurtleff, the famous casting director, estimates real people look at each other only 10 percent of the time. He may be right. Connecting with your partner does not mean staring at her relentlessly. In fact, if there is only one other person in the scene, eye contact tends to lower, because there is no need to signal to whom your remarks are being directed.

Offstage, even when you're in a position that forces you to face another person (like a restaurant booth), note how often your eyes dart away or settle on other targets.

When you are in the vast outdoors with a companion, note how seldom the two of you lock eyes and how much of the time you focus on surroundings.

Voice Maneuvers

Although the writer determines word choice, the actor is responsible for adjusting the control knob on each of the other vocal categories (quality, tempo, rhythm, articulation, pronunciation, pitch, volume, and nonverbals) that we covered in Chapter 3. Each of these is worth working on separately offstage. You might pick a day when rhythm is what you are listening for, in others, and experimenting with, on your own. Try working your way through each category, on different days, aiming to expand your range in that particular aspect of vocal life before the day is over.

The most frequent request from directors and coaches is for variety, for the actor to simply use *more* of everything, to break out of a very narrow vocal life. Most actors need to expand their expressive mode by letting the pitch slide into the upper registers and down into the lower, the quality move into different textures as they describe a range of feelings, to speed up, slow down, and hit a middle stride with less predictability. We're not talking about changing your own vocal tendencies, so much as broadening them. Most of us tend to trap the voice in a tiny expressive mode. Actors learn to use more voice, period.

Vocal Directions

The following are terms used for standard requests, made at rehearsals, during notes, and in class critiques:

anticipate To respond earlier than your cue, revealing that the actor knows what is coming, even though the character would not

build To increase any combination of vocal techniques for a speech to reach a climax

curtain line Last line in scene or any other line requiring pointing up, also called **tag line**

diphthong Two consecutive vowel sounds

drop To omit or to say inaudibly

dynamics Energy, color, and variety of speech

elongate To stretch out or take longer to say

emphasis Pointing out, by stress or any other technique, particular words or sounds

inflection A change in pitch

intonation A series of pitch changes on a vowel

melody pattern A predictable use of pitch, which can be graphed like notes on a musical scale

onomatopoeia Characteristic of a word that sounds, in speech, like what it identifies (saying the word *slap* sounds similar to the act of slapping)

overlap To begin speaking during another actor's speech; not to be confused with anticipating, because overlapping may be both deliberate and natural

paraphrase To say words that convey the meaning of the line but are not those of the playwright

phoneme Any single sound of the English language

phrasing Sectioning speech into units for emphasis and breathing

resonate To use as sounding area, usually a request to change

set-up First of three parts to comic line in which subject is introduced, followed by a pause, then the punch line

speed-through Running lines as rapidly as possible while still maintaining sense, mood, and relationships

stress To place greater weight on a particular portion of a word or phrase; *see* **emphasis**

stretch To take longer with a speech, often by elongating individual vowels

substitute To insert one sound in place of another

support Sustaining sound, projected from within, without allowing waste of breath

swallow To fail to project or resonate certain sounds

tap To hit a consonant lightly, firmly, and briefly

top To register more strongly than a preceding line, usually by speaking louder and faster

throw-away To give a line only the slightest emphasis, usually for comic effect, because the words themselves register so strongly

trithong Three consecutive vowels, employed in few standard sounds, but often true of regional speech or dialects

voice/unvoice To vibrate the vocal folds so that a sound reverberates or not, as in *p* (unvoiced) and *b* (voiced)

undercut To deliver line with much less intensity than the preceding one, usually to deflate; the opposite of **topping**

Exercise 6.8

Vocal Changes

1. Pick a line of dialogue. Face one wall of the room. Begin the line in your head voice. When you get to the corner, switch to your sinus voice. When you get to the next corner, switch to your throat or pharyngeal voice. At the last corner, employ your chest voice. In each instance you are trying to resonate from the body part mentioned. Change lines and expand to other resonators until you feel aware of the differences.

2. Play catch with sound. Throw a "one" to your partner, with one of you onstage and the other out in the house. Give the "one" definite weight and shape so he knows what kind of ball to catch. Partner repeats "one" as you catch it. Then throw a "two" back. Vary the distance between you, the weight, and mass of the sound, and the degree to which the receiver needs to move quickly or some distance to catch the sound where it has been thrown.

Vocal Technique

> *If you learn to be truthful first, it's terribly hard to learn to be heard. And if you learn to be heard first of all, it's terribly hard to speak truthfully.*
> —Geraldine Page

Even though mastery of your own voice starts later and happens more slowly than mastery of your body, it's worth the daily grind when your sound is finally really yours. The first step is to expand your own speech repertoire so that you have more choices whenever you start to speak a line. Every time you hear another version of the nine voice elements or of the vocal directions mentioned, play with it and try to capture it. The following exercises, if pursued regularly, will offer you a wider range of possibilities:

Exercise 6.9

Adding Repertoire

1. Go back over the two-line scenes employed for movement exercises and use each of the vocal directions to add yet another dimension to the relationships. Even if the direction appears to imply a negative speech characteristic, see what characterizing it may achieve.

2. In groups of two, draw slips of paper on which are written each of the items on the vocal directions list. Quickly improvise dialogue to demonstrate the concept. Class guesses which vocal maneuver was being employed.

Exercise 6.10

T-shirt Philosophy

These lines appear on T-shirts I have seen. Their humor works without working the delivery of the line. Relax and experiment, knowing that variation can only enhance each line's impact:

"I said maybe and that's final!"

"If a man speaks in the forest and there's no woman to hear him, is he still wrong?"

"You have the right to remain silent. Use it!!"

"I used to be indecisive, but now I'm not so sure."

"I said no to drugs, but they wouldn't listen."

"Caution: I go from zero to bitch in 2.7 seconds."

"You'd look better with duct tape over your mouth."

"Jesus loves you. It's the rest of us who think you're an asshole."

"I'm not a vegetarian because I love animals. I am a vegetarian because I hate plants!"

"I want to do my part to make the world a better place, but murder is illegal."

"I don't have an attitude problem. You have a perceptual problem."

"You. Me. Whipped Cream. Handcuffs. Any questions?"

"I don't know what your problem is, but I bet it's hard to pronounce."

"You call me a freak like it's a bad thing."

"I'm only wearing black until they make something darker."

"I started with nothing. I have most of it left."

Exercise 6.11

Old T-shirts

These are still worth working for timing and inflection:

"Better to remain silent and be thought a fool than to speak and remove all doubt."

"The future isn't what it used to be."

"Having sex is like playing bridge. If you don't have a good partner, you'd better have a good hand."

"Life is a bed of roses, but watch out for the pricks."

"Conform. Go crazy. Or become an artist."

"The difference between genius and stupidity is that genius has its limits."

"I refuse to have a battle of wits with an unarmed person."

"You're twisted, perverted and sick. I like that in a person."

"Obviously, the only rational solution to your problem is suicide."

"A woman without a man is like a fish without a bicycle."

"Don't tell me what kind of day to have."

"Reality is for people who lack imagination."

"You're the reason my children are so ugly."

"Men [or, depending on the speaker, Women] should come with instructions."

"Keep America beautiful—Stay home."

"Sex is like snow. You never know how many inches you'll get or how long it's going to last."

"Stupid people shouldn't breed."

"Experience is what you get when you didn't get what you wanted."

"Onward through the fog."

Word choice is, of course, set, but . . .

1. Which voice quality best brings out the line's impact? (Review Exercises 3.11: Resonators, and 3.12: Classic Voices, *pages 97–98*.)

2. Which lines should be rapidly or slowly delivered? Should some alter tempo as the line progresses?

3. Where should pause be used, and where should a word or syllable be punched for effect? Where should emphasis be placed and how strong should it be? What rhythmic variations are possible?

4. Are there specific sounds that can be crisply emphasized as spoken? Any that might be slurred or thrown away? How might articulation alter?

5. Would any line be enhanced by a dialect or accent, by a pronunciation other than standard?

6. Do any lines seem to cry out for a high or low pitch or for a change mid-thought? Where does a change in pitch prove most effective?

7. Does the line work well almost whispered? Bellowed? With the volume knob adjusted as it progresses?

8. Are there any nonverbal additions that might be amusing or enlightening? Any places for a slight stammer, a growl, a deep sigh, any other sound beyond the words themselves?

Burning

When called upon to play anger, some actors burst into loud, uncontrolled explosions of wild emotion, like the violent yellow, orange, and bright red flames of a very hot fire, striking, vivid, and, if not contained, dangerous. This may feel good, even great, as it happens, because it allows a deeply satisfying barrage of emotion. There is an undeniable rush from getting hysterical in sanctioned circumstances. One of the great highs of acting is to bust out in public with what is often considered unacceptable behavior, even in private! Unfortunately, such bursts can come across as overwrought. They may be all strident angst and too overwhelming for the observer.

As an actor, it can be especially depressing to be told you went overboard after being encouraged all term to go for it. So I wasn't giving enough and now they are telling me I did too much? What's that about?

Were you accused of being a histrionic actor? Did you feel a great rush, but now need to ask yourself how self-indulgent that rush may have been? Was it actually related to your being able to go for it in front of an audience, which is akin to showing off, rather than responding in an honest way in the context of the play? Was there some element of the "Watch me, Mom!" that took you over in other events? It all comes back to truth.

Fortunately our real life experiences can guide us back to truthful acting. We all know how to burn with a great variety of flames.

When you are really "pissed off" what do you do? Unless you are a loose cannon, always tempestuous and explosive, you are more likely to express your anger in ways that are not huge. The first thing most of us do is try to hide how enraged we are until it becomes impossible to hold it in. You may try to joke about it, perhaps with implied venom behind the joking. You may withdraw and expect your partner to pursue your feelings at a distance after dropping hints of how offended you are. You may practice how you will confront the other because you know that without rehearsal, you will collapse and forget what you intended to say. So, you may present a calculated case for your outrage with as much control as you can muster. If you do explode, you almost always also try to take it down at least for a while so that you can communicate and not just rage. In other words, your anger usually has an ebb and flow.

The image of a fire, whether in a fireplace or on an old fashioned stove can assist in understanding anger. A real deep anger is often expressed in a blue flame, which can be the most powerful because it burns at a constant hot level and does not vary.

Consider these burning levels:

> Yellow and Orange—Unbridled rage like forest fires out of control, huge leaping flames, lots of smoke, an apocalyptic sense of non-negotiable anger. You are freaking out.

Red—Furious but controlled. You are way mad but directed. You could revert back to the colors above at any moment and no one near you wants that to happen.

Blue—This powerful anger comes from a place of deep, constant, controlled rage. It burns steady and is hot beyond touching so you do not want to mess with it. Most important it is constant.

What is important to know about blue flame is that it is often the most frightening. People who are freaking out will probably get tired eventually and you can just let them exhaust themselves. They might also realize that they have gone over the top and collapse in embarrassment. The mere fact that they are out of control can, in some circumstances, give you an advantage if you are the recipient of their rage. Think of the hysterical parents yelling at offspring in the grocery store and the offspring who have learned to ignore it because it will soon pass.

But those who threaten with controlled, calm, often deeply subtle menace are those you do not wish to mess with, because they can sustain this for a very long time. They truly embody the "don't get mad, get even" adage. Or, more importantly, they can be profoundly vengeful in a sustained and controlled way.

Ask yourself every time you want just a hot colors burn if it is just you wishing to go for it or if perhaps the character might release anger into the enormous power of blue, lavender, purple—places of less loud but still strong engagement.

Exercise 6.12

Flames

1. Consider these lines in which the speaker is angry:

   "If you do that I will take out you, your family, and every place and person you have ever loved."

   "How dare you? I am so offended I could hurl you into the f_ _king ocean. Just get away from me and never come near me again."

   "What you have done is unforgivable. You have abused me before, but this surpasses any violation I ever even imagined."

   "You are a total piece of s_ _t."

   "Excuse me? Did you just say what I heard? Then you are such an unbelievable asshole that I just have to tell you."

   "You have lost every ounce of trust, faith, or respect any of us ever had for you."

2. Select a context for each line, a circumstance where saying this would be easily motivated.

3. Try each line in each of the three categories noted above:

   —orange and yellow
   —red
   —blue

4. Analyze what was effective about each choice. Now go back and start the line at one level of anger and allow it to change somewhere to one of the other levels.

5. Continue to observe and experiment with the various ways anger is expressed, always seeking variety and surprise.

Coining

The problem some actors run into after they memorize lines is that those lines *sound* memorized. Their delivery may be too flat, too slick, too lacking in discoveries. It does not seem fresh or spontaneous. The actors may also *look* memorized, because of a lack of facial activity particularly in the eyes. In life, we briefly consider our choices before speaking, evaluating the situation and the consequences of choosing among the alternative statements we might make, during which our eyes are very active. This may happen in a second, but it is a very *full* second.

Coins are created when metal is stamped with a pattern, also called minting. But another major definition of coining is "to make up, invent or fabricate, as to coin a new word." While you may not actually be inventing a word that no one has ever used before it is important that you go through the process of searching and discovering what you want to say and then metaphorically "stamping" it as you say it. You are inventing your phrases or the way you put words together. It is also important to forget that these words were ever printed in a script and have been spoken by other actors before. In your imagination, you are the first person ever to say them.

Here is an example of a speech that may involve coining:

> "I value our friendship more than I can say, so it is hard to me to tell you that while I welcome your visits most of the time, I really need you to let me know before just stopping by. I should probably be more flexible. But I just like to know if someone I care about is coming over beforehand. Can you live with that? I hope so."

Because the speaker is asking a friend to change behavior, words will be carefully chosen so as not to offend. Here is an example of other words that might be considered before those selected.

> "I (care about, cherish, like) value our friendship more than I can say, so it is (challenging, uncomfortable, nerve wracking) hard to me to tell you that while I (am ok with, like, enjoy) welcome your visits most of the time, I (totally, absolutely, completely) really need you to (call, phone, contact me) let me know before just (showing up, popping in, surprising me) stopping by. I should probably be (less fussy, easier going, not so concerned) more flexible. But I just like to know if someone I (love, like, think is important) care about is coming by beforehand. Can you (tolerate, not get pissed, accept) live with that? I hope so."

In life, we are creating our script as we go along. When we act, we need to at least create the illusion that we do not quite know how the sentence will end when we begin.

Here are other signs of coining:

1. There is just the slightest retard as you swiftly scan your options and then pick one.

2. The eyes are moving, sometimes even darting, as you seek to 'see' the right word choice.

3. If your character is lying and not good at it, there will be a great deal of extra eye movement as the character searches for cover or false answers that might come across as true.

4. There is an instant of reaction *after* the word is spoken, in which you may be satisfied, even thrilled with the word you chose or still not entirely happy with it, even way disappointed, but need to go on, a second retard similar in length to the one you took before jumping in with what you said.

5. If you are satisfied with your choice, the eye activity will abruptly halt and you will regain focus on your listener. If you are not satisfied, your eyes may continue to search for something better or you will simply avoid eye contact lest you reveal your dissatisfaction. This will be equally true if you are lying or just not that happy with how you have expressed yourself.

6. If it is not going all that well (you are not making your points as eloquently as you would wish and/or your partner is not responding at all the way you hoped, you are likely to get even more careful and take more time with up-coming choices. So the retards, particularly those preceding speech, will be extended in length.

7. If your listener is unfamiliar to you or reacting in a way you did not expect and therefore *becoming* less familiar, you may also gauge to see how he or she is taking it and then allow that information to influence how tender, harsh, candid or diplomatic our next choice might be, both in word choice and tone of voice. So your eyes move from word searching to sharp focus on the other person and then back to word search mode, back and forth until you are reasonably sure of how things are going again.

8. Sometimes you actually punch, extend or chew on a word to help make it better than it would be with a fairly flat delivery, to give it more oomph. The word itself you know is not all that brilliant but you will make effort at a brilliant pronunciation to compensate, or it is brilliant already and you will rise to that by your delivery.

9. If you are insecure and tentative, you may end a speech with an upward inflection so that a declarative statement sounds more like a question. You are giving yourself away by in essence asking the person if this is OK even though you have not posed a question per se. Use this very selectively as there may be nothing more irritating than perpetual "up speak".

10. If your character loses confidence as the speech continues, your volume may drop and your diction turns to mumbling as you finish the sentence. The assertiveness level simply trickles off, which is the opposite of 8 above.

11. If you choose a metaphor or simile (for example: "Whenever I criticize you I feel like this yipping, pesky little dog who just can't shut up, especially because you always listen and take it patiently like a wise old St. Bernard.") there will be more time just before and after because you are moving out of everyday straight speech into a somewhat less natural mode that requires some creativity. It isn't just a matter of choosing words, but of pulling the experience out of human into dog universe to make the point more vivid and clear.

12. Metaphor is a powerful way to get people to listen because it removes the experience just enough from direct confrontation to another world. If your statement is more far fetched or creative than dog/human parallels (I feel when we are together that . . . we are galactic travelers who have left this planet and this time . . . we are on another moon, but it is . . . many years ago . . .) there will be even more retards as you create the imagery because it requires preparation and reaction time for both you and your listener as you check in to make sure you are sharing this metaphoric journey.

13. When you breathe, you are also likely to be doing an internal assessment of how it is going that plays across your face. Your inhalation may communicate relief in just being able to breathe, your exhalation will be more likely to be accompanied by self-evaluation and checking in with your partner.

14. If your character is struggling, you may insert stalling sounds, that is, nonverbals such as "uhh," "ah," "er," "oh," "ooh," sighs, and sharp intakes of breath. Playwrights often fail to include or suggest these.

15. If you actually do invent something, that is you "coin" a particularly witty, original or vivid phrase or comment), you are likely to stop and relish it for a moment right afterwards, almost as if you are patting yourself on the back.

The best way to become a better coiner as an actor is to sharply observe yourself and others in life. You already do many of the items above offstage. You just need to insert them into your acting.

Exercise 6.13

Coining

Take an actual monolog and write out the alternative words or phrases not selected as in the example at the beginning of this section. Pick six lines in a scene you are working on that are giving you some trouble. Do the same for them.

Go through either a scene or monolog concentrating entirely on:

1. The various eye movements described above.
2. The retards described that occur just before and after a statement.
3. The tendency to strongly emphasize, let fade away, upward inflect, and other variations in terms of delivery described.
4. Experimenting with when and how you breathe and what is going on inside for you when that occurs.
5. Adding crucial non-verbals whenever they will assist in transitions.

Onscreen versus Onstage

> *Film work is about trying to ignore all the things that are suspended above my head and those 50 people who aren't supposed to be there, but actually aren't.*
>
> –Mamie Gummer
>
> *Stage is much more intimidating than going before the cameras because you can really screw up, and you can't do a retake.*
>
> –Daniel Radcliffe
>
> *Much of filming is really boring. It may take six hours to set up a single shot. You're sitting around forever and then they call and you've got to be on! Instantly on! On the stage, you have two and a half hours of intense concentration. But then it's over.*
>
> –Anna Paquin
>
> *In films there is no performance. You just shoot a lot of rehearsals and pick the best.*
>
> –Laurence Olivier

More and more frequently, actors are onscreen before they are onstage. Many never act in plays at all. The professional union for screen actors (Screen Actor's Guild [SAG]) has three times as many members as that for stage actors (Actor's Equity Association [AEA]). Most basic acting principles apply to both circumstances, but there are also distinct differences that you should know when attempting to perform for a camera instead of a live audience.

Repetition

> *I always ask for one more take.*
> —Nicole Kidman

A key contrast between acting for camera and stage is one of repetition. You can do retakes until you get it perfect (or give up), but a live performance is a one-take-only event where the audience is not interested in your second or third attempt.* However, your stage performance is likely to have been repeated so many times in rehearsal that retakes are not needed. The film actor may have a newly memorized, newly revised script never spoken out loud in front of anyone before the moment the cameras run. It may be fresh but raw. Stage actors are also generally expected to stay letter perfect on lines, whereas screen actors may be expected or even encouraged to alter lines for various takes.

Theatre directors have an average of three to six weeks to evolve the production. (*See* Chapter 8.) Any film rehearsal is rare (when the film of the musical *Chicago* rehearsed before filming, it was major news) and costly, so it is far more important to cast actors perfectly and expect them to arrive on set ready. Stage actors get run-throughs and work-throughs, rehearsing the story in the exact order it is written. They have ample opportunity to experience everything from start to finish; to feel and understand the arc of their performances. Screen actors may have to do the ending first. Film shoots wildly out of sequence, sometimes starting with the most intimate encounter or climactic moment. You may divorce someone before you've even met her. You may discover a cure for cancer before you've ever seen a laboratory. You may even die in battle before the war has been declared. Wise film actors often prepare cards for each scene, even placing these cards on a wall in their trailers, so the actors can see the way the story should unfold. The card includes the scene number and page, day, time, and location it takes place, conditioning forces, where you've just been, what you've been doing, where you're going, what you will be doing at the end of the scene, your objective, who will be in the scene with you. Actors can grab the card and take it to the set with them so they have a sense of context.

Screen and stage also differ radically in repetition of performance.

---

*The exception is when some disastrous event (such as a major piece of scenery falling over) or a wild card (such as a wayward animal or child) has paralyzed the show, recovery has somehow happened, and everyone is eager to support you, even cheer you on as you give it another shot.

You do a scene on TV or in movies and that's it. Onstage you get to do it differently the next night.

–Kyle MacLachlan

Theatre is like exercise. It's healthy. But I don't love it as much as movies. A bad experience in the theatre can be so depressing. You've got to do it every night, even if the production is not working.

–Clive Owen

You get to do it differently, but you also "get" to do it over and over. The stage actor has to sustain and repeat a performance for several hours, then again the next day, sometimes twice on matinee days, and again the next week for the entire run. He must, even with some spontaneous shifts in night-to-night interpretation, repeat essentially the same creation over and over. The film actor may be asked to do a single take repeatedly, but that is usually in the course of one day and then it's on to something else. Ironically, although the film actor will probably never have to (or get to) repeat that scene again, it is now permanent, giving her a small degree of immortality (or alas, perhaps infamy). Viewings can be repeated long after her death. The live performance is truly over when it's over.

Size

Theatre is like exploring the universe through a telescope and film is like examining the atom through a microscope.

–Mel Churcher

Stage actors need to project, sometimes all the way to the third balcony of a huge opera house, with much of the audience at some distance. They may need to pantomime reactions so that the performance will "read" to those who cannot clearly see their facial expressions. In contrast, the camera can envelope you in close-up, and the boom or body mike can pick up your subtlest sound. There is usually no need to raise the volume and diction of your speech to be understood, nor to find gestures that define your reactions. You can usually speak as you do in normal conversation or lower still. Even in a small, intimate theatre, no one is as close as a close-up. Your audience may be one very intimate camera lens, catching just your eyes, or it could be hordes of people who will not get any message at all from you unless you make a big, full body gesture that will be clear to the back of the auditorium. For film work, you may need to be more still than you tend to be in real life because even tiny mannerisms and miniscule movement are amplified to the point of distraction.

The size of your performance may be larger onstage, but the size of your filmed image is another matter altogether. It may be projected onto an enormous screen where you will have a head as large as 50 feet tall—and the possibility of facial blemishes of Olympian proportions—which brings us to the issue of scrutiny.

Scrutiny

> *In my 20 years in the theatre, I never got to see myself except through the reaction of the audience, so I was under the impression that I was really hot s_ _t. But the minute you actually see yourself onscreen, the bubble is burst forever!*
>
> —Morgan Freeman

A stage actor can calculate an effect and pull it off impressively, but film tends to expose your technique and effort. So film acting tends to support internal work, whereas stage acting demands external attention to detail. This is not to imply that film is truth and live is technique but, rather, that the stage actor's truth must always be supported by technique.

It is sometimes said that stage acting is based on finding the right activity, and film is about finding the right thoughts or feelings and then just letting the camera in. Some advise film actors to just "be," because anything more can be too much. Screen performers are often asked to move closer to other actors and props than would be normal for everyday interaction because the camera creates space. The camera not only takes in what those close to you do. It takes in more. Those moments when you and a lover are entwined or when a parent who knows you all too well is in your face? It is that close and often closer. Because the camera may take in and enlarge only your eyes, your hands, your feet, your mouth, your butt, it can have an intimacy unavailable to even your closest friends who are usually at least as far away as the other end of the couch. The camera swoops in and scrutinizes your parts and sometimes your soul.

> *The lens has psychic strength. The camera can see beneath the skin.*
>
> —Martin Scorsese

You may have heard or read that Laurence Olivier was widely believed to be the greatest actor of the past century. But when you see one of his films, you may wonder how that could be. This assessment comes largely from those who saw him perform live. He was an amazing and brilliant technician who took big risks and thrilled audiences far enough away not to be able to sense his technique. He rarely reached that impact on film where his work sometimes looks calculated. Richard Burton, also revered as one of the twentieth-century greats, had a voice so huge that it would sometimes overwhelm the camera, the microphone, and all the intimacy of film acting. To this day, many audience members and critics maintain that if you did not experience either of these men in the theatre, you did not experience their magic.

Because of the intensity of the lens and what it notices, it is relatively uncommon for film actors to demonstrate astonishing range. Both Charlize Theron and Nicole Kidman transformed themselves enough to be almost unrecognizable in recent Oscar-winning performances. Meryl Streep has made a career as a chameleon actor. But can you come up with a dozen film actors who consistently morph and shift to demonstrate surprising versatility? Most do not change much externally and are not expected to. It would be unfair, however, to claim that film actors show no range. When you see a retrospective of the work of legends like Katharine Hepburn, Cary Grant, Jimmy Stewart, or Bette Davis, whom one tends to remember as being mostly the same in every film, their versatility is quite stunning. But the range is in nuance rather than an astonishingly different look, sound, inner life, way of moving or relating. There is some way in which we recognize film actors, accept their familiarity, and then let them lead us more quietly to places they may not have taken us before.

The Stanislavski principles outlined in Chapter 4 may shift in prominence because of the differing levels of scrutiny. A skilled screen actor may rely heavily on using public solitude to shut out all the whirling studio or location activity and be completely in the moment. The stage actor will probably more actively employ circles of concentration. As a performance progresses, she sometimes needs to be very aware of the audience out front and the technicians offstage, then mostly on the stage space and her scene partner. At other times she needs to circle in to a private moment that is a constant for her film counterpart. This circle will narrow and expand regularly. The stage actor needs dual consciousness.

Feedback

> *There are more distractions in live theatre. During the most important moment, someone's cell phone will go off, playing the national anthem. Some audience members whisper loud enough that you can hear, and crinkling candy wrappers are ungodly! It's a battle to keep your concentration.*
> —Laura Linney

For better or worse, the stage actor gets constant audience response, whereas the camera is neutral. Though it loves some actors more than others, it never utters this love audibly. It will reveal it later, but tell you nothing as it films. In live theatre, responses during rehearsal and previews as well as director's notes give actors some idea how it's going before opening night and reviews. With film, those present don't actually know how it's going until they see what the camera found. They know little of this day's work until they see the dailies and then still are not certain how this moment fits into the whole. So feedback may be wisely cautious.

There is a constant interplay among stage actors who have been together from the first read-through. They hang out with each other backstage. They offer each other encouragement and advice. Even when they clash, it is genuine tension coming out of mutual experience. The rehearsal period allows you and each of your scene partners to meet often to discuss details and to experiment. The feedback of this partner as you "feed" off each other exchanging dialogue is invaluable. Unless you have scenes with an actor in a film, however, you may co-star with him and never meet him until the publicity jaunt or premiere. And your scene partner may not even be present during the filming of your big speech to her because the only thing on the agenda is your speech. In voiceovers for animated films, even actors with scenes together do not work together, but record each of their lines without any other performer present. In fantasy films, you may perform with a blue screen and need to simply envision your dragon or angel scene partner.

Control

> *If you want someone else to take responsibility away*
> *from you then it's great to be a film actor, because we are*
> *basically pawns.*
> —Goldie Hawn

A stage actor has considerable choice about how each performance will go. A film actor is taken out of the loop earlier on, after which the director can completely control what an audience watches. Your big moment may never make it into the film or it may end up being just the sound of your voice while someone responds to what you are saying, thus the scene ends up being all about how they hear what you say rather than how you say it. Stage performances mostly focus on the speaker. Film just as often chooses the listener, some object in the room, or even the weather outside.

The stage director has to let go of the show as it is gradually turned over to the cast and crew, who will be largely on their own after opening. This director may return to check in occasionally during the run or delegate a staff member to police performers who take too many liberties, but the cast has a great deal of freedom to play. The stage director cannot stop an actor from altering any single performance as the live show runs, but a film director has that performance in the can and can control and transform it by the way it is edited. She can continue to tinker and refine the product: cutting, scoring and tightening, and choosing one shot over another long after filming has ceased and even after initial showings. Some claim films are largely created in the editing room.

Cheating

In stage acting, we are frequently asked to cheat out to the audience by opening up our body positions so that we are something halfway between facing them and our partner. It is used most often in a proscenium space (*see page 188*) where the audience is looking through an opening. This is a position taken in life most often by men who are feeling uncomfortable actually facing each other directly so they focus on either the object of their discussion or the universe in general. In the theatre, it is essential to not shut the audience out. Cheating is often used in film as well but with very distinct conventions. We think of film behavior as entirely natural and lifelike, but each of these adjustments is anything but that. You may be asked to do any of the following:

1. *Moves:* To slow down whatever you are doing to give the camera operator warning to shift and follow you. You must usually make crosses slightly more slowly than in life; the same will be true for rising from a chair, including a bit more preparation before you do so. In movements with props, such as picking up a glass or answering the phone, you may be asked to linger just a bit longer than you might in life as you grasp the prop before you pick it up and then to make the movement less rapidly.

2. *Eyes:* You may be asked to cheat just your eyes. If you are in a shot where your partner's back is to the camera and your face is, you may be asked to look into just one of your partner's eyes, the one closest to the camera to keep your eyes more open to it. The term "eye-line" has developed to guide actors in this form of cheating.

3. *Position:* The camera absolutely hates empty space between actors so it tends to exaggerate this gap, making the two of them seem miles apart when they are actually in normal proximity. You may be asked to move much closer to your partner than you would normally be in life. Sometimes you may actually be pressing against the other person bodily so that your heads can appear to be in a normal relationship on-screen.

Each of these six elements—repetition, size, scrutiny, feedback, control, and cheating—makes a fascinating topic to study as you move back and forth between attending films and live theatre. When you read reviews and anticipate going to a film, consider how it would have been different as a play. When you go to a play, ask the opposite.

Silver Screen versus Tube

Acting for any camera is different from live performance, but there are also key differences between the big and little screens. Film usually has a larger budget, which means more time and more takes. On the average, a TV drama hopes to get five to six minutes of screen time a day, but a film intended for general release goes for one or two. So the process will go much faster in TV filming. But *fast* in this world is a relative term. One big myth of moviemaking is how electrifying and exciting it is. All you need is one visit to the set as hours and hours go by for a few seconds of film to know that it requires extraordinary patience and the capacity to become focused after hours of distraction. Because actors have to be ready and waiting while lighting setups can go on forever, a favorite line film actors use to capture this situation is, "Hurry up and wait!"

Your likeness in close-up can be of King Kong proportions in a movie theatre, but until we all have giant screens at home, it will be considerably smaller on most televisions. Filming decisions are made accordingly. TV films rarely use the ultra close-up. They are designed for distractions because many audience members half-watch in a lit room with more free-flowing conversation than would be tolerated in a movie theatre.* The result is that TV scripts are, for the most part, wordier, with points being repeated for those who may have briefly left the room, with less opportunity to simply show reaction. Film and TV are relatively realistic, but the TV more often goes for a more heightened reality.

Even within the tube world, there are various levels of playing customs. Most films and dramatic series are done with a single camera, but two kinds of shows always shoot with three cameras. Sitcoms (which are generally fast and broad) and soap operas (which tend to be slow and internal) may seem miles apart, but both are closer to live theatre than to single-camera filming because scenes are played all the way through beginning to end. So actors get at least the full sense of a scene during a single taping.

Film Terms

Film actors need to learn a completely new and extensive vocabulary for the staff, equipment, process, challenges, and customs of filmmaking. Many of these terms ("Abby Singer" for the second to the last shot of the day, "Martini" for the last shot,

---

*HBO has often proved the exception in both budget and ambition. Some HBO films have achieved success in general release after being broadcast on the channel.

"Walla" for adding human sounds later, and "Rhubarb" for background conversation) will seem quite eccentric.* Here are just a few that involve the acting process itself:

action Cue, usually given verbally, that the camera is rolling, the shot has begun

ADR Automatic Dialogue Replacement, also called looping, where dialogue on the sound track is re-recorded later.

Big close-up Also ECU (extreme close-up), the tightest shot possible with just your face or part of it

board The order in which scenes will be shot

boom Pole on which the mike is suspended usually just above your head

cheat it Similar to stage acting where you are asked to turn slightly more open to the camera (*see page 202*)

close-up Relatively tight shot from your neck up

close shot Also called *medium close-up*, from your chest up

corpse To laugh while performing

coverage Tight shots filmed out of sequence in a scene to be inserted later

cut Verbal cue that the shot is over

dailies Processed footage from the previous day's filming

dry To forget your lines

eye-line Imaginary line from your eye to whoever or whatever you are looking at

favor Camera position that is going to give more focus or favor one actor in a shot over the other

fix it in post Some element of the performance that is not right but will be altered through technology later in editing

hit your mark Being in the right position on the mark at the right time so you are in focus for the shot. Your mark may be a sandbag or a piece of wood or tape, but most often is somehow arranged in a T shape in which you will be expected to stop straddling the lower line of the T with your toes touching the top.

pickup A portion of the scene that has to be re-shot

print Announcement that the take was satisfactory; sometimes, "in the can"

pull back Shot will start in close-up and slowly widen

---

*Abby Singer was a production assistant who always wanted the current shot to be the last, but somehow one more was always taken. "Martini" is what everyone can go drink if they want now that it is over, so actual "last shot" might be booze. "Walla" and "Rhubarb" sort of approximate the sounds of crowds or generally reactions. Supposedly, a crowd couldn't think of anything to say, and the director said, "Just say rhubarb over and over again, but with great enthusiasm and quietly and it will seem like you are commenting on the action."

radio mike Also called body mike, hidden on your clothing

reverse shot Scene will now be shot from the opposite angle of what has just been done

shot size Distance of the camera that tells you the edges of the frame

signaling Showing (usually too much) overtly what a character feels

single The shot will contain only one actor

take it down Perform more subtly

tight The shot will be so close that you will probably not be able to move at all

traveling shot The camera will follow your movement

wild lines Dialogue recorded with no picture, for possible inclusion later by the film's editor

To Study More

I recommend taking a year of basic acting before enrolling in a specialty Acting for the Camera class, which may not be available on your campus in any case. It helps to have core acting concepts mastered before adapting them to any special context, including film. Or check to make sure the course in question will train you as an actor, not just as a film technician. You can also study independently.

A host of books and at least a dozen instructional videos on acting for the camera are available. I would start with these two fairly recent books, which deal succinctly with the process of making peace with camera and studio process and offer lots of good advice on simply being a good actor:

Robert Benedetti. *Action! Acting for Film and Television.* Needham Heights, MA: Allyn & Bacon. 2001.

A short handbook from a producer who used to be a teacher, this is clear, concise, and easy to follow. Divided into two parts: (1) Working with the Camera; (2) Preparing Yourself and Your Role. Offers exercises for you and a friend working with a home camera.

Mel Churcher. *Acting for Film.* London: Virgin Books. 2003.

A longer, more in-depth examination by a British former actor, who has served as acting coach on films around the world, this book offers an international and a woman's perspective on the process. Lots of entertaining anecdotes.

Even though there are newer videos, the best first one to view is probably still:

Michael Caine—Acting in Film. New York: Applause. 1990. Caine is the consummate production-proof actor, always good even when he is acting opposite muppets or sharks. His careful, personal instruction is clear, humble, and empathetic. (Book available as well.)

More and more student films seem to be made each year. Watch for notices of chances to get involved in these bare-bones projects that help you adjust to the camera without adding in the entire studio and massive production team distractions.

Making peace with the camera itself is also a worthwhile endeavor, especially if you are not a "video baby" whose every major transition has been recorded by your family. And even if you are, it is quite different to adjust to seeing yourself perform a character other than the one you evolved in your household over the years. If you have regular access to a camera, use it as a rehearsal tool for acting class projects and observe how you adjust your work for it to be most effective on tape rather than what works best in class.

Scale

> *To Kate [Winslet] I would say, "Go bigger, bigger, bigger,"*
> *but I couldn't say that in front of Jim [Carrey], because he*
> *would hear that and react to it. I would go to Jim and say,*
> *"This needs to be dark."*
> —Michael Gondry (on directing Eternal Sunshine
> of the Spotless Mind)

A common actor adage is, "Less is more." This is a warning to beginners not to push or try too hard and a reminder to more experienced actors to trust themselves and not to haul out all their ammunition. It is encouragement to allow simplicity and perhaps mystery into the performance, with less showing and more being. Many young actors take this advice so strongly that they have difficulty being both big and honest when both are clearly needed. The fear of being inauthentic or giving a "cheesy" performance often inhibits actors from doing enough to communicate fully to an audience by reaching the emotional heights a character demands. They end up being smaller than life.

> *Minnie Driver would keep running up to me between takes*
> *and asking, "Do you think I'm over-the-top here?" And I*
> *said, "Well, no one ever paid to see under-the-top."*
> —Joel Schumacher (on directing the film *Phantom of the Opera*)

Even though film acting *generally* tends to be smaller and stage acting larger, both need to vary in size under specific circumstances. The term "scale" is borrowed from architecture, where small cabins may be "scaled" to intimate proportions and grand palaces to enormous ones and where furniture may vary from dollhouse to giant size. The size of an actor's performance may be minuscule to monumental. Scale is influenced by these factors: style of show, size of character, type of space, and size of shot.

Style of Show

Most actor training starts with contemporary realism, the style that dominates our culture. But even within what seems like a reasonable facsimile of real behavior, scale may vary. You may have noticed that the acting in TV dramas tends to be more contained and subtler than that in sitcoms. You may have also noticed that performances in sketch shows (such as *Saturday Night Live*) are usually broader than that in sitcoms. The latter two are often taped before live audiences, which tends to heighten the playing energy and make them hybrid performances, neither pure stage nor screen. Within comedy itself, terms like *farce*, *slapstick*, *satire*, *parody*, and *screwball comedy* are all used when human behavior is played big and reactions are scaled high. Refined drawing room comedies of manners, sometimes called high, genteel, or character comedies, may be pitched more subtly. So even though comedy may generally be bigger than drama, it has its own continuum.

Realism itself did not emerge until the middle of the nineteenth century. Many so-called classical (sometimes called "period style") plays are about characters who are larger than life (at least larger than most of our lives). They may be monarchs, warriors, witches, fairies, even gods, and they function in a universe that demands performing on a relatively grand scale. Actors need to heighten their own personas to measure up to those of the characters. When a show is not realistic, it is often described as done in a certain style. Because their names, such as Naturalism, Expressionism, and Romanticism, end with the same syllable, these styles are sometimes called "The Isms." Of all of these, only Naturalism encourages playing on a smaller scale. The others tend to exaggerate or distort what passes for everyday behavior into something more extraordinary. It would be a mistake, however, to assume that all eccentric, offbeat text automatically requires large-scale interpretation. Often the absurdity of a particular world can be most effectively realized with low-key acting. You need to look for actual evidence in the script that the world it creates should be larger than life.

Size of Character

Within any given script, some characters may be drawn more broadly than others are. The eccentric, zany neighbor who pops in with some offbeat interlude is fairly standard in tube cultures as is the way-over-the-top, uber-villain in action movies. In Shakespeare's comedies, there is almost always one buffoon whose behavior is far broader and more ridiculous than the rest of the dramatis personae. A character consistently under extraordinary pressure may react bigger than do those less challenged. And the actor's own tendencies need to be placed against those of the character. In the previous quote, director Michael Gondry was dealing with Kate Winslet, an actor whose impressive body of work had never included a character as wildly eccentric and free spirited as Clementine. He was also dealing with Jim Carrey, whose work has largely been the opposite—huge, zany, signature characters. Playing Joel, who is by far the more subdued and depressed of the two main characters, was a challenge. The director not only had to make sure that Winslet and Carrey were in the same film, but that in many ways they traded actor tendencies.

> *In this film, I'm playing "the Jim Carrey part" and Jim's playing "the Kate Winslet part."*
> –Kate Winslet
>
> *My gonzo acting style? That's the only way I know to go about it. Do it strong or do it wrong.*
> –Will Ferrell

Few actors have succeeded more in playing large scale than Will Ferrell, whose characters, though huge, never seem to be commented on, never seem to come from a mean-spirited place. Actually, his biggest jerks often come across as relatively lovable. It will be fascinating to see if he chooses characters of a smaller scale in the future.

Type of Space

The need to change the size of your performance is not limited to whether you are on-screen or off. Actors may audition in small hotel rooms, hallways, or giant auditoriums. They may perform in intimate spaces where fewer than fifty people can be seated or in huge opera houses, outdoor amphitheatres, and coliseums for thousands of audience members. Unfortunately, many of us rehearse in one space and then perform in another and fail to adjust our performances accordingly. I have often had the experience of actors preparing for major audition competitions, working in an intimate rehearsal room and then they "play small" even though they audition in a vast theatre where their auditors are now at least 50 feet farther away from them than I ever was as we coached. As a judge at such competitions, I have sometimes felt overwhelmed with volume, intensity, and sheer size of performance even though we were in a small classroom and I was only 3 feet away from the artists in question, whose presentations gave new meaning to being blown away. No one wants to feel too close to be comfortable. The reverse can also be true if actors have recently rehearsed in a large theatre and are now auditioning in a normal-sized classroom. Actors always need to think about where they prepared and where they are now.

So big spaces need large scale and small spaces tiny scale, right? Alas, it's not that simple. Some huge theatres are brilliantly designed with the seats stacked so that each audience member is very close to the stage and have acoustics that allow the most intimate use of the voice. Conversely, there are small theatres where the audience is spread out on a single plain and sound is dreadful, demanding far more projection/diction by performers. The height of the ceiling, attention to sound-friendly wall and ceiling surfaces, and backstage masking are just a few factors that can alter the playability of a space. Is there amplification of sound? If so, it may be unnecessary to push vocal work, while still using large physical expressiveness, so you pump up one part of your performance but not the other. It is important to know the reputation and history of the space for scaling a performance to work best there.

Size of Shot

Although much film work involves close shots and close-ups where intimacy and subtlety are essential, as the camera moves out for a medium or long shot, the actor may be asked to engage the whole body and to respond as if the listener is some distance away. The longer the shot, the more similar the acting demands become to those in a traditional theatre space.

You cannot tell the size of the shot from the location of the camera because you do not know to what degree a zoom or telephoto lens will be employed. When auditioning or working on camera, it is important to find out what the size is. You need to know the terms, repeated from the vocabulary list; if in doubt, you can ask to move your hands to the top and side edges of the frame so you can determine the limitations of your movements.

Camera shots fall into seven basic categories, moving from great distance to practically under the skin. These shots parallel categories that social scientists sometimes use to categorize distances for human or offstage contact:

1. *Distant—Extreme long shot.* The camera feels remote and almost indifferent. You are almost simply part of the scenery, nearly difficult to pick out. In life, only someone really looking for you would see you.

2. *Public—Long shot.* The shot is more than 12 feet, and relatively impersonal. You probably need to project as you would at a public gathering. This is also called a full shot—all of your body, head to toe, is included in the frame.

3. *Formal Social—Medium shot.* Camera is 8 to 12 feet from you. The distance is one employed in many casual or business encounters, where we are engaged

but not too intimate. We can see much of your torso, probably above the knees. This shot is good for showing expressiveness of the whole body and is what audiences in small theatres generally have in their frame as they observe you.

4. *Familiar Social—Medium close shot.* Camera moves in to 4 to 8 feet, cutting you off just below the waist, which puts more emphasis on facial expressions and begins to allow us to read feelings and thoughts. There are the beginnings of hints of trust, though perhaps danger, if the distance is not mutually acceptable. Socially we are more comfortable in this setting than in letting others in. This is the most widely used shot.

5. *Personal—Close shot.* The lens is one and a half to four feet away, which is a friendly distance. This shot cuts you off at the collarbone or chest and begins to allow us into your inner life, though in a relatively safe and unobtrusive way.

6. *Intimate—Close up.* Only your head and neck are in the frame, and the top of your head may be out of it. Only those closest to you or threatening you are ever in this space. Subtext becomes as important as text. This shot is used for reaction shots, discoveries, and important moments of realization or change.

7. *Internal—Extreme close up.* This is even closer than intimate. Only your face or part of it is on-screen. No person can be this close to you and still observe you as the lens can. This is used for very powerful, high-emotion moments, and there are often no lines because the moment is almost always too powerful for words.

As you move through various situations in life, from being part of a crowd to the utmost intimacy, note the progression: distant, public, social formal and familiar, personal, intimate, and internal. As you watch films, note the progression. Remember that in numbers 1, 2, and 3, you may be scaling your film performance very similarly to that you would use in a live theatre, then scaling back for 4, 5, 6, and 7. Everything looks different and sometimes this even changes the "look" of the character:

> *I've never worn a hat that worked because I have a relatively small head for my shoulders. For Van Helsing, the costumer tried more than 30 hats before solving my problem. It turns out there is one hat that really suits me in long shot as a silhouette but then when you come into close-up, I have to have a hat that's considerably smaller.*
> —Hugh Jackman

What Happens?

What exactly happens when the scale of a performance enlarges?

- The face tends to be more animated and expressive.
- The body tends to more engaged, expressing emotion with its entirety instead of just from the neck up.
- Physical reactions (such as gulping, doing a double take, gasping for air) are more likely to be inserted between cues.
- Gestures may not be more frequent but they are likely to be more pronounced, moving farther from the torso, with fuller commitment to making a point or expressing a reaction.

  All vocal ingredients will tend to embrace variety:
- Pitch will move between high and low notes more often.
- Projection will tend to come more naturally when enthusiasm is needed, and shifts between loud and soft are more likely.
- Quality will move more often from mellow to harsh, rich to strident, and other timbres to express shifts in attitude.
- Diction will sharpen as points are being made more precisely.
- Tempo will veer between fast, slow, and medium more frequently as mood and energy shift.
- Rhythm will alter from very pronounced strong emphasis to smoother, more fluid expression. The place in each line where stress is placed will switch less predictably.
- Pronunciation may be more playful, with the actor elongating some words, perhaps even deliberately mispronouncing some of them for comic effect, imitating one's partner for irony or playfulness, extending vowels for more overtly emotional responses, and punching consonants to make points more strongly.
- Nonverbals will more likely be present with gasps, sighs, growls, and other explosions of sounds that are not words being inserted into dialogue to further express emotional content and shifts in mood.

When a performance diminishes in scale, each of these elements involves greater restraint and subtlety. The eyes and small shifts of expression become more telling, but they are all still very much alive. Too often actors lower scale and become lifeless, instead of alive with nuance. Unfortunately, taking it down for screen close-ups involves a series of don'ts: don't fidget, don't blink much, don't look down much, don't move your hand or props in and out of the frame, don't do sudden, surprising moves, don't shift your weight—the list goes on and on. Instead of fearfully avoiding these distractions, it is better to decide that you do not need them. Channel the energy that might normally be defused in any of them into really looking, listening, and feeling. Do not play to the camera. Rather, let it observe you and read your mind. The stillness that you need is not empty, but a seething, churning, turbulent, whirlpool of inner excitement and connection. The phrase "Still waters run deep" is never more true than with effective film acting. Let yours run deep.

Unfortunately, many actors cannot decrease the scale of their performance without going dead and listless. Others often have difficulty increasing the scale of a performance without seeming to be sending the material up and stepping outside of it as their embarrassment leads them to make decisions that are not just big but false. Others may get caught in the trap of "enlargement carryover." They raise their volume and, alas, their pitch also goes up. They increase intensity but somehow sound more whiney as their quality shifts from resonant to nasal. They try to use the whole body, but end up just leaning their heads forward to make all points (sometimes called "chicken neck") and shift positions on every line, doing a sort of desperate dance instead of focusing the energy into the words.

Scale presents a particular challenge for technique and truth. How does one manage to be big or small enough and still seem real? Some actors will adjust their performance point by point through each of these techniques, creating a rich large-scale tapestry or a delicate piece of embroidery, but most prefer to start inside by going deeper into the character for motives that will make a large or small performance inevitable and therefore both easy and believable. When a large-scale performance works, it is often because the character is so full of the joy of life that his exuberance is not forced but simply an expression of who this person is. Or so full of resentment, envy, passion, frustrated boredom, or fury that no small behavior would express the urgency the character feels within. If you can find an inner state to allow a larger response to the world, scale adjustment is more likely to come naturally, without self-conscious effort. If you can find a powerful inner truth, much of your outer technique may fall into place, so that you need to make only a few rather than a vast number of external adjustments. For character analysis, you may want to raise the stakes to a more dynamic, super objective and more lively, even off-center strategies. In using your own recall, it may help to collect memories of the times when you were most lively, expressive, and bold, the times when you yourself were larger than life. If you are that very rare actor who tends to over scale and gets notes to pull back, then you simply reverse this process.

Adjusting

How do you adjust? As a film actor, make sure you know the exact context of the section being filmed and the nature of the shot. As a stage actor, whenever you enter a room, size it up. Stage acting would include giving a speech, making a report, being interviewed, chairing a meeting, reading out loud, or any context in which you are performing for an audience in a space that is not necessarily one in which you prepared. Notice how far you are from the back wall, where your primary listeners are, and how many of them there are. If you get a chance, practice to see how much sound and energy it takes to fill this space without overwhelming it. Identify differences between where you practiced and where you are now. If you have a chance to observe actors who tour regularly, note how some get to know the hall they will play in tonight. They will often throw lines out to the back wall; some will even play catch with sound. If you can get into the space alone (or better yet with a friend to help you gauge appropriate scale), use that chance. If others go before you, note carefully which of them adequately fills the space and how. Note if any overwhelm the room or fail to occupy it fully. What adjustments should they have made?

This is something you can study whenever you are in an audience, and it can make a less than riveting presentation more interesting while you analyze it! Always be aware, as well, of your personal tendencies and how these may be right or wrong for the performance.

Reactions

If a performance is scaled large but doesn't work, it is likely to be called ham acting, scenery chewing, histrionic, self-indulgent, embarrassing, or simply overacting. If it works, it may be called spellbinding, brave, dangerous, electrifying, stunning, or even a tour de force. When it is called "over the top" or "larger than life," these are not necessarily insults because they may be either expressions of gratitude for a bravura piece of work or a statement of reservations about scale appropriateness. A performance scaled small may be dismissed as dull, inadequate, or lackluster or praised for its depth, subtlety, and nuance. The key is knowing the right time to make the right scale choice and how to do it.

Offstage Scale

We need to adjust the acting of our lives to our surroundings, but some of us have no space sense. A friend of mine used to say, "This place has gotten too small for us," when the exuberant rowdiness of our group was beginning to bother other patrons. It was time for us to "get smaller" or find another place. Those celebrating in public as if they were in private can be irritating. So can that guy four booths away who speaks so loudly that you can hear every word. Have you noticed that this person is almost invariably also boring so what is being said is both loud and dull?

The same spatial and audience awareness should come into play in daily life. Do you consistently exude a crocodile hunter level of enthusiasm? Others may find you fun to be around when they are in the mood, but exhausting when they are not. Are you so low-key as to seem nearly comatose? Others may appreciate the peace and quiet you send off, but not when they want some spark in their lives. There are those whom one always knows, no matter how far away one is, that they have entered the building, and there are those who can seem to disappear and still be in the room. Most of us would prefer not to get stuck in these or any other scale traps but, rather, to shift with circumstances.

Ask yourself what kind of energy the room, the group, or a single listener may need from you. Sometimes we raise our vivacity level to cheer someone up or go over the top to get the party started. Sometimes we drop it way down to be a good, sensitive listener. We may shift scale to get others to change. A hyper, pushy sales-person or someone hitting on us may get an extremely subdued, low-scale response. We are saying to them that they need to take it way down if they want to stay around us or they need to go away. If this doesn't work, we may need to punch the scale of this rejection up to something even larger than they are putting out to get them to shove off once and for all.

Some of us are so fearful of coming off "perky" (perky people being almost invariably large in scale) that we pull everything so far down that we come off sullen instead. Or some of us are so fearful of making fools of ourselves that we put out nothing around strangers. When forced to respond, we are poker faced, poker voiced, poker bodied—great for playing poker, not so good for relation-ships. You may resent having to be anything but you and balk at the need to take part in space adjustment, but ask yourself: Should others always have to adjust to you? At least spend time developing the awareness to choose not to adjust instead of blindly ignoring the whole issue. It is one thing to make a decision not to put others at ease and join them. It is quite another not to develop the tools to do so if we so choose. Most of us prefer to fit in effortlessly wherever we are. It usually takes some initial effort before the habit of adjustment soon becomes genuinely effortless.

Exercise 6.14

Scale Observation

Write down the answers to these questions:

1. Who are the largest- and smallest-scaled persons you know?
2. Who is strongest at adjusting to various circumstances?
3. Who is the weakest at noticing or making any effort?
4. Are there circumstances in which you are more or less likely to forget to make adjust-ments yourself?

5. Now go back and check the behaviors of everyone mentioned to see if they are consistent with your impressions.

Exercise 6.15

Over the Top and Bottoming Out

Take a monolog or a series of short speeches from a scene. Rehearse them, moving back and forth between the largest and smallest performance possible. If class time allows, present both versions. Both performances should be good; neither should parody the material.

Version 1—You are in a huge opera house, with terrible acoustics, and are feeling full of bravura. You will make everyone in the house listen and feel for this character. Let it rip. Kick out the jams. Give them all their money's worth. You will need to move to accomplish this. Go for tour de force. (This works well if the class is seated in a traditional audience space, and you make an entrance as a great star to tumultuous applause and exit to even more of the same.)

Version 2—You are in close shot on mike or in the most intimate theatre in the world. You just need to connect with the inner need of the character and let all thoughts come as honestly as possible. Take all the time you need. Let it come from the heart. You do not need to move at all. (This works best with the class just seated on the floor in a circle, each actor taking a turn, with no interruption or feedback until the end.)

Exercise 6.16

Who's the Biggest? Who's Smallest?

After the first showing of monologs or scenes in class:

1. Discuss which are the largest and smallest characters being played. For which ones does the actor need to scale large to reach the demands of this larger-than-life personality?

2. At the other end of the scale, which characters are the most repressed, subtle, or timid? Be sure to separate actor from character.

3. Form a line that moves from largest to smallest and through the middle ground of characters. Discuss and negotiate who belongs where in line.

4. Readjust the line so that it reflects the personalities or acting tendencies of the actors themselves. Who has the most adjustment to move from personal to character scale?

Exercise 6.17

Changing Spaces

Working with a partner, using open scenes or short excerpts from scripted scenes, perform them with these variations:

1. Make the performance space in class as intimate as possible with audience chairs very close to the action, surrounding the actors on three sides and making the acting space itself minimal.

2. Change the configuration so audience members are at one end of the room in rows as close to one wall as possible and the actors are at the other end.

3. Move to other theatre spaces in the building. Is there a small black box theatre? A large proscenium house? A medium-size lab or a huge lecture hall? Play the scenes in as many varying spaces as possible.

4. If time allows, go to at least one huge outdoor arena. A track or football field will work well. Scatter the audience among the bleachers with the actors center field.

Discuss what adjustments had to be made in each venue and what that felt like. If class time does not allow, this could be an extra credit assignment reported in a journal.

Exercise 6.18

Camera, Action

Tape several monologs in at least four of the seven major shot set-ups. Review and discuss how effectively the actors adjusted to the various kinds of camera scrutiny. (This might also be an extra credit assignment for those with access to cameras, either to share with a video or a written analysis of how their work changed.)

Exercise 6.19

If Our Scene were on Film

Imagine that your open or scripted scene was a film instead of a live performance. Where do you think the camera would primarily focus? Would it bounce back and forth between the two of you? Would it favor one of you? Would it be likely to move out and include both of you in the same frame? Are there times when it would more likely focus on a prop, an isolated body part, or some part of the set instead of the actors? Would you need to keep any of your blocking or could the camera tell the story? Knowing what the camera (or an insightful director) would choose, how can you use this information to tell the story better?

Improvisation and Freedom

> *Life is improvisation. Classes in improv were like church to me. The training seeped into me and changed who I am.*
> —Tina Fey

In the search for the healthy blending of truth and technique, no activity can be as liberating as *improvisation*. Once the basic language and maneuvers of the body and voice are comfortable, and the actor begins to feel playful again, improvisation can channel that playfulness and help renew a sense of spontaneity. Without some playfulness, how can you do plays?

Improv (which is how it's always abbreviated) gets a bad name when the games don't lead anywhere. Some theatre groups spend a lot of time improvising, and none of it shows up in the final product. Original works, created exclusively through improv, tend to be amusing, even satiric, but rarely memorable. Some people only want to improvise, nothing else, so they drive everyone else crazy with their refusal to set anything. Ever. It is easy to abuse it, but when properly focused, few activities can be as invigorating.

Improv is aimed at tapping your intuition, your knowledge that does not rely on reason or rational processes. It can help sharpen insight, the capacity for guessing accurately. And it can help you dare to decide quickly, and dive in, without wasting time speculating or reflecting unnecessarily. All of us would like to make better decisions, faster, without mentally debating an issue to death. On the other hand, no one wants to turn into a reckless fool. Improv can help you avoid the extremes of careful and careless, in favor of carefree.

Improv Ground Rules

Any game needs rules, or there is no structure to the freedom. The more wild and freewheeling the game, the more important are those rules that keep it from chaos. In improv, actors agree to the following:

1. Always Say Yes

Accept whatever another actor brings into the scene as true. Never say no. If an actor enters an improv scene, looks at you, and shouts, "Brother!" with open arms, you do not answer, "I've never seen you before in my life." All new information is accepted. You are his brother. Hug him. If a new actor comes on while you are holding a broom and asks you whether your baby is a boy or a girl, your broom is indeed your baby. You get to decide the sex.

2. Just Do It

Participate without instantly evaluating your work and judging it. This is exploration without judgment. Listen and respond spontaneously. Go with the flow.

3. Stay Honest

Play to solve the problem, not find the clever line or cute ending, which may be untrue to the character. The more ridiculous the situation ends up being, the more you take it seriously. Don't go for jokes.

4. Stay in the Game

Keep being fully involved until the session is over, either because the situation has resolved itself or because the teacher/coach calls it to an end. Do not step outside the action or drop your concentration. Accept side-coaching, without breaking focus. Live in the moment.

5. Give Up Control

Remove preconceptions or planning ahead. Don't try to run the scene or dominate others. Don't try to be a playwright. Be a person in a predicament.

In addition, the following is useful advice from those who have been using improv for a long time.

- Once you have the basic outline, don't continue to ask questions and engage in more discussion. Whatever you do not now know, assume.
- Don't bother with excessive exposition. Start in what might normally be the middle of the scene, not the beginning. Avoid too much backstory and set-up.
- Keep props to the barest minimum possible. They can quickly bog you down.
- Don't babble and don't do endless monologs where others have no chance to jump in. Keep your answers short and sweet with lots of chances to stop and listen.
- Keep the scene physical and active. Do more and say less.
- When you are at a loss for words, turn to your own senses: How do you feel? What do you smell? Taste? Hear? See?
- Nothing should be regarded as a mistake, just an interesting turn of events.
- Keep filing away twists and turns in the scene for possible later connections because these elements might emerge again.

Most important:

- Treat your partners as if they were poets and geniuses and they will be. Accept everything they bring to the scene as if it is not just OK, but brilliant and inspired.

The more you give, the more you get. Never make them look bad. The best way to make yourself look good is by making them look good. And the best way to do that is just to decide they are awesome.

Basic Awareness Improvs

Earlier chapters in this text have improvs designed to illustrate basic acting concepts. The following improvs are designed to help your concentration and tune up your responses.

Exposure

This exercise is almost universal in an introductory improv session because its lessons are fundamental to performance situations of all kinds.

Exercise 6.20

Being and Doing

1. Stand in groups of five or more onstage; look at the rest of the class and have them look back at you for at least three full minutes. Everyone should get a turn up there.
2. Repeat the process with these tasks: Count the number of book bags in the room, the number of women versus men, the number of people with each hair color, the number of people wearing running shoes. Take suggestions from the audience of what to count. Try to beat the other members of your group and shout out the answer when you have it.

Exercise 6.21

Changing

In the same groups, follow these directions, remaining onstage in a line:

1. Be interesting.
2. Be sexy.
3. Try to appear indifferent.
4. Look intelligent.
5. Be mischievous.

Now replace each of these instructions with:

1. Think of a secret that no one here knows.

2. Quietly scan the room and note those people who turn you on and which qualities especially appeal to you.

3. Count the number of separate items of clothing you have on.

4. Decide which controversial topic intrigues you most at the moment. What is the best argument for each side?

5. Find someone in the room you know you can play a favorite trick on.

Discuss the differences in relative relaxation and the reasons. This is a lesson every actor needs to learn deep in his bones.

Reactions

The capacity to respond with all the senses to an imaginary event calls on the full range of your ability to remember, deep inside the mind and body. It also requires a complete return to a state of, "Let's pretend." Perform in groups of five to ten:

Exercise 6.22

Spectator Sport

Agree as a group on the sport that is going on at a great distance from you. Watch without interacting with each other, but feel free to speak and move around. Accept whatever changes the teacher adds.

Exercise 6.23

Sounds of Music

Same situation as Exercise 6.22, only at a concert where you are enthralled by what you see and hear.

Exercise 6.24

Senses Alive

Pick an agreed-on eating or drinking task and concentrate fully on the act, with as many senses involved as are needed.

Exercise 6.25

Weather Watch

Add to Exercise 6.24 a change in weather that breaks, to some extent, your *dwelling* on the task, dividing your focus between consuming and climate.

Exercise 6.26

Five Alive

Agree on a spectator situation that will allow you to combine all the reactions in the previous four exercises. Several groups layer them in one by one. Later groups try to begin with all reactions working, never allowing any single influence to disappear for long from your consciousness. (*Example:* Group watching square dance at county fair, add sound of fiddler, midway noises, bright glaring sunlight, mix of cooking smells, odors from animal exhibits, eating corn dogs, drinking lemonade.)

Joining

Working as a unit, balancing and supporting each other, and using each individual's contribution is what makes acting the ultimate collaboration.

In groups of five to seven, do the following exercises:

Exercise 6.27

Where are We?

Focus is on establishing an environment. First actor enters an open space and starts a task. Second actor does not enter until he is absolutely sure where scene takes place and how he might fit into the space. Public places (supermarkets, student unions, libraries) should be selected so that the actor can choose any characterization he wishes and still fit it into the location. All interact with the environment and use all the senses.

Exercise 6.28

Helping Out

First person goes onstage and begins an activity, such as yard work or house painting, which can be done alone but can also benefit from help. The task should be physically involving and apparent even to someone who speaks a foreign language. Others join, one by one, concentrating on completing the task with free-flowing group interaction. Every person's objective is to effectively accomplish the basic shared task at hand.

Exercise 6.29

Building

First person enters, assumes an identity, and starts an activity, but he is the only one who knows both of these. Others join as they are called on and given identities by the person preceding them until the group is complete and functioning on the task. (*Example:* Detective calls in assistant who calls in eyewitness who spots and calls in a suspect who calls her lawyer . . .) Everyone is concerned with accomplishing the shared objective, unless the person calling you gives you an identity that justifies your working against the others.

Exercise 6.30

Changing

Variation on Exercise 6.31, with each new person arriving and deciding *both* who she is and her relationship to others onstage. They don't know until the entering actor reveals her connection to them and the task at hand. Character entering is free to decide whether to help or hinder the task at hand.

Concentration

The actor always faces the double task of pursuing two activities at the same time or doing one thing while thinking about another, which means constantly juggling or splitting his focus.

Exercise 6.31

Who Am I?

Done with two actors. First is onstage, seated on a bench, and second (who is the only one who knows their relationship) enters. The first actor needs to find out who she is and what her connection to the second is, by studying the other's behavior toward her without revealing her ignorance. If time allows, actors should switch once relationship is clear, so each gets a chance to initiate.

Exercise 6.32

Eat, Drink, and be Merry

Two to four actors. Same as Senses Alive (Exercise 6.24), but this time actors agree on a topic of conversation that engages them actively. Consume a large meal at the same time. Keep all the areas of concentration balanced. Once secure, add sounds, sights, and weather conditions to the scene.

Exercise 6.33

Preoccupation

Two actors. A shared physical task is undertaken that necessitates that the two people interact. But each is totally preoccupied with his own subject, and neither listens to the other at all, except for matters related to the mutual task. Alternate which person is chattering and which is silently thinking of something else, with moments where both are talking or momentarily drifting away. Keep the task active.

Exercise 6.34

I've Got a Secret

Five actors. Two actors decide on a topic, which they must discuss in the presence of the other three without revealing the topic. They are trying to mislead the others, without saying anything that is actually untrue. Others join, one by one, when they think they know, but never ask if they are right. Two talkers may challenge any participant to a huddle and if the joiner is wrong, she has to leave. Everyone gets two chances to join before being permanently on the outs.

Selectivity

It is important to know what *not* to think about, so that distractions do not get in the way of objectives, onstage or off. The mind can hold only so much at once, so only the essentials can stay.

Exercise 6.35

Drawing and Drawing

Entire class in two teams. Each team has a pile of scrap paper and pencils. Each team sends forward its champion to be shown the name of an item, written on a slip of paper that the scorekeeper has drawn from a hat. Each champion runs back and tries to draw a sketch of the item fast enough but clearly enough so that his team guesses it first. Get only the essentials on the paper. Keep score between teams until everyone has had a turn.

Exercise 6.36

Slow Motion Tag

Entire class. Begin by simply forcing all movement to slow down, even though someone is chasing and others are escaping. Once this becomes comfortable, each person who is "it" sets a particular movement, which everyone imitates, while still trying to keep from being caught. Each new "it" changes the mode of movement.

Exercise 6.37

Passing Sounds and Moves

Entire class. First, everyone stands in a circle and one person starts a peculiar sound, accompanied by a movement. He carries these across the circle, to someone else who catches both, until they are perfectly imitated. When the new person reaches the middle of the circle, both sound and motion evolve into others, which the new initiator carries to another actor. Neither sound nor move should just jerk into a new mode but, rather, selectively move out of the former set, into the new one. Once the group is responding fully, transfer into tag, this time with both sound and movement involved and everyone required to imitate the person who is "it" both vocally and physically, while avoiding being caught.

Exercise 6.38

Coming and Going

Entire class, but one actor at a time. Each person picks a place she just was, and another place she is headed toward, but all we see is the moment between. The actor tries to be selective enough that both are clear. (*Example:* A man zipping up his fly and then pressing an imaginary button on the wall has come from the men's room to the elevator.) Once procedure is clear, actors should draw slips of paper that assign one of the two places, then finally draw both places. *Variation*: Actors work in pairs.

Nonsense

The use of gibberish or nonsense syllables forces you, just as when you are traveling in a foreign country where you don't know the language, to call out the full range of body language and vocal expressiveness. In each following exercise, even your partner is simply making an informed guess about the precise meaning of what you have just said. Remember to use sounds with no recognizable meaning at all (not even letters and numbers), so all information is nonverbal.

Exercise 6.39

Help Me

Work privately, in pairs. Alternate asking favors of your partner, warming up your sense of freedom from words. Ask for specific physical tasks so that your partner is able to literally help you out.

Exercise 6.40

Translating

One of you is demonstrating some product in nonsense, while the other "translates" to the audience at large what he believes his partner has just said. Not even the identity of the object is decided on beforehand. The object should have little relationship to its usual function (so a pail may be the latest in hats or an open notebook may be a bathing suit top), but the nonsense-speaker should try to be as clear as possible physically about intentions and new function.

Exercise 6.41

Selling

Working in pairs to persuade the audience to buy some product, the two of you alternate physical demonstration with the sales pitch, helping each other out, until the end of the commercial.

Exercise 6.42

Interplay

Working in pairs, select any of the conditions in Exercises 6.39–6.42: a request for assistance, a demonstration, or a sales pitch. This time the audience is free to ask questions (in English), which you comprehend, but always answer in your own language.

Calls

As you have probably already figured out, a *call* is a signal that is given to you by some other source: drawing a slip of paper, side-coaching, or the audience itself. Calls usually involve the given circumstances of the scene.

Exercise 6.43

Three P's

Groups of two to five. Each group draws three slips of paper from three containers marked People, Places, and Projects. People will be members of the same profession (Doctors? Hairdressers?) or background (Martians? Elizabethans?). The Place (A stadium? A sauna?) may or may not have anything to do with what they share. The Project (Spring cleaning? Playing poker? Having a quilting bee?) may also be unrelated to their backgrounds. It's all in the luck of the draw. Audience shouts out guesses. Stick with the task until it is finished or well under way.

Exercise 6.44

Audience Coaches

Groups of two to five. Those not in the group decide on the setting, an identity for each participant, the occasion, and the basic conflict, as we have done in earlier chapters. Audience is free to side-coach the scene as it progresses.

Exercise 6.45

Audience Handicaps

Same group sizes. Actors decide on everything except the conflict, which comes from audience. At various points in the scene, the audience layers in no more than five handicaps (someone cannot speak, a dark secret, a case of amnesia), which are incorporated. Keep within the character's perspective, and don't succumb to parody.

Transformations

The ultimate effortless skill of childhood, which every actor needs to recapture, is changing whatever you look at by just believing it is now something else.

Exercise 6.46

Play Ball

Entire class in pairs. Begin tossing an imaginary ball back and forth between you. Teacher will call out changes as it turns into a football, medicine ball, and others as you let size, weight, and attitude influence you. Later, the ball may become other objects of varying shapes, values, and complexity, which are still sent through the air.

Exercise 6.47

Passing Objects

Entire class in a circle, sitting on the floor. First chosen actor creates an object out of air so that her fellow actors can see it, then passes it to the person next to her, who handles it until it transforms into something else, and is passed again.

Exercise 6.48

Passing Masks

Groups of five to seven. Sit in a tight circle. First person picks up an imaginary mask from the floor in front of him, puts it on and lets it change him, takes it off, returning to himself, passes it on to the person next to him. Each person gets to try on this particular mask and each person gets to initiate a mask of his own.

Exercise 6.49

Magic Clothes

Entire class. Everyone wanders around room ignoring others until discovering before you a magic pair of shoes. You decide what they look like and what their power is, but once you put them on, they control you and change how you move and relate to the world. After a time you spot a magic sash, belt, or girdle, which again takes you over and dominates not only that area of the body, but your entire relationship to the space around you. Finally, you encounter a headdress, hat, helmet, or crown, which you put on and it sends your energy up while transforming how you move and what you feel about the area around you. After allowing the headgear to dominate who you are for a while, the three garments begin to fight each other and your sense of self is pulled in different directions. You remove the influence you like the least, then the second choice, and finally allow the one discovery that seems to have freed you most to transform you completely.

Exercise 6.50

On and Off

Groups of five to seven. First actor begins a task and establishes an identity, which, once clear, second actor enters and changes, by virtue of his first line. Once the two of them fall into the new pattern, actor three enters and again changes everything. Allow each new relationship to function before the next change. Once the entire group is on and involved, first actor finds a reason to leave, which transforms the group again, and each actor departs, leaving a change behind. The last actor transforms himself before leaving.

Just for Fun

Although the following exercises will certainly help actors concentrate and make quick decisions, they are basically intended to give everyone a chance to enjoy themselves and play, once actors are comfortable with improv as a theatrical form.

Exercise 6.51

What Are You Doing?

Entire class, standing in a circle. Someone (*A*) enters the circle and starts doing an action. After a moment, someone else (*B*) enters and asks, "What are you doing?" *A* answers something other than what she is actually doing physically at that moment. *B* begins doing the action described. *A* then drops out, and *C* enters with the same question, until everyone has taken part.

In this form, this exercise is kind of a group warm-up. It can also be done with *A* staying and converting to the new activity and actors being eliminated only for stalling, saying something that has already been said, or in any way not responding instantly to what the last person said. In this case, it may go on until there is a designated winner as last person left.

Exercise 6.52

Boss Is Gonna Freak!

Four players—two co-workers, one boss, one late worker. Uh-oh! Somebody was late to work. The two co-workers are the only ones who know what happened to make her late. (The audience makes three wild suggestions, and the two of them pick one while both boss and late worker are out of the room). Boss confronts the late worker about why she was late. The two co-workers are behind the boss pantomiming the actions so the late worker will give the right answer. If late worker does not get it right in three minutes, another pair of co-workers should step up from the audience and try. *Note:* Co-workers cannot be caught acting out by the boss and must freeze or get busy if he turns around. Late worker has to make it seem like a normal conversation.

Exercise 6.53

Freeze Tag

Two initial players, with as many as ten total. Two actors are given a suggestion from audience for a situation, and they start a scene. After the scene is established, someone else yells, "Freeze!" The players freeze in whatever position they are in, and the actor who called it picks one of them and takes his place, tapping him on the shoulder and then taking his exact physical position onstage. A new scene, very different from the preceding one, begins, initiated by the new player. The scene shifts continue until all ten players have played.

Exercise 6.54

New Choice

Same as Exercise 6.53 plus a designated "ref." Two actors start suggested scene. At any moment ref can call "new choice," at which time the actor must revise his line and or movement so that it is entirely different than what just came out. (Ref can call "new choice" as many as four times on the same bit.) In this way, the scene continues with constant on-the-spot re-writes. Actors may be eliminated for hesitating too long or making a new choice too similar to the old one.

Exercise 6.55

Changing

Two players plus "ref." Audience shouts out suggestions for a list of differing emotions, dialects, and film genres, which the ref jots down. (Alternative to save time: Audience begins with a handout of possible choices.) Then audience suggests scene context to actors who start. At any moment, the ref can shout out a new suggestion, such as "hate," at which time that emotion dominates the scene, or "Western," at which time it shifts into that genre, or "French," at which time it shifts to Paris. If time allows, limit the first round to one of the three (emotions, dialects, film genres) lists and then when the group is warmed up, use all three and let them overlap.

Exercise 6.56

Party Quirks

Four players—one host, three guests. While the host is out of the room, the audience gives each guest an unusual trait, fetish, or personality. The host enters and prepares for the party. The guests arrive one at a time and interact with the host who must guess their traits. The host has a minute with each guest before the next enters and then three minutes with all guests present.

Exercise 6.57

Countdown

Four players. The audience provides three scene suggestions. Players agree on one. They are given three minutes to do the scene. Then they are required to repeat the scene over again in smaller and smaller frames of time, by speeding up, editing details, or sharpening transitions.

Exercise 6.58

Rhymes

Two starting players with entire class possibly joining. Player 1 starts a story by offering a first line. Player 2 needs to respond with a line that rhymes and then offer her own first line to Player 1, who must create a rhyme. Actors who hesitate or fail to rhyme "die" (the audience shouts this out) and are replaced by other players. The challenge is to keep both rhymes and the continuity of the story going.

Exercise 6.59

World's Worst

Four players. Players stand in line. Audience shouts out various professions, hobbies, or sports. Each player should try to be the worst example, the most inept, inappropriate, or perverse way of going about the tasks associated with the topic.

Exercise 6.60

Only Questions

Two starting players, with entire class possibly joining. Taking the scene suggestion, two actors must proceed so that any sentence they use must be a question. Actors using statements instead of questions "die" and are replaced by others. New actors need to exactly replace the characters who die rather than bringing in new personalities.

Blending and Balancing

This particular marriage of truth and technique, like most marriages, requires time and adjustment, but is worth it. Every conscientious actor experiences moments that in themselves are tiny miracles. There are few things more wonderful than finding yourself in rehearsal with an impulse you know you can support. Let's say your heart wants to cry out to your partner with a desperation that suddenly seems absolutely right for the character. You know how to extend an *s* sound masterfully, how to support a plaintive vowel sound so it is mournful but not weak. You know how to land on a consonant like *p* so that it seems to explode. You have learned to focus almost all your energy momentarily in your eyes. So when you call out, "Stop!!" to your partner, the other actor is frozen, feels a chill, and turns, mesmerized, looks up, and is locked into your eyes. Your sense of truth launched you, and your technique carried what you felt to capture your partner. Then you feel a chill. Of power and delight.

7

Scene Study

Finding character through script

I study the material kind of like a detective, looking for the clues that might lead me into the character's interior life.

—Helen Mirren

It's all about the text. Some need to be invented or re-imagined or teased out. Some just need to be unlocked.

—Cate Blanchett

You have to respect the script, learn your lines and tell the truth.

—Josh Duhamel

I'm like an investigative reporter. I start with the script. Instead of going straight to the core, I circle my subject.

—Denzel Washington

Immersing yourself in another personality, starting with what the writer has put on the page, that's the important, satisfying part of the job.

—Russell Crowe

A character is first created by the writer. It comes through you, it's not you. As an actor, you have to be more humble than to think it's just all about you.

—Juliette Binoche

Regardless of where your performance ends, it starts with the script. Actors are rec-reative artists, not purely creative ones. Actors start with the playwright's vision and attempt to realize or *complete* that vision. A great actor moves beyond completion into extraordinary *discovery* and may even *reinvent* a role, but the actor does not start with a blank sheet. The work begins with the text.*

This chapter will deal with working on an excerpt from a play in a class or workshop situation, and the next chapter will deal with working on an entire play in production. Scene study may be broken down into seven steps. You never leave one step behind; you add new ones.

1. *Scene selection:* What is the best material for my partner and me? What excerpt is worth several weeks of our lives?

2. *Script analysis:* What is this play really about and how does our scene fit into the whole?

3. *Cutting:* How can we edit the scene to serve time and to favor both actors?

4. *Character analysis:* How can I get to know this character well enough to deserve to play her?

5. *Staging:* How can we use the stage to tell the story? How can our characters' relationship become clear through space?

6. *Script awareness improvs:* How can we use improvisation to help us own our roles?

7. *Shaking up the scene:* How do we keep from getting complacent, bored, or predictable? How do we keep it fresh?

Scene Selection

The following guidelines are the most common for class assignments with scripts. Things that may appear to be limitations are actually freeing. They get rid of distracting hurdles and allow you to concentrate on the basic character truth. The best first scenes for actors beginning their training are those fairly close to home.

Exercise 7.1

Scene Project

1. Select a scene of no less than five and no more than seven minutes in playing time

2. From contemporary American realism (or from another country if accents are unnecessary and the play is more about universal human concerns than those unique to that culture)

---

*The obvious exception would be those extraordinary creators who always improve, devise, or generate text themselves. Most of the rest of us end up working on someone else's script most of the time.

3. With characters rarely more than five years (and *never* more than ten years) outside the actual ages of the actors

4. With neither actor cast against type

5. With dialogue divided fairly equally between the two (or at the most, three) characters

Scene Suggestions

The following scenes meet the basic guidelines and offer interesting conflicts. Some of these scenes veer slightly into the seriocomic or mild stylization but all are close enough to basic realism to use as a starting point. The ages of the characters rarely exceed thirty, though a few go down to twelve. Most actors find it easier to play younger than older because they've been there. Most of the scenes are set in the last part of the twentieth century. Those set in earlier eras are basically timeless so that the encounter remains universal. In other words, none of these scenes requires you to stretch beyond reasonably familiar territory.

All My Sons by Arthur Miller (Chris and Ann)

All the Way Home by Tad Mosel (Jay and Mary)

Am I Blue by Beth Henley (Ashbe and John)

The American Plan by Richard Greenberg (Nick and Lili)

Amongst Barbarians by Michael Wall (Bryan and Ralph)

Angels in America by Tony Kushner (Joe and Harper, Joe and Louis)

Anything for You by Cathy Celesia (Lynette and Gail)

Apocalyptic Butterflies by Wendy MacLeod (Trudi and Hank)

April Snow by Romulus Linney (Gordon and Milly)

Approximating Mother by Kathleen Tolan (Molly and Fran)

The Art of Dining by Tina Howe (Elizabeth and David)

At Home by Michael Weller (Paul and Carol)

The Author's Voice by Richard Greenberg (Todd and Portia)

Away by Michael Gow (Meg and Tom)

Baby with the Bathwater by Christopher Durang (John and Helen)

Bad Habits by Terence McNally (Benson and Hedges)

Beauty by Jane Martin (Carla and Bethany)

Beggars in the House of Plenty by John Patrick Shanley (Johnny and Joey)

Beirut by Alan Bowne (Torch and Blue)

Bent by Martin Sherman (Max and Rudy)

Beyond Your Command by Ralph Pape (Diane and Danny)

The Big Knife by Clifford Odets (Charlie and Ann)

Big Time by Keith Reddin (Fran and Peter)

Birdbath by Leonard Melfi (Frankie and Velma)

A Bird of Prey by Jim Grimsley (Monty and Thacker)

Blue Denim by James Leo Herlihy and William Noble (Janet and Arthur)

Blue Earth by Arthur Winfield Knight (Jim and Cole)

The Blue Room by David Hare (He and She)

Blue Surge by Rebecca Gilman (Curt and Beth)

Borderline by John Bishop (Karen and Charles)

The Boys Next Door by Tom Griffin (Norman and Sheila)

Boy's Life by Howard Korder (Lisa and Don, Don and Jack)

Breaking Legs by Tom Dulack (Terrence and Angie)

Brother by Mary Gallagher (Charlie and Kitty)

Buddies by Mary Gallagher (Theresa and Bo)

Buried Child by Sam Shepard (Vince and Shelly)

Burn This by Lanford Wilson (Larry and Burton)

Candy and Shelley Go to the Desert by Paula Cizmar (Candy and Shelley)

Careless Love by Len Jenkin (Marie and Wife)

Cheating Cheaters by John Patrick (Angelica and Theresa)

Class Action by Brad Slaight (Tina and Robby)

Closer by Patrick Marber (Anna and Larry, Anna and Dan, Alice and Larry, Alice and Dan, Larry and Dan)

Club Hellfire by Leonard Melfi (Slice and Silky)

Coastal Disturbances by Tina Howe (Lee and Holly)

The Coming World by Christopher Shinn (Dora and Ed, Dora and Ty)

Coyote Ugly by Lynn Siefert (Scarlet and Dowd)

Danny and the Deep Blue Sea by John Patrick Shanley (Roberta and Danny)

Darcy and Clara by Daisy Foote (Darcy and Tom, Darcy and Clara)

Dates and Nuts by Gary Lennon (Donald and Eve)

Days of Wine and Roses by J. P. Miller (Kris and Joe)

Division Street by Steve Tesich (Yovan and Chris)

Dolores by Edward Alan Baker (Dolores and Sandra)

The Dead Boy by Andrew C. Ordover (Cop and Wife)

The Death of Bessie Smith by Edward Albee (Receptionist and Intern)

Dirty Hands by Jean-Paul Sartre (Jessica and Hugo)

The Diviners by Jim Leonard (C. C. and Jennie Mae)

Dolly Would by Jocelyn Beard (Dolly D and Dolly Z)

The Dreamer Examines His Pillow by John Patrick Shanley (Tommy and Donna)

Duet for One by Walker Owen (Feldman and Stephanie)

Early Dark by Reynolds Price (Rosacoke and Wesley)

The Early Girl by Caroline Kava (Jean and Lily)

Eastern Standard by Richard Greenberg (Stephen and Drew, Peter and Phoebe)

Echoes by N. Richard Nash (Tilda and Sam)

Erotic Scenes in a Cheap Hotel Room by Michael Hemmingon (Shella and Tina)

Extremities by William Mastrosimone (Raoul and Marjorie)

The Family of Mann by Theresa Rebeck (Belinda and Ren)

Far East by A. J. Gurney (Bob and Sparky)

Fatal Attraction by Bernard Slade (Tony and Blair, Doris and Blair)

Ferris Wheel by Mary Miller (John and Dorie)

Final Placement by Ara Watson (Luellen and Mary)

Fishing by Michael Weller (Rob and Mary Ellen)

Five Women Wearing the Same Dress by Alan Ball (Trisha and Georgeanne)

Flop Cop by Laura Cuningham (Officer Murphy and The Playwright)

The Food Chain by Nicky Silver (Amanda and Serge)

Fool for Love by Sam Shepard (Eddie and May)

The Foreigner by Larry Shue (Ellard and Charlie, David and Katherine)

The Four Seasons by Arnold Wesker (Adam and Beatrice)

Fragments by John Jay Garrett (Jack and Rachel)

Fresh Horses by Larry Ketron (Jewel and Larkin)

The Game by Laura Henry (Man and Woman)

Gemini by Albert Innaurato (Francis and Judith)

Geography of Horse Dreamer by Sam Shepard (Beaujo and Cody)

Ghost on Fire by Michael Weller (Michelle-Marie and Julia)

Goose and Tomtom by David Rabe (Goose and Tomtom)

The Gift by Simon Fill (Jones and John)

The Girl Next Door by Laurence Klavan (Jill and Bill, Page and Bill)

The Glass Menagerie by Tennessee Williams (Laura and Jim)

Golden Boy by Clifford Odets (Lorna and Joe)

A Good Time by Ernest Thompson (Mandy and Rick)

The Good-Bye People by Herb Gardner (Nancy and Korman)

The Guest Lecturer by A. J. Gurney (Fred and Hartley)

Half Court by Brian Silberman (David and Susan)

A Handful of Stars by Billy Roche (Jimmy and Tony)

A Hatful of Rain by Michael V. Gazzo (Polo and Johnny)

Hazelwood Junior High by Rob Urbanati (Shanda and Amanda)

The Heidi Chronicles by Wendy Wasserstein (Heidi and Sandra)

Hello Out There by William Saroyan (Girl and Young Man)

Here by Michael Frayn (Phil and Cath)

Here We Are by Dorothy Parker (He and She)

High Tide by Brad Slaight (Connie and Brian)

Hooters by Ted Tally (Cheryl and Ronda, Clint and Ricky, Ricky and Ronda)

Hope of the Future by Shannon Keith Kelley (Dennis and Rex)

Hothouse by Megan Terry (Jody and Roz)

The House of Yes by Wendy MacLeod (Lesly and Jackie-O)

I Am a Camera by John Van Druten (Sally and Christopher)

I Won't Dance by Oliver Hailey (Don and Kay)

In On It by Daniel McIvor (Brad and Brian)

In the Boom Boom Room by David Rabe (Chrissy and Susan)

Isn't It Romantic by Wendy Wasserstein (Janie and Harriet)

Judgment Call by Frederick Stroppel (Harvey and Frank)

Keely and Du by Jane Martin (Keely and Du)

Laundry and Bourbon by James McClure (Elizabeth and Hattie)

Lemon Sky by Lanford Wilson (Alan and Ronnie)

Lend Me a Tenor by Ken Ludwig (Maggie and Max)

The Less Than Human Club by Timothy Mason (Amanda and Dan, Davis and Larley, Kirsten and Davis, Kirsten and Julie)

A Lie of the Mind by Sam Shepard (Beth and Frankie)

Life of the Party by Doug Holsclaw (Jay and Curtis)

A Little Like Drowning by Anthony Minghella (Leonora and Alfredo)

Live Spelled Backwards by Jerome Lawrence (Frank and Woman Who Knows)

Living at Home by Anthony Giardina (David and John)

Living in Paradise by Jack Gilhooley (Butch and May)

Lonestar by James McClure (Roy and Ray)

Long Day's Journey into Night by Eugene O'Neill (Jamie and Edmund)

Long Walk to Forever by Kurt Vonnegut (Catharine and Newt)

Look Homeward, Angel by Ketti Frings (Eugene and Laura)

Look, We've Come Through by Hugh Wheeler (Belle and Bobby)

Loose Ends by Michael Weller (Paul and Susan)

Love Nest for Three by John Patrick (Veronica and Norton)

The Love Talkers by Deborah Pryor (Bun and Read Head)

Lovely Afternoon by Howard Delman (Alan and Pam)

Lovers by Brian Friel (Meg and Joe)

Lovers and Other Strangers by Joseph Bologna and Rene Taylor (Cathy and Hal)

Lu Ann Hampton Laverty Oberlander by Preston Jones (Lu Ann and Billy Bob)

Lunch Hour by Jean Kerr (Carrie and Oliver)

The Man Who Couldn't Dance by Jason Katims (Eric and Gail)

Marvin's Room by Scott McPherson (Bessie and Lee)

Meeting the Winter Bike Rider by Juan Nunez (Mark and Tony)

Mimosa Pudica by Curt Dempster (Diane and David)

Minnesota Moon by John Olive (Alan and Larry)

The Miss Firecracker Contest by Beth Henley (Tessy and Carnelle)

Misreadings by Neena Beber (Simone and Ruth)

A Modest Proposal by Selma Thompson (John and Mer)

Mr. Melancholy by Matt Cameron (Olie and Delores)

The Normal Heart by Larry Kramer (Ben and Ned)

North of Providence by Edward Allan Baker (Bobby and Carol)

On Tidy Endings by Harvey Fierstein (Arthur and Marion)

Once a Catholic by Mary O'Malley (Mary and Mary)

One More Zero by Timothy Mason (Heather and Eddie, Heather and Miriam)

Only You by Horton Foote (Estaquio and Katie Bell)

Ordinary People by Judith Guest and Alvin Sargeant (Karen and Conrad)

Orphans by Lyle Kessler (Phillip and Treat)

Out of Gas on Lovers Leap by Mark St. Germain (Mystery and Gruper)

The Owl and the Pussycat by Bill Manhoff (Felix and Doris)

The Paper Chase by Joseph Robinette and John Jay Osborn (Hart and Ford)

Patio by Jack Heifner (Pearl and Jewel)

Perfect by Mary Gallagher (Tina and Kitty)

Period of Adjustment by Tennessee Williams (Isabel and Ralph)

The Philadelphia by David Ives (Al and Mark)

Phyllis and Xenobia by Christopher Durang (Phyllis and Xenobia)

Prelude to a Kiss by Craig Lucas (Peter and Rita)

Private Wars by James McClure (Gately and Silvio)

Proof by David Auburn (Catherine and Hal)

A Quiet End by Robin Swados (Jason and Max)

Railing it Uptown by Shirley Lauro (Woman in White and Woman in Black)

Reckless by Craig Lucas (Rachel and Lloyd)

The Red Coat by John Patrick Shanley (John and Mary)

The Reincarnation of Jaime Brown by Lynne Alvarez (Jaime and David, David and Jimmy)

The Rimers of Eldritch by Lanford Wilson (Robert and Eva)

Road Trip by Jason Milligan (Ron and Lisa)

Safe Sex by Harvey Fierstein (Mead and Ghee)

The Saint Valentine's Day Massacre by Allan Knee (Cheryl and Kenny)

Sally and Marsha by Sybille Pearson (Sally and Marsha)

Savage in Limbo by John Patrick Shanley (Savage and Linda)

Say Goodnight, Gracie by Ralph Pape (Jerry and Steve)

Seascape with Sharks and Dancers by Don Nigro (Tracy and Ben)

Seven Strangers in a Circle by Eric C. Peterson (Masha and Robert)

Sexual Perversity in Chicago by David Mamet (Danny and Bernie)

Shivaree by William Mastrosimone (Chandler and Shivaree)

The Sign in Sidney Brustein's Window by Lorraine Hansberry (Sidney and Iris)

Skin by Naomi Izuka (Lisa and Mary)

Slam by Jayne Nixon-Willis (Linc and Mel)

Someone Who'll Watch Over Me by Frank McGuiness (Edward and Michael)

Sorrows of Stephen by Peter Parnell (Stephen and Christine)

Sorry by Timothy Mason (Pat Wayne and Katie Bell)

The Speed of Darkness by Steve Tesich (Anne and Joe)

Speed-the-Plow by David Mamet (Charlie and Bobby)

Spike Heels by Theresa Rebeck (Andrew and Edward, Georgie and Lydia)

Splendor in the Grass by William Inge (Bud and Deanie)

The Square Root of Love by Howard Delman (Alan and Pam)

Stars by Romulus Linney (He and She)

Stargazing by Nancy S. Chu (Jeanine and Gillian)

Strange Snow by Stephen Metcalfe (Martha and Megs, Martha and Dave)

Streamers by David Rabe (Richie and Billy)

Summer and Smoke by Tennessee Williams (Alma and John)

Talk to Me Like the Rain and Let Me Listen by Tennessee Williams
(Man and Woman)

That Midnight Rodeo by Mary Sue Price (Cindy and Bo)

There Is No John Garfield by Ernest A. Joselovitz (Edgar and Margo)

This Is Our Youth by Kenneth Lonergan (Warren and Dennis, Warren and Jessica)

The Tiger by Murray Schisgal (Ben and Gloria)

The Time of Your Life by William Saroyan (Joe and Mary)

Torch Song Trilogy by Harvey Fierstein (Arnold and Laurel)

Tracers by John DiFusco (Williams and Baby San, Professor and Doc,
Professor and Baby San)

The Trestle at Pope Lick Creek by Naomi Wallace (Dalton and Pace)

True West by Sam Shepard (Austin and Lee)

Twelve Dreams by James Lapine (Sanford and Miss Banton)

Two Eclairs by Joe Pintauro (Maud and Mark)

Two on an Island by Elmer Rice (John and Mary)

Uncommon Women and Others by Wendy Wasserstein (Kate and Rita)

Voices from the High School by Peter Coe (Senior and Freshman)

The Voyeur and the Widow by Le Wilhelm (Elgin and Edwina)

The Wager by Mark Medoff (Leeds and Ward)

When You Comin' Back, Red Ryder? by Mark Medoff (Angel and Stephen)

Women and Wallace by Jonathan Marc Sherman (Lili and Wallace)

Women of Manhattan by John Patrick Shanley (Billie and Rhonda)

The Woolgatherer by William Mastrosimone (Rose and Cliff)

The Wrong Man by Laura Harrington (John and Nadia)

Wrong Turn at Lungfish by Lowell Ganz and Garry Marshall (Anita and Dominic)

You Can't Trust the Male by Randy Noojin (Laura and Harvey)

Zero Positive by Harry Kondoleon (Himmer and Patrick)

These plays have three character scenes for instances when there are an odd number of students:

The Author's Voice by Richard Greenberg (Portia, Todd, and Gene)

Baby with the Bathwater by Christopher Durang (John, Nanny, and Helen)

The Baltimore Waltz by Paula Vogel (Anna, Garcon, and Carl)

A Bird of Prey by Jim Grimsley (Tracy, Donna, and Chris)

Blue Window by Craig Lucas (Boo, Alice, and Griever)

Burn This by Lanford Wilson (Burton, Anna, Larry)

The Chopin Playoffs by Israel Horovitz (Fern, Irving, and Stanley)

Hold for Three by Sherry Kramer (Bartiey, Scottie, and Ed)

Independence by Lee Blessing (Sherry, Jo, and Kess)

Last Summer at Blue Fish Cove by Jane Chambers (Rae, Annie, and Lil)

Laundry and Bourbon by James McClure (Elizabeth, Hattie, and Amy Lee)

Life Under Water by Richard Greenberg (Amy-Beth, Amy-Joy, and Kip)

The Miss Firecracker Contest by Beth Henley (Carnelle, Delmont, and Elaine)

Sensual Intelligence by Michael R. Farloash (Tom, Felicia, and Betty)

Strange Snow by Stephen Metcalf (Megs, Martha, and Dave)

Sunday on the Rocks by Theresa Rebeck (Jen, Elly, and Gayle)

A Thousand Clowns by Herb Gardner (Murray, Sandra, and Albert)

T-Shirts by Robert Patrick (Marvin, Kirk, and Tom)

The View from Here by Margaret Dulaney (Fern, Maple, and Carla)

The War Boys by Naomi Wallace (David, Greg, and George)

The Widow's Blind Date by Israel Horowitz (Archie, George, and Margie)

Multicultural Scenes

The generic scene list presented involves characters that could be played by actors of any race, but the original productions featured Caucasian performers. The following scenes feature Asian, Hispanic, African American, or Native American characters. Many focus on identity issues connected with heritage.

Acts of Faith by Marilyn Felt (Ahmed and Barbara)

Alchemy of Desire/Dead Man's Blues by Caridad Svich (Simone and Miranda)

And the Soul Shall Dance by Wakako Yamauchi (Kiyoko and Masako)

An Asian Jockey in Our Midst by Carter W. Lewis (Nathan and Alice)

Baby Jesus by Isaac Bedonna (Elizardo and Rudy, Berto and Marlon)

The Ballad of Yachiyo by Philip Kan Gotanda (Yachiyo and Osugo)

The Basement at the Bottom at the End of the World by Nadine Graham (Naneen and Paul)

Before It Hits Home by Cheryl L. West (Wendal and Junior)

Birds Without Wings by Renaldo Ferradas (Carlos and Claudia)

Blackbird by Adam Rapp (Froggy and Baylis)

Borderline by Hanif Kureiishi (Amina and Haroon, Ravi and Susan)

Boxcar by Silvia Gonzalez (Roberto and Bill)

Breath, Boom by Kia Corthron (Prix and Cat, Prix and Angel)

Buba by Hillel Mitelpunkt (Elie and Rachel)

Cage Rhythm by Kia Corthron (T. J. and Avery)

The China Crisis by Kipp Erante Cheng (Mickey and Lola)

Clean by Edwin Sanchez (Gustovito and Father)

Cloud Techtonics by Jose Rivera (Celestina and Anibal)

Columbus Park by Karen Huie (Chrissy and Jimmy)

The Conduct of Life by Maria Irene Fornes (Leticia and Olympia)

The Dance and the Railroad by David Henry Hwang (Lone and Ma)

The Darker Face of the Earth by Rita Dove (Augustus and Phoebe)

De Donde? by Mary Gallagher (Alirio and Sister Kathleen, Felicia and Teto, Felicia and Victor)

Dos Amigos by Paul Morse (Juan and John)

Down Payments by Tracee Lyles (Nia and Fancy)

Dutchman by Amiri Baraka (Clay and Lula)

Eddie "Mundo" Edmundo by Lynne Alvarez (Alicia and Eddie)

Fallen Angel by Elois Beasley (K. C. and Kathryn)

The Fat-Free Chicana and the Snow Cap Queen by Elaine Romero (Amy and Silvia)

Five Scenes from Life by Alan Brody (Nina and Bobby)

Full Moon by Reynolds Price (Ora Lee and Kip)

Gleaning/Rebusca by Caridad Svich (Sonia and Barbara)

Graffiti by Nilo Cruz (Bruno and Lucy)

The Guitarron by Lynne Alvarez (Guicho and Michaela)

The House of Ramon Iglesia by Jose Rivera (Javier and Caroline, Javier and Charlie)

The House on Lake Desolation by Brian Christopher Williams (Iggy and Janna)

How I Got That Story by Amlin Gray (Guerrilla and Reporter)

In the Heart of America by Naomi Wallace (Fariouz and Remzi)

Jelly Belly by Charles Smith (Mike and Barbara)

Joe Turner's Come and Gone by August Wilson (Reuben and Zonia)

Latins in La-La Land by Migdalia Cruz (Laly and Margo)

Letters to a Student Revolutionary by Elizabeth Wong (Bibi and Karen)

Marisol by Jose Rivera (Marisol and Lenny)

The Matsurian Mirror by Velina Hasa Houston (Tooriko and Aiko)

The Migrant Farmworker's Son by Silvia Gonzalez (Oliverio and Henry)

Music Lessons by Wakako Yamuchi (Kaoru and Chizuko, Aki and Chizuko)

My Children! My Africa! by Athol Fugard (Thami and Isabel)

No Place to Be Somebody by Charles Gordone (Shanty and Cora)

Once Upon a Dream by Migel Gonzalez-Pando (Machito and Tony)

Parting by Nubia Kai (Sudan and Sherrie)

Rain Dance by Lanford Wilson (Tony and Hank)

Rancho Hollywood by Carlos Morton (Ramona and Jed)

References to Salvador Dali Make Me Hot by Jose Rivera (Gabriela and Benito)

Seer from Saigon by Elaine Meredeith Hazzard (Yen and Dr. Truong)

Shadow of a Man by Cherrie Moraga (Lupe and Leticia)

A Shayna Maidel by Barbara Lebow (Lucia and Rose, Lucia and Hannah)

The Shrunken Head of Pancho Villa by Luis Valdez (Pedro and Ming)

The Signal Season of Dummy Hoy by Allen Meyer and Michael Nowak (Dummy and A. C.)

Slaughter City by Naomi Wallace (Tuck and Baquin)

Songs of Harmony by Karen Huie (Emily and Suzanne)

Struggling Truths by Peter Mellencamp (Rinchen and Dorje)

The Suit by Can Themba (Philemon and Matilda)

T-Bone N Weasel by Jon Klein (T-Bone and Weasel)

Take a Giant Step by Louis Peterson (Christine and Spence, Iggie and Spence)

Take Me Out by Richard Greenberg (Darren and Kippy, Darren and Davey, Kippy and Shane)

Takunda by Charles Smith (Takunda and Chipo)

Talking Pictures by Horton Foote (Estaquio and Katie Bell)

Tango Palace by Maria Irene Fornes (Isidore and Leopold)

Thin Air by Lynne Alvarez (Anya and Johnny)

Tomorrow = X2 by Myrtle Nord (Diana and Russ)

Turning Yellow by Curtis Chinn (Frank and William)

Walls by Jeannie Barroga (Stu and Dave, Sarah and Morris)

Welcome Home, Jacko by Mustapha Matura (Zippy and Gai, Zippy and Jacko)

Wipe That Smile by Kay M. Osborne (Putus and Phanso)

Yankee Dawg You Die by Phillip Kan Gotanda (Bradley and Vincent)

Yellow Fever by Rick A. Shiomi (Sam and Nancy)

Three character scenes:

Black Girl by J. E. Franklin (Norma, Ruth Ann, and Billie Jean)

Marisol by Jose Rivera (Marisol, Lune, and Lenny)

Mixed Babies by Oni Faida Lampley (Dena, Reva, and Shalanda)

12-1-A by Wakako Yamauchi (Koko, Ken, and Harry)

Yesterday's Window by Chiori Miyagawa (Woman, September, and Delivery Man)

A quick glance at the lists shows that you will have a far easier time finding a scene for a man and a woman than any other combination. So if you decide to work with a same-sex partner, know that your choices will be more limited.

Script Analysis

Understanding the text as a whole will help you see how your character fits into the big picture and relates to other characters, the words, and the audience. Here are categories to consider:

1. *Classification:* What kind of a play is this? Try to come up with a phrase (for example, "a light, romantic comedy" or "a raw slice of life drama") to describe the script. If you do not know dramatic literature terms, find your own words to describe the overall feeling of the text.

2. *Style:* Even though all scenes for this assignment will come from contemporary American realism, there will be variations on this form. Is the play more like totally uncensored life (naturalism), somewhat more beautifully extravagant life (romanticism), life totally out of whack (absurd), life making fun of certain targets (satire), life as a largely physical joke (farce), as a series of

overblown coincidences (melodrama)? Ask yourself how probable the behavior of the characters is and if it is at all improbable, in what direction does it lean? Are people in this play wittier, weepier, more cruel, or clumsier than they are in your offstage world?

3. *Structure:* How is this play put together? Is it a one act or a full length? If full, how many acts is it divided into? How many scenes within each act? Are these scenes lengthy, short, or some combination? If you had to give a title to each act, what would it be? Where does your scene fit into this overall pattern? How close is it to the climax of the play and how much new information does it provide compared with other scenes?

4. *Theme:* What does this play say about life? What is the author's message? What issues are raised and what position does the writer take regarding the human condition? How does the action of the play begin and how does it end? How are central characters different because of the journey? What does the title mean? Do you think the writer is trying to get the audience to change in some way or just divert them? Try to put the theme in a single sentence. Remember that all plays say something even if it is only, "Isn't middle class life great?"

5. *Cultural binding:* This play was probably written between the 1940s and the turn of the century. When? Do the social customs, attitudes, and language seem tied to the date of writing? Is the play better served by moving it into the present or by placing it in its own time? Was it written from a strong geographical, economic, or ethnic bias? How do these intersect with that of you and your classmates?

6. *Production history:* What can you find out about this play in performance? Has it been popular? Obscure? Have any well-known actors played your roles? What kinds of critical reviews has it received? Were there any choices made by previous performers that you might also try? Are there mistakes other actors made from which you might learn?

7. *World of the play:* Just as a character has given circumstances, so does the play as a whole. It's important to know who your character is and how she fits into the play. If your character is gregarious, bubbly, and personable, it's a lot more significant if all the other characters do *not* share those traits and if being outgoing is not rewarded behavior in this play. You may have heard a performance described as striking but not in the same *play* as everyone else.

Here are some questions to use to find out what play everyone else is in. Ask yourself how close or far away your character is from the majority:

1. *Time:* How rapidly does it move for most people? What lengths of attention spans do these people have?

2. *Space:* How large a bubble do most people carry around? To what degree is privacy and open space respected?

3. *Place:* Do people feel connected with where they live or indifferent to it? How aware are they of other places?

4. *Values:* What are the beliefs most widely shared? What ideals? How do people define sin, consequences, forgiveness, ethics?

5. *Structure:* Who rules and who follows? How easy is it to bring about change? How is the pattern of daily life ordered and followed?

6. *Beauty:* What look is most aspired to in this group? Who are the contemporary ideals of male and female perfection?

7. *Sex:* How is seduction defined and sexuality communicated? How much tolerance is there for deviation, infidelity, promiscuity?

8. *Recreation:* What is most people's idea of fun? What would be an ideal social occasion in this world?

9. *Sight:* How does the world look in shapes, angles, light, shadow, and color? What are dominant patterns of movement and gesture?

10. *Sound:* What is the common mode of speech and use of nonverbals? To what degree are listening and speaking prized?

How close is your character to the average member of the group? How likely would he be to defend his right to be different if pressured to conform? Analyzing the world of the play becomes more crucial the farther that world is from the one you live in offstage.

Exercise 7.2

Analyzing the Script

Prepare answers of no more than a single phrase or sentence in each of these categories:

1. *Classification:* Single phrase capturing what kind of play this is

2. *Style:* Degree of probability; types of improbability

3. *Structure:* Script length; acts; scenes; place of your scene in the whole

4. *Theme:* Author's message on life

5. *Cultural Binding:* Date written and set; cultural bias present in text; challenges for performance here and now

6. *Production History:* Possible lessons from those who have done it before

7. *World of the play:* Majority choices made by characters for

Time	Beauty
Space	Sex
Place	Recreation
Values	Sight
Structure	Sound

Exercise 7.3

Fitting into the World

Create a situation in each of the ten world-of-the-play categories described where your character is confronted with a group that conforms to the expected behavior in the world. React as your character would and either give in completely, make an adjustment, or defy the standards altogether. Complete, in some other way for each category, your sense of how your character will or will not blend with all the others.

Cutting the Scene

Time limits on acting class scenes have to be enforced, simply because there are so many people in class and so little time for vital individual attention. If you present a scene that goes way over the assigned limit, you have wasted time in a number of ways. You're eating into your own period of being critiqued or having your scene worked. You're probably eating into *other* people's time, which is worse. You've also spent all these valuable rehearsal hours working on a giant, unwieldy rock of a scene, when what was wanted was a little jewel glistening in the sun. You've probably heard the standard theatrical adage, "Leave them wanting more." As advice, it has no peer. It stands to reason that the shorter your excerpt, the more times you can run it, work it, try something else, polish it, right? No epics allowed.

Time the scene regularly as you work. You will probably add time as you get more layers, find inspired pauses, consider incredible alternatives during your evaluations, and so on. So if your scene timed near the limit at first reading, you will inevitably have to cut. It is very common for a scene to run fifteen minutes and for actors to say "But it was only ten last week." Last week? That was before you found all that glorious subtext.

What can be cut? Every line is perfect? Here are some standard edits:

1. Anything connecting with other parts of the play, but not directly connected with the scene. The scene can have a life of its own.

2. Start closer to the climax than you originally intended, or consider ending with more of a cliff-hanger, rather than full closure. Find the portion of the scene that gives you the best acting workout.

3. Any passages where you have found you can imply, or communicate physically, without stating specifically. Some speeches may be overwritten; others you simply find can be edited, once your subtext is clarified.

4. Cut for balance, if one character has been given lengthy monologs, so that the scene becomes more of a duet. This experience should serve both partners.

5. Lines you have trouble with: trouble pronouncing, motivating, clarifying. *Not* until you've tried to make them work, but eventually to relieve yourself from unnecessary pressure. There's no point approaching a word or phrase with dread because you've rarely been able to say it right.

6. Dated or obscure references that the audience is unlikely to grasp.

7. Bleed the scene, instead of looking for giant amputations. Sometimes you do need the entire body of the scene, but can ease out a word here, a phrase there, so you have a cleaner script but a complete one.

Exercise 7.4

Edit Three Minutes

Imagine that your scene is overtime and must be shortened by at least three minutes. Go over the text in each of the categories above. Find the cuts that will serve both the script and actors best. Get a sense of how each of the categories may create a slightly different piece of work.

Cutting is a valuable skill for actors. Too many leave it all up to directors. You are much closer to each line, more intimately aware of potential nuances within each speech. In play rehearsals, if you are able to offer suggestions for cuts, you are also far more likely to be able to keep your favorites. Respecting a text isn't synonymous with needing to present it all. Some magnificent texts can be enhanced with surgery.

Character Analysis

By doing character analysis and research, you feel secure in what you are playing. The audience may not see what you did, but they see the confidence and security.

—Benicio Del Toro

When you take on a character, you need to get to know him at least as well as a close friend. You need to analyze him enough to understand the choices he makes. Texts offer different amounts of information about the people in them. Some playwrights, such as George Bernard Shaw and Eugene O'Neill, give microscopic character details, down to the titles of books the characters keep on their shelves. Other playwrights simply give your role a name such as THE BOY, minimal dialogue, and leave a lot for you to discover. To make certain all evidence is examined, go through the following stages:

The Three "I"s: Investigation, Inference, Invention

1. *Investigation:* This is just facts. You find evidence in the script. If the character is well known, it's crucial to make sure you are looking at the person the playwright *wrote* and are not overly influenced by some famous actor's performance, by an acting tradition for this part, or by the public image of this character. There will still be gaps, so you move to inference.

2. *Inference:* From facts, you draw conclusions. If everyone keeps calling you "child," you assume you're younger than they are. If your stage directions are filled with indirect movements and pauses, you infer you're hesitant and nonassertive. This is a fascinating process and easy to confuse with investigation but inference must be *based* on facts. Now blanks can be filled in with invention.

> *Acting is interpretive by nature. An architect may have an overall vision, but it takes the attention of craftsmen like plumbers, carpenters, sheet-metal men and roofers to bring it to life. I'm quite happy being a craftsman. I don't feel lessened by that at all. It's the facts, Jack.*
> **—Harrison Ford**

3. *Invention:* Some actors are tempted to skip to this stage, without earning their way through the first two. Others neglect it, contented with unactable generalizations like "she's in her teens" or "she's in high school." Remember, no real person thinks of herself as *in* her teens, but is concerned with precisely where. Remember Stanislavski's admonition that "in general" is the *actor's greatest enemy.* After inferring an approximate age, this is where you decide you are eighteen and you were born on March 4, on a still, moonless night, by Caesarean—the whole picture.

Following this progression (investigation to inference to invention) ensures the actor that the writer's will has been served, and leaves her free to discover. The list that emerges is filled with *technical details* to rehearse and master, plus *emotional conditions* to plant and let develop. The document you prepare is often kept with the *score* and strongly connected to it.

Exercise 7.5

Character Past

Complete the statements from the character's perspective with a strong need to tell the truth. Fortunately, you have already done a character analysis on yourself in Chapter 3 so you are familiar with the standard questions and can compare yourself with your character. This time, each category is phrased with acting vocabulary developed in the last few chapters (*see* Appendix I).

I come from . . .

My childhood was . . .

Family conditions were . . .

Experiences making the most lasting impression on me were . . .

Ten most important given circumstances are . . .

Five most powerful members of my private audience would be . . .

Crucial actions before scene were . . .

The moment before my entrance in complete detail involves . . .

Exercise 7.6

Character Present

Complete the statements from the character's perspective with a strong need to tell the truth:

Immediate conditioning forces are . . .

Others in script (and/or playwright) describe me as . . .

I describe others as . . .

In groups I tend to . . .

I would describe myself as basically . . .

My usual style or clothing and type of accessories include . . .

My most distinguishing characteristics are . . .

My favorite things are . . .

My temperament could be described as . . . For example . . .

I am most and least interested in . . .

My physical life varies from the actor playing me in . . .

My vocal life varies from the actor playing me in . . .

The actor playing me needs to use the Magic If for this role in . . .

Three examples where endowment must be used in the scene are . . .

The location of this scene can be described as . . .

The most crucial moment of evaluation (including all alternatives considered and rejected) is . . .

I make the following discoveries in the scene . . .

Exercise 7.7

Character Future

Complete the statements from the character's perspective with a strong need to tell the truth:

My super objective is . . .

My intentional hierarchy would include . . .

My immediate scene objective is to . . .

Obstacles I face are . . .

My strategy in the scene could be described as . . .

Specific tactics I employ are . . .

My best possible future would be . . .

My worst possible future would be . . .

My wildest dreams come true would be . . .

Once you do your homework, build your character's biography, immerse yourself in the period—do all the conscious work—then a moment of ease and effortlessness may come. You are transcendent, you lose your self-consciousness. All ego concerns go away and you're free.

–Annette Bening

Abstracting

Much analysis work is systematic and logical, so a useful balance can be achieved by also working in an abstract and fanciful mode. The following questions should be answered, not thinking of what the character would *choose* to wear, drink, or drive but, rather, which qualities sum up the character's essence.

Barker [the director] said to me, "Lear should be an oak, you're an ash; now we've got to do something about that."
—John Gielgud

A person may choose the finest champagne to consume but still be warm draft beer to those who know him. Another may drive a truck, but clearly be thought of as a Rolls by everyone she meets.

Exercise 7.8

Character Abstracts

This exercise is based on a party game, sometimes called Abstracts or Essences. The class may wish to play. In the first version, one person picks one other in the room and then everyone poses a question, until someone guesses who is being abstracted. In another, a guesser leaves the room, while everyone agrees on a subject in their midst. When the guesser returns, she questions each person there until she guesses correctly or gives up. It's always surprising how often people agree on these indirect ways of describing others, and how clear the final image emerges. Ask yourself, if the character were actually one of the following, which would he be?

1. Fabric
2. Animal
3. Beverage
4. Mode of transportation
5. City
6. Tree
7. Color
8. Play
9. Scent
10. Song

11. Type of day

12. Decade or era

13. Film or TV series

14. Landmark or building

15. Snack

16. Mythological or fantasy figure

17. Spice

18. Musical instrument

19. Painting or photo

20. Toy

Abstracting helps you discover some images to snap you into character, to help drop the day's distractions, especially if you're not in the mood. You walk into rehearsal feeling like "milk" and a "bus shelter" but you think of "dry sherry" and the "Taj Mahal," and you shift your *sense* of yourself. It is whimsical but it works. Abstracting also provides a way of communicating when traditional terms are inadequate. Gielgud, the actor, really *is* an ash, and the character King Lear is truly an oak. There is no clearer, kinder way to make that distinction, than in abstract images.

Exercise 7.9

Character's Autobiography

1. Take all the information you've accumulated and write an autobiography, no longer than one page, in the voice of the character.

2. There's way too much available material to include, so pick what the *character* would consider important.

3. Take the character only up to her first entrance in the scene and end the essay by completing the statement: "What I want most out of life is . . ."

4. Give yourself a strong motive for speaking the character's truth as he sees it. Maybe the essay is being written for a psychiatrist who can only help if the answers are genuine. Maybe it's written for a priest, with the complete conviction that the man of God will see through any deceptions. Maybe it's written to a child, who deserves to know the truth about her parent and you are determined to finally tell it. If the only way the character would ever prepare a manuscript of this kind is to write a letter to someone, then use that format. Try to find a condition that suits who this person is.

5. Use the character's language, spelling, and sentence structure. Experiment with altering your handwriting (if the character would not type this document) to suit the writer. Pick the texture and color of paper and pen this person would choose. The difference

between using lavender stationary, purple felt tip pen, all small letters, and i's dotted with circles, maybe even some smiles in those circles (which would be the right way to express some characters) and a legal size document in triplicate, from a word processor (which would be right for another), is a vivid way to express differing personal approaches. Enjoy the process of finding the right mode of presentation.

Exercise 7.10

Analysis into System

1. Score the scene based on Stanislavski's concepts

2. Armed with new information about your scripted character, go back and execute each of these exercises in Chapters 4 and 5 from the perspective of the person you're playing:

Others' Givens (4.2)	Imaging (4.13)
Planting (4.3)	Naming Members (5.11)
Hierarchies (4.5)	Group Bias (5.12)
Tiny Triumphs (4.7)	Adding Conditions (5.13)
Adding Consequence (4.9)	Open Futures (5.15)
Bringing It Back (4.10)	Playing Against (5.16)
Release Album (4.11)	

Work with your scene partner when appropriate. Work alone when you need time and space and no pressure to react quickly. Make a promise to yourself to let none of your analysis and research remain theoretical, but to actively apply the results in rehearsal.

Exercise 7.11

Warming in

Pick the most evocative images from your character analysis, those that seem to thrust you most vividly into the character's experience and feelings. While warming up to present the scene, let these particular images drift over you so that as your body and voice prepare, your mind releases your own biases and accepts those of your character.

All this homework finally takes when the character is an inevitability in your life.

It's like a woman getting pregnant. This character, this person that I am to become, starts to grow inside me and I listen. If I don't listen, he will die in me.

—Marcello Mastroianni

Staging

It is not impossible to block your scene yourself. You start with a floor plan as a map and work your way step by step. Again, some scripts give you finite details and others only vague references. Write down every item (entrance, piece of furniture, prop) you know must be present. As a shortcut, see if some variation on the generic floor plan in Figure 7-1 will work. Though the possibilities are infinite, when you sit in the audience, you usually see some version of this set: Why? Because it is simple, and provides most of the opportunities to explore relationships, while keeping everyone easy to see. It has:

1. A strong up center entrance
2. Two "islands" that can become territories so that any actor may assume one space as his and the other as his partner's
3. Opportunities for actors to play space invasion or space sharing games
4. Easy movement around the furniture so actors can protect themselves at one instant, then step forth the next
5. A couch and an arm chair, which offer the widest possible range of leaning, sitting, reclining, and lying possibilities
6. The smooth and effortless use of figure 8s around the two main sections, as well as employing other curving patterns
7. Two isolated areas upright and left for retreat and reflection, as well as an alternative, if weaker, entrance/exit

This is not a bad space to start exploring with your partner as you begin work on a scene, especially if you know little about scene design. Alter it, as the scene requires, but try to keep the same opportunities for variety and visibility. What it

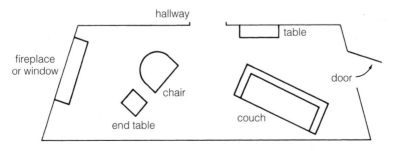

Figure 7-1   The Generic Floor Plan

lacks in originality, it offers in reliability. Ultimately, the space is made compelling by what people do there.

1. If your scene has other requirements, make the adjustments on paper along with a list of what absolutely must happen physically.

2. Review the section on Stage Movement in Chapter 6 (*pages 189–190*), this time with the context of your scene in mind. What pieces of *business* are necessary? What *bits* might be fun to try? Where can you tell you will have to remember to *cheat* so you don't close off a crucial moment from the audience? Are there places where it feels as if one character is likely to *cross*? Where another should *counter*? Is it evident where one of you needs to *give* and the other *take stage*? Some patterns should immediately emerge to give the scene a rough outline.

3. Review Exercise 6.3: Living Pictures- (*pages 191–193*), asking yourself if some moments are best served by one of you sitting and the other standing, where you may not be looking at each other at all, and so forth.

4. Review Exercise 6.5: Adding Motion (*pages 194–195*) to see if there are movement patterns that might contrast between your characters, where one may be more active generally? Is one more likely to cover space but the other more likely to gesture actively?

5. Remember that the most effective actor-generated staging is organic. It evolves as you rehearse and get to know these people and this space better. You need to get on your feet and rough out something that will do early or you will be tempted to postpone too long, but once the scene has a physical outline, let yourself explore and trust your intuition.

Script Awareness Improvs

Anything that appears in your character analysis could become the basis for an improv to help get the information fully assimilated, especially if you wrote it down but you are not yet using it in the scene. Some possibilities follow.

Characters Offstage

Exercise 7.12

First Meeting of the Characters

Set up all the circumstances of the first time the two of you laid eyes on each other. Then enter the scene from a point of innocence and discover your partner. Leave the encounter when you have some idea when you will see this person again.

Exercise 7.13

Crucial Offstage Event

Select the single most influential experience, either before the play begins or away from the script, on your actions. This may or may not involve your partner. Set yourself up to simply respond without scripting the experience. Solo examples: a character anticipating an abortion goes to an actual clinic for counseling, an alcoholic attends an AA meeting, an expectant mother goes to a birthing class. What matters is not how many demands you place on yourself but, rather, the range of *feelings* the experience allows you to share with the character.

Exercise 7.14

Character Wake-up

On the morning of the beginning of the play, move from sleep to the character's anticipation of the day ahead. Get a strong sense of the bed (if it is a bed), the space, your feelings about where you sleep, the time you wake up, your expectations about the coming day, and all the circumstances that launch you into this event. Go through each detail of bathing, choosing what to wear and eat, what to take with you. Arm yourself with everything the character carries onto the stage.

Exercise 7.15

Typical Time

Spend an evening or an afternoon as the two characters, doing something they would likely do together. Agree on the exact point at which you leave yourselves behind and take on the characters. Try to view each event and line heard from the character's perspective and to relish the change. Pick up a sense of how the two of them deal with each other and others outside the script itself.

Exercise 7.16

Character Interview

If possible, this exercise should be performed in class, but it can be done with your partner or a friend playing the interviewer. You decide the circumstances. Are you interviewing for a job, a deposition, a biography, an article, a grant, a TV show? The group is free to ask you any question, and you must answer at all times from the character's point of view.

Exercise 7.17

Character Encounters

In character, go through the list used for Partner Sharing in Chapter 5 (Exercise 5.18). Imagine the circumstances under which these two would do this together (to save their marriage, to satisfy the urging of one of them, to help them get over a misunderstanding?). Answer fully as the character would, and later note where you and the character intersect and where you divide.

Characters Onstage

Exercise 7.18

Scoreboard

Place a blackboard (or some other prominent means of visibly displaying who scored the last point) somewhere on your set. Play the scene with particular attention to one-upping your partner.

When you know you have scored, walk up to the board and give yourself the point. Take time out if the point is contested. Relish each point you score. At the end, tally who wins and by what margin.

Exercise 7.19

Unrelated Activity

As you run lines with your partner, pick a variety of ways to involve yourselves physically at the same time. You might set the table for dinner or do laundry or clean the rehearsal hall or any task that will involve the two of you equally. Let the lines and the activity influence each other so that neither is independent of the other.

Exercise 7.20

Stop Partner from Leaving

Imagine that one of you simply wants to leave and not deal with the encounter at all. Using the actual dialogue, one actor should employ any tactic available to keep the partner from going. The partner should actually walk out of the space, if not stopped by some riveting sense of urgency, need, or power. Reverse positions and run the scene the other way around. Then alternate every four lines whose turn it is to feel the need to get away.

Exercise 7.21

Talking Beats

Walk through the scene, negotiating, in character, about where each beat begins and ends, and what it should be called ("This is the beat where I show what a fool you've been and it should be called 'Sheila's Revenge'"). Disagree as your character might ("What is really shown here is your mindless cruelty and it should be called 'Sheila the Bitch'"). Negotiate until you find a mutually acceptable spot, for the beat's beginning and end, and a title that both parties can deal with. Try it with larger clusters of beats (measures or subscenes), giving titles to them as well.

Keys

Actors are always searching for the key to a character. They often discover what they are looking for in a costume prop (a hat, a handkerchief, a pair of shoes or glasses) or some physical characteristic (set of the jaw, hands deep, deep into pockets, feet turned in slightly when walking) or vocal quality (a slightly nasal quality, a hum, a startling laugh) characteristic. The actor will talk of searching and searching ("until I put on this scarf and that was the key") when suddenly the door to the whole characterization opened.

This search and discovery represents vividly the way in which a single technical element can unlock an emotional awareness. It also shows how much technique the actor needs, to experiment with all those physical and vocal traits, to know what to *do* when he picks up the hat or the cane, to even recognize the *value* in picking it up. Stanislavski refers constantly to "unconscious creativeness through conscious technique" where the actor earns the right to discover by carefully opening herself up to possibility. A simple physical object or tiny change can suddenly make her feel like another human being, with detail after detail rushing in to complete the character.

> *Actors are always searching for the key, because then you have the secret behind the door and permission to go in and soak it up.*
>
> —Edward Norton

Try to explore whether there is a particular piece of clothing or prop that tends to unleash more for you. Then you can go there often. For an amazing number of actors, shoes are very important for unlocking different qualities in themselves for each role. For others, it's props:

> *When I wear high heels, I can have a great vocabulary and speak in paragraphs.*
>
> —Meg Ryan
>
> *I like to totally familiarize myself with the props I'm going to use and feel compelled to know how to make all of them work. Okay, maybe I obsess over it but this is where I get crucial information.*
>
> —Taye Diggs

Exercise 7.22

Key Searching

1. Select a character and spend a half hour wandering around your own room (or, if available, a prop room) trying things on, picking up and handling props, examining small objects, letting each work on the character's sense of self. Keep the best of what you find, but keep your personal antennae out everywhere you go for objects that might open character doors.

2. Do the same thing with isolated physical and vocal characteristics and techniques. Try them on like glasses or scarves, seeing if they fit (or even release) the character.

Shaking Up the Scene

Not all improvisation work has to be done in early stages, as groups begin to form or as the scene is just taking shape. Some rehearsal experiments should come later in the process, when the scene is relatively solid, and ready for some new life. The following exercises work best when lines and blocking are quite secure. In class, these fit best when the work has been shown once, been critiqued, and gone back into rehearsal.

Your teacher and classmates may suggest some specific ones, based on the first showing, but all are worth trying. Sometimes the very aspect of the scene about which you feel most complacent turns out to benefit from a jolt of a different kind of energy. If this experimenting is not done in class, it helps to have some observers at your rehearsal to help you identify your discoveries. It is possible to become so caught up in doing an exercise that you fail to register the benefits. After each of the following exercises is an indication of what often happens when it is accomplished.

Don't *force* that result, because in your case it may be something altogether different. Or like any improv, it may fizzle out. Not all mining trips lead to treasure. Not all lead to the *same* treasure. Leave yourself open.

Character Explorations

Exercise 7.23

Spoken Silent Script

Actually speak your continuous interior monolog in addition to the lines themselves, so you are speaking both text and subtext. Take all the time you need, to recognize inner thoughts and get them into words. Go ahead and overlap with your partner, as your tapes run simultaneously.

Remember, a lot of your silent script won't make sense to others, and that's as it should be. Speak the "silent" parts in a slightly less projected voice than the actual lines, which can be more projected for clarity. This exercise starts rough, but once you get it, it rolls. Stanislavski suggests trying it in four stages:

1. Speaking the silent script, in a lower tone of voice
2. Merely whispering the script
3. Speaking the script soundlessly
4. Expressing the script only with the eyes, moving the benefits gradually back into the traditional performance mode

What Happens: You find out where your thinking is muddy and some gets cleaned up. Some awkwardness drops away because you are so busy. You discover busyness and movement as your body takes over.

Exercise 7.24

Shadowing

Hand two other actors your scripts, and have them go through the scene. You and your partner shadow them, telling them where to move, asking to have some words punched, to repeat some lines or moves, with greater emphasis, encouraging before an important moment and after a maneuver is accomplished successfully, acting as alter ego and coach. When you are ready for your "stand-in" to read the line, press her lightly on the back.

What Happens: You get a new perspective. Countless little insights come out of just peering over another's shoulder and seeing the scene from another place altogether. You are able to put this alter ego onstage with you in places where encouragement would help.

Exercise 7.25

Isolating

Pick any two charm or threat tactics from Chapter 1 (pages 21–22) and use them exclusively in the scene. Don't let your partner know which ones you choose. (This may also be done by simply drawing slips of paper so the decision is made for you.) Make sure every inch of mileage is gained from each tactic.

1. Both of you employ the same tactic on each other.
2. Both select tactics you are relatively sure your character does *not* employ in the scene.

What Happens: Focus shifts from lines to maneuvers. Evaluations have more excitement. You see tactics as possibilities that you failed to consider before. The scene becomes more like a game, and partners are studied more carefully.

Exercise 7.26

Role Reversal

1. Switch parts with your partner and run the scene.
2. Keep the major shape of the scene the same, but feel free to use your own line readings and character business whenever you wish to do something differently.
3. Listen closely to your partner when he gives a new and interesting twist to a speech, when it sounds the same as the way you usually do it, when your sense of timing is altered.
4. Most important, enjoy playing the other role and doing all the things you might wish the other actor would do, but would never "direct" him to do.

What Happens: You learn immediately how well you know the whole scene and how often you have simply been biding time and not really listening when your partner speaks. There is a thera-peutic release in getting to say the words and do the other part the way you want. Whether or not your partner hears, notices, or decides to use anything of yours, at least you've had the chance. You tend to feel somehow freer. You find places you may have been making the other guy wait forever, or where you may have been anticipating his cues, or a cross you have been making more difficult than necessary. You get all the benefits of the Magic If for your partner. If you are alert, your partner will show you some better alternatives and will give you permission to try things.

So I said, "Okay, let's just switch roles." You have to trust the other person, because when he plays your role, he's gonna be telling you how you should play it . . . well, we just flew. Raul [Julia] was the one who took off first. I was dazzled by his flamboyance. So I took up the gauntlet and made that revolutionary one tough son of a bitch. We were giving each other what we needed from each other.

—William Hurt (on Kiss of the Spider Woman)

Exercise 7.27

Passing

Start with a simple object, such as a rubber ball, beanbag, or tennis ball, and run the scene, passing it to the other person at the very end of each speech. Use the object to punctuate your lines while you have it, and literally pass it to your partner the way the cue is passed (violently, slyly, flirtatiously, with outrage, and so on). Let the relationship between the characters central-ize in the object. Remember you don't just have to hand it to the other person, you can put it in his pocket, on his head, down his pants. You can nudge it over to him with your foot or your little pinkie. You can do more than hold it while you speak. You can crush it, roll it, bounce it, or put it down your own pants.

Variation: Move to a game that is most appropriate to the conflict in the scene (ping-pong or croquet if it is witty repartee, boxing if it is all frontal assault, wrestling if it is gutsy and noncere-bral, chess if it is sly) and explore the same way.

What Happens: Line readings tend to have more color. As the energy goes into the object, it also goes into the words, so variety and clarity both rise. Individual consonants and vowels, within words, get more liveliness and variety of attack. Both partners become more alert hearing and receiving cues.

Exercise 7.28

Animal Abstractions

Assume the animal images you have chosen for your characters and perform the scene with all the animal's physical characteristics you can summon, with an animal voice (animal-sounding but with real words, punctuated by a generous dose of non verbals). Your animal can be a com-bination of animals instead of one that exists in real life. Let the blocking of the scene change in any way that seems right, and go ahead and scratch where it itches. Open up the scene to all the non-intellectual sensory, sensual, sexual, purely physical realms. Repeat the scene immediately without any effort to animalize.

What Happens: A greater playfulness often emerges as well as some pure animal carryover. This can effectively counterbalance actors who tend to talk a scene to death or to act too much with the head.

Exercise 7.29

Contact

Touch your partner at some point during each of your lines in the scene. Take your time and find some way to physically connect with her every time you speak. Touches may be anything from traditional moves (slapping on the shoulder, nudging, pointing into someone's upper chest) to those that are simply discovered (touching elbows, pulling someone's shirt untucked, even pressing your nose to someone's knee). Some combination of the conventional and the new will probably emerge. Don't try to be clever, but let your body tell you some way to connect at the same time your words do.

What Happens: A surprising number of these moves end up being serious possibilities to put into the actual scene. Others provide an emotional memory for the body to suppress interestingly later. The emotional contact is inevitably heightened by physical contact. And some unexpectedly pointed line readings are discovered.

Exercise 7.30

Gibbalogue

Select agreed-on nonsense syllables and run the scene, using these limited lines instead of the actual dialogue. Make sure you have communicated as fully through the gibberish as you would through the words, maybe more so. To accomplish this you will need to intensify your physical and nonverbal responses. The face will need to get involved and the range of vocal life will need to be more vivid. Do not go on to the next line until your partner has made your cue perfectly clear.

What Happens: Much as when struggling with a foreign language, the body gets engaged. As in the Nonsense section of Chapter 6, the communication suddenly has higher stakes for both participants. Often you decide to keep some of these vivid choices at moments of high intensity.

Exercise 7.31

Handicaps

1. Play the scene sitting back to back, with your partner's arms and yours locked at the elbows and neither of you having any possibility of seeing the other.

Communicate everything through your voice and whatever pressure you can manage on the other person's back and your arms, where looped.

2. Sit against the wall, facing each other at opposite ends of a large classroom or rehearsal hall. Communicate over the vast space, keeping the scene intimate and complex, not allowing it to become loud and flat.

3. Invent a handicap for the scene, based on removing anything you agree either of you has grown to rely on heavily. If that is different for each of you, try it both ways.

What Happens: Just as those who are sight or hearing impaired tend to gain, by necessity, a heightening of other senses, adding some limitation to the scene can sharpen the intensity of communication in other areas and get both actors thinking again.

Exercise 7.32

Counterpoint

Decide what your character is not and play the scene as if she is just that. Deliberately interpret each line so that it conveys a meaning opposite to that which seems intended by the text. Create a character who would be the polar opposite of yours and relish the difference. You may need to repeat this once, for the obvious amusement you will experience, then for listening very carefully, to determine once and for all what you know is absent from the scene and also to find the occasional contrast within people, which makes them interesting, the touch of villain in the saint and vice versa.

What Happens: Initially, there is a relief of laughter as in seeing a parody of something taken deadly serious before. Then a security comes from eliminating some options completely from the scene. Finally, some spice and unexpected twists may be discovered.

> *There are great lessons in playing opposites. If you've got an unsympathetic role, try playing him like the hero. The script won't let you succeed, but you'll find something worth keeping.*
> —Jeff Daniels

Exercise 7.33

Layering

Gradually add extreme conditioning forces into the first beat of the scene. Make the space arctic cold or swelteringly hot and humid, blindingly light or all dark shadows. Makes the characters dreadfully late or having had to wait forever. Give yourself an extreme physical condition (a dreadful cold, the worst hangover of your life, a devastating injury). Manipulate various combinations, then back off to more subtle, nuanced circumstances, but those with constant influence.

What Happens: If you tend to play in a bland, neutral state, this will shake you out of that. It opens up the senses. Even though the exercise choices may be too extreme to retain, an intense physical awareness tends to linger. Also, with the concentration so strongly on the body, some surprisingly natural readings emerge.

Exercise 7.34

Rally squad

1. Select four class members to serve as a cheering section for each actor. Each "squad" stands on a separate side of the acting area.

2. Perform the scene, turning continuously to your squad for encouragement and advice before returning to give your next line. Squads should react to the other side much as you did to opposing teams in high school. They should cheer their hero on to victory. They should speak out encouragement and comfort to their player.

Variations: Split the class down the middle and have the actor play, each to his own half of the house. If the actors are a man and a woman, let each sex root for its own. Or divide the class between those over and under the age of twenty. Find some group identification that gets adrenalin flowing.

What Happens: All the competitive elements of the scene are suddenly quite clear. The scoring of points is sharper. The rally squad can carry over into the private audience, so that each character feels supported in her part of the conflict. Most important, there is an infusion of relish, each actor savors her chance to play, and the resulting scene tends to have a greater feeling of playfulness, once the shouting dies down.

Exercise 7.35

Speed-through

Run the scene as rapidly as the words and moves will come, keeping all the values present and playing it in the same emotional key as always. Save this one for the very final stage of rehearsal, close to the last time the scene will be presented in class. Try to go through all your normal evaluations and interior monologs, as well as the script and blocking itself, so that all ingredients are included, only faster.

What Happens: Suddenly indulgent pauses or subtext work that has become labored is revealed.

You find places where the lines *do* work that fast because of the urgency of the moment. You may even find some places to overlap each other's lines, as people often do in life. You discover you can evaluate *during* lines, instead of doing all your alternatives between speeches. Conversely, you find out which pauses and extended evaluations are absolutely essential to the scene.

Character Confidence

These next two exercises, in which each actor faces the audience as the character, but without the script, can make you feel you own the role. If your preparation has been inadequate, they can also make you aware of how much more you need to dig in. Most actors develop real confidence when they can take the character before an audience without the absolute necessity of the playwright's words. When you go back to the security of those words, a new surge of authority tends to accompany them.

Exercise 7.36

Character Hot Seat

A variation on the Character Interview (Exercise 7.16), but with somewhat greater intensity, more like a grilling by a district attorney. The audience gets to ask any questions they want of the character, but should focus on forcing him to justify his behavior. A class member may be chosen to play head prosecutor. Any ethically questionable act by the character should receive particular attention.

What Happens: By this time, actors are secure enough to enjoy the confrontational challenge and take on all comers. The Magic If gets a genuine workout because it is essential to become the character from a completely nonjudgmental perspective. You retain the character's own sense of conviction regarding the appropriateness of her acts.

Exercise 7.37

Comparisons

The character appears before the class and speaks about the actor.

1. What does the character think of this person presuming to play him?
2. What does the character feel the actor still needs to work on to get it right?
3. What does the character feel the two of them have most and least in common?
4. Would the character like to know and hang out with the actor in real life or would they probably not get along?

After the character presents her basic opinions, the audience is free to ask questions about the actor being described.

What Happens: The perspective is pleasurable and illuminating because the actor is being discussed as if he is not there. The actor tends to feel he has finally got the character down if he can actually discuss himself as the character. The immersion is finally complete.

Exercise 7.38

Character Encounter, Part II: The Sequel

Unlike most sequels, this one can be as good as the original. Now that the actors have been together as the characters for some time, a more challenging encounter is possible and productive. Review these questions the night before doing the exercise because your answers may involve actually creating shared experiences between your character and that of your scene partner. With the same format as the Partner and Character encounters from Chapters 4 and 5, complete these questions as the character you are playing:

1. You tend to hurt me most often when you . . .
2. The single time you hurt me most was when . . .
3. What I love most about our relationship is . . .
4. The part of my life I prefer not to discuss with you is . . .
5. I cannot stand the way you . . .
6. I was proudest and most moved to know you and be part of your life when . . .
7. You and I are most similar in . . .
8. You and I are completely different in . . .
9. I envy the way you . . .
10. If I could wish and make something happen for you, it would be . . .

Variation: Repeat the exercise with your partner as your actual selves.

What Happens: The relationship is explored with greater depth and emotion than in the past. The shared histories of the two people emerge with more layers. If the actors choose to do the variation, their own working relationship often has more depth and dimensions.

Exercise 7.39

Meet Another Character

1. Either the teacher or groups of classmates should pick characters from different scenes and set up circumstances in which they might encounter each other.
2. A public place where these two might actually run into each other works best.
3. Keep your character's point of ignorance, regarding the other person, and respond without your audience knowledge of the scene you watched your classmates perform earlier.

The characters you have seen in other contexts now provide enjoyable challenges to yours. Actors inevitably begin to think about how their characters would respond to all the others, expanding their sense of those characters at large.

Scene study provides a great chance to take a small part of a script and come at it so many ways that both you and the script seem to grow. No matter what you discover, there is always another possibility.

Exercise 7.40

Offstage Action: Analysis

What new information do you have from this chapter that could influence your progress in each of the OA areas? If needed, review, the subcategories on pages 29–37.

1. Negating newness
2. Pleasant as possible
3. Keeping cool
4. Sensing signals
5. Winning ways

6. Image
7. Richer relationships
8. Social savvy
9. Prediction potential
10. Career capabilities

Specifically: What have you learned from playing your scene character that may be useful in playing yourself?

Anger isn't just yelling. Anger has a thousand faces. That's what acting is. Which of those thousand faces? Often the least obvious is the most interesting.

–Steve Martin

8

Performance Process

What to expect from first audition through closing night

The process is me going into my bag. You want funny, deep, smart, musical? I'll dig it out for you.
—Jamie Foxx

The acting process is a lot like sex. Fun to do. Hard to talk about.
—Paul Bettany

The director's job should be to open the actor up and, for God's sake, leave him alone.
—Dustin Hoffman

I call myself an actor, not an actress. I mean, when did you last go to the doctress?
—Alfre Woodard

Acting taught me everything I know about writing and directing. Most directors don't know s_ _t about acting. Actors are used to dealing with directors who don't understand what they do or how they do it or how to talk to them about it.
—Quentin Tarantino

Theatre has powerful protocol. Learn it if you want to join the family. Every year talented newcomers get well cast, offend many, and become immediate history. Or it takes a long time for anyone to risk working with them again. Often the offending newcomer is just a victim of ignorance. The actor's talent is ready, but not his work ethic, daily communication, and sense of proportion. He has learned how to act but not how to "act." He gets overwhelmed and blows it. I once heard a veteran actor refer to this phenomenon, while watching a recently fired young actor depart, as "choking the baby on meat."

Some things you are better off not having too early. You don't play King Lear when you're seventeen, and you don't want to play *anything* until you understand basic behavior in the theatre. This chapter more than any other will deal with what makes onstage different from off.

Acting Etiquette

> *Acting is horrible, painful, and yet also intoxicating and emotionally liberating.*
> —Jodie Foster
>
> *Childbirth is easy compared to giving birth to a role in a play.*
> —Helen Hayes
>
> *I am an actor. An actress is someone who wears boa feathers.*
> —Sigourney Weaver

Most actors call themselves actors. Most of us only use the term "actress" when discussing awards shows. Actors expect to become self-sufficient, knowing that they cannot necessarily depend on a director to do any of their work for them. Actors are as generous, supportive, and loving as any group in the world. Forced to compete against each other for parts, they nurture each other in every other way. They have a huge tolerance for personal eccentricity and almost no tolerance for laziness, stupidity, or disloyalty. Because we are so widely (and wildly) different from each other and encourage each other to be so, it is easy to miss the areas where we are all alike. There are standards we all share. The process of putting together a play has a (often unspoken) code of procedure and behavior.

Taking Time

If you have some theatre experience, use this chapter to review, brush up, and most important, look for some gaps in your own acting etiquette or some factors you may not have considered before. If you are new to theatre, study how to join the club before you join.

The biggest surprise for most newcomers is, inevitably, the enormous time commitment. Although the process of putting together a production varies wildly, the following will do as a model of traditional rehearsal patterns.

1. *Audition notices:* Posters and ads describing when, where, and how tryouts are to be conducted.

2. *Auditions:* Basic tryouts, often spread over more than one day, usually held in the evenings.

3. *Callbacks:* Smaller group narrowed down by director for another look, possibly a different set of audition activities. Often no one is actually "called" on the phone, but rather a list is posted. Know where and when it will appear.

4. *Cast list posted:* Notice of casting, may involve initialing next to your name by way of acceptance.

5. *First company meeting:* Introductions of participants to each other, and sharing of director's production concept with the company.

6. *Show and tell:* Costume and set designers (plus other possible specialty designers) demonstrate their renderings and explain visual concepts.

7. *Read-throughs:* Exploratory sessions, often sitting in a circle, just reading aloud, focusing on script, possibly stopping to cut some passages and discuss relationships.

8. *Blocking:* Physical staging, slow and laborious, may range all the way from director meticulously preplanning and simply instructing actors, to director planning none of it and weeks of exploration.

9. *Fittings:* Costume pieces tried on you and adjusted at various points in construction process.

10. *Character/Ensemble development:* Rehearsals geared toward getting individuals into character and feeling like a group.

11. *Coaching:* Sessions devoted to individual acting problems, seldom involving more than director and one or two actors at a time.

12. *Intensives:* An "anything goes" period, usually working very small portions of script, over and over, in great detail and out of sequence.

13. *Polish:* Work on flow and builds for whole show, more and more running through an entire act or whole script, without stopping.

14. *Promotion:* Taping media ads, doing interviews, taking scenes to special events, posing for publicity photos, selling the show.

15. *Tech-ins:* Adding lights, props, sound, set pieces, all technical elements— lengthy sessions requiring infinite patience from everyone.

16. *Dresses:* Rehearsals just before opening, done as close as possible to actual performances, with all ingredients present, seldom more than three rehearsals, one of which is sometimes a preview.

17. *Opening:* Official first night, after months of prior work.

18. *Run:* Scheduled performances, usually with adjusted calls or times you are expected to arrive at the theatre.

19. *Brush-ups:* Rehearsals called, when considerable time exists between performances, to review lines and get it back in shape, often done without technical elements, unless cues are tricky and also need review.

20. *Closing and strike:* Final performance, followed by taking down set, storing props and costumes, cleaning make-up and dressing rooms, taking down lights, and so on. Process involves both actors and technicians.

Usually, audition notices go out two to three weeks before tryouts, the audition process takes under a week, the show itself rehearses at least four weeks, and rarely runs longer than three weeks if it is a college or community theatre production. (Commercial productions may close after a single performance or run for years. In fact, all time frames vary wildly in commercial theatre.) So the entire process takes, on the average, a few months, but this time can be greatly expanded if the show is large and complex. Big musicals and Shakespeares often rehearse at least twelve weeks because of all the extra dance, singing, fighting training, and special skills needed to develop the styles of performance. Most shows rehearse at least five evenings a week for three to four hours, and in the final stretch may rehearse daily, weekends included, with tech and dress rehearsals going into the wee hours.

A popular statistic for minimum play rehearsals is one hour for every minute of running time. So a small cast, single set, contemporary, realistic play that runs 2 hours (120 minutes) plus intermission would rehearse a bare minimum of 120 hours. This figure could easily quadruple with large casts and difficult scripts. You need to determine if you have the time to do all this before you ever attend auditions.

What follows are some basic questions to consider at each stage of the performance process.

Auditions

Audition Preparation

- Are scripts available to check out and read beforehand? Find out where and for how long. Why go in blank?

- Is there a definite production concept that might affect how you could be used? Is there something about yourself that you can punch up? Ask around.

- Are any roles pre-cast and not worth shooting for? Ask only people who know. There are always false rumors on this one.

- Will there be cold readings or are you to prepare material? If you need to present something memorized, need it be from the script? Even if it is cold readings, there's nothing stopping you from practicing and making your reading at least lukewarm. Does "prepared" mean a polished reading or a fully staged, memorized, finished presentation?

- Can someone who knows your work and the play advise you where your best casting potential is in this show?

- Does this director regularly use certain audition methods, ask certain questions, show definite preferences? What kinds of actors does this director seem to admire? What kinds of procedures are known to be standard when this person is in charge? You can research the director, not just the script.

- Can you get into the space beforehand to get comfortable and maybe have a friend help you check your projection?

- What to wear? Something that will not get between the director's imagination and visualizing you in the final production. Full costume and make-up are too much, but try not to look all wrong for the play. If it's an elegant drawing room comedy, your sweats and your sneakers are a bad choice. Pick the closest thing, in your closet, to the spirit of the play.

- Have you thought of all your potential time conflicts over the next few months, so that you can list them? Have you thought of your responses to questions that might be on the forms?

Audition Behavior

- Which night(s) are you going to attend? Most people suggest going the first night, especially if you're new. Directors go home with actors in their minds, after the first night, no matter how hard they try to wait to cast.

- How early should you get there? Right at the beginning, when a series of instructions are often given and questions answered.

- Is there someone in charge here besides the director? Is there a stage manager or assistant or some troubleshooter? This is the person to ask things.

- Is the director the only one who can help you? Leave him alone until there is a break. Never, ever talk to him while another actor is up there reading.

- Are there instructions written down? Read anything handed out carefully so you don't need to request info that's already been given to you.

- What if you're asked (on a form or in person) if you will accept any part? If you'll work on a crew? If you can miss work for some rehearsals? If you will change your hair color? Lose some weight? Grow a beard? Gain some weight? These are fairly standard requests, and no one can tell you how to answer. But give yourself some time to think about it, so you are not so staggered by the question that you can no longer concentrate. It is always OK to say you will think it over, and let them know by the end of the evening or the next day.

- Are you tensing up? It is always all right to warm up. Are you getting too loud and chatty because you're nervous? Remind yourself to support every person who reads. Don't ever get so thrilled that a hotshot actor you admire is talking with you that you distract from someone else struggling onstage.

- Are you studying the other actors? This session can turn into a master class if you observe closely. Watch not only those who do well, but those who don't. You probably have tons of examples of what to do and what not to do right before your eyes.

- Do you need to leave? Make sure it's all right. If you can't do that, tell at least one person, who plans to stay, that you've gone and where you'll be.

- Do you know when you might hear something?

- Where the list will be posted? Are you absolutely sure of all details for callback time, place, procedure?

Audition Activities

- Are you asked to do something weird? Think of it as a game and give yourself permission to have fun. Often your poise, imagination, and sense of adventure are being tested. It doesn't all have to make sense.

- Do you get a chance to choose a partner to read with? Check out everyone for those who look right with you, people who make you comfortable. This is a real chance to use your insight instead of just grabbing someone.

- Are you being asked to change your reading? This is always a good sign. Respond positively. Directors rarely direct people at auditions who do not interest them.

- Are you puzzled by the range of activity? Remember, anything that could happen in acting class can happen here in a highly condensed form. You study improv to release your spontaneity. If improv is used here, it is probably to test your spontaneity.

- Do you sometimes just have to stand there while the director studies you and others? She is looking at combinations: families, lovers, ages. Let yourself relax and try not to look like a hunted animal. You *are* being considered.

- Is there a chance to volunteer? Take it. You've just been up there. Fine. They'll see you again. Within reason, actors are aggressive, and enthusiasm to be onstage now says you will carry this enthusiasm through rehearsal.

- Are you rushing and not connecting when you read? Stop and ask yourself what you want, what's in the way, what your plan is, how much the person opposite means to you, the quick basics. Don't let yourself forget the way you always act most effectively. Take time to feel the words and to see the person reading opposite you.

Callbacks

- Is there something you need to prepare, check out, a person you are to work with in advance, information you still need to provide? Read the notice with incredible care, so your joy over making the list doesn't cloud your sense of detail.

- Are you not on the list? You still need to check the cast list, because some directors only call back people they are undecided about, and do cast some roles based on the initial reading.

- Is there something the director would like to see from you that you have not yet shown? Ask. If you make callbacks, you are a contender. Is there a mannerism she would like you to modify, a quality to punch up, some alteration in your appearance? You have a golden opportunity to show the kind of actor you will be if cast.

- Any last-minute reservations? This is the time to get out. If you drop out after the cast list is posted, you do serious, possibly irreparable, damage to your reputation. You inconvenience many. And no matter how thrilled the person is who replaces you, he and everyone else will always know he was not first choice. All because of you.

Rehearsal

Preparation for First Rehearsal

- Are you supposed to check out a script beforehand? Probably. This is a good time to mark your lines with highlighter or in some way that helps you focus.

- Is there a callboard for this production? Start checking it daily. This is where they tell you they need to take your measurements for costumes and each time you're needed for a fitting. This is where you may get a deadline for a form that needs to be filled out, so something can be sent to your hometown newspaper. This is where last-minute messages of all kinds are posted.

- Do you have your rehearsal supplies? Several pencils (not pens; you may need to do a lot of erasing), a notebook or journal, basic supplies (mouthwash, mints, whatever you need to "feel good about being close"), script, special clothing or shoes that may be needed? It helps to keep all this stuff together and ready.

Rehearsing Outside of Rehearsal

A common error made by new actors is to schedule yourself so tightly that you can fit in rehearsal but very little else during each day. This is what you are generally expected to do outside of rehearsal:

1. Analyze the character.

2. Memorize lines.

3. Research the role for background information on further understanding the world of the play.

4. Apply the director's notes from last night.

5. Experiment with character approaches.

6. Develop the vocal life of the character.

7. Develop the physical life as well.

8. Brush up on material that hasn't been worked in a week.

9. Attend costume fittings.

10. Participate in publicity photo sessions and interviews.

This list could expand if you need to work with a coach on a particular skill or if you and one of your acting partners need to explore some aspect of your characters' relationship together.

To keep your bases covered, it's a good idea to plan on an hour of offstage re-. hearsal, usually by yourself, for every hour spent onstage with the rest of the company. You may not need this much every day, but sometimes you may need more. And few things are worse than having a director say to you, "Your work was sluggish tonight. You've got to get more rest." Then, after she walks away, you turn to your crammed schedule, and ask yourself, "When?"

Rehearsal Behavior

- What is the scheduled starting time? Whatever it is, it means that you have already arrived, unpacked, gone to the restroom, warmed up as necessary, and taken care of chitchat. It's not the time you breeze in the door out of breath. It's not a bad idea to aim to arrive a half-hour before the scheduled time and take care of business.

- How long ahead will you know when you are called? There is no guarantee. Some directors post each day what will be on that night and never post ahead. That's an extreme, but even if you have what looks like a detailed schedule, check the callboard daily for last-minute changes. Someone may be sick, and your scene is going to be worked instead of hers.

- Some of your favorite lines are cut? Try not to gasp, moan, or collapse on the floor. Strive for grace. Should you try to get these words put back in? Only if you are completely convinced they are essential to your character. Not just because you like them. Think about this for a while.

- Feeling inhibited by some big guns in the cast? Get to know them as soon as possible. Work past the image to the real people. Feeling cautious generally? Don't let yourself start bottling up. No one expects a performance yet. Rehearsal is where you need to feel free to experiment before finalizing, where you dare to be foolish and vulnerable.

- Conflicts with class demands and show demands? Can you expect theatre teachers to let you out of assignments or delay them because you are in a play? No. You can ask, but realize you are asking a big favor, and it is because of your own failure to structure your time.

- Missed a fitting? Beg the designer's forgiveness. Go volunteer to work in the shop. Costumers can put pins places you would rather not feel them. Need help in feeling like your character? Wear the closest you can come up with to the right rehearsal clothes, either checked out from the costume shop or from your own closet. If the character wears heels and fitted skirts, don't wait. Get into these the first week. The character is a cowboy? Get in boots. Even throwing your coat over your shoulder, in place of the cape that will eventually be there, is better than nothing. Don't underestimate the power of clothes to transform you. Don't be embarrassed by adding these things. Some in the company may tease you, but secretly recognize you as a serious actor.

- Blocking coming at you fast and furious? Write it in shorthand. There is standard code for common stage movements. In addition to using only the initials (DR for downright, UC for upcenter, and so on), of stage areas, the symbols shown in Figure 8-1 are often employed:

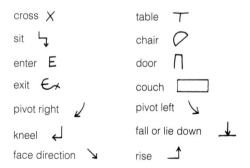

Figure 8-1 Stage Shorthand

Exercise 8.1

Stage Shorthand

Write the following directions as quickly and economically as possible:

1. Cross down left to the table, pivot right, and exit.
2. Cross to the door and face upright.
3. Enter up center and sit on the couch.
4. Move from the table to the door to the chair, then exit left.
5. Enter down left, kneel at door, rise, cross down, and sit.

Practice ways of getting lengthy directions down on paper with the least possible amount of writing.

- Or make up your own. Confident you'll remember the movements without writing them down? Don't be. There may be lots of time before this scene is called again, and you may be struggling with lines by that time, so your concentration will be scattered. Write it down. And check it again before you sleep tonight to make sure you've got it.

- Are you being asked to do things you don't understand? Are you unclear about the objectives of some rehearsals? Ask, right away. Unlike an audition, there should be no hidden agenda here. You have a right to know why and wherefore.

- Tech staff or crew members attending rehearsals? Contact with box office and front of house staff? Treat every person on this show with maximum respect. Don't succumb, for an instant, to acting as though these people are your servants. They are fellow artists. And they don't get curtain calls.

- Feel like a haircut? Lightening your hair color? Going on a crash diet? Clear any potential change in your appearance with the director beforehand. Do you have any idea how many actors have foolishly altered the very thing the director liked best about their looks?

- What to eat and drink before rehearsal? Keep it light, so you don't get sluggish. Most actors choose long-term energy food, instead of stuff that gives you a surge that dies long before the end of rehearsal. No, don't even consider arriving even mildly drunk or stoned (or stunk and droned, a combination). Any experimenting (like rehearsing a character who drinks heavily by drinking) is on your own time, or by mutual agreement with the director and anyone else involved.

> *I had a lot of trouble working with my co-star, who was*
> *from the Cocaine School of Acting.*
>
> —Shirley MacLaine

- Getting bored or tired waiting for your scene to come up or to be called in to work? Bring other work (stop-and-start stuff) that can be done while waiting. Write in your acting journal! See if the costume shop needs someone to sew on buttons. Or work on your character in these stretches. Keep yourself energized and occupied.

Likely Deadlines

- For your analysis work? Usually about two weeks into the rehearsal period. Handed in? No, not usually, but shared with the group or just integrated into the rehearsal process by this time. Be prepared to answer all the character questions noted in Chapter 7.

- Outside research? Varies. Anything you don't know about the historical period, country, art, music, or styles of the people in the play is worth a few trips to the library. Will others feel disdain for you as an eager beaver? Only the motivationally impaired and the jealous.

- Lines? Some directors want them as soon as possible; most expect them the second time a scene is called after it is blocked. Rarely are there less than two full weeks with everyone off book before opening. If you are a slow study, start scheduling daily line workouts from the first day. Realize you tend to lose a lot of solid memorization once you are in front of the other actors, so consider checking memorization with the other people in your scenes before the actual deadline.

- Running lines? Usually an assistant director will help you. Other actors will usually be glad to. Calling for lines? Stay in the scene. Try not to look at the prompter. Give yourself a beat for the line to come. Try not to break character or concentration. Lines will come much faster if you stay in the moment itself, even when the words are rough.

After Opening

- Adjusting performance? Only in consultation with the director and anyone else influenced by being onstage with you.

- Reviews? Look for trends, if reviewed by a number of publications. If by one not-very-respected local critic, ignore altogether. Never take a copy to the theatre or quote it or grumble about it, or in any way inflict the review on others, who may wish to rise above it.

- Let down? It's inevitable after the rush of opening night. Don't succumb to second night blahs. Consider yourself a source of energy and fresh air for everyone you work with. It is always opening night for the audience. Always. Renew that night every night. These people deserve nothing less than your miraculous best.

> *I want to come out of a theater feeling that someone has touched me. The whole point is to have a revelatory experience, to be carried to the heights.*
>
> —Kathy Bates

- Brush-ups? May be called if show has been dark for a while. Lots of plays just perform on weekends, so may go Sunday through Wednesday or Thursday dark, and need at least a run-through before going to an audience again. Give yourself the same charge as just described.

- Some performances better than others? Inevitably. But these things happen for a reason. Try to make sure you aren't the reason. Which performance is best? Ideally, closing night. You grow a little bit every time you go out. And on closing, you look forward to the next time you will get to work with this script or develop further this kind of character.

- Strike? All actors become crew members until everything is put away. It's a tradition and not to be violated. This is not the moment to suddenly decide to have a fling with being irresponsible. See the experience through to the end.

Exercise 8.2

War Stories

Many of us learn the etiquette discussed by messing up once or twice. This is a good time for the more experienced members of the class to share their experiences in failing to plan well or to show maximum consideration for others in the process. Describe the event, what you got out of it, and the particular vows you made to yourself about working on productions in the future.

Adaptations

Adapting Show Process to Class Process

What happens in a production can simply be scaled down for a course in acting. How? You just look at the time frames, responsibilities, and deadlines, then modify them. The number of actors who function brilliantly when someone else imposes the schedule, but then collapse when they have to do some of this themselves is alarming.

It's a ten-minute scene? That means the bare minimum rehearsal period before the first time it's done in class is ten hours. Remember? The operative phrase here is "bare minimum." Full productions develop a cumulative effect. Scenes late in the play sometimes require less rehearsal because so much groundwork and layering has preceded them. Once you really know these characters and have experienced them in previous situations, you somehow earn the right to discover quickly in the final stretches. Obviously, a scene never has this advantage. So you only add time. Also your entire rehearsal period is more likely to be a few weeks, so you are condensing the performance process.

Shortcuts? You and your partner have discovered you are soul mates and probably are really brother and sister separated at birth? You are so well cast that each line of dialogue sounds as if it rolled off your very own tongue? A shining light descended on a rehearsal and every word uttered for the next five minutes was magic? There are no shortcuts. You can always rehearse a few more times, and discover some more values.

Look at each stage of the traditional preparation of a play and make sure that, to some extent, that period exists for your scene. Any chance to develop and share your work with an audience is a very big deal. Your scene is an important production, in miniature.

Schedules and Objectives

As soon as you get a partner, sit down together and map out a rehearsal period. Reserve generous time frames between now and the due date. You can always cancel an unnecessary rehearsal more easily than you can squeeze in an unanticipated one at the last minute. In class, you often have a partner before you have a scene, so selecting one may be your first objective, with a definite deadline.

Many actors just sit and read through the script for lots of sessions without any progression. Then one day, it becomes obvious that they've got to stand up and do some blocking, so they do that, and from then on in they just run through again and again, without progression. A certain amount of progress takes place despite this vapid approach. But not nearly as much as if you establish an objective for each time you get together. One meeting might be for no purpose but to get to know each other better, another to work on vocal technique and line delivery, another to clarify only subtext, another to develop the characters' shared history. There are so many tasks to be accomplished that the main problem is just which one today.

Stated objectives will also make you feel, when you leave, that you know why you were there. A great deal of acting is magical and mysterious. There is always plenty of that, no matter what. Some organization will actually free you to unlock the magic.

Exercise 8.3

Setting a Schedule

1. With your partner, copy a calendar and identify how many days you have until the "opening" of your scene, and if it is to be presented twice, how many days between "opening" and "revival."
2. Identify a specific meeting time with never more than two days between rehearsals.
3. Identify specific goals for some of the rehearsals, leaving others for pure experimentation.
4. Overdo the time commitment because it will be easier to cut back later than to cram in rehearsals not planned.
5. Consider working with a copy of a rehearsal schedule for a full production, crossing off irrelevant items like photo calls, but keeping some version of everything else.
6. Make sure you each have a copy and that you both understand not only the schedule itself but those times (such as memorization or analysis) when both of you agree to commit to considerable time outside of rehearsal as well.

Memorization

Some actors are quick studies and others are painfully slow. There is a definite trend to ask for lines earlier and earlier in rehearsal. It used to be thought that if actors memorized too early, they would lock the actual delivery of the line as well. So many exercises are now designed to liberate and vary delivery that the problem of locking is rare. If you have trouble getting lines down, here are some suggestions.

For Both Scenes and Monologs:

1. Highlighting lines, rather than underlining them, can make the lines seem to jump off the page and make a more vivid impression on your memory.
2. Work on lines for short periods (under half an hour) ideally a single beat mastered at each session. Marathon sessions are rarely retained.

3. Always memorize according to what the character *wants*, rather than doing words by rote. Memorize thought clusters and intention clusters rather than word clusters. Actors who forget or "go up" on lines are invariably those who have just placed the words in their heads, with narrow computer logic, so that when the word is gone, so are they.

4. Try getting up and moving in some way to load the words in after you have memorized them. If the scene has been blocked, go through your exact movements and lock the words in direct association with your staging as you speak them.

5. After you get through about a half a page, go back over and drill, then drill again. Never assume you've got lines without backtracking.

6. Place a card over your upcoming lines and reveal only as much to yourself as absolutely necessary as you cue yourself and master each line.

7. Use images to get a vivid film and/or still shot to associate with each group of words. The visual image as it pops back into your mind will tend to bring the lines with it. Add sharp physical and emotional sensations on key words as well.

8. Every time you memorize, review everything else you've memorized in the last few days as well. Go back to the beginning for a brush-up, which serves as a warm-up to get you in memorization mode.

9. Vary the tempo-rhythm with which you run the lines so you are open to different attacks in rehearsal. The variety of pacing will also make it less likely that you will forget when some surprise comes up during rehearsal that might tend to break your rhythm and concentration there.

10. At least every other day run lines as a speed through, as fast as you can without losing sense or emotional connection. You will find some places where you can speed up in performance, but more importantly doing it fast tends to solidify the words in your head.

For Scenes:

1. Start memorizing from your *cues*, not from the first word of your lines. Memorize at least the last half of your partner's speeches and listen closely as they near the end of each. Do not become one of those actors who are paralyzed because they were not expecting their partners to stop talking.

2. Cue yourself off motivating words (action cues) within your partner's speeches, the words that stimulate response, not off the last word (line cue) of his speech. Start gearing up to respond on a word or phrase while the other person is still talking.

3. Invest in a small hand held recorder that will fit in a pocket and that you can take anywhere. Tape record your partner's lines with spaces to run yours or, if your partner is feeling helpful, have her tape her lines, so you can run yours when she's not around but still wish to hear the right voice, giving you cues.

4. Make a second tape of everything, both your parts. This allows you to listen to a complete text while doing other tasks (driving, shaving, getting dressed) so you can let the words act on you without having to stop other activities. It also allows you to walk through your blocking without having to speak, which can enhance your sense of subtext.

5. Try using flash cards, with the other actor's lines on one side and yours on the other. Putting the cards together is time-consuming, but the mere act of writing them can speed memorization.

6. Ask a friend to hold the book, reading your partners lines to cue you, and correcting where you may have inadvertently re-written a line. Most people enjoy this and are glad to help.

7. If you are running lines at home or in any space with enough room, set up furniture so that it is close to your set and actually walk through your blocking, even looking at the empty space where your partner would be and endowing it with her presence.

8. To test how well you both know the scene when your partner is present, do a role reversal. This has many other rehearsal advantages but it definitely solidifies your mastery of the words.

For Monologs:

1. Divide the speech into parts. Most monologs have three to five sections. A subject might be introduced, a solution or two or three might be considered, and then some kind of conclusion might be made so the speech falls into a reaction-exploration-decision pattern. The parts may be places where you achieve new realizations. There is always a structure that can be subdivided into smaller manageable chunks.

2. Tape the speech very early and re-tape it as your interpretation grows more interesting and textured, really listening to and adjusting to the changes.

3. Tape the speech a half dozen times in succession so that you can just let the tape keep running and the words float over you while you go about some other task.

4. Highlight crucial words, using different colors for key verbs, nouns or important modifiers. Get a strong image of what these key words look like on the page.

5. Paraphrase the speech so you have a clear idea of what the character *might* have said but decided instead to use the words in the script. This will help you seem to actually choose the words.

6. Identify the reactions of your imaginary partner or listeners and use these response moments as places where you rest and re-evaluate before going on.

7. Run your speech while doing some physical exercise, such as jogging or riding an exercise bike. Sometimes the rhythm and exertion can help load in the words, as you multi-task.

8. Whenever you get stuck on a particular line or phrase, take time to give it an extra dose of visual and kinesthetic information. Make sure you have a highly vivid picture as well as a powerful sensation, an emotion, a physical impulse, a scent, a taste, a temperature—anything that can reinforce your memory of the line kinesthetically.

Working with a Teacher, Coach, or Director

All three of these guides attempt to help you, but in different ways. It's important to distinguish their functions, so you know what to expect. There are many exceptions to the following distinctions, but they hold true most of the time.

An acting *teacher* creates an environment (physical and emotional) and provides exercises, to help you explore and discover your own potential. The teacher rarely inflicts his will or forces change. He is aiming to make you self-sufficient, and, particularly in beginning acting classes, is usually more concerned with your overall awareness and growth as a person than with technical precision.

An acting *coach* functions much like a coach in sports, working with you on specific problems, having you try a number of solutions, fine-tuning the same moment, over and over, driving you a little farther than you thought possible. You go into a coaching session with definite problems to be solved. If it's a good session, you leave with some solved, and more to work on, because the coach has stimulated you to move ahead in specific areas. A coach's attention is in many ways the most direct or personal, and the efforts the most precise.

A *director* is the most likely of the three to impose her will on yours. She is the most likely to tell you (at some point, sooner or later in the rehearsal process) exactly what she wants and (very late in the process) to lock much of what you do. This is because she has an opening night, and a huge group of other company members to think about. In a show, you are part of a much larger package, a package that will ultimately be, in some way, marketed. One of my favorite directors said regularly to casts, "You are all like hands on a clock, very important, but I'm standing out here, and I'm the only one who can tell what time it is." The director is ultimately concerned, to a larger degree than the coach, and much larger than the teacher, with a finished product. The teacher is the most concerned with process.

These distinctions are arbitrary and often contradicted. Sometimes a director is mounting an experimental work that is highly process-centered, for example, with no interest in slick surfaces. Some teachers act as gurus, and instead of making their actors self-sufficient, they make the actors highly emotionally dependent on them. A director mounting shows involving styles or skills unfamiliar to his cast may move through all three roles. He may start by teaching, then evolve into coaching each performer, and only toward the end become a traditional director. The distinctions between the three are useful, however, for your own anticipation. Actors are sometimes naively disappointed because their work isn't "polished" in a class, failing to realize that surface is not the purpose. Others will go for a coaching session, expecting everything to be "fixed," upset when they leave, aware of even more work that needs to be done. All of these people, if they are conscientious artists, are trying to help make you strong. Even the director will only "fix" things for you, because he has an audience to think about. Work with all three guides, with realistic expectations, for long-term growth.

Working Without a Director

For years I went around saying, "What I really like is a strong director who knows exactly what he wants and will tell me." It took me quite a while to realize that what I was really saying was, "I don't know what I'm doing so I want to be told." The ideal relationship with a director is collaborative, full of mutual strength and support. No one has summed up the ideal more vividly than Stanislavski, who said, "A talented director may come along and drop just a word, the actor will catch fire and his role will glow with all the colors of his soul's prism." How's that for a good working relationship?

A director who tells and shows you everything, with no exploratory encouragement, is hardly treating you like a collaborator. Such directors are probably eagerly awaiting the time when robots get sophisticated enough to use them instead of you.

At the other extreme, any actor should be prepared to survive the absence of a director's help. There are many productions where someone is listed in that capacity, but that person did precious little to provide vision and coordination. And remember, the director can leave the theatre, the town, the country. You are the one who has to go out in front of the audience.

So, if you're lucky enough to have help, grab it and relish it. But if you are on your own, you can do it. You can survive. The primary switch you need to make is in attitude. Every time you have to block yourself, or go to a friend for feedback on a speech, or make up a rehearsal objective, without being told by the resident authority figure, think of it as one more chance to grow self-sufficient. "I need a director" is too easy to say and impossible to survive.

Working with a Non-Director

Sometimes you simply get no feedback whatsoever from the person in charge. It doesn't usually work to go up to her and say, "Give me some feedback." You tend to get an answer like, "You're doing fine." It doesn't usually work to stop her after rehearsal and ask, "Got any notes for me?" You'll probably be told, "No, I'll let you know."

Now, it's important to remember that if everything is going smoothly, *no notes are good notes.* Many directors only address what is wrong, and you may indeed be doing well. But if you feel insecure and awkward, you have to devise a strategy. Your best bet is to ask questions that *must* be answered, like, "Why do you think my character does this?" or "Which of the ways I tried that sequence has been working best?" or "Tonight, I'm going to try this. Tell me if you think it adds, or if we should go back to the other approach." Always, of course, keep it friendly and respectful. You need to be not only aggressive, but a bit clever. If you are getting no help, you can take the initiative. But you must provide the framework for a reticent director to respond to you.

All directors find it easier to edit your work than to relentlessly feed you with ideas, energy, and courage. Actors who bring a lot into the process allow a director to add shape and nuance, which is the director's ideal function. It is a good idea to bring a lot of choices to rehearsal.

> *I do not believe acting should be smaller than life. I just enjoy throwin' myself at stuff, risking being too much. I'd rather have someone say, "Tone it down, Hunter, whooaah!" than not feel I'm giving enough.*
>
> —Holly Hunter

Working with Untrained Observers

Almost anyone who lives observes human behavior. And most people are quite good at detecting when that behavior is dishonest, phony, stiff, or distracting. So you do not need to go to a supposed theatre expert to get feedback while working on a scene or monolog. Sometimes friends and family, who are completely unconnected with the theatre, can give you some of the best information and a fresh perspective on your work.

You don't want to drown them in actor lingo, or in any way make them feel less than experts. Just show them what you're working on, and have them respond, human to human. Below are some questions that you can ask absolutely anyone about your scene.

Exercise 8.4

What You See

Show your work to a friend with no specific theatre background and use the following questions as the basis for soliciting feedback:

1. What kind of a person do I seem to be?

2. How old am I? What kind of background? Beliefs?

3. Where am I when this speech takes place?

4. What had happened to me just before the scene? Where did I come from? What had I been doing?

5. What do my movements and gestures say about me? When do my moves look unnatural?

6. How would you imagine me dressed and looking if the show were fully produced?

7. To whom am I talking? What is my relationship to her? What is her reaction to me? Does my listener ever move or respond? When? How?

8. Which moments do you find hardest to understand? Which are most difficult to believe?

9. What do I seem to want in this scene? What does this person seem to want out of life?

10. What do you notice going on between my words? What am I deciding *not* to do or say?

11. What, if any, changes do I seem to go through? How do I modify my behavior?

12. Is there anything getting in the way between me and what I want? What is it?

13. What about this character is just like me? What is different?

14. Do I remind you of anyone else when I do the speech?

15. When do you find the whole thing least interesting?

16. How would you feel about being friends with this kind of character?

17. What effect did my imaginary surroundings have on me? Any you could see?

18. Does this scene take place right now, in the present time? If not, when? How can you tell?

19. What kinds of feelings did listening and watching me create in you?

20. At what points did you think my concentration seemed to be more on myself the actor than on the needs and desires of the character?

Notice that all these questions are open-ended, the same kinds of questions needed with non-directors. Nothing can be answered, "Yes," "No," or "Maybe." The person you're talking to has got to give you information. There are also almost no value judgments or implied requests for compliments. Why? Most people want to tell you what you want to hear.

So if you just do your speech and say, "What do you think?" your friend is likely to say, "Great."

YOU: Any suggestions?

FRIEND: No. Boy, I could never do that.

YOU: Was I believable?

FRIEND: I guess so. Sure.

YOU: The character is younger than I am. Was I young enough?

FRIEND: Oh, right . . . Absolutely.

YOU: Could you see the wind blowing?

FRIEND: Wind? . . . Uh . . . Yeah, wind. Whatever.

You can see that this goes nowhere. You are implying a desired answer. If you just ask how old the character is, you get exactly what the other person really thinks. If your friend says fifty-three, you know you have some "youthening" work ahead of you in rehearsal.

Clearly, you will not want to ask everything on the list of everyone you know. Expand or contract the list according to the needs of the scene and your personal respect for the opinions of your auditor on life in general. Substitute other questions based on your character analysis. An added benefit to sharing your work regularly with friends and family is that the unveiling in class is less tense, because you have already unveiled in bits and pieces. Don't neglect this source. You may get a lot of the help you need right at home.

Exercise 8.5

A Little Help from my Friends

1. Pick three friends or family members who know nothing about theatre.

2. Identify what you particularly value about each of these people for their wisdom or understanding of human behavior. Where are they wise and compassionate?

3. Share your scene or monolog with them, using the questions in Exercise 8.4 as a guide.

4. Think of your friend as an expert on truth, and use that expertise to help you shape the scene.

Criticism: Give and Take

Criticism in acting class is a free gift that actors give to each other. It is especially important in assignments that will be repeated, to give your classmates all the reactions you have so you can help them go back into rehearsal, armed. If terms aren't coming as quickly as you want them to, just revert to the kind of vocabulary and categories described earlier. If you say to a fellow actor, "I wasn't always sure what you wanted from him," that's a valid expression, which may mean the actor's objectives weren't clear, and it could also mean that you weren't looking very carefully, but at least you have shared it. What the actors do with these free gifts is up to them.

Many beginning actors simply will not take part in critiquing a classmate's work, leaving it all up to others. It is one thing if you're simply drawing blanks, but if you're still worried about others thinking you're cruel, opinionated, or out of line, you are sabotaging yourself and them. It's selfish to keep to yourself and not dare to risk disapproval. Remember you are invested in these people and they in you. Shying away from generous confrontation is not generous at all.

> *I've worked hard as a person and as an actor, to fight my*
> *way through shyness. It's our responsibility as human*
> *beings to share with others. Being shy and withdrawn is*
> *selfish.*
> –Michael Douglas

How to take criticism that seems harsh? Remind yourself that nobody criticizes unless he cares; it takes too much energy. Being criticized beats not being noticed at all. And it goes with the territory. Drama critics have the right to print comments about actors that would get other writers sued for libel. And many abuse that freedom.

> *The terrible thing about reviews is that they're never good*
> *enough. The bad reviews lodge in your heart like a poisoned*
> *arrow . . . I remember the reviewer who first panned me.*
> *And he's still out there writing—the bastard.*
> –Helen Mirren

The healthiest actor I know carries the following review with him in his makeup kit and puts it up on the mirror in each new dressing room he occupies:

> Mr. _____ spends the entire evening onstage making a pitiful attempt to prove his masculinity. The attempt is pathetic, boring and a complete failure.

The actor manages to find humor and solace in this old review. He's home free. No one will ever write anything worse about him.

Critiquing

I believe everyone in class should be engaged in critiquing the performances of others. The teacher brings experience and training. Everyone else brings empathy and peer support. This is an invaluable combination. Vital critiques involve the whole group. Learning to offer in a way that others are able to receive it will serve you in countless other contexts. Sometimes you learn as much observing and analyzing what others do as when you yourself perform and receive criticism. It also keeps you engaged in class if you know you are going to be asked to respond. It prevents you from tuning out, getting overly nervous about your own upcoming performance, or being too self-absorbed. Because there is more objectivity when someone else is on the spot, you can often take in the ideas comfortably and transfer them to their own work. A critique needs to be nurturing but candid and supportive but challenging. Following are a few ideas to consider:

1. *Hits and Misses, Roses and Thorns*
   A critique session should always establish what is already working *before* you move on to suggestions for change. If a scene is like a house, starting with "hits" is like laying a foundation on which to build the rest of the structure. It is vital to identify what is already working so the actors can take that and build the whole house on something solid. This also creates an atmosphere where those who have just performed feel validation that makes them more responsive to the suggestions coming up. My students call these Roses and Thorns (some refer to them as Hits and Misses or Strokes and Pokes) wherein students are presented with the fragrant, colorful accolades before the class moves down the stem to the more prickly, but essential, points in order "to make it even better."

2. *Why Always Positive Strokes?*
   Some actors just want the suggestions for improvement and find the positive strokes syndrome somewhat perky and "Pollyana-ish" in its insistence on the affirmative. But there is a very practical, pragmatic reason for this praise phase. There are actors who, if you don't stroke them for their strong suits, will go back to the drawing board and throw out all the good stuff! Most of us lack the judgment, particularly at the beginning of our training, to recognize when we are doing our strongest work and what about ourselves we should continue to nurture. Never regard the roses phase of critique as superfluous, as it truly offers you a sense of your own strong suits and building blocks.

3. *Having Students Be Responsible for Each Other*
   It can sometimes help critiques to have classmates assigned as lead critics or first respondents. This can be especially effective in partnerships where two groups are responsible for observing closely each other's work and finding a way to lead off the critique sessions. These observers will watch closely and

often share acute insights. This also eliminates the syndrome of shy students vs. those whose hands and voices are always bursting forth. Everyone has a moment of stepping up first, before others join in.

4. *Difference Between First and Second Class Showings*
If scenes or monolog are shown twice, keep your comments distinct for each. The first time something goes up in class, be precise and specific. It's about getting this particular project better. The next time, you don't say things like, "That bit still didn't work," or "I didn't believe you loved him." These are too specific to the presentation that just happened. Think more about what your classmates can learn to expand their work generally. Instead, "keep working on small details" or "on really connecting with your partner" are useful because they give actors goals for future work, dealing with their tendencies and your wishes for their continued growth.

5. *Teachers Last*
Many are waiting for judgment from the leader and are dying to hear what the teacher has to say. But if classmates respond first it is more encouraging and helpful as all of you are learning the critique process. And if the authority in the room was also first respondent, many would be reticent to disagree or offer alternative suggestions. Teachers will monitor feedback and diffuse that which is irrelevant or mean spirited, translate vague responses and make more palatable severe criticism. They will actively finesse the critique, but still wait to offer direct feedback. It is always best for the teacher to render judgment last.

6. *Teaching Vocabulary and Concepts Through Critique*
When new terms have been recently introduced, it is often a good idea, before plunging into hits and misses, your teacher may ask right out of the gate, for example if a scene has been presented, what the most important given circumstances, objective, strategies and changes in tactics were for each of the performers involved. Or even simper, where the character were, what was their relationship and how they changed during the scene. If you are reticent to claim something was not clear, raise your hand and ask something like, "What did the class feel these characters wanted most?"

7. *Time Constraints*
Sometimes classes do not allow time for projects to be evaluated in the group as a whole in which shortcuts must be employed. If it is a short project, those of you sitting around the performers may be asked to offer them quick Roses and Thorns with your teacher using a stopwatch for when it is time to make a switch. Sometimes, your instructor may ask for quick roses from the group, "What is the very best part of this presentation we have just seen?" then segue into, "What would make it better?"

8. *Effective Critique Forms*

Sometimes time limitations make oral critiques impossible. In these cases the class may be asked to fill out written responses instead, possibly half sheets of paper sectioned into a Roses and a Thorns part for quick, open-ended comments. There may also be key vocabulary terms in a side column for you to circle if you thought these were unclear or put stars next to them if you thought they were successful.

9. *Employing Present/Future Tense*

When you speak of the work just presented in the past tense it seems in some ways a dead event. When you speak in the present/future tense it has a sense of ongoing dynamics. So it is always more effective to say, "I don't think you are joyous enough at that amazing news, so just go for it," instead of, "You were supposed to be happy but just seemed kind of blah at the news." The former suggests potential for growth, the latter a sort of mini death sentence. Always consider the scene and the actor as a living, dynamic work in progress, so all feedback is based on how it will be presented next time, or in a larger sense how this actor will continue to grow in the future.

10. *Receiving Criticism*

If you have rarely been publicly critiqued before, the experience can feel quite devastating. And if twenty classmates are all offering advice, it can seem as if you under radar attack. But understand first of all that only those who care offer criticism, others make no effort, and, while it might have been lovely to bask in adoration, this is all about growth. Always ask yourself, "What am I getting here that will help me get better?" instead of all the other mind traps like, "Why do they hate me so much? Why do I suck? Why don't they understand what I am trying to do?" None of these are going to help you, so prepare yourself in the following way:

Before the scene or monolog goes up, ask yourself honestly if you did everything you could to make it awesome. If you slacked at any point in preparation, own that this may be caught and called out. Remind yourself that what you *think* you put out is not necessarily what others *receive*. So your job may be to take your brilliant ideas and make them more clear next time. And tell yourself to be grateful for anyone's ideas, even if you consider them bogus, because they are paying attention to you.

As the critique occurs, here is the protocol:

Grace Under Fire

Never, ever object, defy, deflect or in any way disagree with anything being said. Do not speak at all unless it is to clarify your understanding of what has just been said.

Do not reject critiques in any fashion, either verbally or by rolling your eyes or giving the critic a look that says how you are appalled and offended. Under no circumstances ever challenge or oppose your critics. Realize that what they experienced may have been different from your intentions, and you will always lack the objectivity to be where they were during your presentation. It may have felt a great deal differently than it came across. Accept all with grace.

All Feedback is a Gift

Many classmates sit silent and offer you nothing. Some may give you harsh feedback out of jealousy or some other non honorable motivation, but the majority who rise to the occasion do so because they care about you and your work. Recognize this. How easy is it to just sit there? How challenging is it to try to offer constructive suggestions for change? It is way too easy to resent the negative feedback. Remind yourself of everyone who does work no one ever notices and to be grateful for being noticed.

Record it as Spoken

Write down *everything* said. Research shows that from a general critique of our work, most of us will only remember seven comments at most and often edit or change those we do not want to hear. Because comments can be both forgotten and wildly distorted in your memory, it is important to get them exactly right, especially the ones that you feel are most "offensive" or "challenging." Especially write down, word-for word, the comments you find most objectionable, because your imagination may escalate them into wildly inaccurate and offensive versions that never happened.

Sleep on It

Study the hardest remarks to accept or comprehend. As you sleep on it, ask what wisdom is there even if you still totally disagree. Often you didn't like them because they struck some deep chord of truth. In my own experience, the feedback that I thought was a total crock at the time given was often the most deeply helpful the next day. And I recognized that finding it hard to hear simply meant that it was more true. Decide later which components may have some merit and which are worth ignoring. But do not cave to every criticism without any center or standards. Do feel free to reject suggestions, simply not before extended reflection.

Process versus Product

Process does not stop one day in rehearsal, as product suddenly replaces it. If the distinctions between these two are too sharp, the work changes radically, rarely for the better. People who do lousy, lazy shows often say they are concerned with process as a rationale for a complete lack of quality and polish on opening night. Others refuse to tolerate exploration because "we have a product we need to get out here." Everyone involved in such a show is forced to set work at the earliest possible moment, without a chance to grow or discover.

In the rehearsal of a play or a scene, as opening or class due date draws near, a shift in energy often occurs among actors—a sort of panic that undoes a great deal of earlier work, as if now is the time to get serious and lose all the delight and spontaneity of our past weeks together. Then there is the procrastinator-actor, who does absolutely nothing until a performance date looms on the horizon, then suddenly crams—a very bad idea. A performance is not like a term paper, where you can write all night, then drop the product off and collapse. Remember you are it. Not only can you not do work worth watching, if you are exhausted and stressed, but your performance will have had no chance to grow. You need to start working seriously early, then give yourself rest periods where you let things work on your imagination, where you allow the character to visit you. The famous actress Laurette Taylor (the original Amanda in *The Glass Menagerie*) used to compare it to bread dough rising. Making bread from scratch is an apt comparison for a performance because there are interludes where you have to stop forcing the product and just let the process take its course for a while. If you always just look for results, you fail to savor the moment.

> *Fame is fun for a minute, but it gets very boring. I think the real fun part is the actual work. There's not a feeling in the world like manipulating yourself into feeling something and knowing you were honest for that one moment.*
> —Winona Ryder

If you expose your evolving performance in bits and pieces, as suggested earlier, to your loved ones and some of your classmates, it will help the gradual nature of your performance process, so there isn't this tremendous shock when suddenly you show it to people. Presenting work at least twice in class helps. Previewing scenes and speeches from a production and having an invited audience or a preview performance also help. Process is a way of thinking. Opening night is like a rehearsal, where the new problem is adjusting to the change in acoustics and to playing the house. Each night of the run is a chance to set a personal, process-oriented objective during rehearsal. An ideal to shoot for is that your best will be on closing night. Looking beyond closing is an even better idea. Keep yourself future-focused, looking ahead to the chance to repeat this role or play another of this type again sometime. There should be no moment in the process where growth stops and fear or sentiment replaces it.

Kiss the Line Good-Bye

There is a great temptation at the close of a play to get maudlin. You love these people, and this project has engaged you for a long time. A constant in your life is being eliminated. Actors sometimes go out onstage, and relish each moment (usually a good idea), to the point where the performance is much like a memorial service. "Good-bye little line. Good-bye little prop. I'll never use you again. Good-bye little upstage turn." We all tend to do this. I have been one of the worst offenders. If you have loved it, how can you let it go? At least without saying good-bye?

The answer is the audience. They deserve nothing less than your opening night best on closing night. What have they done to deserve attending a wake? Your memory deserves better too. You want to remember this last performance as crisp, strong, full of control, a work of art. Backstage, afterward, during strike, that's where you've earned the right to get messy and mushy.

Exercise 8.6

Offstage Action: Process

What new information do you have from this chapter that could influence your progress in each of the OA areas? If needed, review the subcategories on pages 29–37.

1. Negating newness	6. Improving your image
2. Pleasant as possible	7. Richer relationships
3. Keeping cool	8. Social savvy
4. Sensing signals	9. Prediction potential
5. Winning ways	10. Career capabilities

Specifically: In reviewing theatre protocol and process, what might be helpful as you anticipate joining any specific group (social or professional) in the future?

Offstage Performance Process

You decide to join a club, a co-op, or a corporation. You seek membership in a fraternal order, team, party, family, secret society, navy, monastery, or the Daughters of the American Revolution. What do you do? Follow the exact process outlined in the preceding pages. Each group has particular quirks, but also universal questions to be answered. Those who don't do well, socially and professionally, haven't done their research. Because theatre has so many restrictions, freedoms, and peculiarities, if you can case it out, you can case anything.

In any group you join, you will probably be a better member for having studied acting. It is easy to lose sight of all the skills you pick up as you pursue theatre because they fall in place so naturally and enjoyably. If your family or friends suggest to you that this is not the best use of your time and you should be looking at something more useful, share this Offstage Action, particularly the Career Capabilities list, with them.

One of the largest employment agencies in the country has reported their greatest success placing students who have studied acting, in other fields, because they have such highly developed skills in each of the areas most valued by every organization, whether the context is the arts, communications, education, law, politics, or business. The theatre teaches these topics by necessity. Getting involved in a play does more than take up a lot of time and be lots of fun. Theatre is the ultimate arena for developing polish, precision, and creative thinking on your feet. It can teach you both fundamental survival skills and advanced marketable skills.

The following standard items appear on recommendation forms. Those recommending you are asked to rank you from the top to bottom percentage of those they have worked with or taught: socially mature, self-reliant, self-motivated, perceptive, self-assured, adaptable, cooperative, poised, well-mannered, and articulate. Can you think of anything that will more notably increase one's capacity in all these areas than the study of acting?

Your parents may well be concerned (not without reason) about the huge unemployment rate in the theatre. Theatre training cannot guarantee you a place in the theatre. Yet there are no subjects you can study that will better prepare you for a wider array of other professions. Onstage training equips you for a productive, resourceful life offstage.

Acting takes way more time, work, energy, concentration, collaboration, initiative, courage, and drive than most "civilians" ever imagine. Acting is one demanding endeavor. So why do so many of us want to do it? Need you ask?

With acting, you get to do things that are normally illegal. There are no repercussions and nobody doesn't love you.
—David Duchovny

I love acting! You get to be psychotic and get paid for it.
—Rosie Perez

We have the best job. When we do it, people applaud! They don't do that for accountants.
—Rosie O'Donnell

Acting is a pisser! You get to put on costumes and run around like an idiot. Acting is Halloween 365 days a year.
—Liev Schrieber

Acting isn't work. I remember work. That's when you hated to get up in the morning.
—Jamie Foxx

Acting Anticipated

Setting goals for growth and satisfaction

Sure there's pressure, but that's the way I want it, man. I prayed for this pressure. This is willed! Bring it on.

—Shia LaBeouf

Once you can say, I've moved someone: I've made something think differently through my acting, then it becomes like a drug and you want to keep doing it.

—Daniel Craig

The future is scary but inevitable. The best we can do is accept it for what it is and take it gracefully.

—Scarlett Johansson

I can't wait to see what is next. If I'd been told I'd be where I am now, I wouldn't have believed it.

—James McAvoy

All those imaginary games I played with friends in the neighborhood, entering all different worlds. I don't have to put those games away. As an actor, I get to keep playing them!

—Kevin Spacey

I believe if I had not become an actor, I'd probably be in some f_ _ _ing institution somewhere.

—Whoopi Goldberg

For so many years, you're just waiting to hear yes. Then you have to learn how to say no.

—Jude Law

Looking to the Future

Everyone who takes a beginning acting class wants two things:

1. An increased level of self-awareness and confidence: the capacity to take an actor's poise, command, and concentration into your own life, even if you never go near a theatre again.

2. An increased understanding of what needs to be done if you do decide to enter the theatre again, a sense of how you might be able to make onstage acting a part of your life.

Most onstage awareness can be taken off and used. And the theatre waits patiently, ready to have you back when you're ready to return.

Is the Art for You? Are You for It?

> *I found that the only way I could cope with life was to remove myself from social mores and routine and run my own track. So I became an actor.*
>
> —Jeremy Irons

A primary question about acting right now is whether you want to stick around. Expressing yourself artistically somehow is essential to living fully. Those who don't see the performing arts as basic, like the three Rs, fail to see the need to feed the spirit. Many walk around, still breathing, but with starved, dead spirits. You probably realize this, or you wouldn't have chosen to take an acting class. But is this the right place for you to feed regularly?

Ask yourself if acting has rewarded you, and ask yourself if you can collaborate. This art form has pronounced pressure and constant candid criticism. It's communal; the group has to be put above the individual. It's uneven; it's always starting and ending, as another play goes into production or closes. There is no slow, steady flame, but rather bursts and explosions of light and intense heat.

Are the bursts, the explosions, and the groups what you love? Or do you find yourself frustrated and stressed by them? The god of the theatre is Dionysus, who embodies the irrational, the powerfully emotional, who gave the world wine. The actor who puts on the mask may take on the power of the god himself, but he risks the mask overcoming him. Unable to take it off, he flirts with madness. Do you need something less frantic and more constant? When you think back on your time so far, were you unsettled during much of it? Lots of performers are acting addicts.

They are so desperately unhappy that acting seems more like a needle in the arm than a source of strength. They are wrapped up in acting, but without joy.

Do you find acting a source of strength and joy? Or do you have trouble being on time, not letting partners down, not flirting with irresponsibility? Was it a strain meeting obligations and deadlines involving all those partners? If you're a flake, get out of the theatre. You can always go write verses on the beach, strum a guitar, get out the easel and oils—none of these objects can be hurt by your irresponsibility.

Discipline is always the key. Why do so many people fail to understand that?

–Sean Connery

If you can't collaborate, get out of the theatre.

–George Abbott

There are lots of reasons to stay with acting. The two big reasons for leaving it are the recognition of how easy it is to hurt yourself and to hurt others. The biggest reason for staying is because it feels like home.

Most of us need to keep training. We're like a dull knife. We have the tool, but we need to sharpen it.

–Luis Guzman

Acting was the first thing that made the work and the commitment effortless.

–Michelle Pfeiffer

I found that acting was like a virus, growing stronger and consuming me. My true calling came out. And it came with great force.

–Andy Garcia

Training Objectives

If you decide to stay, take your new self-awareness and translate it into goals, including the following possible training routes:

1. Pursue a theatre degree where you are now, assuming each course in the sequence will address areas of concern.

2. Transfer to a school that is larger, smaller, more or less professionally focused, closer to an academy or to a scholarly university, to match your needs.

3. Take courses in dance, movement, singing, and voice to release and express your physical and vocal instruments.

4. Study privately, with a coach, on areas in which you particularly want to move quickly ahead.

5. Set up sessions with a specialist, counselor, or therapist who is trained to address the tension or inhibition that is standing in the way of your exploration.

6. Pursue a tangential therapy that addresses your own special concern and also appeals to you: bioenergetics, functional integration, Feldenkrais or Gestalt therapy, yoga, Zen sports, shiatsu, reflexology, Rolfing, relaxation response, biofeedback, meditation, aikido, t'ai chi ch'uan, hakomi, Alexander Technique, psychodrama, visualization, or some of those dealt with later in this chapter.

7. Turn acting into an avocation or serious hobby, with no more formal training but some involvement in your theatre community.

8. Spend some time as a newly aware audience member, studying the work of actors from a distance, determining how much you miss the activity itself.

9. Postpone any decision until you've had a chance to take another course or two and determine whether your infatuation survives a test of time and familiarity.

10. Learn everything you can about auditions, because they are the next hurdle if you stay involved. In fact, they are always the next hurdle to leap over (and over) throughout an actor's life.

Before you pack your bags, take a good look at where you are. If you are learning here, you should stay. When you stop learning is the time to go. The most pathetic actors are those who keep transferring to smaller and less reputable programs so that their casting chances improve. Is it really worth it to be surrounded by mediocrity?

Many actors never stop taking classes, even repeating the local version of Acting 1 in different locations, just to stay in touch. Each acting class is a separate event because the people are so different. And acting is not like the measles, where you have it and then it's over. A veteran once explained to me that his penchant for always taking class was "just like going to the gym to stay in shape. No one would ask why someone still does sit-ups." Acting class is where your emotional muscles and imagination muscles can always get a good workout. And who knows what changes may occur soon in actor training?

New Directions

Where will actor training go in the future? Six directions present strong possibilities. All come from the imaginations of powerful, innovative, and creative practitioners. All have already affected many of us. None of these "approaches" is so complete that it could be called a "system," but all move beyond Stanislavski's basic ideas. Some have already been integrated into graduate programs, and any could be incorporated into basic training. If you study acting further, you'll want at least passing familiarity with each. They may well shape the way actors work in this new century.

Alba Emoting

> *This is a method of inducing real emotion through precise patterns.*
> –Richard Gere

Neuroscientist Susana Bloch studied real people experiencing the most powerful basic feelings (joy, sexual arousal, tenderness, grief, fear, anger) under hypnosis. She used sophisticated equipment to monitor their breathing patterns, areas of muscle tension/relaxation, shifts in posture and gesture, and their tendencies to make or avoid sound. The result is an accurate, systematic guide to how emotion is expressed. Her work, amazingly, shows that the "big" emotions are expressed identically among all the cultures of the world. Even in a relatively restrained culture (such as Great Britain), or a more extravagantly expressive one (such as Italy), powerful feeling manifests itself in the same way. We do not need to speak your language to understand how you feel.

Bloch found that emotions are biological and manifest through physical changes she calls "effector patterns." She has isolated the universal characteristics of major states. For each emotion, she has determined the following:

1. A breathing pattern, characterized by amplitude and frequency modulation, and whether you inhale or exhale through the nose or mouth.
2. A muscular activation characterized by a set of contracting or relaxing muscles, particularly those of the abdomen, and defined by a particular posture.
3. Facial muscle patterns forming particular expressions.

Bloch has taken her work to the theatre, often teaching companies of actors how to stimulate or evoke emotional expression based on solid scientific evidence.

More than a century ago, a major theatre figure named Delsarte attempted to do what she has done, but because he lacked the technology and precision of observation, he merely produced a series of clichéd poses. He was right in the observation that many people make identical choices when they have these feelings. He was wrong in making sweeping generalizations based on external impressions rather than on respiratory patterns and muscular tension behind them. Today "Delsartian acting" is the worst insult for someone making tired and trite choices. But Bloch has captured the universal rather than the cliché. Her observations are 100 percent accurate, recreated repeatedly in the laboratory with widely varying subjects.

Alba Emoting provides an amazingly effective blend of inner and outer technique. If you beckon emotion and it is not coming, simply reminding yourself of the breathing pattern and muscle tension of the feeling will make it very likely that the emotion will come and will also give you the power to present the characteristics, if you so choose, without letting the feeling overwhelm you. If something is missing in your portrayal of an emotion, a review of the Alba characteristics can often diagnostically enhance the believability of your portrayal.

Before attempting any of the Alba processes, it is important to learn how to get out of any emotion you do not want to trap you.

Exercise 9.1

Stepping Out

1. Stand up very tall, keeping your eyes lifted and focused out toward an imaginary horizon. Do not allow your gaze to drop down.

2. Take three deep, slow breaths. As you inhale through the nose, lace your fingers together in front of you, and with as little muscular tension in your arms as possible, lift your elbows up and bring your hands behind your head to the back of your neck. As you exhale through the mouth, return your hands forward and down and let them flop at your sides.

3. Shake out your appendages.

4. Wipe and massage your face with your hands, relaxing all facial muscles as you do so.

5. Stretch with arms extended and legs wide.

Repeat this pattern several times as needed.

The reason Stepping Out works so well (and it will work equally well in an off-stage situation when an emotion is potentially overwhelming you) is that none of the actions in the exercise are those of primary emotions. We don't do any of those things when we are in prime feeling mode. So the motions of Stepping Out break the connection. This exercise is also a good one to use at the end of a rehearsal or performance, to leave the feelings of the show behind and not experience "emotional hangover" later.

Exercise 9.2

Archetypal Action I

1. Take a relaxed position, open to approaching others and to being approached.
2. Weaken, loosen, or reduce the muscles you use for stretching.
3. If you feel an impulse to sit or drop down, follow it.
4. Allow the outer corners of your mouth to turn up.
5. Let your eyes relax, even half close.
6. Take a deep, abrupt inhalation through the nose.
7. Exhale rapidly through the mouth. At the point where your lungs seem almost empty, engage the abdominal muscles in a series of twitching "grabs" that remove the rest of the air and continue for some time after the lungs seem empty. Follow this with a series of short, twitching exhalations.*
8. Allow your breath to become uneven, with the exhalation phase invading the inhalation phase.
9. Extend your breath into sounds.
10. Step out.

Exercise 9.3

Archetypal Action II

1. Take a relaxed but heavy posture, withdrawing from or avoiding contact with others.
2. Let your body tend slightly downward. Relax your shoulders and let them cave forward.
3. Feel as if you are very long and narrow.
4. Let all the muscles you would use to stretch completely relax.
5. Allow the outer corners of your mouth to turn down and your mouth to fall slightly open.

*As in Chapter 5, the exercises here are inspired by the artists themselves, but I have designed or adapted them for a basic class. These exercises are "in the style" of the innovator, but not necessarily ones that would occur in that person's class or rehearsal. They sometimes simplify concepts to give you a taste of what work of this kind is like.

6. Allow your eyes to close at least halfway, and if the impulse comes to close them altogether, allow it. Bring your eyebrows together and upward at the center. Feel a slight downward pull on the corners of your mouth.

7. Take rapid inhalation through the nose, twitching very slightly as you do so. Exhale through the mouth. When your lungs seem completely empty, engage the abdominal muscles in a strong inward and upward "tuck." This contraction may make it difficult to breathe in again, creating a conflict between tensing abdominal muscles and the need to relax them to take a breath.

8. Allow the inhalation phase to totally dominate your breathing, even invading the exhalation phase.

9. Extend breath into sounds.

10. Step out.

The first pattern involves the universal physiological characteristics of happiness or pure joy, so if you felt like laughing that was a natural response. The second is pure grief, so simply doing the actions may have saddened you. Note that the breathing patterns for laughing and crying are in exact opposition, even though both involve a gravitational force that gradually pulls one down to the ground. Crying involves dominating inhalation invading exhalation, whereas laughing is about exhalation invading inhalation. When crying, we experience a twitching on the inhale and when laughing on the exhale; both can "bind up" the breathing pattern, and result in a gasping for breath.

It may take several times through to be comfortable enough to let all the parts of the pattern take hold. If Bloch or one of her associates trained you, you would learn the patterns in considerably more detail and variation. It is also important to realize that the pattern is to be used in a diagnostic way when a performer is being challenged in playing an emotion, rather than as a building block to the emotion. The patterns help you adjust.

As you study the patterns, you notice that all emotions except fear are centered in the abdomen, and that concentrating on lowering the breath to that area can be an effective antidote to encroaching fear. You also begin to learn blends of emotions. You begin to recognize your own tendencies toward "entanglement," getting trapped in a mixed pattern, such as always crying when you are angry rather than finding other more direct ways to express your anger. You also study blends or mixes of emotions, such as pride (a combination of anger and joy) and jealousy (involving elements of anger, sadness, and fear).

Alba (Spanish for the color white) Emoting (expression of emotion) combines science and art in a way that suggests phenomenal potential future collaborations, as we learn more about how emotion happens. Anyone who has ever felt out of control or frightened when asked to produce powerful emotion in performance can benefit from it. So can anyone who has trouble producing believable laughter or tears onstage or anyone experiencing an "off night" and in need of some solid help.*

To Read More

Rix, Roxane. "Learning Alba Emoting." *Theatre Topics* 8.1 (March 1998).

Chabora, Pamela. "The Method and Alba Emoting," *Method Acting Reconsidered*. Edited by David Krassner. New York: St. Martin's Press, 2000.

Web sites: www.albaemoting.com, www.albaemotingna.org

Augusto Boal

> *This is a different kind of theatre—a kind of social therapy. . . . It focuses the mind, relaxes the spirit, and gives people a new handle on their situations.*
> –Richard Schechner

Augusto Boal has brought the art of the actor into the realm of social consciousness and provided tools for changing our lives. For him, acting has a double definition. It is not just about performing, but also about taking action.

After escaping an oppressive military regime in Brazil and while in exile in various European nations and the United States, Boal developed methods for combating oppression through theatre. His work also breaks down the barriers between actors and audience, leading us to a theatre where observers become active spectators, whom he calls "spect-actors," offering ideas, even stepping into roles. Boal uses theatre to confront all the "offstage" problems that permeate our lives, with particular emphasis on those (sexual harassment, homophobia, racism) where one group oppresses another.

Boal worked for many years on audience involvement, but he did not fully find his process until one, now legendary, performance during which a woman in the audience became so angry that an actor onstage could not understand what she meant by a suggestion that she came onto the stage and showed him. His form of theatre was born.

---

*Personal testimony. In the last few years, I have played two different characters (in the plays *Art* and *Shadowlands*) who needed to burst into tears during a scene onstage. I do not do this frequently in life, so it is not a response I can pull up with absolute reliability. I found if the emotion was not completely there at the needed moment, that adjusting my body and facial tension and breathing invariably activated it. The patterns provided a reliable safety net. The physical response was always present, and it was up to me how much I actually chose to "feel" the emotion inside.

Boal sees theatre not as spectacle but rather as a forum designed to analyze problems (usually of the misuse of power) and to explore group solutions. Seeing a problem enacted, debated, then seeing solutions enacted can have high and lasting impact. He has established numerous participatory companies that develop community-based performance for those engaged in the struggle for liberation. Most are called Centers for Theatre of the Oppressed (CTOs). Activities are of three kinds:

1. *Forum Theatre*: Short scenes representing problems of a community are shown unsolved, and audience members are invited to suggest, interact, and enact, sometimes by replacing characters in scenes and improvising new solutions. Sometimes the "problem" scene (sometimes called the "anti-model") is presented once, then again (possibly speeded up) until someone yells, "Stop!" and steps in. It may be repeated several more times as others step into the role of protagonist. The events are presided over by someone called the Joker, so named for the joker in a pack of cards, not because she will play jokes on participants. The Joker defines and enforces the rules of the game in the manner of a stage manager/referee. A Joker may often stop a scene saying, "That's magic," meaning that the actors have contrived a solution (such as discovering a hidden fortune or a sudden change of heart) that does not involve step-by-step problem solving.

2. *Image Theatre*: This exercise uses bodies and tableaus to sculpt events or relationships. Human forms are employed to create images, helping participants explore power relations and collective solutions. As much as possible, the process is done without words, though it may begin with an individual recounting a personal story of oppression of some kind or a group discussion of the issue that will be explored. Titles are suggested. Then individuals mold participants, like clay, to form an intense visual representation of the power relationships, and other tableaus are created to change the status quo. Two major tableaus emerge: one the Real Image of things as they are now and the other the Ideal Image of things as they could become.

3. *Invisible Theatre*: Prepared scenes are presented, as in Forum Theatre, to stimulate action, but in this case, they are performed in public spaces for an unsuspecting audience that does not recognize the event as theatre. In addition to the actors in the scenes themselves, several may infiltrate the crowd as provocateurs, stimulating debate and discussion. For example, a scene is created and rehearsed regarding a cross-dresser. The actors go into a store and one of the men tries on women's clothing. Another actor responds by being overtly appalled at what he is doing, while another defends his rights. Everyone present is drawn into a discussion about the parameters of individual rights.

The three techniques may overlap, and all of Boal's processes share three characteristics:

1. Problems are always presented in a nondidactic way, without the suggestion in the initial scene of a solution.

2. As solutions evolve, the issues always move outward to include a larger group rather than inward to individual or smaller ones. The oppression is examined in a larger context.

3. Debate/discussion never stays long in verbal exchange (or what Boal calls "radio forum"), so that at every possible moment participants are asked to stop talking, get up, and express their intentions or interventions in theatrical forms. The formats are designed to negate the trap of endless talk blocking solutions and the advantage of the slickly verbose members of any group.

Although most exercises used to train CTO actors are standard (many appear in this text), the actor who will thrive on this approach is one who is extremely comfortable with improv, socially/politically aware, able to play opposing points of view without bias, and as Boal himself says "dialectical and free of narcissism, with a strong sense of give and take."

Of course, trained actors and theatre personnel constitute only part of those who participate. Boal's process engages social service workers, labor and union organizers, educators, and community activists. It employs classic improv techniques as well as those of sociodrama and playback theatre.

If acting students are taught Boal techniques, they will all have the tools, in whatever community they might find themselves, to offer the art of acting as part of a solution. Many people regard theatre as frivolous and improvisation as the single silliest, least substantial part of theatre, so what an amazing antidote such resourcefulness could offer! It could actually change the way our art is regarded by the populace at large while making a huge contribution to that populace. And the techniques are equally useful for solving problems within an acting environment or theatre company, where power issues often abound.

Exercise 9.4

Real to Ideal

1. As a group, determine your most immediate instance of an unfair power/oppression issue. Keep it close to home: departmental or campus politics, management issues regarding the theatre, a local crisis—something that directly influences the lives of people in the room. Or pick a more universal, unresolved issue that affects the lives of those present every day.

2. Someone volunteer to create a group of statues from other participants, creating in visual form the conflict itself.

3. Anyone who disagrees with a detail may adjust the sculpture until there is consensus that it now represents the Real Image.

4. Then the statues are altered (again with someone starting and others adjusting) to create the world in which the oppression has stopped and the problems have been overcome—the Ideal Image.

5. Return to the Real Image. Each spect-actor now has the right to modify it to show how it may get from Real to Ideal, which stages it may have to go through, or events that must occur. Each of these must also resolve into a sculpture.

6. Finally, the statues return to the Real Image tableau and move, either in slow motion dissolve or through a series of freeze-frames, until the Ideal is reached. Thus, an Image of Possible Transition emerges.

NOTE: If two different groups present have entirely different perceptions of the problem, then each can form its own Real Image and try to work them into one of agreement. The same can happen with two Ideal Images that become one.

Exercise 9.5

Forum Fundamentals

If time allows, the entire class could create scenes for this assignment. If not, a volunteer group of four or five can work on it outside class as extra credit or in class while others are engaged in alternative projects. Each group finds an issue that concerns all of you enough to be worth your time.

1. Work privately on first improvising, then scripting a scene where the issue is clear and the protagonist in the scene at one point makes an error of judgment. Design it so that a solution is not suggested. The problem is simply presented. Keep the scenes three minutes or less. Select a Joker outside the scene to moderate.

2. Run the scene once to clarify the problem, then start a second run until someone feels they can step into the role of the protagonist at a crucial decision-making moment. This spect-actor indicates the direction she would like the scene to move, and it resumes with her in the role.

3. Others in the scene will not cave to the new actor but actually intensify the pressure to demonstrate how difficult a solution may be. If the new protagonist gives in, someone else can take her place with a different solution.

4. If the scene is now enacted to a more satisfactory conclusion, others in the class may still jump into the roles of oppressors to demonstrate any aspect that the group may not have thought of.

5. Once all input and potential blocks have been acknowledged, a somewhat newly formed cast enacts what Boal calls "a model of action for the future."

To Read More

Boal, Augusto. *Aesthetics of the Oppressed*. New York: Routledge, 2006.

Boal, Augusto. *The Theater of the Oppressed*. New York: Theatre Communications Group, 1985.

Boal, Augusto. *Games for Actors and Non-Actors*. New York: Routledge, 1992.

Boal, Augusto. *The Rainbow of Desire*. New York: Routledge, 1995.

Cohen-Cruz, Jan and Mady Schutzman (editors). *A Boal Companion*. New York: Routledge, 2005.

Anne Bogart

> *In a culture where the best acting is done from the neck up,*
> *Anne's work is an obvious antidote. . . . It's dance done by*
> *actors in the service of dramaturgy.*
> —Jon Jory

"A great actor seems dangerous, unpredictable, full of life and differentiation," says Anne Bogart, who has affected theatre as an innovative director and teacher. Here, we will deal with her actor training and its most defining component—a series of exercises called "Viewpoints."

Vsevolod Meyerhold recognized early on that Stanislavski-trained actors do not always move in the space and worked to create flexible actor/athletes, but Bogart has gone a step further and conceived a whole vocabulary of body use that can train actors to respond to a wide range of challenges and provide them with tools for performing distinctly nonrepresentational works. The nine Viewpoints are points of awareness each performer has while working.

Four of them relate to *time*:

1. *Tempo:* The speed of movement
2. *Duration:* How long a movement, gesture, or sequence actually lasts
3. *Kinesthetic response:* The timing of your responses to stimuli
4. *Repetition:* Repeating something onstage, both internally (within your own body) and externally (something picked up outside your body).

The final five Viewpoints are those of *space*:

5. *Shape:* Lines, curves, and mixtures of these two, stationary versus moving shapes, all of which take on one of three forms: the body in space, the body in relationship to architecture, and the body forming a shape with other bodies.

6. *Gesture:* Work involving two different kinds: behavioral (everyday real ones) and expressive (abstract, large ones).

7. *Architecture:* The physical environment where the acting occurs. It includes solid mass (walls, floors, ceilings, furniture, windows, door), texture (wood, metal, fabric, changing or unchanging textures), light (sources and shadows), color. Within architecture, spatial metaphors (such as "I'm up against the wall" or "lost in space") are created.

8. *Spatial relationship:* Distances between all things onstage, implications of clustering, spreading, focusing.

9. *Floor pattern* (sometimes referred to as "topography"): How the landscape is created by movement, with various areas perhaps assigned greater or lesser density or simply being declared off limits.

Bogart has continued to evolve her ideas, and like Stanislavski, sometimes can be misrepresented by someone who caught her at an earlier point in development or is "three degrees of separation" from a teacher trained by her. Vocabulary and process continue to shift and have yet to be codified in a way that does not lead to potential misuse.

Viewpoints training is like scales for a pianist, structure for practice, keeping needed "muscles" in shape, alert, and flexible. Viewpoints goals are listening with the entire body, achieving spontaneity, taking in and using everything around you, finding larger possibilities, eliminating any "My character would never do that" tendencies, giving up overly cerebral work, and giving yourself surprise, contradiction, and unpredictability.

Viewpoints training is strongly related to using whatever space you are working in as a source, responding fully to all the elements within it. Some of the suggestions, such as conditioning forces, in the following exercises would not be used in the training, but are offered here as a substitute for a known environment to be discovered and to give you a sense of the flavor of the work.

Exercise 9.6

Exploring Space

1. Divide the classroom into four quarters, each being a place where one of the following emotions dominates: Joy, Hate, Fear, Anger. As you move through the spaces, let each hit you and influence your continued movement and attitude.

2. Now divide the room into four sensations: Sticky, Wet, Freezing, Bouncy. Repeat.

3. Next, have everyone gather onstage, and divide the space into two contrasting states such as Heavy and Light. Those on the Light side find a way to help those on the Heavy pass over without moving into their area. Continue to experiment with various contrasts between areas of the room.

Exercise 9.7

Points of View

This exercise is designed to prepare a group for Exercise 9.8 by exploring some of the tools employed.

1. Begin exploring the acting space, weaving in and out of other people. Explore both the tempo and the duration of your movement. Begin making sharp turns and changing directions more frequently as you continue to explore.

2. When a turn causes you to face someone else, let her movement influence yours to change in some way, either adopting hers or just letting it alter you.

3. Keep your eyes in soft focus, not really looking at others, and continuing to move, restricting yourself to no more than two or three gestures. From your peripheral vision, gradually pick up moves from others and allow some repeated move to be shared by everyone who is doing the exercise.

4. Break the group movement and begin exploring again, this time only moving in straight lines on a grid. Play with tempo, moving at different speeds, always responding to and taking care of the other people in the space. At the signal of a side coach, switch to only curves, then finally to altering between lines and curves. Again, gradually pick up movements around you and repeat the same pattern in unison with others.

5. Freeze and begin a fairly casual gestural pattern, working through some of your most standard gestures, particularly those you use when you talk with your hands. Then at a signal, let a huge gesture come out of you. Alternate between mundane everyday gestures and larger, exploratory ones.

6. Explore all the available surfaces in the space, both for their visual impact and for what they are like to touch. Rediscover all of them.

7. Move around and let colors in the room grab you, then either project toward or propel away from them.

8. Decide for yourself on one-third of the space as a place so heavy that you are just this side of frozen in it, one-third as so light you could dance on your tiptoes, and one-third where the energy changes constantly, both aiding and preventing freedom of exploration in alternate patterns.

Exercise 9.8

Closing and Opening the Open Scene

Part A

1. Begin by working with one partner. Take the reduced open scene dialogue from Chapter 4 (pages 134–135). Quickly create a scene with the following in it in any sequence:

   A kiss

   A jump

A push

A catch

Running away

Part B

2. Next, work in groups of four with the same dialogue. Each group should create a scene with the following elements:

   a. A very rapid tempo except for one crucial moment

   b. Using almost all curving shapes in space

   c. With three large expressive gestures at key moments

   d. Using the entire acting area in the room but strongly favoring one side

   e. With one color-related item that has a powerful impact on all who pass its way

   f. Using two objects that are passed around by the entire group and that each change identities at some point

   g. With one area of the stage so dense or thick that only slow laborious movement is possible and another so light or non-gravitational that leaps, skips, and other buoyant moves are fostered by it

   h. Do not worry about the linear sense of your scene. Take ten minutes in one class period to brainstorm, at least one night to dream, and then fifteen minutes of the following class to put it together for class presentation.

Part C

Agree on the needed ingredients for a scene but this time simply start with a title, such as "The Rehearsal" or "New Apartment," and one line of dialogue that must appear somewhere in the scene. Proceed to create the scene including the remaining dialogue.

Exercise 9.9

Viewpoint Event

This is a more advanced exercise where teams may be given the assignment, sent home to think about it, and then given twenty minutes to a half an hour to prepare it in class.

1. Working in groups of five, create a five-minute presentation called OUR TOWN, which will have three parts: Part 1—How Our Town looks, Part 2—How Our Town sounds, Part 3—How people who live in Our Town really are

2. The event must include all nine Viewpoints plus:

   • Ten seconds where everyone is doing the same thing

   • Someone getting hurt

- Three sudden changes within the Viewpoints
- A cough, a shout, a hug, and a silent gesture
3. The script will be limited to six lines agreed on by all the participants. Write these down at your group meeting and then proceed to create the event.

As you can see, these processes can make you vividly aware of movement generally, can refine your capacity for working closely with others, and can enhance your sense of how space is altered by choice.

In training or rehearsal, actors may work on a single Viewpoint for an extended period, then begin to layer them. Viewpoints may be used purely abstractly or they may be centered around themes or ideas in a script you are working. Viewpoints may be used as warm-ups or ensemble exercises, but can also be employed to create the basic staging for a play script as well. In any script, even highly realistic ones, Viewpoints might be employed to define the use of space and to specifically stage dream sequences, fantasies, and other flights of imagination within the whole, whenever nonfacsimile performance is appropriate. It can also expand one's sense of facsimile, pushing even realistic behavior to find the contradictions that we commonly express even under ordinary circumstances.

Bogart's work is extremely movement-centered, with the spoken word less a key player than the body. Her way of working encourages actors to create a physical score that exists independently from the verbal expression of their characters. In fact, she actively seeks tension between action and word, rather than coherence. She fills up the stage like a moving painting; words sometimes become superfluous. Her work has been strongly influenced by Asian culture, particularly theatre forms and martial arts. Her teaching methods draw heavily from t'ai chi—nonautocratic, noninterference, being open to what every other has to offer, letting go of restrictive investments of self. Yet, she also identifies American vaudeville and dancer Martha Graham as primary influences. Regarding her distant inspirations, she says, "I get closest to my American roots by going away."

Because every movement in one of her shows is eventually precisely set, the actors are free to feel differently and therefore respond differently to one another in every single performance. Freedom inside the strict form is a fundamental principle of all Asian aesthetics. Bogart has more recently developed Vocal Viewpoints, which will take her work in an important new direction. These are tempo, pitch, timbre (a synonym for quality), volume, silence, repetition, and gesture (actually vocal gestures, often called nonverbals: coughs, snorts, sniffs, giggles, etc.). In learning these, actors may be asked to repeat a short monolog while exaggerating the contribution of each viewpoint.

Through her "technique of dissociation," she discards Western representational conventions and is regarded by many as our most postmodern innovator. She tends to describe herself as at odds with much Stanislavski-based work, but she shares with him a powerful urge to keep working to "unfreeze tradition." In some ways, her work is the antithesis of Strasberg's because he focused so heavily on individual feelings and memories and she on the individual's commitment to the total ensemble.

To Read More

Bogart, Anne. *And Then You Act*. New York: Routledge, 2007.

Bogart, Anne and Tina Landau. *The Viewpoints Book*. New York: Theatre Communications Group, 2005.

Bogart, Anne. *The Director Prepares*. New York: Routledge, 2002.

Dixon, Michael Bigelow, and Joel A. Smith (eds.). *Anne Bogart Viewpoints*. Lyme, NH: Smith and Kraus, 1995.

Neuro-Linguistic Programming

> *NLP is the most powerful vehicle for change in existence.*
> —Psychology Today

NLP started when two researchers studied three legendary therapists (Virginia Satir, Milton Erickson, and Fritz Perls), asking, "What do brilliant communicators do that can be taught to others?" The resulting system—Neuro (brain and nervous system), Linguistic (language and nonverbal communication), Programming (shortcuts and codes)—includes a series of exercises for identifying and changing behavior and learning patterns. It is now taught at more than 100 institutes in the United States and a similar number throughout the rest of the world. NLP has significantly affected the fields of therapy, business, law, and both early childhood and elementary education. It is new to theatre arts but offers strikingly original processes for the training of actors.

Often called "software for your brain," NLP was developed by a linguist (John Grinder) and an information scientist (Richard Bandler), who examined the exceptional communicators mentioned to figure out how excellence could be transferred. NLP is learning how others code information in order to connect with them better and learning to recode our own information process so we can function more effectively.

The part of NLP that is best known is the idea of determining whether you are primarily a visual, auditory, or kinesthetic learner (V, A, or K).

1. Do you like to study using lists and outlines? Do you use words like *see*, *shows*, *focus*, *perspective*, *looks*? Are you straight-backed, even when sitting, with raised, tense shoulders, a dropped chin, minimal facial expression, and

few gestures? Is your speech rapid, breathy, high-pitched, uninflected? You may be visual.

2. Do you like to study and run lines with others, having them ask you questions and hearing yourself answer? Do you favor phrases like *tell myself, rings a bell, I hear you*? Do you like to sit when talking, touch your own face, tap out rhythms, and sometimes turn your ears toward others when they speak to you? Do you really like to talk, nod often when listening, and sometimes repeat exactly what you've been asked before answering? Is your voice pleasant and your speech varied? Auditory.

3. Do you have trouble studying? Do you need to get up and pace and do things to take in info? Would you always build a model rather than write a paper if you had a choice? Do you say *grasp, handle, feel*, and other similarly physical verbs? Do you need space, gesture big and often, like to be up acting out experiences and feelings, but slump when sitting? Are you highly expressive and emotionally available, but also sometimes lose the thread of a speaker's (or your own) main points, so you alternate between energized and comatose? A kino.

Note that the three descriptions represent those who are extremely likely to be in a particular mode, but most of us (and actors in particular) shift between modes as our experiences vary. Still, it is valuable to begin to recognize your own tendencies. As soon as you know yourself and recognize others, you raise your capacity to connect positively. A visual-learner acting teacher may correct a kinesthetic actor on the pronunciation of a word a thousand times, explaining how it is spelled (because she "sees" the word) over and over. Once she recognizes the actor is a kino, who will only pronounce the word differently if she explains how it feels to move the lips, teeth, and tongue into the correct pronunciation, Eureka! Communication! The actor pronounces the word right, and the teacher no longer wants to kill him. This tension could also exist between you and your scene partner and any other working combination.

A visual actor will wish to highlight his script and return to looking at the words frequently during rehearsal. An auditory actor may wish to record and playback often. A kinesthetic needs to get into the right shoes and rehearsal garments and start using props and making contact with others at the earliest possible moment. An outstanding actor will work to access learning modes he does not habitually employ, so that he can join any partner.

NLP is also about reframing experience. When you have a positive memory, is the visual component a photo or film? Are you in it or just watching it? Is it in color or black and white? Sharp or blurry focus? You can restructure positive memories into sharp, richly colored films where you are the camera, totally reliving it from inside. You can place unpleasant memories into small, out-of-focus, black and white shots stuck in a photo album. However, many of us have, out of habit, done the reverse, with painful, brightly colored films and out-of-focus, tiny still shots of joyous times! Think of the potential for the actor in simply reprogramming her own audition memories to bring victories into stronger focus and soften the defeats.

And simply experimenting with making a character V, A, or K can shake up the work in evocative, productive ways.

Exercise 9.10

What's my Mode?

1. Take the previous information and determine your primary preferred mode. Many of us blend two modes, so first identify the one you rarely use, and try, of the two you favor, to pick one that is more prominent than the other.

2. Observe yourself in numerous situations where you feel tension.

3. Identify those that are caused by your needing to interact with someone who does not share your preferences. Ask yourself if those instances where a scene partner or someone else in a show seemed like a jerk to you may have been simply a matter of clashing modalities.

Exercise 9.11

Pure Modes

Working in groups of four or five, converse in a circle until the leader gives some signal that it is time to switch.

1. Be a group of auditories discussing/arguing about what is the best song ever recorded.

2. Be a group of visuals debating the most beautiful color in the entire spectrum.

3. Become kinos talking about who should have been chosen MVP in a sport of choice last season.

Exercise 9.12

Switching Modes

1. Pick a fairy tale well known to everyone in the circle to tell and someone to start it.

2. The starter picks V, A, or K and starts to tell the tale entirely as a series of pictures, sounds, or feelings.

3. At the switch moment, the person to the speaker's right picks up the story, but in a different mode.

4. Continue around the circle. The next speaker must always pick it up in a different mode from the person who has just spoken.

NLP has the potential to assist the whole acting process: greatly reducing performance anxiety, helping actors communicate more clearly, intensifying character analysis, stimulating imaginative rehearsal choices, and helping everyone involved in a project let go when the time comes for it to end.

To Read More

Ready, Romilla and Kate Burton. *N.L.P.* for Dummies, Chichester, England: John Wiley & Sons, Ltd 2004.

O'Connor, Joseph, and John Seymour. *Introducing N.L.P.* London: Aquarian Press, 1990.

Acting Somatics

> *It explodes the traditional mind/body split and restores us to our essential selves. What a joyous reunion!*
> –Elizabeth Carlin-Metz

Barbara Sellers-Young has developed an exciting, innovative, movement-based approach to acting. She is probably the first movement specialist to bring both Eastern and Western wisdom together into a single integrated vision. Asian practices have been used for years in Western warm-ups, but they have only recently been employed in the deeper creative process itself. Like Bogart and Suzuki (*see following section*), Sellers-Young found inspiration in the way the arts (both performance and martial) were taught in Japan. But she also draws on the work of Constantin Stanislavski, F. Matthias Alexander, Moshe Feldenkrais, Rudolf Laban, and other Western guides. She has even drawn ideas from African dance, employing a "whole body" approach, in which you as a performer do not see yourself as a set of individual parts but as a total unit, a mind-body integration to be deepened with training.

Somatics refers to the *soma*, a rich and constantly flowing array of senses and actions that are occurring within the experience of each of us. Sellers-Young's work leads to *chi* (Chinese) and *ki* (Japanese), an invisible energy state (often sought in martial arts) that combines outer and inner layers of perception, conscious and unconscious levels of awareness, so that one is both inside and outside the self at the same time, analogous to the center of Stanislavski's circles of attention and to his creative state.

Like Bloch, Sellers-Young recognized breath as the basis for any kind of significant emotional expression. She has developed breath-focused exercises in a "feel, fuse, follow" pattern. You feel inhalation, fuse with the top of the breath, and follow it through your body. The "three Fs" become a somatic skill with a wide range of uses.

The three key somatic processes are:

1. *Exploration:* An attitude of exploration immerses you in an experience of yourself as a perceptual being who uses conscious and associative memory to reflect on your present and to create a future.

2. *Breath:* An aide in exploration expands your awareness and enlarges your image of self. Breath not only transforms through the three Fs, but is also the key to stillness at your center (*chi, ki*) from which your creative energy emanates.

3. *Imagery:* The use of metaphors provides impetus to the creative process, ongoing sensory states, and a primary stimulus for exploration.

Sellers-Young seeks to help students integrate external action with internal motivation when creating a physical character and to move beyond a tendency to play themselves or to only act from the head. She has found a connection between the phrase, "When mind moves, *ki* moves," from Japanese philosopher Yasuo Yuasa and Stanislavski's statement about physical action that, unless it is purely mechanical, there is always concealed inner action or feelings behind an outer action, so that inner and outer levels of life are created and intertwined through an unbreakable bond.

Imagery, particularly metaphor, plays an important part in her work. She learned actors could grow by uniting *chi/ki* with an image, just as Stan's actors unite inner experience with outer physical action. Acting Somatics allows actors to transcend personally limiting images. Performers explore myths, childhood stories, fairy tales, even TV programs that played a central role in their childhoods and their self-images, possibly still influencing the way they act. *Examples:* Your favorite story was *The Little Engine That Could*, and now you play all characters as if you are single-handedly pushing a train up a hill. You are a serious, longtime karate student and tend to make each gesture strong, sudden, and direct. Your personal myth is Cinderella, and you perform with great hesitancy, as if waiting for something to happen. The process finds the "controlling" images and then gradually replaces them with those that free the actor and expand her range.

Exercise 9.13

Feel, Fuse, and Follow: Touch

Inspired by a technique first described by martial arts instructor James Kapp, this exercise integrates your sensory and mental systems through focus on a task. Perform this exercise alone or in a class where a number of objects have been brought in and randomly spread around the room.

1. Pick up an object. If the object has a standard use, ignore that information and "discover it" as new. Begin to feel the size, shape, and texture of it.
2. While touching the object itself, become aware of your breath moving through your body and out your hand.
3. Extend the feeling of breath into the object, allowing the breath to fuse with your experience of touching it.
4. As your hand becomes comfortable with the object, follow the impulse to manipulate or use the object derived from that fusion.
5. Try not to plan the action at all but, rather, to allow it to evolve from the experience of feeling, fusing, and following your internal impulses to explore.
6. Whenever possible, explore other ways of discovering other objects beyond touch. For example, you might employ eyes, ears, and nose, substituting *see*, *hear*, and *smell* as the opening guide words instead of *feel*. Allow each sensory system to increase your awareness of another. You can actually learn to listen to your muscles, hear through your feet, and smell with your skin.

Sellers-Young is interested in creating actors with a thinking body or a body-minded brain, with movement as the unifying bond. Acting Somatics integrates acts of contemplation with acts of exploration. Actors thus trained can take in, at any moment, new information through their senses and process it through their deeper sensory modalities. Somatic knowledge is not just knowledge *of* the body but knowledge gained *through* the body.

To Read More

Sellers-Young, Barbara. *Breathing, Movement, Exploration*. New York: Applause Books, 2002.

Tadashi Suzuki

> *Suzuki's actors have stunned the world with their ability to sustain characterizations of tremendous intensity, depth of feeling and range. The combination of expression and control has amazed and moved audiences.*
>
> **—Richard Brestoff**

Suzuki (who was brought from Japan to the United States by Jewell Walker and John Dillon) has made an impact on theatre with stunning productions of Shakespeare and Greek tragedies, where actors have shown awesome intensity, achieving grandeur and power rare on the contemporary stage. He desires actors who "can make the whole body speak even when one is silent."

He shares with Bogart, his co-founder of the Saratoga Theatre Institute and frequent collaborator, a strong desire to change the status quo and a powerful belief that naturalistic acting is too limiting for the future.

Suzuki is a much tougher taskmaster in his approach. (His classic and notorious inquiry to struggling actors in rehearsal: "Why you so bad?") His work is more about the actor checking herself and developing her internal energy than about the facing of others that characterizes Bogart. He is less postmodern than she, though still basically modern in his search for one man's vision and his demand for unity of expression. He aspires to channel "animal energy" with a completely integrated expression of verbal and body language, in contrast to her willingness to break connections. Suzuki focuses on the actor's relationship to her own body, whereas Bogart's Viewpoints focus on the acting ensemble as a single unit. He sees much of "modernized" theatre as a place of non-animal energy, including an over-reliance on technology, that has essentially "dismembered" us from our essential selves.

He has taken classical Japanese theatre and Indian Kathakali dancing and blended them with Western ballet. His training seeks an ideal form, an impossible perfection, with rewards in the attempt. His forms require balance, stamina, strength, and concentration for heightened theatricality and presence. One of the reasons his work is so powerful is that he has actors discover their characters' greatest desire and then magnify that desire many times over.

Suzuki work always begins with feet as the root of expressivity (Michael Chekhov placed the same emphasis on feet, and Meyerhold did so on the knees). There is a powerful sense of grounding, or what Suzuki calls "the attraction for the ground which the lower half of the body feels." Tremendous demands are placed on the lower body, while the upper body is often relaxed. The traditional vectors of Japanese theatre, sky and earth, heights and depths, are honored with full awareness that "when we die we return to the earth." His work honors the most ancient Japanese rituals of feet stomping to arouse energy and activate life, going back to the earliest Japanese stages, which were built on land where the dead were believed to dwell.

Exercise 9.14

A New Way of Walking

Perform this exercise in heavy socks (*tabi* if you have them) or very soft shoes.

1. Move around the room in the lightest possible way, with images of yourself as a butterfly, a cloud, an angel, chiffon fabric, a gentle breeze. Continue to find imagery

that gets you to lift and float. Remember to engage your entire upper body, head, shoulders, arms all in the sensation.

2. Now switch to heavy walking. You are Godzilla or King Kong stomping out everything in your path, your feet are giant boulders, you are marching in weighted boots, your feet are pounding gavels. Do not lock your knees, but allow the sensation of power and gravity to dominate.

3. Now break your torso in half, with your upper body light and airy and your lower body strong and rooted. Practice until you feel a genuine contrast, as if your feet are planted on the earth with each step, while your head, in contrast, is in the stars.

4. Move across the room, not going forward or backward, but on constantly shifting diagonals, with your feet almost stomping, concentrating on your lower body, with your upper body unchanging and relaxed.

5. Experience the contrast between constant motion below and stillness above, each state complementing the other.

6. Remember this contrasting sensation, and continue to look for stillness in movement and movement in stillness in other aspects of your work as an actor.

Suzuki classes are often accompanied by loud percussive music. While the music plays, actors are expected to fiercely beat the floor with their feet, then when it stops, to relax, perhaps even to fall, and achieve complete quiet and stillness. Perhaps the most vivid difference between his classes and most actor training is that instead of relaxation and avoiding strain, he asks actors for mastery over strain.

His work so far is a healthy antidote to actors who tend to equate making small decisions inevitably with honest ones. He offers assistance in achieving large moments of heightened expression and total commitment way beyond a prosaic, everyday believability.

Because Bogart's and Suzuki's work has so often been interwoven, probably the best comparison of what they do comes from Bogart herself: "The results I see (from Suzuki training) are incredible concentration, focus, strength, and the ability to change quickly. Viewpoints deals with spontaneity and flexibility and being in the moment—it's a magic, chemical combination. . . . The Suzuki is like a barre class for a dancer and the Viewpoints is a way to practice creating fiction using time and space. One is vertical, the other is horizontal. One is you and God; the other is you and the people around you."

To Read More

Allain, Paul. *The Art of Stillness: The Theater Practice of Tadushi Suzuki.* New York: Palgrave Macmillan, 2003.

Suzuki, Tadashi. *The Way of Acting.* Translated by J. Thomas Riner. New York: Theatre Communications Group, 1986.

Summary

Each of these six approaches is uniquely specialized, but there are some interesting connections. Notice a tendency to draw from the wisdom of the East and to integrate these ideas with distinctly Western concepts for new, genuine fusion. There is also an emphasis on the body and a highly physical approach to acting, with breath as the basis for both creation and expression of feeling. And there is attention to moving beyond the traditional acting process itself, into improving relationships between actors, between all theatre participants, and between members of communities, where the actor/citizen can contribute. Whether or not any of these specific approaches finds widespread acceptance as part of basic actor training in the future, the ideas that they represent—fusion of global knowledge, deep body and breath work, and a higher level of collaboration—are all worthwhile goals for any acting program to pursue.

In the meantime, any individual performer can pursue immediate objectives. The most important of these is to become an actor who has such a clear working process and vision that she is not dependent on those around her and can survive under a huge variety of conditions.

Production-Proof Actors

As an audience member, you have surely identified a few performers who always seem to do good work, no matter what vehicle they're in. The film or play can seem like chicken poop, but the actor always transcends and illuminates the material. This is a good goal for any novice performer. Too many actors go down with the ship in an ill-conceived vehicle that bombs in a big way. Too many go down with the dinghy, in smaller, inept projects.

Transcending the material means managing to work with or without any kind of director and having enough security in all areas of production to survive everything that touches your performance. The more production tasks you learn, the better able you'll be to save yourself. You don't study props or costuming just to fulfill course requirements, you need to be able to clearly communicate with the design team to get the best work possible from them. It's insulting to their art for you to fail to understand how they work. Or you could keep yourself ignorant, increasing your chances of wearing a dumpy frock, lit like a cadaver, holding a pathetic prop while sound effects drown out what you're saying. Is it kind of hard to choose?

Post-Audition Mortem

Why deal with auditions at the end of the book? Because the audition is always the next step. If you know you want to be a professional actor, you audition to move on. If you know you want to leave the theatre for a while, you audition to come back. In Chapter 8, the process of performance went directly from auditions to beginning rehearsals. For many actors, there's a stop between these steps because they weren't cast. On a professional level, acting has the largest unemployment rate in the entire world. And even on an amateur level, there are many more people than parts. So there's a lot of auditioning going on that doesn't lead directly to rehearsal. What then?

You audition for a show and give it your best shot. You're not called back. Or you're called back, but not cast. What to do next? (For the moment, we'll omit giving up because you can't stand the rejection. That's always an option.) In educational theatre, to learn from the experience and train for next time, the actor may naturally seek out the director for feedback. Asking is appropriate, because these people are there to educate you. Don't feel that discussing your audition with a teacher or director is a terrible imposition. This is our job. But review the following guidelines before you do:

1. Never talk to the director until after the show is cast. Her efforts are entirely focused on that task. She doesn't have time right now.

2. Wait a good two or three days until after the final cast list is posted, to give yourself time to put the entire experience in perspective. Only time will give you some objectivity. Only time will help you minimize responses that are purely emotional.

3. Use this waiting period to put together your own list of reasons why you may not have been used. Move beyond "no talent" as an explanation, to real, concrete events that occurred during tryouts and to the specific needs of the production. Review your own participation in the audition process, step by step. Try to determine when you were functioning most and least effectively. When you consider all the decisions you made, which were most and least appropriate?

4. Use this checklist against your own castability:
   • *Cultural binding:* You have a conspicuously contemporary, regional, ethnic, or any other characteristic that makes it hard to imagine you outside your own culture and inside that of the play.
   • *Wrong appearance for this show:* You don't have the shape, size, bone structure, capacity to look right in the costumes, to seem like a member of that family, to fit into the visual world of the play.
   • *Company balance:* Sometimes an actor is very good, but would throw off a sense of focus, would be distracting, or would alter the dynamics of the ensemble.
   • *Movement limitations:* Some demands, such as mastery of intricate dance routines, handling period costume pieces, or radically altering your physical bearing, might be outside your range right now.

- *Voice limitations:* You haven't yet mastered specific skills, such as handling verse rhythms, singing in a certain range, or speaking in a different register.
- *Inexperience:* You simply lack essential experience, both in training and in living, to possess the technical and spiritual capacity for certain roles.

5. Extend the list using your knowledge of this particular show. Separate those things you can't do anything about from those you can. Use the "can" list to set some of your training objectives.

6. You may find that you don't need to see the director after all because you've answered your own questions. If you still need feedback, go in with your own list of conjectures, regarding your audition and needs for growth. Ask the director to verify, clarify, or help alter your own perceptions, not to do all your thinking for you.

7. Focus your conversation on the future. Consider the difference between these requests:

> *Why didn't you use me? What did I do wrong? What is it about me you don't like? Why did you pick her instead of me? What did I do to blow it?* and *I'd like to work with you as a director sometime, and I'd like to work in this play sometime. Can you offer me suggestions for how I need to train? What would you like to see from me in future auditions that you didn't see in this one? Where do you see me needing the most growth?*

The same information is being asked for, but the spirit and the focus are entirely different. The show is cast and auditions are history. You want to move into the rest of your life, with a sense of obtainable objectives. You want to leave this office with some idea what to do next.

8. Don't expect the kind of detailed response you would get in an acting class or a coaching session, where work is centered on how to improve a performance. Remember, a director has been doing eliminations, not pondering how to fix things. She has not been asking herself why various readings did not work; she has been looking at those that did. There are only so many categories possible to focus on at any moment. The director is not thinking about critiquing work presented.

9. As you prepare for next time, don't let the cloud of an unsuccessful audition hover over your efforts. There is no such thing as an unsuccessful audition if you learn from it. Far from going into the next round negatively predisposed toward you, those who might direct you will be thrilled if you show any progress or development from last time. The most common reaction to weak

auditions, however, is that, with the exception of the actor himself, *nobody remembers them!*

I have been visited by actors who apologize for lousy auditions they gave a year or two ago. I draw blanks. I ask others who were present, and they don't remember either. While casting, one is so clearly an editor that inept work simply fades away. You almost need to walk out, knock over a few pieces of scenery, mistakenly assume that Juliet is the boy's role (Julio?), and interrupt your reading with painful personal anecdotes, explaining why you think these lines are poorly written (especially if they're Shakespeare's), before you register in a powerfully negative way. Take comfort in this.

> *They ask you basically to make a fool of yourself, which I was very good at. I made enough of a fool of myself that they thought they could work with me.*
> —Mel Gibson (On Auditioning)

Constant Reminders

For future auditions, you should develop a strategy based on your own responses to pressure. If needlepoint samplers were put together, to frame and hang on the wall, regarding auditions, I would like to offer two contenders. The first:

1. Life is unfair.
2. Theatre is less fair than life.
3. Acting is the least fair part of theatre.
4. Humans submit themselves to nothing less fair than the audition.

If your experience has not led you to believe that number 1 is true, it will. Regarding 2, look at the number of times that superb writers, directors, and actors collaborate for months of their lives and still come up with a bomb. Look at the number of unquestionably superb, critically lauded works that are ignored by the public and die. Look at the virtual crap that can rake in $90 million at your local cinemas.

You can set out to be a theatre designer, stage manager, box office manager, shop supervisor, publicist, technician, or historian, and find a reasonable path to follow for career development, as well as actual employment potential. Superb actors run into career snags and unemployment for interminable stretches. Terrible actors who are good at marketing themselves work all the time. There's number 3.

1. *Life Is Unfair.*
2. *Theatre Is Less Fair Than Life.*
3. *Acting Is The Least Fair Part of Theatre.*
4. *Humans Submit Themselves to Nothing Less Fair Than the Audition.*

Figure 9-1 Life

And 4? When you go out on opening night, at least you know you were chosen for the part. Even if you bomb, someone designated you as better than someone else. You own the role, even if it may shortly be repossessed. At an audition, you are as vulnerable as at any moment in your life. You lay out your skills and sensitivity with no guarantee of anything beyond a curt "Thank you" and the memory itself. You may prepare for weeks for an exposure that may not last minutes. Yes, Auschwitz and Hiroshima were worse than auditions, but the participants did not willingly submit themselves. Yet, auditions are the best way anyone has found so far to cast, and though technology surges ahead so rapidly as to take your breath away, auditions have remained virtually unchanged for the last 200 years.

> *I'm not good at auditioning. I'm not a good salesman.*
> —Aaron Eckhart

The second contender:

> Auditioning is like being a Fuller brush man. Only you are the brush.

Selling yourself without feeling crass or immoral is tough. It takes a firm belief in who you are and a capacity to separate essential marketing strategy from the artist within.

Making the Rounds of Auditions Is Like Being a Fuller Brush Man. Only You Are the Brush.

Figure 9-2 Rounds

The water of the art of acting and the oil of the business of acting don't mix painlessly. Consider these three testimonies from one of the more respected actors in the world:

> *Acting is the most minor of gifts and not a very high class way to earn a living. After all, Shirley Temple could do it at the age of four.*
>
> *Being an actor is such a humiliating experience, because you are selling yourself to the public, your face, your personality, and that is humiliating. As you get older, it becomes more humiliating because you've got less to sell.*
>
> *But if you survive, you become a legend. I'm a legend. I'm revered, rather like an old building.*
>
> —Katharine Hepburn

So what's your strategy? The audition is a separate entity from the performance. The world is full of brilliant actors who cannot audition and brilliant auditioners who cannot act. Theatre shares this irony with politics, business, and many public service professions. Many actors give in to their own worst tendencies in an audition. Things they got over long ago and blocks they surmounted early in Acting 1 loom again like giants as they go to try out for a show or interview for a summer job. The same self-sabotaging occurs in offstage application or interview encounters.

I used to be terrified of auditioning. Then something happened. I went to an audition and someone was being an asshole and I thought, "I don't really want this job." I wasn't working at the time, but I thought, "I don't think I could bear to work for you." After that I always auditioned better. I no longer ran at it saying, "Like me!! Want me!!"
—Cate Blanchett

Some of the greatest actors in the world just cannot audition well. They get nervous and self-conscious, so they act weird around people. Some people who aren't great actors are great auditioners. You wonder why they're getting work when they're not that exceptional, but it's a different talent.
—Penelope Ann Miller

Those who succeed in jumping the audition hurdles find ways to psych themselves and keep themselves out of their own mind traps. They recognize that something more than talent is needed and they find it.

I walk into auditions thinking about "Wow," asking what's gonna make me different from the other girls here. They're looking for the next star to walk into that room. It's about being alive, open, electric, confident—that's the "Wow."
—Jennifer Lopez

I saw all the other talented actors and started freaking out. But then I thought, "I survived the social welfare system of New York City. Surely I can survive an audition!"
—Rosie Perez

> *I'm probably just above average in talent, but where I think*
> *I excel is psychotic drive. All I need is for somebody to say*
> *I can't do something and this crazy switch inside me makes*
> *me attack whatever I'm doing. Psychotic drive is where I*
> *excel over people that are probably more naturally gifted.*
> —Will Smith

What do you do? You find warm-ups, ways to focus your energy, philosophical positions that get you back to the creative state you have achieved onstage. You personalize and adapt warm-ups to serve you in multiple circumstances. You develop a playful attitude toward the audition experience itself that allows you pleasure. You put this into perspective. You step out of the center of the universe. You decide to enjoy being there.

General Casting

Early in your training, almost every audition you go to is *specific*; you know the play being cast and often the parts for which you are being considered. If you decide to pursue acting further, the *general* audition is inevitable. The format and objectives are different because a much broader look is being taken. Your preparation level is expected to be quite a bit higher. The general audition is often used for:

1. Moving on in an acting program where there are large numbers of applicants
2. Transferring to another school
3. Gaining admission to an academy or professional school
4. Studying with a private instructor
5. Getting into a restricted seminar or master class
6. Being accepted for a Master of Fine Arts program
7. Winning a scholarship or some other acting competition
8. Employment in summer stock
9. Seasonal contracts in regional repertory.

You need to learn this format, even if you're not yet sure how big a place acting will have in your life. Even if you're just a serious shopper, this audition is needed to get into most of the sales.

In *general casting*, instead of saying that you fit into one play or part perfectly, you're saying that you are interesting, versatile, disciplined, and gifted enough to be taken on by the auditor for some long-term venture. If the season has a variety of plays, you'll fit in them all. If the program takes a series of approaches to acting, you'll adapt well to each of them. If the agency deals with various media, you fit them all.

In offstage terms, it's similar to being hired by a company to function in a wide range of tasks (troubleshooter, Person Friday, fund-raiser, spokesperson) instead of a narrowly defined desk job. When you looked for your very first job, the requirements for delivering papers, pumping gas, or frying burgers seemed quite specific. Becoming a public relations representative or cultural ambassador is general. You are demonstrating a wider scope.

Fortunately, the format is almost identical for all these auditions, so that once your basic presentation is in hand, you can use it repeatedly. Usually the conditions are

1. You are given less than five minutes to present two memorized monologs, and time limits are enforced.

2. Strong contrast between the two pieces is encouraged, so that your range can be examined.

3. One monolog should be quite close to you and your evident type, while the other should have some surprise. Often, one of them is requested to be classical or verse, to show technical mastery and a sense of style.

4. All choices should involve material for which you are well cast now. The versatility should not come by playing radically out of your age or from shock value.

5. Introductory and transitional material should be kept at an absolute minimum.

Why should this concern you if you are still in Acting 1? Because the search for the right material is endless. It is almost impossible to start the search too early.

There are two main exceptions to the format presented:

1. Auditions for teachers and coaches will sometimes involve only one monolog. You may be worried about demonstrating your range, but trust the perceptions of the observer. Do the monolog that is closest to you. The feeling, shared by many teachers, is that if the person comes across as interesting, truthful, and focused, versatility and virtuosity can come later.

2. The Irene Ryan Competition of the American College Theatre Festival requires that one of your two pieces be done with a partner. This is a rare opportunity and one to be relished. You normally spend so much of your effort trying to play to your imaginary partner in an audition that having a real partner there to support you can be wonderful.

Exercise 9.15

Audition Observation

The best way to quickly assimilate the general audition is to watch one. Ask around for local versions. Then watch in the following categories, which tend to be employed to evaluate actors. Ask yourself which decisions you would make in the actor's place. A glance will show you that these exact same categories can be used to evaluate any presentation in almost any line of work. This exercise is worthy of consideration for any presentation of self, offstage or on.

1. *Appearance/Attire:* Care, attractiveness, appropriateness
2. *Selection of material:* Suitability, originality, scope
3. *Control of material:* Understanding, analysis, credibility
4. *Use of voice/speech:* Quality, clarity, variety
5. *Use of body/space:* Movement, staging, focus
6. *Dynamics:* Stage presence, energy, imagination, poise, attitude
7. *Flow:* Set-up, introduction, transitions, ending

1. Appearance/Attire

- Does it look like the actor gave some thought and preparation to how he looks today?
- Does this look suit this person? Does it seem to fit who he is?
- Is it the human being we're looking at or are we watching clothes and hair? Is hair out of eyes and the actor fully visible?
- Is the outfit in any way fighting with the actor for attention?
- On the other hand, is the look so bland that it is impossible to remember?
- Is there a balance between stiffly dressed up and so casual that the performer does not seem to respect the occasion?
- Is the look versatile enough that it works for both characters and the actor herself?
- Does the actor accomplish any changes in appearance during the audition?
- Were these changes creative or merely distracting?

2. Selection of Material

- Has the actor picked pieces that seem to reflect herself?
- Do either of the choices indicate a lack of self-awareness?
- Are either of these characters too familiar or done too often?

- Are the roles too strongly associated with famous actors to view without being too reminded of the great original performances?
- Is there a feeling of having searched and uncovered new material?
- Do the lines have a sense of the unexpected and the fresh?
- Do the pieces provide the opportunity to share two entirely separate human beings?
- Do the monologs satisfy? Do they seem complete, clear, and fully realized?

3. Control of Material

- Do you feel the actor fully comprehends his characters and that each word is under his control?
- Is it evident that homework and research have taken place?
- Do you ever question the thoroughness or accuracy of the analysis behind the presentation?
- Are either of these characters outside the actor's range at this point in his growth?
- Is the actor believable as these people?
- Are you watching real human beings in crisis, or are you always aware that this is a performance?

4. Use of Voice/Speech

- Does the voice seem comfortable and pleasant to listen to?
- Do you ever have any trouble understanding?
- If so, is it because of volume, articulation, or any other cause you can identify?
- Does the voice change enough between roles for you to hear a new person?
- Is there any tendency to make predictable or regular choices that are tiresome?
- Is the sound varied enough within the body of each speech?
- What is your response to the actor's sense of timing?
- Are any vocal effects labored or forced?
- Does this actor possess a rich, expressive instrument? Does it serve him fully?

5. Use of Body/Space

- Does the actor move with assurance and authority?
- Does the actor appear agile and coordinated?
- Is there enough use of the space so that you can tell if the actor knows how to move?

- Is the action so busy that you cannot tell whether she can be still?
- Does action ever make you tense or uneasy?
- Can you see the imaginary listener(s)?
- Is the focus consistent or do you ever lose track of listener relationships?
- Can you always see the actor's facial expressions? Does she focus down or off-stage too frequently? Does she ever upstage herself or throw attention elsewhere?
- Does the actor have any trouble staying in the light?
- Does the actor appear at home in the acting space?
- Did you ever feel the need for more or less physical activity?

6. Dynamics

- Does this person compel you? Does he command your attention?
- Do you want to watch him? Are you curious to know more about him?
- Is the actor the primary source of energy in the room?
- Is that energy contagious or pushed?
- Do you feel you are in the presence of a lively, creative spirit?
- Does the actor seem to like being here, being an actor?
- Does the actor appear gracious and friendly to the observers?
- Do you ever get a sense of defensiveness or tightness?
- Is there any feeling of apology or self-deprecation?
- Does the actor put you at ease with his effortless assurance?

7. Flow

- Does the audition proceed with a smooth efficiency?
- Are there awkward adjustments of furniture, clothing, or lines? Any unfilled pauses?
- Is the introduction brief, pointed, but conversational?
- Does each person go through realizable changes?
- Do you get to watch a metamorphosis between characters?
- Are you ever confused in a way that is clearly not intentional?
- Do vocal and physical changes appear in sync with each other?
- Does the actor bring it to a definite, clear close, so that the curtains can close in your own imagination?
- Does the actor return to herself after the last character so that you get to see the real person again?

- Does the actor leave the stage with a sense of completion and pride?
- Does the audition last all the way offstage?

Exercise 9.16

Choices

See Appendix J: Audition Observation for an optional format to use with this exercise.

1. Note at least two instances in each category where you feel an actor made vividly appropriate and inappropriate choices. Debate with friends. Justify your reactions through the questions listed. Avoid simple rating words in favor of concrete information.

   Which auditions linger in your mind now and which rapidly fade away?

   Why? What separates outstanding from adequate work?

2. If you know any of the actors, ask if the person you know really appeared in the audition. Were there any essential qualities that you find appealing in the human being that were missing in the presentation? How can these be integrated?

Post-Application Mortem

Everything in the previous section has a direct parallel in those offstage situations where you have put yourself on the line for the scholarship, the grant, the job, the admission to a certain school or program, the fellowship, the contract, or the commission, and it doesn't come through. Don't retreat from a defeat. Force it to teach you.

Whether or not the person making crucial decisions is available to counsel you, a systematic review of your participation, objectivity gained from some passage of time, and careful development of positive objectives are still the secrets to recovery and growth and the way for setbacks to set forward. Auditioning is what you're doing whenever you are in a situation that is now tentative/temporary, but may or may not become definite/permanent. Learning to audition is learning to open up the full range of your offstage life.

Exercise 9.17

Offstage Auditions

Pick one of the following events and observe choices made in exactly the same categories employed for the previous two exercises. After observing others, make decisions regarding your own habitual choices that will help you the next time this kind of event comes your way.

1. An important social occasion
2. A public hearing on a controversial issue
3. A committee meeting where varying proposals are considered
4. An instance where competing bids or designs depend on rehearsed presentations
5. An informal or private encounter where the stakes are high enough to involve careful preparation.

Interviews

Being questioned is standard procedure when you are applying to move ahead. Here are some of the most commonly asked questions for actors, which you should be able to quickly adjust for situations outside the theatre:

The Dreaded Thirteen

1. Tell me something about yourself.
2. Why do you want to be an actor?
3. What have you done?
4. Why should we use you?
5. What's special about you?
6. What can you do for us?
7. Can you be . . . (funny, sad, sexy, commanding, and so on)?
8. Why do you think you're right for this . . . (part, company, agency)?
9. How do you feel about . . . (subject that follows may be anything from impossibly vague to controversial or private)?
10. Would you be willing to . . . (change something about yourself, play a role that is demeaning to your heritage, sex, and so on)?
11. By next week, can you . . . (relocate, leave your family, learn to do some tricky skill)?
12. What are your real strengths as an actor? As a person? What do you like best about yourself?
13. If you could change one thing about yourself, what would it be?

Oddly enough, the ones with the widest choice of answers (like 1 and 2) seem to unhinge people the most. The good news is that almost any interview comes down to this list or some variation. Think about all the ways you might answer, and feel no need to always answer the same. Realize that what you say matters far less than how you respond to the question. Interviews, from politicians stepping into press conferences to beauty contestants stepping out of soundproof booths, come down to attitude. No one expects the Senator or Miss Ohio to have a startling, illuminating, pungent response (and they usually don't). What is expected is that neither recipient will be rendered comatose by the question, that both will keep a sense of poise, humor, perspective, and a willingness to give it a go. Almost any answer is better than drawing blanks. Just give yourself permission to respond like a reasonable human being.

What if you want to be startling, illuminating, and pungent? Remember *l'Esprit de l'Escalier* or the Spirit of the Stairs? The beauty of interviews is that they are so relentlessly predictable that you can start reading, borrowing, quoting, shaping, practicing now for an answer you may not be called on to give for years. I attended an audition once where the director (who had a reputation for unsettling actors) stopped the woman who was reading and asked her what she had done. She answered that, and then he asked, "And what is your favorite sexual position?" There was an audible hush and sudden tension in the room. The rest of us were in a state of shock. She paused, smiled, and said, "Number twenty-three." Everyone laughed, and the audition went on in a normal way.

Was the director really trying to get personal information from her? Maybe, but I doubt it. He was testing her poise, humor, and reaction. She managed to say to him (subtextually), "You can't unhinge me. My humor is in good shape. And I'm not telling you a thing." The question is only a variation on number nine from the list of thirteen.

> *You pack your suitcase. You outline possibilities, lines you might use, turns and changes that may happen. People expect you to be on the button. You don't want to be caught saying "Uhhhhh. . . ." So you pack your suitcase, putting all your stuff where you can find it.*
> —Billy Crystal

The spirit of adventure essential in an audition can be carried into countless moments of your life. If you approach a job interview with a sense of the person on the other side of the desk functioning like a casting director (Can you comfortably costar at IBM?), a great deal of this process can be fun. You're always auditioning in life for further chances. A first date is, in many ways, an audition for a second. And when you go home to visit the family of your current companion, you are, without doubt, auditioning for the role of son- or daughter-in-law. Even if you aren't sure if you want the part, you are auditioning. If what you have now is temporary/tentative, but it could become permanent/definite, you are auditioning, even if you are nowhere near a theatre.

If you are looking at an acting career, should you plan now for being famous? I'd recommend instead that you plan for being good. And remember, fame and fortune do not come without a price:

> *One time I went to the movies with my mother in Georgia and I was in the bathroom. All of a sudden this voice says, "Excuse me? The girl in stall No. 1? Were you in Mystic Pizza?" I said yeah and she goes, "Can I have your autograph?" and slides a piece of toilet paper under the stall. I just said, "I don't think right now is the time."*
> –Julia Roberts
>
> *When someone follows you twenty blocks to the pharmacy where they watch you buy toilet paper, you know your life has changed.*
> –Jennifer Aniston
>
> *Reporters always ask you a question like "What are your deepest secrets?" As if, I'm thinking, that's funny. I'd really like to discuss this in a national magazine.*
> –Tom Hanks
>
> *I love to hang out in cafes by myself and people-watch, stealing tics and mannerisms for future characters. But if you're a big cheesy movie star, you can't do that. Everybody's looking at you.*
> –Gwyneth Paltrow

Personal Objectives

Even if you never again darken the door of the theatre, you should now have a sense of the kind of figure you cut in space, the sort of sounds you generate, the impressions (accurate or not) you leave on those you encounter.

> *I never thought I'd be making a life for myself in this acting business. I went into it to shore up my weaknesses— the ability to read and memorize and stand up in front of somebody.*
> –Edward James Olmos

You may also recognize circumstances where you are easy and exploratory contrasted with those where you are inhibited or stiff. A basic knowledge of self and of what constitutes a character should clarify certain life choices:

Choosing Partners and Playmates

Most of us search for a life partner with whom we need to do a minimum of acting, someone who makes it easier to deal with what the world wants or who helps us not care. Feeling comfortable in a relationship because everything is so predictable, however, is hardly the same as feeling comfortable because unqualified love and acceptance are present and whatever comes will be all right. The ideal companion for the full journey of life is one with whom we don't need to act at all but who will also, when we get the impulse, be there as an enthusiastic audience or as a dynamic scene partner, who will join the fun. So why do so many people pick the wrong mates, friends, even the wrong one-night stands? Many fail to recognize the difference between having a relationship and playing scenes. Many cast companions based on surface impressions and misread signals. Sure, some "professional actors" are the worst cases of multiple failed marriages and destructive relationships. But these victims are rarely students of acting, who should be better armed and needn't be anyone's victim.

> *Theatre has a connection with the human condition.*
> *You learn things about yourself through the plays. Your*
> *character's circumstances and emotions cause you to examine what is going on inside yourself.*
> —Nick Nolte

Your understanding of acting principles can help you choose better who you want to play with, to make informed selections regarding friends and lovers. You should be better able to recognize playful performance versus destructive self-deception, and to distinguish between nurturing comfort and mere predictability. The more you know about acting, the more you know how much you want it in your relationships.

Using Theatre in Your Life

There is plenty of opportunity for theatre in your offstage interactions.

> *The oldest form of theater is the dinner table. The same*
> *people every night with a new script.*
> —Michael J. Fox

You can always continue to train yourself to perform your life better:

1. Take what you have learned about your body, voice, and personality and set up goals to clean up what is misleading in your behavior.

2. Identify the suggestible conditions present when you've given your most memorable life performances so far. Aim to set up those conditions deliberately more often.

3. Seriously scrutinize any role models you've been using and ages you've been lingering in too long. Make edits and replacements. Start shooting to become someone's role model yourself.

4. Either accept and acknowledge your own dominant influences (of your private audience and cultural binding), or free yourself from them. Make peace with them in any case. Take the long-running, dueling performances of your life and make a judgment in each, deciding which will win and freeing yourself from the tiresome pressure.

5. Examine those strategies and tactics that you overuse in your life and those you neglect. Freshen your strategic choices. Expand your own working repertoire. Stop playing tired, worn-out tapes that nobody listens to.

6. Warm up for potentially difficult encounters, rather than just thinking about them.

7. Observe all the performances being given around you more intensely, for both enrichment and pleasure, and to avoid being taken for a ride.

8. Conquer space! Not necessarily in a space ship, seeking unbridled intergalactic ambition. Start with just keeping cool in any medium-sized room. Any space you enter may or may not become yours. You now understand what personal bubbles are and the various means people use to break or invade them. You know how movement, composition, and business all make an impression. You understand the varying powers of sustained, intense, varying, indirect, and darting eye contact. You can, if you will, stage yourself.

9. Conquer sound! Dare to use your voice to influence others' behavior. Let your voice be known to you, useful to you, no longer a stranger. Devote at least as much time to "working out" your voice as you do your body.

10. Confront the way life has typed you so far and the various parts that you've been cast in whether you wanted them or not. Cast yourself more assertively. Vow not to accept some roles.

Casting Yourself

Probably most actors would like to be viewed by the world as a romantic leading man or a leading lady. Those types, on the other hand, lament the fact that interesting, offbeat character roles aren't open to them. Why are they forced, role after role, to be commanding, attractive, romantic? Why will the public not allow them to scratch and itch? It's obvious that no one is completely delighted with what he or she's got. You can waste an enormous amount of time lamenting. Or you can separate "can change" from "can't" from "don't want to anyway" and get on with your life. And you can begin to savor what is extraordinary about you. Sometimes it takes a while for others to recognize it.

> *My first acting job? Dressed as an El Pollo Loco chicken,*
> *I clucked customers in to the restaurant.*
> —Brad Pitt
>
> *I got my Equity card playing a duck.*
> —Kathy Bates

There are roles that life has undeniably and sometimes cruelly cast you in. Some guys look and sound like Woody Allen, others more like Jude Law. From the way you look and sound, the world expects certain behavior from you. In case you haven't noticed, many people look more like one of those two, but feel more like the other. Their lives are often chaotic. Certain genetic, cultural limitations are placed on each living creature. Motivational and spiritual limitations are more often placed on the creature by the creature. Although genetics are undeniable, your capacity to transform yourself is considerable. I don't mean plastic surgery or psychotherapy (sure, those are alternatives), but rather the simple way you think about yourself and elect to present yourself to the world.

> *Acting is something that most people think they're incapable*
> *of but they do it from morning to night.*
> —Marlon Brando

Transsexuals are vivid examples of people whom the genetic game has dealt a tough set of cards. Most people are lucky enough to be able to discover their true selves with less radical measures than surgery. Surely you have discovered something as simple (and at first glance superficial) as a hat, a pair of shoes, a hair style, a way of moving, a song, a new color that suddenly made you feel you had found a way of expressing who you actually are. These items can be far more than trite indulgences. Like the keys to a character, they help you find you and help you feel much more as if you live inside your own body.

Some actors even change what they call themselves. Years ago, most changed their names to suit their images. So Harold Crosby became Bing, and later male starlets were christened Rock, Rip, Troy, or Tab. Now far more are keeping their own names, but quite a few still decide that a new name is needed to match who they feel they really are. Imagine if Irving Rhames had not shortened it to Ving? Or if Caryn Johnson had not become Whoopi Goldberg? Can you picture leading ladies with names like Mary Lou Streep (who became Meryl), Susan Weaver (Sigourney), or Cherilyn La Poire (Cher)? Or legendary actor Maurice Michelwaite (Michael Caine)? Maybe Winona Ryder would have had the same career if she had remained Horowitz, but what if Thomas Mapother IV had not become Tom Cruise or Laura Jean Witherspoon did not morph into Reese? What if Eric Bishop never changed his name to Jamie Foxx? Or if Queen Latifah had remained Elaine Owens? Who knows?

One thing is certain. With an actor's awareness, you can be far more alert, not just to finding keys to unlock other characters, but also keys to your own.

Now I'm managing to carry performing power into my
personal life and taking some personal life things onstage.
The lives are starting to feed each other.
—Robin Williams

Here is one extraordinary story of an actor's transformation for the stage. For much of his career Paul Newman was considered film's major heartthrob (ask your grandmother what she thinks of him and watch her eyes glaze over), but he did not start out that way:

> Paul Newman's Broadway debut was in *Picnic*. He did not play the command-
> ing hunk leading man, Hal, who mesmerizes every woman in town. He played the
> well-meaning, ineffectual rich boy who loses the leading lady to a man of physical
> magnetism. The director (Joshua Logan, one of the most respected and successful
> in Broadway's history) wouldn't even let him read for Hal. He said Newman had no
> sexual charisma or danger. "At that point I probably didn't. That sort of thing has a
> lot to do with *conviction*."
>
> The director also told him to get in shape. "The way I translated that was
> six hours in the gym every day." He eventually won the role on the show's national
> tour after working diligently on both pectorals and presence. How? He studied acting
> and women. "You can measure a woman and find ways of being gallant, of listening,
> of crowding and pursuing."

Similar offstage metamorphoses are accomplished all the time. If Paul Newman could lose a role because he was insufficiently sexual and commanding and still become Paul Newman, what might others do? What might you do?

Have women always considered me fine? Well, there was nobody knocking when I was a senior in high school or a freshman in college. Where were they all then? Power is attractive.

–Denzel Washington

When I was younger nobody thought I was much. I was spacey, mediocre, goofed up. And now suddenly all this attention!

–Josh Hartnet

It's amazing how much better looking I've gotten since I've been on "Alias." I didn't have that many fans when I was 19 and working as a waiter.

–Michael Vartan

All these enthusiastic female fans are sweet, but they don't know me. They've just seen characters I play, but that's not me. I never got that before and I still don't. The characters do.

–Orlando Bloom

We are all looking to cast ourselves in the world. But much casting is just thrust upon us. The groups you deal with daily may force you into Earth Mother, Trusted Confidant, Charming If Bubbly Airhead, Somber Companion, Brick, or Jaded Sophisticate, depending on the needs of those around you. Now is the time to identify those roles that you have had long runs in and are ready to close. Now is a good time to promise yourself some overdue performances that you've wanted to give for a long time. Now may be the time to decide to star in your own life, instead of doing only featured roles and cameos in the lives of others. Or, if you've been phenomenally self-centered, now may be the time to do just the reverse. Now may even be the time to create an altogether new type: The _____ (fill in your own name) Type.

And remember, if you do get to work as an actor, you get permission to go all sorts of places where nothing else allows you to go and sometimes you get to be very naughty:

By the time I was 25, I had been a pizza waitress, lawyer, prostitute, and I died and came back all by acting. Acting is a fascinating way to live inside someone else's life.

–Julia Roberts

> *First I wanted to be a quarterback then a rock star, then a lawyer. I am so thankful to find something that lets me be all these and more, and then walk away when I want to.*
> —Matthew McConaughey

> *The excitement for me is to dig down into diverse realms of experience without ever having to choose those lives or take those consequences.*
> —Edward Norton

> *I was a very good girl for a long time. That's what really drew me to acting. The stage is the perfect place to be outrageous, sad, angry, to be all these different things.*
> —Joan Allen

> *I'm a small guy who was picked on and got beat up a lot as a kid. When a little guy finally gets to beat somebody, boy, it's hard to stop him. That's me onstage.*
> —Chris Rock

Exercise 9.18

Offstage Action: Anticipation

What new information from this chapter could influence your progress in each of the OA areas? If needed, review the subcategories on pages 29–37.

1. Negating newness
2. Pleasant as possible
3. Keeping cool
4. Sensing signals
5. Winning ways

6. Improving your image
7. Richer relationships
8. Social savvy
9. Prediction potential
10. Career capabilities

Specifically: What knowledge can be carried over from an audition for a play to other crucial moments in your offstage life? Which of the OAs remain challenges for you? Put these on your To Do list, and continue pursuing them in other classes as well as on your own, because you always have time to learn to act your own life better.

Living Fully: Onstage and Off

> *You can become a better actor by becoming a more complete human being and you can become a more complete human being by becoming a better actor.*
> —Ted Danson

Acting can liberate you as easily as it can imprison you. It can give you a wide range of choices and the means of cleaning up distractions that are cluttering your communication. You can enjoy watching tactics being employed that you might not have recognized before, taking pleasure that you are seeing and hearing more around you. You can look across a room and savor the compositions, enjoy the body language, which may now make more sense, catch bits and pieces of conversation and idly analyze how a point might have had a different effect with a drop in pitch or by twisting the final consonant. The small details accumulate into a wealth of perception and pleasure. Acting can help you play your own life better, and it can help you more playfully observe others living theirs.

The tools are now at your disposal. There is no doubt that you will continue to act, offstage at least. How well you act, or how long each performance lingers in the memory of those who observe it, is largely up to you. How much you discover and how much you enjoy yourself is also up to you. If you are open and alert, acting will offer you the potential for profound insight and a phenomenally good time—not a bad combination.

> *There's not a lot an actor can do to make things right. I can't solve the homeless problem or cure a disease. But I can give people hope, I can make people laugh, I can make people feel, I can humanize our dehumanized condition for a couple of hours. That's how I can contribute.*
> —Kevin Kline
>
> *Acting is simply my way of investigating human nature and having fun at the same time.*
> —Meryl Streep
>
> *It's never too late to have a happy childhood.*
> —Tom Robbins

APPENDIX A　MY ACTING HISTORY

Ages Experienced, Ages Observed

Infant

_____

_____

Schoolchild

_____

_____

Lover

_____

_____

Soldier

_____

_____

Justice

_____

_____

Pantaloon

_____

_____

Second childhood

_____

_____

Rejected alternative 3

_____

_____

Rejected alternative 4

_____

_____

Choice (actually spoken)

_____

_____

Beat Change
Describe one moment where a beat ended and another began (for a reason other than the entrance or exit of a character):

_____

_____

_____

APPENDIX C | **PHYSICAL LIFE OBSERVATION**

Habits (Still)

Standing

_____

_____

Sitting

_____

_____

Expression

_____

_____

Habits (Active)

Tempo and Rhythm

_____

_____

Motion

_____

_____

Gestures

_____

_____

Adaptations

Groups

_____

_____

Contact

_____

_____

Mood

_____

_____

Cultural Binding

Geography

_____

_____

Family

_____

_____

Conditioning

_____

_____

Interests

_____

_____

Age _____

Sex _____

APPENDIX D   **VOCAL LIFE OBSERVATON**

Habits

Quality

_____

_____

Tempo

_____

_____

Rhythm

_____

_____

Articulation

_____

_____

Pronunciation

_____

_____

Pitch

_____

_____

Volume

_____

_____

Word choice

_____

_____

Nonverbals

_____

_____

Adaptations

_____

_____

Cultural Binding

_____

_____

How does this person's physical life influence (restrict, set, determine) the vocal life?

_____

_____

APPENDIX E   OPEN SCENE SCENARIOS

Scenario 1

Actors _____ and _____

Characters _____ and _____

Tentative title _____

Conflict _____

What happens?

_____

_____

_____

_____

_____

_____

How is each character different at the end?

_____

_____

_____

Scenario 2

Actors _____ and _____

Characters _____ and _____

Tentative title _____

Conflict _____

What happens?

_____

_____

_____

_____

_____

_____

How is each character different at the end?

_____

_____

_____

_____

APPENDIX F	**OPEN SCENE SCORE**

Actors _____ and _____

Characters _____ and _____

Scene Title/Headline _____

Setting _____

Time _____

Conditions _____

Activity   Intention

1. _____ to _____

2. _____ to _____

3. _____ to _____

4. _____ to _____

5. _____ to _____

6. _____ to _____

7. _____ to _____

8. _____ to _____

9. _____ to _____

10. _____ to _____

11. _____ to _____

12. _____ to _____

13. _____ to _____

14. _____ to _____

15. _____ to _____

16. _____ to _____

17. _____ to _____

18. _____ to _____

19. _____ to _____

20. _____ to _____

21. _____ to _____

22. _____ to _____

23. _____ to _____

24. _____ to _____

25. _____ to _____

26. _____ to _____

27. _____ to _____

28. _____ to _____

29. _____ to _____

30. _____ to _____

31. _____ to _____

32. _____ to _____

33. _____ to _____

34. _____ to _____

35. _____ to _____

36. _____ to _____

37. _____ to _____

38. _____ to _____

39. _____ to _____

40. _____ to _____

41. _____ to _____

42. _____ to _____

43. _____ to _____

44. _____ to _____

45. _____ to _____

46. _____ to _____

47. _____ to _____

48. _____ to _____

49. _____ to _____

50. _____ to _____

51. _____ to _____

52. _____ to _____

53. _____ to _____

54. _____ to _____

55. _____ to _____

56. _____ to _____

57. _____ to _____

58. _____ to _____

59. _____ to _____

60. _____ to _____

61. _____ to _____

62. _____ to _____

63. _____ to _____

64. _____ to _____

65. _____ to _____

66. _____ to _____

67. _____ to _____

68. _____ to _____

69. _____ to _____

70. _____ to _____

APPENDIX G   **STANISLAVSKI OBSERVATION**

Character _____

Event _____

Given Circumstances

1. _____

2. _____

3. _____

4. _____

5. _____

6. _____

7. _____

8. _____

9. _____

10. _____

Conditioning Forces

Conditioning forces on first entrance _____

_____

_____

_____

Changes in conditioning forces

_____

_____

_____

_____

How You Would Use the Magic If to Play This Role

_____

_____

_____

_____

How You Would Employ Grouping

_____

_____

_____

_____

Objectives

Character's super objective _____

Primary obstacle(s) _____

The Character's Rehearsed Futures

Best possible _____

_____

Worst possible _____

_____

Wildest dreams come true _____

_____

Endowment

Props or set pieces

1. _____

2. _____

3. _____

Other people

1. _____

2. _____

3. _____

APPENDIX H   SCRIPT ANALYSIS

Play title and author _____

Characters

_____ played by _____

_____ played by _____

1. Classification

_____

2. Style

Degree of probability _____

Types of improbability _____

_____

3. Structure

Script length _____

Number of acts _____ Number of scenes _____ Length of scenes _____

Place of your scene in the whole _____

_____

4. Theme

_____

_____

5. Cultural Binding

Date written _____ Date set _____

Cultural biases in text _____

_____

_____

6. Production History

_____

_____

_____

_____

7. World of the Play

Time _____

Space _____

Place _____

Values _____

Structure _____

Beauty _____

Sex _____

Recreation _____

Sight _____

Sound _____

Actor _____

CHARACTER ANALYSIS

Character _____

Play and author _____

Character Past

I come from _____

_____

My childhood was _____

_____

_____

Family conditions were _____

_____

_____

Three experiences making the most lasting impression on me were

1. _____

_____

2. _____

_____

3. _____

_____

Ten most important given circumstances are

1. _____

2. _____

3. _____

4. _____

5. _____

6. _____

7. _____

374

8. _____

9. _____

10. _____

Five most powerful members of my private audience would be

1. _____ because _____

2. _____ because _____

3. _____ because _____

4. _____ because _____

5. _____ because _____

Crucial events prior to this scene were _____

_____

_____

Details on the moment just before my entrance include _____

_____

_____

_____

Character Present

Immediate conditioning forces are _____

_____

_____

Other characters and/or the playwright describe me as _____

_____

_____

I describe others as _____

_____

In groups, I tend to _____

I would describe myself as basically _____

My usual style of clothing and type of accessories include _____

_____

My most distinguishing characteristics are _____

_____

My favorite things are _____

_____

My temperament could be described as _____

For example _____

I am most interested in _____

I am least interested in _____

My physical life differs from the actor playing me in that _____

_____

_____

My vocal life differs from the actor playing me in that _____

_____

_____

The actor playing me most needs to use the Magic If in _____

_____

_____

Three examples where endowment must be used in the scene are

1. _____

2. _____

3. _____

The location of this scene can be described as _____

_____

In the most crucial moment of evaluation in the scene, my cue, rejected alternatives, and choice are

Cue _____

First reject _____

Second reject _____

Third reject _____

Fourth reject _____

Choice made (My answer or action) _____

_____

I make the following discoveries in the scene: _____

_____

_____

My scene breaks down into the following beats *(number and label each, use back of sheet if needed):*

_____

_____

_____

Character Future

My super objective in the play is to _____

My intentional hierarchy would include _____

My primary objective in the scene is to _____

Other important objectives include _____

_____

_____

The obstacles I face are _____

_____

My strategy in the scene could be described as _____

_____

Specific tactics I employ in two pages of text are *(mark script copy if you prefer)*

_____

_____

_____

My three rehearsed futures are

Best possible _____

_____

_____

Worst possible _____

_____

_____

Wildest dreams come true _____

_____

_____

Character Abstracts

Helpful images _____

_____

_____

_____

_____

_____

APPENDIX J **AUDITION OBSERVATION**

Event _____

Actors observed _____

Try to identify *why* you felt a choice worked or did not, through the impact it had on you as you watched.

Appearance/Attire

Appropriate Choices	Inappropriate Choices
1. _____	1. _____
2. _____	2. _____
3. _____	3. _____
4. _____	4. _____
5. _____	5. _____

Selection of Material

Appropriate Choices	Inappropriate Choices
1. _____	1. _____
2. _____	2. _____
3. _____	3. _____
4. _____	4. _____
5. _____	5. _____

Control of Material

Appropriate Choices	Inappropriate Choices
1. _____	1. _____
2. _____	2. _____
3. _____	3. _____
4. _____	4. _____
5. _____	5. _____

Use of Voice/Speech

Appropriate Choices   Inappropriate Choices

1. _____   1. _____

2. _____   2. _____

3. _____   3. _____

4. _____   4. _____

5. _____   5. _____

Use of Body/Space

Appropriate Choices   Inappropriate Choices

1. _____   1. _____

2. _____   2. _____

3. _____   3. _____

4. _____   4. _____

5. _____   5. _____

Dynamics

Appropriate Choices   Inappropriate Choices

1. _____   1. _____

2. _____   2. _____

3. _____   3. _____

4. _____   4. _____

5. _____   5. _____

Flow

Appropriate Choices   Inappropriate Choices

1. _____   1. _____

2. _____   2. _____

3. _____   3. _____

4. _____   4. _____

5. _____   5. _____

SAMPLE SCENE: *THE REHEARSAL*

(Two actors enter the room tentatively)

FRED: I can't believe there's no one in here.

ETHEL: It's freezing in here.

FRED: You know what Katharine Hepburn insists on whenever she rehearses?

ETHEL: No. What?

F: She insists that the temperature is always 60 degrees.

E: Really?

F: Yeah.

E: Why didn't you ever tell me that before?

F: I just read it. She says it keeps actors from getting sluggish. She also brings sweaters for those who need them. A box full of sweaters.

E: Well, Fred, you're a good actor, but you're no Katharine Hepburn. At least not yet. And you haven't brought me any sweater. It's still freezing.

F: Maybe we need to warm each other up.

E: *(pause)* What do you mean?

F: I mean that we both need to read this scene so well, so brilliantly that we get the blood rushing. You know.

E: Oh. Right. Well, let's read it and see.

(They begin reading Beatrice and Benedick from Shakespeare's Much Ado About Nothing, *Act II, scene iii)*

F: "When I said I would die a bachelor, I did not think I should live till I were married.—Here comes Beatrice. By this day, she's a fair lady: I do spy some marks of love in her."

E: "Against my will I am sent to bid you come in to dinner."

F: "You take pleasure in the message?"

E: "Yea, just so much as you may take upon a knife's point. And choke a daw withal.—You have no stomach, signior: fare you well."

(Exits)

F: "Ha! Against my will, I am sent to bid you come to dinner—there's double meaning in that." *(to Ethel)* Do you think I should give those first and last lines to the audience? Like I'm confiding in them?

E: *(re-entering)* Sure. I would. Do you think she knows she loves him yet?

F: I think she loves him, but I don't think she knows it. She thinks she hates him.

E: Yeah. That's what I think too. Let's just take it from my entrance. Okay?

F: Right. I'll cue you in. "I do spy some marks of love on her."

E: "Against my will, I am sent to . . ." Have you noticed what's going on in this assignment?

F: What do you mean?

E: We're all working with our first partner from back in the first acting class. At least I'm pretty sure that's true.

F: My god, I think you're right. Karen and John and Tim and Ralph and . . . I think you're right.

E: I wonder why.

F: Probably supposed to give us some sense of perspective or something. *(He discovers a jacket someone has left in the room)* Hey, look!

E: What?

F: Who says there's no sweater here for you? *(Puts it around her shoulders)*

E: Do you even remember our first open scene?

F: Sure. The best thing I ever did. *(She looks at him witheringly)* Just kidding. But we did Okay. How come we were never partners again? Until now?

E: You mean why didn't I ever ask you?

F: Yeah. I asked you the first time.

E: Well, as I recall you missed two rehearsals altogether, you were late more than a few times, and you didn't even get your lines until the day before it was due. How could I resist working with you again?

F: But I matured a lot after that term. You know that. I got much more disciplined. So how come we never worked together again?

E: I don't know. We're together now. Or . . . I guess it was our names.

F: Our names?

E: Fred and Ethel. I didn't like the idea of anyone thinking of us as the Mertzes.

F: The Mertzes?

E: Lucy and Ricky's neighbors.

F: Oh. Is that the real reason?

E: I don't know. Let's get back to it. From my entrance again?

F: Right. "I do spy some marks of love on her."

E: "Against my will I am sent to bid you come in to dinner." Did you know that Katharine Hepburn played Beatrice?

F: She did?

E: At the Stratford Festival. I just thought I'd impress you with some Hepburn trivia of my own.

F: "You take pleasure in the message?"

E: Now I can't stop thinking about all the rehearsal time I've spent in this place. And it's just about over. From open scenes to Shakespeare.

F: And next comes graduation. Then we have to deal with "real life."

E: Alright. What the hell. It's almost over anyway. The real reason I avoided working with you is . . . God, I can't believe I'm going to say this. I always thought you were attractive. I mean I was attracted to you and I just didn't want to get distracted so . . . Well, you know.

F: Seriously? *(She nods)* 'Cause I've never been exactly indifferent to you either, but I never thought . . . No kidding?

E: "Against my will I am sent to bid you to come to dinner."

F: "You take pleasure in the message?" Don't you think we should talk about this?

E: No. I think we should rehearse. "Yes, just so much as you may take upon a knife's point . . ." *(She is getting emotional, skips lines)* "If it had been painful I would not have come . . ." *(She can't go on.)* I'm sorry. . . . I guess it's all this end of the year stuff and it's . . . *(She moves away from him to collect herself. Pause.)*

F: May I give you a hug? A very nonthreatening, nonsexual, supportive friend-type hug?

E: Please. *(They hug, at first tentatively, then relax into it)* Listen, this room has more memories than I'm up to today. Do you think we could go somewhere else?

F: Sure. Let's find someplace more Shakespearean. Then we can say we used sense memory in rehearsal.

E: And then, sometime soon, we'll talk.

F: Right, first we do a brilliant scene. Then we work on . . . then we talk about . . . us. Okay?

E: Good. Let's go. *(Exit. She returns as soon as they leave, having remembered the jacket she has on. She removes it, replaces it, and starts to leave)* Thanks for the sweater, Katharine. Uh . . . Kate. Ummm . . . Ms. Hepburn. God, it's freezing in here. *(Exits)*

Index